TROUBLESHOOTING INTERNETWORKS

Tools, Techniques, and Protocols

TROUBLESHOOTING INTERNETWORKS

Tools, Techniques, and Protocols

Mark A. Miller, P.E.

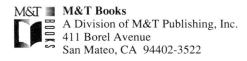 **M&T Books**
A Division of M&T Publishing, Inc.
411 Borel Avenue
San Mateo, CA 94402-3522

© 1991 by Mark A. Miller

Printed in the United States of America

Library of Congress Cataloging in Publication Data

Miller, Mark, 1955-
      Troubleshooting internetworks: tools, techniques, and protocols / by Mark A. Miller.
          p.   cm.
      Includes bibliographical references and index.
      ISBN 1-55851-236-5
        1. Computer networks—Maintenance and repair. 2. Computer network protocols. I. Title.
      TK5105.5.M56 1991
      004.6—dc20   91-41578
                                                       CIP

94 93 92 91   4 3 2 1

Trademarks:
All products, names, and services are trademarks or registered trademarks of their respective companies. See "Trademarks" section at back of book.

Cover Design: Lauren Smith Design   **Project Editor:** Sarah Wadsworth

---

To Nathan and Nicholas

Contents

WHY THIS BOOK IS FOR YOU 1

THE COMPLEXITY OF INTERNETWORKS 3
1.1 A Historical Perspective on Connectivity 4
1.2 Wideband Requirements 8
1.3 Advances in Workstations 9
1.4 Protocol Interoperability 11
1.5 LAN/WAN Connectivity 14
1.6 Network Management Trends 17
1.7 Economic Considerations 20
1.8 Analyzing the Resultant Mixture 21
1.9 References 22

THE ULTIMATE ANALYZER 25
2.1 A Brief History of Internetworking 25
2.2 Internetwork Analysis 26
2.3 Internetwork Analyzer Requirements 30
    2.3.1 Expert Systems 31
    2.3.2 PC-Based Analyzers 35
    2.3.3 Enhanced Graphical User Interfaces 37
    2.3.4 Combination LAN/WAN Analyzers 37
    2.3.5 Multiport/Multiprocessing Capabilities 39
    2.3.6 Emerging MAN/WAN Protocol Support 40
    2.3.7 Network Management Protocol Support 42
    2.3.8 Remote Data Gathering or Analysis 43
    2.3.9 Integration with Network Simulation/Modeling Tools 45

2.4 Selecting Your Ultimate Analyzer 47

2.5 Using Your Ultimate Analyzer 60

2.6 References 62

TROUBLESHOOTING APPLETALK INTERNETWORKS............65

3.1 AppleTalk Architecture and Protocols 65

   3.1.1 AppleTalk Physical and Data Link Layers 65

   3.1.2 AppleTalk Network Layer 67

   3.1.3 AppleTalk Transport Layer 68

   3.1.4 AppleTalk Higher Layers 69

   3.1.5 AppleTalk Addressing Conventions 70

   3.1.6 AppleTalk Packet Formats 73

3.2 AppleTalk Analysis Techniques 74

3.3 AppleTalk Internetwork Troubleshooting 75

   3.3.1 AppleTalk Nodes Entering a Token Ring Network 76

   3.3.2 AppleTalk Node Accessing a Remote Host 80

   3.3.3 AppleTalk Phase 1 to Phase 2 Transition Services Impact 91

   3.3.4 AppleTalk Internetwork Additions 95

   3.3.5 AppleTalk and the IBM 8209 Bridge 107

   3.3.6 AppleTalk with an SNA Gateway 120

   3.3.7 EtherTalk to LocalTalk Wiring Problems 129

3.4 References 134

TROUBLESHOOTING BANYAN VINES INTERNETWORKS.135

4.1 VINES Architecture and Protocols 135

   4.1.1 VINES Physical and Data Link Layers 137

   4.1.2 VINES Network Layer 137

   4.1.3 VINES Transport Layer 139

   4.1.4 VINES Higher Layers 139

   4.1.5 VINES 5.0 139

   4.1.6 Addressing the VINES User Process 140

   4.1.7 VINES Packet Formats 142

4.2 VINES Protocol Analysis Techniques 143

4.3 VINES Internetwork Troubleshooting 146

    4.3.1 VINES Internetwork Login Sequence 146

    4.3.2 VINES Intermittent Server Operation 152

    4.3.3 VINES SMTP Gateway Service 160

    4.3.4 VINES SNA Gateway 166

4.4 References 174

TROUBLESHOOTING DECNET PHASE IV

INTERNETWORKS **177**

5.1 DECnet Architecture and Protocols 178

    5.1.1 DECnet Phase IV Physical Link and Data Link Layers 178

    5.1.2 DECnet Phase IV Routing Layer 180

    5.1.3 DECnet Phase IV End Communication Layer 182

    5.1.4 DECnet Phase IV Session Control Layer 182

    5.1.5 DECnet Phase IV Higher Layers 182

    5.1.6 DECnet Phase IV Packet Formats 184

    5.1.7 DECnet Phase IV Internetwork Addressing 187

    5.1.8 DECnet Phase V Protocols 188

5.2 DECnet Phase IV Protocol Analysis Techniques 190

5.3 DECnet Phase IV Internetwork Troubleshooting 192

    5.3.1 DECnet Ethernet Frame Errors 192

    5.3.2 DECnet Erroneous LAT Packets 196

    5.3.3 DECnet Lost Connection 202

    5.3.4 DECnet Invisible Connection 212

5.4 References 220

TROUBLESHOOTING IBM TOKEN RING/SNA

INTERNETWORKS **223**

6.1 Token Ring/SNA Architecture and Protocols 223

    6.1.1 Token Ring Architecture and Protocols 224

    6.1.2 Source Routing Protocol 224

6.1.3 SNA Architecture 228

6.1.4 SNA Physical and Data Link Layers 230

6.1.5 SNA Path Control Layer 230

6.1.6 SNA Transmission Control Layer 231

6.1.7 SNA Data Flow Control Layer..231

6.1.8 SNA Presentation Services and Transaction Services Layers 232

6.1.9 The SNA Packet Format 232

6.2 Token Ring/SNA Protocol Analysis Techniques.........................234

6.3 Token Ring/SNA Internetwork Troubleshooting.........................236

6.3.1 Token Ring/SNA Terminal Emulation 236

6.3.2 Token Ring/SNA Source (mis)routed Frames 253

6.3.3 Token Ring/SNA Multiple NetBIOS Broadcasts............273

6.3.4 Token Ring/SNA RS/6000 Gateway to TCP/IP Environment........284

6.3.5 Token Ring/SNA Gateway Response Time Problems 294

6.4 References 299

TROUBLESHOOTING NOVELL NETWARE INTERNETWORKS

TROUBLESHOOTING NOVELL NETWARE
INTERNETWORKS..305

7.1 NetWare Architectures and Protocols 305

7.1.1 NetWare 286 Architecture 306

7.1.2 NetWare 386 Architecture 308

7.1.3 NetWare Physical and Data Link Layers 309

7.1.4 NetWare Network Layer 310

7.1.5 NetWare Transport and Higher Layers 311

7.1.6 NetWare Internetwork Addressing..................................312

7.1.7 NetWare Packet Formats...314

7.2 NetWare Protocol Analysis Techniques 315

7.3 NetWare Internetwork Troubleshooting 319

7.3.1 NetWare Internal Routing 319

7.3.2 NetWare Preferred Server Operation 327

7.3.3 NetWare Addressing Confusion......................................333

7.3.4 NetWare Source Routing Bridges 341

7.3.5 NetWare Extraneous Frame Copied Errors 348

7.3.6 NetWare SNA Gateway 353

7.4 References 357

TROUBLESHOOTING TCP/IP-BASED INTERNETWORKS...361

8.1 TCP/IP and Related Protocols 362

   8.1.1 DOD Internet Architecture 362

   8.1.2 DOD Local Network Layer Protocols 363

   8.1.3 DOD Internet Layer Protocols 364

   8.1.4 DOD Host-to-Host Layer Protocols 365

   8.1.5 DOD Process/Application Layer Protocols 366

   8.1.6 DOD Internet Addressing 367

   8.1.7 DOD IP Datagram Format 367

8.2 TCP/IP Protocol Analysis Techniques 371

8.3 TCP/IP Internetwork Troubleshooting 373

   8.3.1 TCP/IP Server Login Failure 373

   8.3.2 TCP/IP Incompatible Frame Formats 378

   8.3.3 TCP/IP Incompatible Terminal Type 388

   8.3.4 TCP/IP Router Problems 395

8.4 References 414

THE COSTS OF TROUBLESHOOTING INTERNETWORKS.419

9.1 The Costs of Network Ownership 420

9.2 The Cost of Telecommunications Circuits 422

9.3 The Cost of Network Downtime 422

9.4 Saving Internetwork Expenses 428

   9.4.1 Saving Workstation Expenses 428

   9.4.2 Saving Protocol Interoperability Expenses 430

   9.4.3 Saving LAN/WAN Connectivity Expenses 430

   9.4.4 Saving with Network Management Systems 431

9.5 References 432

APPENDIX A: ADDRESSES OF STANDARDS
ORGANIZATIONS 435

APPENDIX B: SELECTED MANUFACTURERS OF
INTERNETWORKING PRODUCTS 439

APPENDIX C: LAN AND WAN ANALYZER
MANUFACTURERS 469

APPENDIX D: ACRONYMS 475

APPENDIX E: ETHERNET PROTOCOL TYPES 489

APPENDIX F: LINK SERVICE ACCESS POINT (SAP)
ADDRESSES 497
    IEEE-Administered LSAPs 497
    Manufacturer-Implemented LSAPs 498

APPENDIX G: DATA LINK LAYER FRAME FORMATS 499

APPENDIX H: PHYSICAL LAYER CONNECTOR
PINOUTS 505

TRADEMARKS 515

INDEX 519

Table of Illustrations

Figure 1-1   Traditional Distributed Processing 4

Figure 1-2a   Local PC to Host Connection 5

Figure 1-2b   Remote PC to Host Connection 6

Figure 1-3   Connectivity with Ethernet/IEEE 802.3 7

Figure 1-4   Connectivity with Token Ring/IEEE 802.5 8

Figure 1-5   Bandwidth Comparisons 10

Figure 1-6   Internetworking and Interoperability within
                the OSI Framework 13

Figure 1-7   Comparing Internetwork Architectures with OSI 16

Figure 1-8   Increasing Internetwork Complexity 18

Figure 1-9   OSI Network Management Functional Areas 19

Figure 2-1   Layered Protocol Control Information within a
                Data Link Layer Frame 28

Figure 2-2   LAN and WAN Analysis 29

Figure 2-3   Rule-based Expert Analyzer 35

Figure 2-4   Combination LAN/WAN Analysis 38

Figure 2-5   Analyzing LAN Traffic on Both Sides of a
                Bridge 39

Figure 2-6   Troubleshooting an ISDN Exchange 41

Figure 2-7   Remote Diagnostics via Distributed Slave Units 44

Figure 2-8a   Distributed Sniffer System Connected to a Network 46

Figure 2-8b   Distributed Sniffer System Overview 46

Figure 2-9   Integrating LAN Analyzer Data with a
                Simulation/Modeling Tool 48

Figure 2-10   Internetwork Troubleshooting Methodology 61

Figure 3-1   Comparing the AppleTalk Architecture with OSI 66

Figure 3-2   AppleTalk Packet Formats 72

Figure 3-3   AppleTalk Node Connecting to Remote VAX 75
Figure 3-4   AppleTalk Transition Router Operation 92
Figure 3-5   AppleTalk Remote Network Connections 96
Figure 3-6   AppleTalk Networks with the IBM 8209 Bridge 108
Figure 3-7   AppleTalk with SNA Gateway 122
Figure 3-8   EtherTalk to LocalTalk Connections 131
Figure 4-1   VINES Elements and the OSI Model (Server Side) 136
Figure 4-2   VINES Protocol Families 141
Figure 4-3   VINES Packet Formats 143
Figure 4-4   VINES Login and SNA Gateway 149
Figure 4-5   VINES Login Sequence 150
Figure 4-6   VINES Intermittent Server Operation 153
Figure 4-7   VINES SMTP Gateway Service 162
Figure 4-8   VINES SNA Gateway Access Sequence 167
Figure 5-1   DNA Modules Resident in a Typical DECnet Node 179
Figure 5-2   DECnet Phase V Architecture 183
Figure 5-3a   DECnet Packet Formats 185
Figure 5-3b   DECnet Phase IV Routing Information Details 186
Figure 5-4   DECnet Erroneous Signal Analysis 193
Figure 5-5   DECnet Erroneous LAT Packets 197
Figure 5-6   DECnet Session Establishment 205
Figure 5-7   DECnet Lost Connection 206
Figure 5-8   DECnet Invisible Connection 214
Figure 6-1a   Routing Information Within an 802.5 Frame 226
Figure 6-1b   Routing Information Field Details 227
Figure 6-2   Comparing SNA with the OSI Reference Model 229
Figure 6-3   SNA Packet Format 233
Figure 6-4   Token Ring/SNA Remote Host Access 237
Figure 6-5   Token Ring/SNA Connection Establishment 242
Figure 6-6   Token Ring/SNA Remote Terminal Emulation 254
Figure 6-7   Token Ring/SNA with FDDI Backbone 275
Figure 6-8   Token Ring/SNA RS/6000 Gateway 286

Figure 6-9   Token Ring/SNA VINES Gateway 295
Figure 7-1a   NetWare 286 Architecture 306
Figure 7-1b   NetWare 386 Architecture 307
Figure 7-2   NetWare Native Protocols 309
Figure 7-3   NetWare Packet Formats 314
Figure 7-4   NetWare Internal Router Operation 318
Figure 7-5a   NetWare Server Connection Sequence 331
Figure 7-5b   NetWare Preferred Server Connection Sequence 334
Figure 7-6   NetWare Misconfigured Addresses 336
Figure 7-7   NetWare Remote Bridge Connection 342
Figure 7-8   NetWare Local Bridges..349
Figure 7-9   NetWare SNA Gateway Architecture 354
Figure 7-10   NetWare SNA Gateway Connections 355
Figure 8-1   Comparing DOD Protocols with OSI and DOD Architectures 363
Figure 8-2   The IP Datagram Format 369
Figure 8-3   TCP/IP Connection Establishment/Disconnect Events 376
Figure 8-4   TCP/IP Incompatible Frame Formats 379
Figure 8-5   TCP/IP Incompatible Terminal Type......................................390
Figure 8-6   TCP/IP Router Confusion 395
Figure 9-1   Cost of Network Ownership Model 420
Figure 9-2   Number of Network Disabilities Per Year 423
Figure 9-3   Network Disability Length 424
Figure 9-4   Lost Productivity Per Year 424
Figure 9-5   Lost Revenue Expenses Per Year 425
Figure 9-6   Direct Expense Costs Per Year 426
Figure G-1   ARCNET Frame Formats 499
Figure G-2a   FDDI Token Format 500
Figure G-2b   FDDI Frame Format 500
Figure G-3   Ethernet Frame Format 501
Figure G-4   IEEE 802.3 Frame Format Including 802.2 LLC Header........501
Figure G-5a   IEEE 802.5 Token Format 502
Figure G-5b   IEEE 802.5 Frame Format 502

Figure G-6   Sub-Network Access Protocol (SNAP) Header Encapsulated
              within an IEEE 802.x Frame 503
Figure H-1   EIA-232-D/CCITT Recommendation Y.24 505
Figure H-2   EIA-449 506
Figure H-3   EIA-530 507
Figure H-4   Interconnecting EIA-530 with EIA-449 508
Figure H-5   CCITT Recommendation I.430 (ISDN Basic Rate Interface) .509
Figure H-6   CCITT Recommendation V.35 510
Figure H-7   CCITT Recommendation X.21 511
Figure H-8   Centronics® Parallel Interface 512
Figure H-9   IEEE-488 Digital Interface for Programmable
              Instrumentation 513

Foreword

In the 1970s, connecting remote terminals to centralized host processors was a typical definition of the term "internetwork." In the 1980s, connecting geographically distributed hosts into a single system became the norm. In the 1990s, more powerful workstations, plus the advent of client/server computing, presented new challenges. Add to this a mixture of both proprietary and open vendor architectures and protocols, and the internetwork manager has quite a challenge on his or her hands. To describe this challenge, an internetworking axiom is proposed:

Internetworks, by nature, are exceedingly complex. When they work, they are marvels of engineering. When they fail, you are in big trouble.

Avoiding "big trouble" (according to the reader's definition of the term) is the theme of this book. This volume discusses "big trouble" from the internetworking point of view. Previous volumes in this series have taken other perspectives. The *LAN Troubleshooting Handbook* (M&T Books, 1989) concentrated on LAN hardware and cabling systems. The *LAN Protocol Handbook* (M&T Books, 1990) discussed the analysis of LAN operating systems. *Internetworking: A Guide to Network Communications* (M&T Books, 1991) touched on all aspects of LAN/WAN (i.e. internetwork) design. This, the fourth volume, concentrates on analyzing the resulting mixture: LANs, WANs, MANs, and all the protocols that glue them together. In other words, now that you have it all designed and installed, here's some guidance on how to keep it working.

This book is structured in a modular fashion. Chapter 1 discusses the complexity of internetworks and why they have evolved into more difficult systems to maintain. Chapter 2 discusses the "Ultimate Analyzer," the device that will analyze all of your links and protocols without missing a bit. Chapters 3 through 8 discuss the internetworking aspects of particular protocol suites. In order, these are Apple

Computer's AppleTalk, Banyan Systems Inc.'s VINES, Digital Equipment Corporation's DECnet, IBM's Token Ring/SNA, Novell Inc.'s NetWare, and the multivendor TCP/IP. Since we are dealing with internetworking problems, the case studies included in each chapter deal with the internetworking layers of those architectures, i.e. primarily the OSI Network and Transport Layers. Chapter 9 concludes the book by investigating the cost elements (both overt and hidden) associated with internetworks. Select and study those chapters that are relevant to your applications.

Appendices A through H provide addresses of Standards Organizations, Internetworking Vendors, and Internetwork Analyzer Vendors; Acronyms, Ethernet Protocol Types, Link Service Access Point Addresses, LAN Frame Formats, and Physical Layer Connector Pinouts. Special thanks to Bill Cohn and Karen Andersen for their assistance with Appendices E and H, respectively.

A book of this nature is a team effort among contributors, editors, artists, and the author. My editors at M&T Books, Brenda McLaughlin, Tom Woolf, and Cheryl Goldberg provided the right balance of encouragement and motivation to keep the work on track. Sarah Wadsworth made sure that an endless number of details did not get overlooked. David Hertzke of Integrated Graphics Communications made hand-drawn sketches into the figures used throughout the book. Thanks to all of you for your assistance.

I am indeed fortunate to have a number of colleagues and friends who provided expert advice and input on various sections of the manuscript. These experts included: Dan Callahan, Randall Campbell, John Case, Al Driver, Paul Franchois, Garry Hornbuckle, Kirk Preiss, Carl Shinn, Jr., Paul Turner, and a host of people from Banyan Systems, Inc.

A number of vendors provided valuable input for the discussion in Chapter 2 on emerging internetwork analysis trends. Thanks to Dan Byrnes, Ben Merritt, Eva Holdenreid, Carole Ann McCarthy, Gary Rohlke, and Irv Witte. Network General Corporation provided the use of a Sniffer Protocol Analyzer for the analysis of the case studies in each chapter. Kent Sterling and Bob Bessin were instrumental in putting this together, and deserve much credit.

The protocol analysis hints in Chapters 3 through 8 were compiled by interviewing a number of people, just like many of you, that spend their days in the internetwork trenches. The case studies included in Chapters 3 through 8 are real problems that were captured from live internetworks. Contributors included: Joe Bardwell, Sam Cicchetti, Stewart Clark, John Cornell, Tracy Currie, Lee Diver, Al Driver, Andre Dubreuil, Ross Dunthorne, Chris Dutchyn, Sherilyn Evans, Paul Franchois, Larry Grover, Garry Hornbuckle, Michael Howard, Steve King, Brent Kuchvalek, Tom LaCorti, Frank Leeds, Kevin LeMay, Al Leveckis, Iwan Lie, Myron McCarty, Doug Parks, Phil Reagan, Mike Rutigliano, Bob Sherman, Gregg Sterner, Ray Swincki, and Evan Trebing.

Nancy Wright did much of the research for Appendices A through C, as well as the word processing on the manuscript. Thanks, Nancy, for an excellent job.

Holly, Nathan, and Nicholas again supplied the much-needed support and encouragement at just the right times. Buster, Brutus, and Boomer did their best not to bark during periods of high concentration. Your love is greatly appreciated.

Mark A. Miller
December 1991

Why This Book Is For You

This book, the fourth volume in the Troubleshooting Series, is written for designers, managers, and administrators who must analyze the health of their internetworks. Sections of this handbook address the following topics:

- The complexity of internetworks and the challenges of a multiprotocol environment.

- How to select the appropriate analyzer for your internetwork, assuring that all the LAN/MAN/WAN interfaces and protocols are covered in that tool.

- The internetworking capabilities of AppleTalk, VINES, DECnet, NetWare, Token Ring/SNA, and TCP/IP.

- Hints on how to analyze each of these protocol suites and what significant events to look for.

- Explanations of the packet formats for each architecture, including detailed figures.

- Thirty case studies describing actual problems, taken from live networks, that illustrate the protocols in use, what can go wrong, and the solutions to the problems.

- Reference appendices showing LAN frame formats, protocol addresses, and connector pinouts.

If you have to maintain a multiprotocol, multivendor internetwork, this handbook belongs next to your protocol analyzer.

CHAPTER 1

The Complexity of Internetworks

For many years, there were two simple axioms in the data communications industry: Computer users never have enough memory; and they're never satisfied with the performance of their systems. Today's PC users still require adequate memory and good performance. But as technologies grow more complex, systems managers must deal with far more difficult issues. For instance, PC users who wish to communicate with a peer, say, to access a bulletin board system (BBS), must now be concerned with the speed of their dial-up modem. PCs connected to a Local Area Network (LAN) are restricted by the memory and speed of devices such as network interface cards (NICs), servers, print spoolers, and so on. And when the PC is on a LAN connected to other LANs via Metropolitan Area Network (MAN) or Wide Area Network (WAN), communication between distant workstations is further constrained by the available transmission facilities.

As the industry moves from "the year of the LAN," which occurred in the late 1980s to "the decade of the internetwork" in the 1990s [1-1], management issues will continue to grow more difficult. Internetworks are, by nature, exceedingly complex. When they work, they're marvels of engineering. But when they fail, you're in big trouble.

This book is designed to help you recover from those inevitable periods of network downtime. No matter how troublesome the internetwork problem, a thorough analysis should restore it to health. But before we jump into network troubleshooting, it's important to understand how internetworks became so complicated to begin with.

1.1 A Historical Perspective on Connectivity

The architecture of the early 1970s consisted of a large, centralized host processor with dumb terminals connected via terminal controllers. One example of this traditional centralized architecture was IBM's System Network Architecture (SNA). By the late 1970s, distributed host processing, typical of Digital Equipment Corporation's (DEC) DECnet, was providing connectivity between geographically dispersed hosts (Figure 1-1). These distributed hosts were linked into a Wide Area Network (WAN) via either Point-to-Point (PTP) or Packet Switched Public Data Network (PSPDN) connections. The transmission links between hosts, typically leased lines running at 56 Kbs or less, were slow by today's standards. (See References [1-2] and [1-3] for more information on these earlier architectures.)

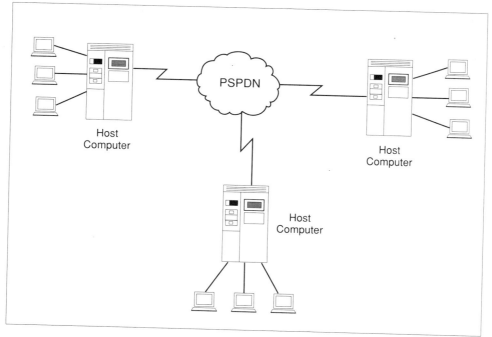

Figure 1-1. Traditional Distributed Processing

With host-based systems, the host's ability to handle input/output (I/O) and information processing requests limited the speed of user applications. WAN links between the user and host further degraded response time. The PC, which was introduced in 1981, addressed the I/O and information processing issues by bringing processing power to the desktop. PCs also pioneered the user-friendly interface. But these early PCs were hardly a panacea. They simply replaced earlier performance constraints with new problems of inadequate memory and slow processing. And PC users who expected the power of a mainframe database were certainly disappointed with the database offerings available for the PC.

In an attempt to combine access to the mainframe database with the PC's ease of use, local processing, and data storage, PCs became emulators of host terminals such as the IBM 3278 and the DEC VT-100. Two options developed to connect the PC to a host: a local connection within the same building or campus via coax or EIA-232 interfaces (Figure 1-2a), or a remote connection, such as Remote Job Entry (RJE), via modems (Figure 1-2b). Both configurations increased desktop productivity. Reference [1-4] illustrates these configurations in greater detail.

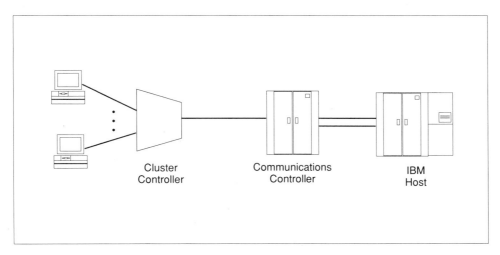

Figure 1-2a. Local PC to Host Connection

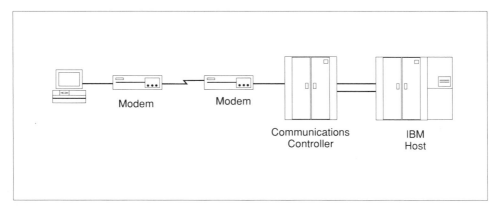

Figure 1-2b. Remote PC to Host Connection

The late 1980s were routinely proclaimed the "Year of the LAN." The initial objective for local area networking was to allow PCs to share printers and files. Yet, access to host applications, such as financial databases, remained a user requirement. This requirement led to a merger of technologies, with the LAN acting as the "glue" that brought the host, peripherals, and workstations together. Two principal types of LANs have emerged. The first, Ethernet/IEEE 802.3, was developed by DEC, Intel, and Xerox in the early 1970s. It originally consisted of a coaxial cable and bus topology (Figure 1-3), but now offers several choices of transmission medium (twisted pairs, coax, or fiber) and architecture (bus or star). IBM has heavily influenced the second technology, the token ring/IEEE 802.5 (Figure 1-4). This topology also supports a variety of transmission media (shielded and unshielded twisted pairs and fiber optic cables) in a distributed star architecture.

Writing in *Business Communication Review* [1-5], Mel Ethem discusses interconnection strategies based upon the centralized or distributed nature of the architecture. Centralized systems become host-centric, with workstations requiring access to just a few data sources. With this architecture, the protocols, transmission speed, physical cabling, and the like of the gateway constrain the design of the internetwork.

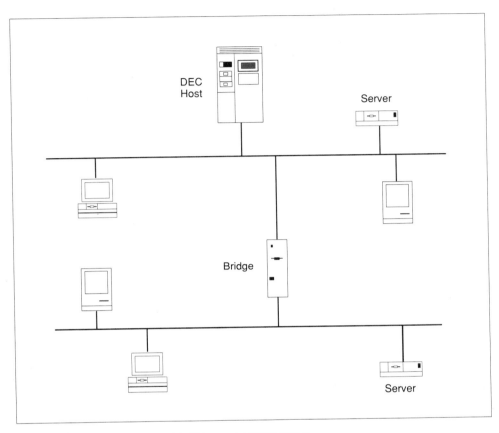

Figure 1-3. Connectivity with Ethernet / IEEE 802.3

In a distributed system, workstations access a number of hosts. Here, a client/ server paradigm emerges in which any desktop client connects to the information on any other desktop or server. In this type of system, the *network operating system* (NOS) that defines the client/server paradigm constrains the distributed computing architecture. For maximum interoperability, choose a single network operating system, such as Banyan System's VINES, IBM's OS/2 LAN Server, or Novell's NetWare, for all LANs within the internetwork.

7

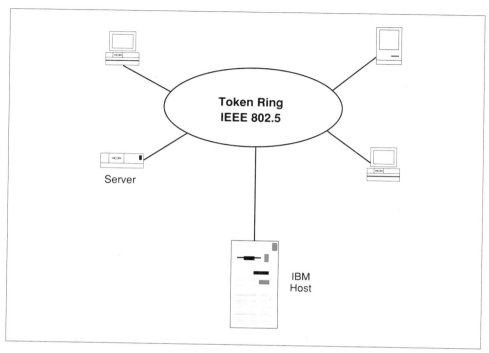

Figure 1-4. **Connectivity with token ring / IEEE 802.5**

1.2 Wideband Requirements

The transmission lines that provide the required bandwidth have also had a major impact on the design and characteristics of today's internetworks. Local Exchange Carriers (LECs), Inter-Exchange Carriers (IXCs), and Packet Switched Public Data Networks (PSPDNs) offer reliable, digital, high-bandwidth pipes for data. These services are defined by the users they serve and the regulations they must adhere to. LECs provide communication services within a Local Access Transport Area (LATA) and are regulated by the State Public Utility Commissions (PUCs). The IXCs offer communication services between LATAs, and are regulated by the Federal Communications Commission (FCC) and the PUCs. PSPDNs, which are unregulated, provide both intra- and inter-LATA services, as well as access to PSPDNs in other countries.

Three transmission technologies address the wideband requirements of faster distributed host processing. Both LECs and IXCs have implemented the Integrated Services Digital Network (ISDN) to provide integrated voice/data transport at 1.5 Mbps. A new service from many LECs, Switched Multimegabit Data Service (SMDS), offers high-speed DS-1 (1.544 Mbps) or DS-3 (44.736 Mbps) data transport within a metropolitan area. SMDS is based upon the IEEE 802.6 standard. The Synchronous Optical Network (SONET) is a Bellcore standard for high speed data transport at rates above DS-3. The basic transport signal runs at the OC-1 (Optical Carrier, level 1) rate of 51.840 Mbps; the fastest defined signal is OC-96, operating at 4.976 Gbps.

As we'll discuss in the following section, as PC workstations and applications become ever more powerful, they need to store and retrieve an ever larger quantity of information. For example, a single page is equivalent to approximately 2,000 characters, and a book around 580,000 characters [1-6]. Graphical information, such as medical images (X-rays, CAT scans, etc.) or engineering drawings (CAD/CAM), can be an order of magnitude larger than character-based information. Transmitting such vast quantities of data across LANs, MANs, or WANs becomes quite a challenge (see Figure 1-5). For example, transmitting a book (580,000 characters) would require 1.7 minutes at 56 Kbps, 3.8 seconds at 1.544 Mbps (T1 rate), 0.06 seconds at 100 Mbps (FDDI rate), or 0.003 seconds at 1.7 Gbps (fiber optic rates). Similar analyses could be made for the bandwidth required to transmit an engineering drawing from one subcontractor to another. Large file sizes demand high-bandwidth transmission pipes. As a result, the market for wideband services such as FDDI, ISDN, SONET, or SMDS is expected to grow rapidly through the end of the decade. References [1-7] through [1-10] contain further information on these emerging transport technologies.

1.3 Advances in Workstations

1991 marked the 10th anniversary of the announcement of the PC. Since its introduction, the available memory, clock speed, processor bus width, and I/O options of the original PC have been eclipsed many times over. A number of factors have affected the direction of workstation evolution, which in turn has impacted the performance of the internetwork.

Document	Characters	Wideband 56 Kbps	T1 1.5 Mbps	FDDI 100 Mbps	Fiber Optics 1.7 Gbps
Page	2K	0.3 Sec	0.01 Sec	0.0002 Sec	0.00001 Sec
Report	60K	10.3 Sec	0.4 Sec	0.006 Sec	0.0003 Sec
Book	580K	1.7 Min	3.8 Sec	0.06 Sec	0.003 Sec
Local Library	56B	116 Day	4.3 Day	1.6 Hr	5.5 Min
Library of Congress	14T	81.5 Yr	3 Yr	16.6 Day	23.5 Hr

Figure 1-5. Bandwidth Comparisons
(©1991, Infonetics Research Institute, Inc.)

These factors include:

- Applications—the prime driver behind the workstation type. For example, graphics-intensive applications, such as CAD/CAM or desktop publishing, require high-resolution video displays and place heavy performance demands on the workstation processor. In addition, graphics applications create large files. When these files are transmitted over the network, they generate a great deal of network traffic, which impacts bandwidth requirements for both the LAN and WAN.

- Operating platform—the prime driver behind the selection of the Network Operating System (NOS). The battle lines between DOS, Macintosh, and UNIX-based workstations have shifted recently due to the success of Microsoft Windows 3.0, which gives DOS applications a graphical, multitasking operating environment [1-11]. The workstation operating system defines many parameters, such as file sizes and video resolution, that have a secondary impact on server memory consumption, network traffic, etc. Whatever the ultimate fate of each of these environments, it's important to make sure the NOS supports the platform or platforms found in your internetwork.

- Hardware performance—Increasingly, the workstations of the 1990s need the power of the minicomputers of the 1980s. Fueling this requirement are the graphics-intensive applications that demand rapid access to large files. Desktop workstations are expected to migrate from the current Intel 80386 or Motorola 68030 processors to the Intel i486/80586 and Motorola 68040 processors in the next few years [1-12]. As workstations become more powerful, they are taking on new roles as servers or interconnectivity devices, such as bridges and routers [1-13]. With these new applications come even more rigorous performance expectations.

Thus, as desktop applications demand a higher level of performance, the connectivity medium (LAN, MAN, or WAN) must offer sufficient bandwidth to respond. Enhancements to workstation processors, servers, and interconnectivity devices will be necessary to meet expanding internetworking requirements. Another complexity arises because many of the internetwork devices operate with different protocols.

1.4 Protocol Interoperability

It's one thing for two workstations to exchange sequences of bits, quite another for them to share meaningful data. The *protocols*, or rules of communication, determine the level of understanding between workstations.

Prior to the development of the International Organization for Standardization (ISO)'s Open Systems Interconnection (OSI) Reference Model (discussed later in this section), most network architectures were proprietary. Because vendors did not use open standards designed by committees of international experts, software from a vendor such as IBM could not interoperate with software from DEC, for instance, which, in turn, could not communicate directly with systems from either Hewlett-

Packard or Wang Laboratories. A gateway was necessary to translate protocols at all levels of these proprietary architectures.

One of the goals of the open systems concept is to provide protocol interoperability between systems from different vendors. Theoretically, if all vendors adhered to a common architecture, communication problems between those systems would vanish.

Most readers probably already understand the concept of the Open Systems Interconnection (OSI) seven-layer Reference Model. Rather than rehashing the functions of the layers, let's consider how each one impacts internetworking and interoperability (see Figure 1-6).

Starting at the bottom, the Physical Layer makes the physical connection to the transmission medium, such as twisted pairs, coaxial cable, fiber optic link, etc. Once the physical connection is complete, the Data Link Layer, which is implemented in firmware on the network interface card, puts the bit transmission in a specific order, called a *frame*, and adds the address of the transmitting and receiving endpoints. The Data Link Layer then reliably and sequentially communicates that frame across the link. Thus, these lower two layers perform *Local Network Connectivity*.

Layers 3 through 7 are usually implemented in software. The Network Layer establishes a path for the data through the WAN or internetwork. To do this, the Network Layer designates local and network addresses. This is similar to the way in which a telephone network operates. For instance, to call an associate next door you would use a local telephone number, NXX-XXXX, where N is an integer between 2 and 9, and X is an integer from 0 to 9. To call across the country, you would add an area code: 303-NXX-XXXX. And to call across the world, you would add a country designator as well: 19-0011-303-NXX-XXXX. Other Network Layer responsibilities include routing the data, which at this layer is called a *packet*, from the source to the destination via the appropriate LAN, MAN, or WAN transmission facilities. The Transport Layer assures the reliability of the connection through the various networks. Thus, the Network and Transport Layers provide *Internetwork Connectivity*.

Just because a LAN or WAN physically connects two workstations doesn't mean that the two workstations can communicate with each other. The workstation you're trying to reach may be engaged in a communications session with another

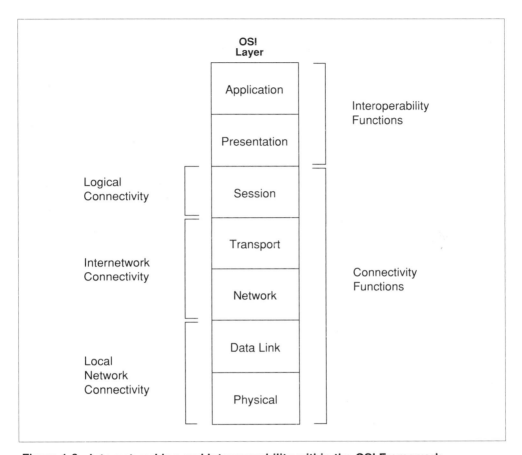

Figure 1-6. Internetworking and Interoperability within the OSI Framework

host, or it may not have enough memory to communicate with two network nodes at once. The Session Layer, therefore, adds a *logical* dimension to the *physical* connectivity of the lower layers. This logical process controls the connection and disconnection of the data communication path (the "session"), and establishes the rules (half or full duplex) under which workstations will converse. Should our session be disconnected inadvertently, the Session Layer will re-establish it where we left off. Taken together, the lower five layers handle *Connectivity*.

Once we get data from another workstation on the LAN or WAN, we need to make sure it's in a format we can read and use. The Presentation and Application Layers assure this interoperability. The Presentation Layer operates with the syntax or form of the data without changing its meaning or semantics. Examples of Presentation Layer functions include data compression, encryption, and code conversion (e.g. ASCII to EBCDIC). The Application Layer provides a standard format for end-users to use to send and receive electronic mail, read and update remote files, or access and change database records.

In theory, the OSI model provides the basis for true interoperability between networks from different vendors. Unfortunately, many vendors continue to add proprietary hooks in order to gain, regain, or maintain market share. These multiple architectures result in internetworks that require additional devices, such as gateways, to assure the level of interoperability necessary for reliable communication. (Chapter 9 of Reference [1-14] discusses gateway operations in depth.)

Figure 1-7 illustrates just a few of the protocols used within various manufacturers' internetwork architectures. As you can see, each of these vendors uses different protocols at every layer. No wonder we have problems with internetworking and interoperability!

One firm, the Clarke Burton Corporation (Salt Lake City, UT), has compared various LAN architectures and developed what it calls the CBC Interoperability Matrix [1-15]. The matrix identifies five key transport protocols: AppleTalk, NetBEUI (IBM NetBIOS), Novell NetWare IPX/SPX, OSI, and TCP/IP. It then compares architectures from various vendors, including Apple Computer, Banyan Systems, IBM, Microsoft, Novell, and 3Com, based upon their support for these and other LAN protocols. If your internetwork requires protocol interoperability, make a similar analysis for your applications before ordering internetworking software.

1.5 LAN/WAN Connectivity

A decade ago, LANs typically connected small groups of perhaps 10 to 20 PCs. WANS were used primarily for voice communication. These WANs acted as analog trunks between distant Private Automatic Branch Exchanges (PABXs). Beginning around 1986, the popularity of T1 circuits, operating at 1.544 Mbps, (the equivalent of 24 voice-grade telephone lines before compression) became the impetus for LAN/ WAN integration. First, the pricing of T1 circuits made their large bandwidth economically attractive. And second, T1 multiplexer manufacturers took advantage of the T1 circuits' bandwidth by developing digital interfaces for their devices that combined voice and data into a single datastream. Vendors of digital PABXs produced similar designs that became known as integrated voice/data PABXs. Thus, the carriers (both LECs and IXCs) developed a new market for their services, while the multiplexer and PABX vendors created a new market for their hardware.

The only missing link was the physical connection between the LAN and the WAN. Not surprisingly, the T1 multiplexer vendors such as Timeplex (Woodcliff Lake, NJ) and Vitalink Communications Corp. (Fremont, CA) were among the first to consider LAN interfaces for their products. Before long, more traditional bridge and router manufacturers such as Proteon (Westborough, MA), Microcom (Norwood, MA), Wellfleet Communications, Inc. (Bedford, MA), cisco Systems Co. (Menlo Park, CA), and Retix (Santa Monica, CA) were also devising ways to make the LAN/ WAN connection.

As LAN/WAN links became more capable, they also became more popular— and more complex (Figure 1-8). On the LAN side of the link, devices such as bridges, routers, and gateways must now support multiple protocols and architectures. *Bridges* are used primarily to manage network traffic in order to optimize the efficiency of the internetwork. *Routers* implement subnetworks, which are, in many cases, geographically distant and connected via WAN links. *Gateways* are used to logically connect an application, such as electronic mail, on one host with a similar but incompatible application on another. It may be necessary to do protocol conversions at multiple layers to make that connection. Chapter 1 of Reference [1-14] discusses these functions in greater detail; References [1-16] and [1-17] discuss the complexities of these devices.

Examples of LAN bridges, gateways, and routers include IBM's 8209 Ethernet to token ring bridge; Ungermann-Bass' (Santa Clara, CA) Ethernet to FDDI bridge; Proteon's routers, which support token ring, Ethernet, or FDDI hardware plus a number of Transport protocols, such as TCP/IP, Novell's SPX/IPX, and DECnet; and Wellfleet's products, whch provide concurrent bridging and routing with a wide range of options for WAN links.

OSI Layer	Apple Computer	Banyan Systems	DEC DECnet	IBM SNA	Novell NetWare	TCP/IP Internets	OSI Protocols
Application	Application Programs and Protocols for file transfer, electronic mail, etc.						
Presentation	AppleTalk Filing Protocol (AFP)	Remote Procedure Calls (Net RPC)	Network Management Network · Application	Transaction Services Presentation Services	NetWare Core Protocols (NCP)	Application- Specific Protocols	ISO 8823
Session	AppleTalk Session Protocol (ASP)		Session	Data Flow Control	NetBIOS		ISO 8327
Transport	AppleTalk Transaction Protocol (ATP)	VINES Interprocess Communications (VIPC)	End Communication	Transmission Control	NetWare SPX	Transmission Control Protocol (TCP)	ISO 8073 TP0-4
Network	Datagram Delivery Protocol (DDP)	VINES Internet Protocol (VIP)	Routing	Path Control	NetWare IPX	Internet Protocol (IP)	ISO 8473 CLNP
Data Link	Network Interface Cards: Ethernet, Token-Ring, ARCNET, StarLAN, LocalTalk						
Physical	Transmission Media: Twisted Pair, Coax, Fiber Optics, Wireless Media, etc.						

Figure 1-7. Comparing Internetwork Architectures with OSI

On the WAN side of the LAN/WAN link, a number of emerging digital technologies have supplemented T1 as a digital pipe for LAN to LAN connections. These include the Fiber Data Distributed Interface (FDDI) for connecting LANs; and T3 (44.736 Mbps), Frame Relay, ISDN, and SMDS (Switched Multimegabit Data Service) for WAN connections [1-18].

As you might imagine, internetworks that use all of these products can become quite challenging to manage. We'll look at these network management considerations next.

1.6 Network Management Trends

When a network came from a single vendor, that vendor was responsible for its support. Thus, AT&T and the local telephone company took responsibility for the telecommunication lines, IBM managed the mainframe in the accounting department, and DEC managed the minicomputers in the engineering department. The network manager simply identified the malfunctioning system, and the appropriate vendor would solve the problem.

Today's internetworks (shown in Figure 1-8) are far more difficult to manage for three reasons. First, centralized data processing has been replaced by distributed systems. Second, the divestiture of AT&T in 1984 dramatically changed the way customers manage their telecommunication circuits. Today's internetwork manager must interface with the LEC, IXC, and other providers, such as Packet Switched Public Data Network (PSPDN). Finally, the economic growth of the data communications industry has dramatically increased the number of vendors in the marketplace. All of these developments increase the likelihood of finger-pointing between vendors.

Both vendors and standards bodies have proposed solutions to these challenges [1-19]. The predominant standard, ISO 7498-4 [1-20], defines five functional management areas, shown in Figure 1-9 and explained below.

- Fault management deals with detection, testing, and correction of network failures.

- Accounting management allocates network costs to the responsible party.

- Configuration management maintains the current status of all elements within the network.

- Performance management collects and logs statistical information regarding system performance.

- Security management protects network resources and controls access to the network.

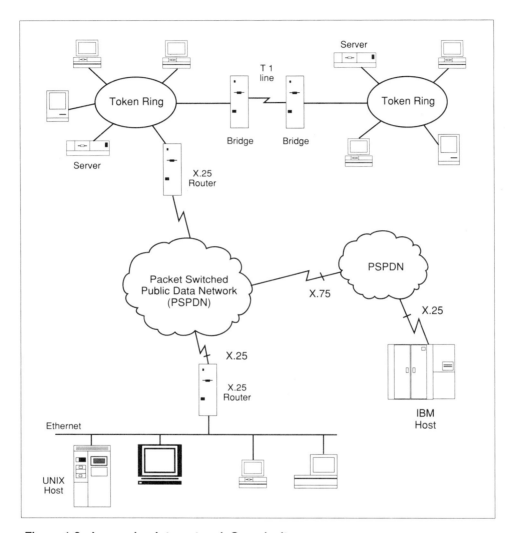

Figure 1-8. Increasing Internetwork Complexity

Various standards bodies have developed protocols to support these standards. The ISO standard, known as the Common Management Information Protocol (CMIP), is described in ISO 9595 and 9596 (References [1-21] and [1-22]). A second is Common Management Information Protocol over Transmission Control Protocol

(TCP) known as CMOT [1-23]. CMOT starts with CMIP as a base, but uses TCP as the Transport Layer protocol, instead of the ISO TP-4. Another derivative of CMIP is known as CMOL, which is CMIP on IEEE 802.2 Logical Link Control; it was developed by IBM and 3Com Corporation (Santa Clara, CA). The IEEE has now renamed CMOL the IEEE 802.1b LAN MAN Management Protocol (LMMP).

The most popular network management protocol, however, is SNMP, the Simple Network Management Protocol [1-24], which was developed by the Internet (TCP/IP) community. Its popularity is largely due to its simplicity: It defines only

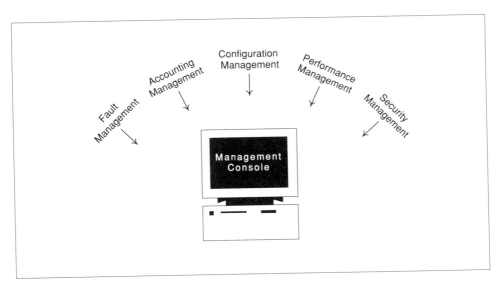

Figure 1-9. OSI Network Management Functional Areas

five commands/responses. Thus, it makes network management as painless as possible by minimizing the amount of management data transmitted between network elements and the management console.

Finally, vendors in the data communications industry have developed network management systems that incorporate standard protocols (CMIP, CMOT, SNMP, etc.) into proprietary architectures. Major players in this market include AT&T (Unified Network Management Architecture—UNMA), DEC (Management Control Center—DECmcc), Hewlett-Packard (OpenView Network Management), and IBM (NetView). Look for growth in this area as internetwork complexity increases. References [1-25] through [1-28] are examples of recent literature describing this growth.

1.7 Economic Considerations

When the PC was announced in 1981, few financial analysts estimated that it would become the $28.4 billion annual market projected for 1991 [1-29]. A large number of these PCs are expected to be connected via networks. The Gartner Group of Stamford, CT estimates that 67 percent of the PCs in the U.S. will be networked by 1992 [1-30]. The Market Intelligence Research Company of Mountain View, CA predicts that the total amount spent to network those PCs will grow from $5 billion in 1991 to $9.2 billion in 1995.

The market for internetworking hardware and software is growing even faster. Infonetics Research Institute, Inc., based in San Jose, CA, is projecting a worldwide compound annual growth rate of 31 percent for the period of 1990 through 1993 [1-31]. This growth represents an increase in revenues from $528 million in 1990 to $1,080 billion in 1993. Multiprotocol routers are expected to account for the vast majority of these sales.

All the money being spent on hardware and software is bound to add to the complexities of internetworks. And analyzing these internetworks will demand new skills from their managers. Just as the speed of the data transmission facilities has increased from T1 to T3 and beyond, so must the capabilities of those who design, install, and implement those internetworks. As Professor John Donovan of MIT's Sloan School of Management has stated, the Chief Information Officer must move into the role of Network Manager [1-32]. Reference [1-33] elaborates on the network management functions that these complex systems will require.

Perhaps a more alarming issue is the cost of internetwork failures. Our society has come to depend on complex technologies. But what happens when these technologies fail? Imagine that you're the internetwork manager for a mail order company selling specialty items to a worldwide customer base. What would be the financial implications of your toll-free (800-number) communication circuits failing for one hour? What if the host maintaining your inventory crashed? How much revenue would you lose before those communication or computing resources were restored to full operation? Pondering this question for a few minutes should inspire you to conduct a thorough reliability and redundancy audit of your internetwork. We will consider these economic costs in detail in Chapter 9.

1.8 Analyzing the Resultant Mixture

All of these factors—centralized versus distributed computing architectures, wideband transmission facilities, specialized workstations, multiple protocols, new methods for LAN/WAN connectivity, and dissimilar network management systems—can result in an interesting mixture. The internetwork may use a combination of cabling types, including twisted pair, coax, and fiber optics. The LAN hardware may include incompatible access methods, such as CSMA/CD (IEEE 802.3) and token passing (IEEE 802.5). Connectivity devices such as bridges may use different algorithms, such as spanning tree (IEEE 802.3) or source routing (IEEE 802.5). The electronic mail package from one network operating system may not communicate with one from its competitor. So how do you analyze this internetwork stew?

The following are some general guidelines that provide a framework to help you get started:

- Define the problem—you can't troubleshoot a problem that you can't clearly describe.

- Develop a solution— proceed carefully and methodically to solve the problem.

- Document your work—so you can learn from the past.

- Disseminate the results—so that others can benefit from your experiences.

With this background into the complexity of internetworks, the rest of this book will focus on methods of analyzing and troubleshooting internetworks. Chapter 2 will focus on the new breed of analyzer that can handle LANs, MANs, and WANs with equal facility. Subsequent chapters will investigate Apple Computer Inc.'s AppleTalk, Banyan Systems' VINES, Digital Equipment Corp.'s DECnet, IBM's SNA, Novell Inc.'s NetWare, and the multivendor TCP/IP. Now that we're motivated, let's begin our study of internetwork analysis by selecting the Ultimate Analyzer.

1.9 References

[1-1] Lippis, Nick and James Herman. "The Internetwork Decade." *Data Communications* supplement, January 1991.

[1-2] Cypser, R. J. *Communications Architecture for Distributed Systems*. Addison-Wesley, Reading, MA, 1978.

[1-3] Digital Equipment Corporation. *Digital's Networks: An Architecture With A Future*. Publication EB-26013, 1984.

[1-4] Madron, Thomas William. *Micro-Mainframe Connection*. Howard W. Sams & Company, Indianapolis, IN, 1987.

[1-5] Ethem, Mel R. "Strategies for LAN Interconnection." *Business Communications Review* (May 1991): 26-32.

[1-6] Infonetics Research Institute, Inc., 1991.

[1-7] Mazzaferro, John F. and Alexa A. Dell'Acqua. "FDDI Technology Report." *Computer Technology Research Corp.*, Charleston, SC, April 1991.

[1-8] Kessler, Gary C. ISDN. McGraw-Hill, New York, 1990.

[1-9] Muller, Nathan J., Robert P. Davidson, and Michael I. McLoughlin. "A Management Briefing on the Emerging Synchronous Optical Network." General DataComm, Inc., 1990.

[1-10] Kessler, Gary C. "Service for Your MAN." *LAN* (October 1991): 47-63.

[1-11] Curran, Lawrence. "A Battle is Brewing on the Desktop." *Electronics* (June 1991): 41-46.

[1-12] International Data Corp. "U.S. Personal Workstation Market Review and Forecast 1989-1994." Framingham, MA, 1990.

[1-13] Blevins, David W., Christopher A. Bartholomew, and John D. Graf. "Performance Analysis of Personal Computer Workstations." *Hewlett-Packard Journal* (October 1991): 92-96.

[1-14] Miller, Mark A. *Internetworking: A Guide to Network Communications.* M&T Books, Redwood City, CA, 1991.

[1-15] Burton, Craig, Jamie Lewis, and Karl DeBrine. "LAN Transport Protocol Interoperability." *Clarke Burton Report*, November 1990.

[1-16] Seifert, William M. "Why Complex Networks Require Routers." *Business Communications Review*, March 1990.

[1-17] Lippis, Nick. "Multiprotocol Gateways: Beyond Internet Connectivity." *Data Communications* (June 1991): 35-36.

[1-18] Burton, Craig, Jamie Lewis, and Karl DeBrine. "LAN/WAN Connectivity Trends." *Clarke Burton Report*, December 1990.

[1-19] Dowling, Suzanne. "Reflections on SNMP, CMIP and Other Notable Network Management Issues." *Network Management Perspective* (January 1991): 1-10.

[1-20] International Organization for Standardization, *Information Processing Systems—Open Systems Interconnection—Basic Reference Model—Part 4: Management Framework.* ISO/IEC 7498-4: 1989.

[1-21] International Organization for Standardization, *Information Processing Systems , Open Systems Interconnection, Management Information Service Definition, Part 2: Common Management Information Service.* ISO/IEC 9595-2, 1989.

[1-22] International Organization for Standardization *Information Processing Systems, Open Systems Interconnection, Management Information Protocol Specification, Part 2: Common Management Information Protocol.* ISO/IEC 9596-2, 1989.

[1-23] DDN Network Information Center. *The Common Management Information Services and Protocol over TCP/IP (CMOT).* RFC 1095, April 1989.

[1-24] DDN Network Information Center. *Simple Network Management Protocol.* RFC 1157, May 1990.

[1-25] Herman, James. "Integrated Network Management: Fact or Fiction?" Communication Networks Conference, January 1991.

[1-26] Vasquez, Bill. "Implementing Integrated Network Management." *Journal of Network Management*, (Winter 1990): 12-20.

[1-27] Salamone, Salvatore. "An Elementary Look at Network Management." *Network World* (April 9, 1990): 1-48.

[1-28] Borsook, Paulina. "Management Wars: NetView and SNMP Battle for Supremacy." *Interoperability* (Fall 1990): 35-38.

[1-29] Mulqueen, John T. "Data Communications 1991 Market Forecast." *Data Communications* (December 1990): 95-98.

[1-30] Carr, Jim. "Forecasting New Highs." *LAN* (May 1991): 36-44.

[1-31] Infonetics Research Institute. "LAN Interconnection Products: User Requirements and Buying Plans." November 1990.

[1-32] Donovan, John J. "Beyond Chief Information Officer to Network Manager." *Harvard Business Review* (September-October 1988): 134-140.

[1-33] Muller, Nathan J. and Robert P. Davidson. *LANs to WANs: Network Management in the 1990s*. Artech House, Boston, 1990.

CHAPTER 2

The Ultimate Analyzer

As we saw in Chapter 1, corporations are relying increasingly on complex internetworks that may be distributed across the globe and might use a wide variety of LAN, MAN, or WAN protocols. Such dependency means that the costs associated with network downtime can only continue to rise. To meet the challenges of these internetworks, network managers must make sure their network management and analysis tools will be able do more, work smarter, and last longer (see Reference [2-1]).

In order to analyze complex internetworks, we need to understand the trends shaping the computer and communications industries. Let's begin with a brief history of these industries and how internetwork maintenance has changed with them.

2.1 A Brief History of Internetworking

The 1960s was the era of the vendor-proprietary, host-centric network. Telecommunications facilities consisted primarily of analog leased lines. Because of the proprietary nature of those systems, internetwork maintenance was dominated by the vendors that supplied the host system and the communication lines. In most installations, communication lines were maintained by the then-dominant Bell System: AT&T and its subsidiaries. Although AT&T published many standards for their analog lines, modems, etc. that third-parties could have used to enter the communications business, this industry did not see significant growth until the AT&T divestiture in 1984.

With the popularity of minicomputers in the 1970s came the growth of distributed processing. For multi-location organizations, it made sense to move the computing power close to end-users. Thus, if the engineering center, manufacturing facility, and distribution warehouse were in separate locations, three computer centers were established. Because those locations invariably required data communication, computer and communications technologies began to meld. As the network became distributed, managers needed to extend their span of control. Vendors, therefore, developed in-hand diagnostics to extend the network control center's reach to modem and multiplexer-based networks.

A major revolution in computer and data communication technologies occurred in the 1980s. Price/performance improvements in personal computers and VLSI (very large-scale integration) components, which made network interface cards easier and cheaper to manufacture, helped fuel the LAN explosion. At the same time, the switch from analog to digital transmission lines such as T1/T3 and ISDN created radical changes in testing methods and practices for WAN facilities.

The 1990s have been described as the decade of internetworking. Three significant developments are expected to impact the networks of this era. First, distributed computing is replacing host-centric architectures in most industries. Thus, processing power is moving closer to end-users, who need to communicate with their peers wherever they may be located. Connectivity devices, such as bridges and routers, therefore, will become more prevalent [2-2]. Second, as workstations become more powerful and graphical applications require more data to be transmitted over the network, the bandwidth needed to connect these devices must also increase. Third, with the move toward distributed computing comes an associated move away from the single vendor network. Open Systems will demand a number of multivendor protocol solutions.

2.2 Internetwork Analysis

As internetworks continue to become distributed, offer higher bandwidths, and support more protocols, network managers must be prepared to adjust their network support departments and to purchase new analysis tools.

Distributed networks will require companies to change the structure of centralized MIS departments. Individual locations will need their own network management staff to handle user-related problems, while the headquarters location will be better equipped to analyze internetwork failures.

The development of high bandwidth connectivity has reduced the economic life of existing network analysis and management equipment. As new technologies, such as fiber optic LANs and high-speed MANs, become more popular, internetwork managers will have to update their diagnostic instruments. When the typical WAN link was an analog circuit, for example, a network administrator suspecting a problem on that circuit would test it for compliance with analog transmission parameters, such as impulse noise, envelope delay distortion, and phase jitter. But today's digital circuits that constitute the high-bandwidth pipes require entirely different analysis techniques to analyze completely different transmission parameters. For example, T1/T3 circuits must be tested for proper data framing, improperly generated signals, such as bipolar violations (BPVs), and special data encoding, such as B8ZS (bipolar with eight zero substitution). If that transmission medium is optical fibers, rather than twisted pairs or coaxial cable, the analyzer needs an optical rather than an electrical interface.

Multiprotocol internetworks will require more intelligent analyzers. Analyzers that once handled a single protocol suite, such as SNA, must now take care of several, such as SNA, DECnet, and TCP/IP. To understand this trend, you need a little background on how analyzers work and the direction in which they have been developing.

A protocol analyzer works as follows. The analyzer attaches to the internetwork in a passive mode and captures the information transmitted between various devices. This information can be divided into two categories: data and control. The data comes from an end-user process, such as an electronic mail message. The control information assures that the data transfer obeys the rules of the protocols. For this reason, the control information is often called *protocol control information* (PCI) and it is unique to each protocol. Thus, if seven protocols were associated with a particular internetwork function, there would be seven unique PCI elements. These elements, usually called *headers*, are transmitted along with the data inside the Data Link Layer frame (see Figure 2-1). The data to be transmitted originates at the Application Layer, and is therefore called *Application Data* (AD). The Application Header (AH) is then appended to the data, and that combination (AH + AD) is passed to the next lowest layer (e.g. the Presentation Layer). The Presentation Layer treats

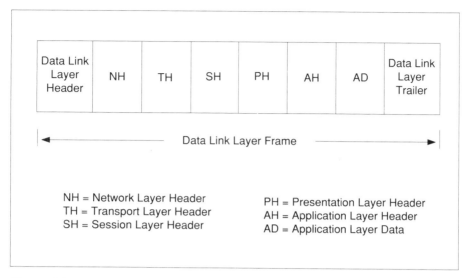

Figure 2-1. Layered Protocol Control Information within a Data Link Layer Frame

this information (AH + AD) as its data, and appends its own header (the Presentation Header or PH). The result is PH + AH + AD. The process continues until the entire frame is constructed with the appropriate PCI from each layer.

The protocol analyzer's job is simply to unravel the PCI and display it in a user-understandable format. However, as we will see from the case studies in Chapters 3 through 8, the unravelling process has become quite complex.

The capabilities of protocol analyzers have been evolving over time. First generation analyzers were actually datascopes that simply decoded a datastream and produced a hexadecimal display on the CRT. They had no user-friendly interface. The second generation added analysis capabilities up to OSI Layer 3. They could decode bit-oriented protocols, and users could program them to perform various tests, based upon their troubleshooting requirements. These tests, for instance, might restrict the data captured to the communication from one specific workstation or one particular protocol, such as the Internet Protocol (IP). Today's third generation analyzers can decode and process protocols up to and including OSI Layer 7 and provide a user-friendly interface that facilitates programming and report generation.

What capabilities can we expect from the fourth generation analyzers? How will they handle various combinations of LANs, MANs, and WANs? This is a crucial question because LANs, MANs, and WANs use protocols of different degrees of complexity. MANs and WANs encompass OSI Layers 1-3, although higher layer information, such as signaling or network management data, may also be present. LANs cover OSI Layers 1-7 (see Figure 2-2). A MAN/WAN analyzer must be able to decode the PCI at the Physical, Data Link, and Network Layers. Thus, it will test the way the packets traverse the communications subnetwork (Layers 1-3), but it won't decode the information contained within those packets. It is the end-users on LAN workstations who are interested in the information inside the packets. Work-

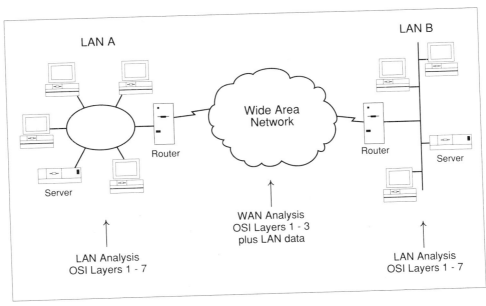

Figure 2-2. LAN and WAN Analysis

stations run an operating system, such as Novell's NetWare, that includes protocols up to and including Layer 7. To properly diagnose a problem between a workstation on LAN A and a server on LAN B connected by the WAN, a LAN analyzer must decode those higher layers.

The testing requirements of LANs and WANs also differ because of the types of failures that typically occur. LAN failures tend to be repetitive, while WAN breakdowns may be one-time events. A final difference is the way the analyzer is physically attached to the LAN, MAN, or WAN. MAN/WAN analyzers are usually used in equipment rooms or central offices where space is limited. (For that reason, they are often designed for both vertical and horizontal use.) LAN analyzers are typically used on a desktop.

2.3 Internetwork Analyzer Requirements

If network managers are to "work smarter, not just harder" to maintain today's distributed, multivendor, multiprotocol networks, they need to have the right tools. Their analyzers must include features such as remote data analysis, the ability to test multiple data links simultaneously, and increased intelligence.

The remainder of this chapter will explore the trends in data communications test equipment. To research these trends, we interviewed the principals shaping this industry and conducted a survey of more than 20 manufacturers of LAN, MAN, and WAN test equipment. (Appendix C lists addresses and telephone numbers of these manufacturers.) The objective of the survey was to look at trends and technologies, not to test products. First, we examined the trends in protocol analyzers to determine the degree of sophistication required by today's internetworks. Second, we looked at support for emerging technologies, such as Frame Relay and SONET, as a benchmark against which to measure the capabilities of the new analyzers. Finally, we tabulated the vendor's responses along with their comments on the direction of this industry.

In the course of our research, we found it difficult to make "apples to apples" comparisons between analyzers due to a thorny, industry-wide problem known as "specsmanship." Specsmanship takes many forms. Some vendors deluge the buyer with volumes of relevant and irrelevant product statistics and details. Other vendors present fundamental measurements (such as frames per second) without the necessary supporting information (such as the size of the transmitted frames). Still others make "apples to oranges" comparisons. For example, many interface modules or cards for analyzers contain an on-board processor, such as an 80186 or 80286. The host machine (for example, a PC) that contains the interface card has its own processor, such as an 80386 or 80486. It would be incorrect to compare the *interface* processor of one vendor's product with the *host* processor of another. Yet such comparisons can, and do, occur. As we examine the trends shaping the analyzer industry, we must filter out the specsmanship that invariably creeps into product data sheets.

Our survey and interviews identified nine trends that apply to LANs, WANs, or both. The remainder of this chapter will examine each trend individually and discuss how the network manager wishing to purchase an analyzer can filter them. Table 2-1 summarizes eight emerging LAN analysis trends: expert systems, graphical user interfaces, combination LAN/WAN analysis, multiport capabilities, network management protocol support, PC-based analyzers, remote data gathering, and integration with simulation tools. Table 2-2 summarizes seven emerging WAN analysis trends: graphical user interfaces, combination LAN/WAN analysis, multiport capabilities, network management protocol support, PC-based analyzers, emerging MAN/WAN protocol support, and remote data gathering. The significance of these trends will be discussed separately, beginning with expert systems.

2.3.1 Expert Systems

In order to maintain good performance on complex internetworks, network analyzers must become increasingly intelligent. All analyzers contain quite a bit of imbedded knowledge of interface characteristics, protocols, interactions between protocols, and so on, that they use to provide help screens, invoke test sequences, or extract protocol information on one port and use it with information extracted from another. But the smartest new analyzers are those that use Expert Systems. Two excellent references on the subject of expert systems are [2-3] and [2-4].

True expert systems are able to use a set of rules, combined with their knowledge of the network and its operation, to diagnose and solve network problems (see Figure 2-3). (In Table 2-1, the term "EXP" indicates an expert system which can develop a list of potential faults within the context of that network.) The expert system's knowledge comes from a variety of sources, including a theoretical database (e.g. the IEEE standards by which the network should operate); a network-specific database (e.g. topological information regarding the network nodes); and the user's previous results and experiences. All of the information then generates a hypothesis about the cause of the problem and a plan of action to resolve it. For example, an Ethernet with an abnormally high rate of collisions would infer further tests of the backbone cable and terminators, and eventually arrive at a conclusion.

Table 2-1. Vendor Support For Emerging LAN Analysis Trends

Vendor	EXP	GUI	L/W	MP	NMP	PC	REM	SIM
BYTEX	F					S	S	S
CABLETRON		S			F	S	S	
CXR/DIGILOG		S		S	F	S	S	
DIGITAL TECH		F		S		S	S	
FTP SOFTWARE						S		
HEWLETT-PACKARD	S	S			F	S	S	F
IDS		S	S	S		S	S	
NETWORK GENERAL	S		S		S	S	S	S
NOVELL		S		S	S	S	S	F
PROTOOLS INC.		S		S	F	S	F	
SPIDER SYSTEMS		F		S	F	S	S	F
TTC/LP COM			S	S		S	S	
W & G	F	S	S	S	S	S	S	

Legend:

S: Currently supports

F: Committed future release

Table 2-2. Vendor Support For Emerging WAN Analysis Trends

Vendor	GUI	L/W	MP	NMP	PC	PRO	REM
ANDO CORP.						S	
AR/TELENEX	S		S	S	F	S	S
CXR/DIGILOG	S					S	S
DIGITAL TECH	F		S		S	S	S
DIGITECH IND.	S		S		S	S	S
FREDERICK ENG.	S		S		S	S	S
GN NAVTEL INC.	F		S		S	S	S
HEWLETT-PACKARD	S					S	S
IDACOM	S		S			S	S
IDS	S	S	S		S		S
KAMPUTECH		F	S	F	S	S	S
NETWORK COMMUN.			S	F	F	S	S
NETWORK GENERAL		S		S	S	F	S
PROGRESSIVE COMPUTING	S		S		S	S	S
REALTIME TECHNIQUES			S			S	S
TEKELEC	S		S	S		S	S
TTC/LP COM		S	S		S	S	S
TTC						S	S
W & G		S	S	S	S	S	S

Legend:

S: Currently supports

F: Committed future release

Abbreviations:

EXP:	Expert system
GUI:	Enhanced graphics/user interface
L/W:	Combination LAN/WAN Analyzer
MP:	Multiport/Multiprocessing
NMP:	Network Management protocol support
PC:	PC-based system
PRO:	Emerging MAN/WAN protocols
REM:	Remote or distributed data gathering
SIM:	Integrates with simulation/modeling software

Hewlett-Packard's LAN Analyzers meet the criterion of an expert system. Network General has an expert system known as the Expert Sniffer, which automatically identifies problems in real time and suggests solutions based upon a combination of expert technologies. Other LAN vendors with plans for expert systems include Bytex and Wandel & Goltermann.

H-P's "expert" is named the Fault Finder. The user or the analyzer furnishes Fault Finder with a fault symptom and the analyzer develops a hypothesis based upon current network conditions and/or analyzer-generated tests. This process continues until the analyzer reaches a conclusion. If the process is inconclusive, the analyzer gives the user a list of potential problems and network symptoms to use in further troubleshooting. Because the expert system automates the hypothesis/testing cycle it should minimize network downtime.

Because of the complex nature of WAN protocols, such as ISDN and Signaling System 7-SS7, third generation WAN analyzers offer very powerful analysis features. For example, third generation analyzers perform statistical analyses of the incoming data stream. A summary of these statistics at either the frame (OSI Layer 2) or packet (OSI Layer 3) level offers a quick diagnosis of the health of the WAN link; a low number of frames with CRC errors or few reject packets indicates a healthy link. Should errors occur, WAN protocol analyzers can help identify the cause by selectively examining the information on that high-speed link through a process known as filtering. For example, if only one workstation was experiencing

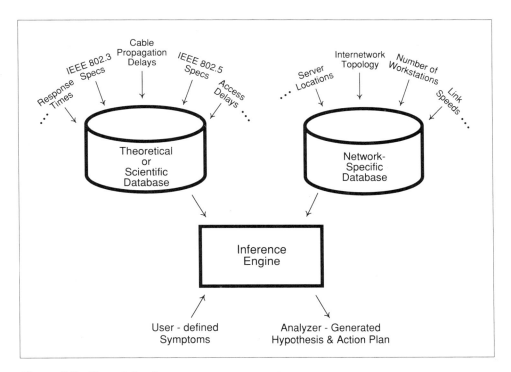

Figure 2-3. Expert Analyzer

a problem, the analyst could set a filter to capture only the data from that workstation. While the MAN/WAN tools studied in this report provided these and other sophisticated analysis capabilities, not one contained an inferencing engine.

2.3.2 PC-Based Analyzers

Intel 80386 and 80486 microprocessors have brought the minicomputer power of the 1980s to the desktops of the 1990s. With their heavy-duty processing power, these lightweight units are ideal platforms upon which to build test equipment. The portability of laptop computers allows you to carry the analyzer to a remote site. The standardized bus, ISA, EISA, or MicroChannel, also allows you to easily add other devices, such as modems, for remote access. As a result, many of the analyzer manufacturers have chosen the PC as their hardware platform. (In Tables 2-1 and 2-2, the designation "PC-based" indicates that the analyzer is based upon a PC or compatible platform; contains a PC or compatible processor and user interface; or, for add-in card analyzers, can operate in a PC or compatible host machine.) The LAN analyzer manufacturers have traditionally supported PC-based systems because of their similarity to a network workstation. WAN analyzers are now basing their products on PCs as well.

When examining analyzers built on the PC platform, you need to ask two questions: How does the manufacturer define "PC-compatible," and how do you implement those capabilities? First, there's a difference between using a PC as the analyzer platform, and having PC capabilities built into the analyzer itself. A number of vendors, including CXR/Digilog and ProTools base their instrument on a laptop, luggable, or desktop computer. Cabletron Systems has an analyzer based on the Apple Macintosh. As a result, you can use these devices for other applications, such as word processing or spreadsheets, when you're not using them for network analysis. Other vendors, such as Wandel & Goltermann, use multiple processors: one for PC applications and another for network analysis. A third alternative, software supported by GN Navtel, allows any PC to analyze data captured by the analyzer. Other products allow you to use standard DOS disk drives for data storage, or an external output to a CRT or printer. Thus, you need to find out what a vendor means when you see the specification "PC-based."

The second issue is implementation: How do I turn my PC into an analyzer? You have three choices here as well. FTP Software's LAN analyzer is a stand-alone software product that you install onto your own PC equipped with a LAN interface card. FTP offers versions of the software for various interface cards, such as 3Com Etherlink, Proteon ProNET, etc. A second option is to purchase a combination hardware/software package and install it in a PC. WAN analyzers from Frederick Engineering and Progressive Computing use this approach. The third alternative, a complete turnkey system, is available from a number of LAN and WAN analyzer vendors, including CXR/Digilog Inc., Hewlett-Packard Company, Network General Corporation, and TTC/LP COM. Turnkey products provide better support because just one vendor is responsible for the system.

2.3.3 Enhanced Graphical User Interfaces

One way vendors are making network management easier is by supporting graphical user interfaces (GUIs). Several interfaces are emerging: the Macintosh (used by the AG Group), Microsoft Windows (used by Progressive Computing), OS/2 Presentation Manager (used by ProTools), X Windows (used by CXR/Digilog), and DESQview (used by Frederick Engineering). (In Tables 2-1 and 2-2, the "GUI" designation indicates that the product is based upon one of these industry-standard windowing interfaces.)

GUIs are known for their user friendliness. Easier interfaces enable people who aren't protocol experts to monitor network health. In addition, GUIs' windowing capabilities can display multiple internetwork test points, for example, to monitor traffic on both sides of a bridge.

GUIs have also provided the basis for analyzers to offer object-oriented capabilities. Typically, these products use an icon to represent an object that performs a specific analysis function. ProTools offers twelve such objects in their LAN analyzer. You can link these objects to perform multiple tasks to make data capture and analysis easier. Thus, the ACQUIRE object captures data from the network; the FILTER specifies the data to be analyzed and stored; and the DISPLAY object controls the visual output.

2.3.4 Combination LAN/WAN Analyzers

As distributed computing merges LANs and WANs into complex multivendor internetworks, analyzers must be able to examine LAN and WAN links and optimize the performance of the combined system, regardless of the number of vendors involved. (In Tables 2-1 and 2-2, the "LAN/WAN combination" indicates interface and protocol support for both LANs and WANs in the same analyzer.) Four vendors—International Data Sciences, Network General, TTC/LP COM, and Wandel & Goltermann—use the Swiss Army knife approach, producing analyzers that combine all the analyzer horsepower into a single box.

Wandel & Goltermann's analyzer provides simultaneous LAN/WAN data capture, analysis, and simulation. The user can select any two options: LAN/LAN (e.g. Ethernet/Ethernet), LAN/WAN (e.g. token ring/SNA), or WAN/WAN (e.g.

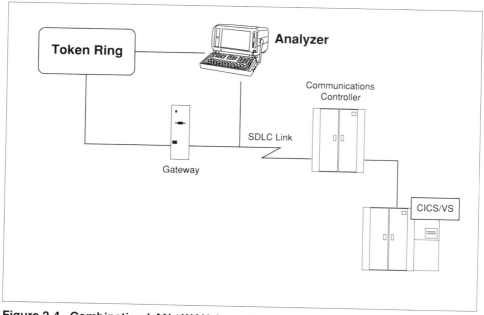

Figure 2-4. Combination LAN / WAN Analysis
(Courtesy of Wandel & Goltermann Technologies, Inc.)

X.25/SNA). This analyzer is built into a modular chassis that can accommodate up to two active analyzer boards and up to four network interface boards (up to two active). The user programs the network interface and selects the protocol stack decodes that will be active for each analyzer module. Output from both analyzer modules can be displayed on the screen simultaneously.

The combination analyzer has advantages and disadvantages. The advantages are straightforward—the analyzer gains economics of scale from having only one analyzer platform, power supply, and so on. In addition, the end user only needs to learn one set of commands, read one manual, and call one technical support line. On the other hand, with all your analyzer eggs in one basket, you better watch that basket. If your vendor doesn't support a protocol or interface that you require after the initial purchase, you could wind up back at square one selecting another analyzer. Fortunately, all four of these vendors offer a wide range of network options that should cover most internetwork requirements.

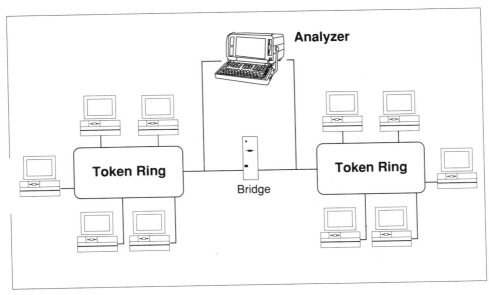

Figure 2-5. Analyzing LAN Traffic on Both Sides of a Bridge
(Courtesy of Wandel & Goltermann Technologies, Inc.)

Do-it-yourself analysts have another option. Several vendors, including Frederick Engineering and Progressive Computing, offer PC-compatible stand-alone WAN analyzers. Select a LAN analyzer based upon a PC platform, assure that no hardware or software conflicts (IRQ lines, DMA channels, etc.) exist between the LAN and WAN products, and plug in the WAN card. Voilá—your own custom LAN/WAN analyzer!

Figure 2-4 shows a combination analyzer. The analyzer is measuring both the token ring and host side of a gateway.

2.3.5 Multiport/Multiprocessing Capabilities

When computing is geographically dispersed, analyzers must monitor multiple networks and transmission links. This is a job for the analyzer's multiport (or dual-port) and multiprocessing features.

Several types of multiport capabilities are available. The first is true dual-port, dual-processing. In this type of system, the analyzer attaches at two points (for instance, either side of a bridge as shown in Figure 2-5) and independent processors analyze the traffic on each side. The analyzer screen can display results simultaneously as well. AR/Telenex, GN Navtel, Kamputech, Realtime Techniques, Tekelec, TTC/LP COM, and Wandel & Goltermann's products are among those having dual-port/dual processing capabilities.

Other analyzers install multiple network interfaces into the analyzer, but only one can be active at a time. Spider Systems operates one network card in the foreground, visible on the display, and the other in the background, invisibly capturing data. Another way to implement multiprocessing is to run multiple analyzers as DOS applications under DESQview or Windows 386.

With many LAN and WAN protocols being combined into a cohesive internetwork, the demand for multiport and multiprocessing analysis will certainly grow. (In Tables 2-1 and 2-2, the "MP" designation indicates multiport and/or multiprocessing capabilities. Simultaneous data capture is required, simultaneous display is not, i.e. background capturing is still considered multiprocessing.)

2.3.6 Emerging MAN/WAN Protocol Support

The internetworks of the 1990s will need to transport ever more data at ever higher speeds. It is likely, for instance, that internetworks will be expected to handle high bandwidth transmissions that include multimedia, voice, and image applications, such as teleradiology. Several MAN/WAN protocols and services are emerging that will significantly impact wideband digital transmissions. These include FDDI, IEEE 802.6/SMDS, ISDN, SS7, Fractional T1, SONET, and Frame Relay. (On Tables 2-1 and 2-2, "Emerging MAN/WAN Protocols" indicates support for at least one of these.)

FDDI has received considerable attention for applications that require inter-LAN connectivity, such as a campus-wide backbone or back-end communications between hosts and peripherals. FDDI's optical transmission means that the analyzer must be attached via fiber optic splitters, rather than an electrical interface. Up to four of these taps can be installed on one ring. Performance statistics defined by the FDDI protocols, such as token rotation time and the bandwidth utilization of a specific workstation, also differ from other LAN or WAN architectures. Digital Technology and Tekelec are among the vendors currently supporting FDDI.

40

Many of the Bell Operating Companies have been testing the IEEE 802.6 standard and the associated Switched Multimegabit Data Service (SMDS). The SMDS' ability to allocate large amounts (T1 or T3 equivalent) of bandwidth to customers on demand has sparked considerable interest among users. However, analyzer vendors have yet to jump on the bandwagon. Our research revealed that Idacom is the only manufacturer that currently supports the IEEE 802.6/SMDS standard.

Two other standards, ISDN and SS7/SS#7, have generated wide interest within the analyzer community. AR/Telenex, Idacom, Realtime Techniques, TTC/LP COM, and GN Elmi are among the vendors in the ISDN testing arena. A number of interesting applications have also been derived. One is the simultaneous monitoring of both B and D channels for either the basic (2B+D) or primary (23B+D) rates. Thus, the D-channel signaling protocol can be monitored along with the B-channel data. A second application is the ability to emulate the ISDN Terminal Equipment (TE). An excellent reference on ISDN testing is [2-5]. A third is the ability to simulta-

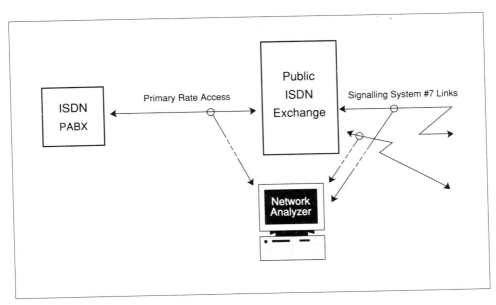

Figure 2-6. Troubleshooting an ISDN Exchange
(Courtesy of GN Elmi)

neously analyze an ISDN PRI line between Local Exchange and PABX, and the associated SS#7 signaling links out of that exchange (Figure 2-6). For example, suppose that the information from an ISDN PABX is not passing correctly from one ISDN exchange to another. To trace this call, the analyzer must be connected to both the incoming PRI and the associated SS#7 links simultaneously. Access to both sides allows the analyzer to trace the signal as it passes through the ISDN exchange, thus determining the accuracy of the protocols.

Fractional T1, the 64 Kbps x n data transport service, can be tested by AR/ Telenex and Network Communications analyzers. References [2-6], [2-7], and [2-8] also explore the technology and testing of WAN circuits.

SONET (Synchronous Optical Network) is supported by both Ando and AR/ Telenex. In addition to the optical interface, these products must analyze SONET framing and overhead information. SONET's high-speed transmission (up to 155 Mbps) places an additional requirement on the analyzer for a high data capture and analysis rate.

Frame Relay has been envisioned as an interconnect facility between a variety of CPE (PBXs, bridges, routers, etc.) devices over T1 and possibly ISDN or IEEE 802.6 lines. A large number of equipment vendors, including Advanced Computer Communications, AT&T, cisco Systems, DEC, Northern Telecom, StrataCom, and others are behind the development of CCITT and ANSI standards for Frame Relay. Digitech Industries, TTC/LP COM, Idacom, GN Navtel, and Wandel & Goltermann have or are planning analysis capabilities for this emerging standard. Reference [2-9] is an interesting tutorial on frame relay implementation; Reference [2-10] addresses the analysis requirements.

2.3.7 Network Management Protocol Support

Volumes have been written about the need for network management standards to assist in the centralized management of complex internetworks. Two protocols are becoming popular for this task: SNMP (Simple Network Management Protocol), which is used widely within the TCP/IP community; and the OSI network management protocol, known as CMIP (Common Management Information Protocol). (In Tables 2-1 and 2-2, "NMP" indicates decoding capabilities for SNMP or CMIP protocols support for the IBM NetView network management protocols.) Of the analyzers surveyed, SNMP was the predominant standard. Although there is some support for CMIP—Tekelec supports CMIP for WANs, and AR/Telenex supports IBM's NetView, but not protocol analyzers via their matrix switch— this standard is in the early stages of acceptance.

SNMP's ability to decode network management protocols serves several purposes. Developers of SNMP Agents or Managers can test their code for accuracy by capturing the Agent-Manager information. The analyzer can also determine response time delays between an Agent report and an associated Manager response. Since management data consumes network bandwidth, the analyzer can also measure the percentage of network management information vs. user traffic on the network.

SNMP can be decoded by Micro Technology, Novell for LANs, Kamputech, Wandel & Goltermann, and Network General for LAN/WANs. Spider Systems also plans to integrate SNMP into their products.

Novell has incorporated SNMP into a network probe, called LANtern. LANtern attaches to an Ethernet/IEEE 802.3 network, and uses SNMP to communicate to an SNMP-compliant network management console. The network itself provides the communication path between probe and console, and the probe is the SNMP agent. Because LANtern is an Ethernet network monitor, not a protocol analyzer, it collects network statistics like collisions, CRC errors, and frame errors, but performs no frame decoding.

Another LAN analyzer vendor, FTP Software, offers an interesting product, known as SNMP Tools, which is based on FTP's well known product PC/TCP. SNMP Tools runs on any DOS PC and is supported by a large number of LAN interface cards. It also offers a development kit for custom SNMP applications.

2.3.8 Remote Data Gathering or Analysis

The ability to gather and/or analyze network information remotely is essential to the effective maintenance of highly distributed internetwork components. (Almost every WAN analyzer manufacturer supports some form of remote diagnostics. This is indicated in the "REM" column in Tables 2-1 and 2-2.)

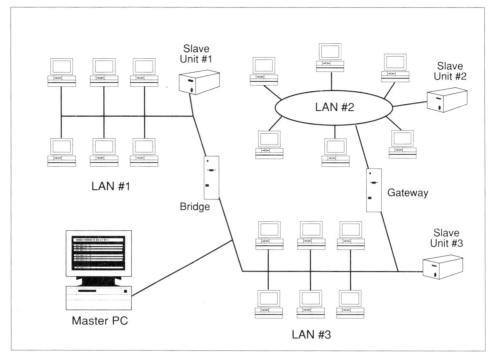

Figure 2-7. Remote Diagnostics via Distributed Slave Units
(Courtesy CXR / Digilog)

Four methods provide remote diagnostics with varying degrees of capability. PC-based administrators can use a program such as PC ANYWHERE (Dynamic Microprocessor Associates, Inc., New York, NY) or Carbon Copy (Microcom Inc., Danbury, CT) to control the analyzer remotely. For example, a PC in Chicago might control an analyzer in New York. As long as an operator in New York is available to make necessary physical interface changes, a user in Chicago could monitor the remote New York network, initiate tests, and perform all other protocol analysis functions as if he or she were local to the network. The only difference will be the transmission delays.

A second option, remote analyzers from manufacturers such as Digital Technology and Wandel & Goltermann, can control a remote analyzer via a LAN. Digital Technology's protocol analyzer connects to both the FDDI ring and an Ethernet.

A third alternative, popular with distributed LANs, is the remote probe. Supported by both CXR/Digilog and Spider Systems, this technique places the probe (sometimes called a slave unit) on remote segments (Figure 2-7). The probe communicates with a central console (or master) over the LAN or via an external serial (RS-232) connection. The serial connection is advantageous when the LAN backbone fails as well as in eliminating non-user traffic.

The fourth alternative, based on a client/server architecture, is implemented by Network General over LAN/WAN architectures. Rather than installing a probe at remote locations, the distributed Sniffer system installs an analyzer on each segment (Figure 2-8a). The analyzer is an intelligent server that processes and analyzes information from that segment, and communicates via the LAN/WAN to a central console, called the SniffMaster. The server analyzes and processes the data before transmitting it to the console, thus minimizing the amount of non-user traffic. This application would be more properly termed remote data analysis rather than remote data gathering. You can also configure each analyzer to capture relevant network statistics and transmit them using the SNMP TRAP command to an SNMP Manager, located anywhere within the internetwork (see Figure 2-8b).

2.3.9 Integration with Network Simulation/Modeling Tools

When networks were host-centric or confined to a single location, it was much easier to calculate delay and response time parameters and forecast network growth. The wide distribution of network resources has made predicting these network performance metrics more difficult. Performing an analysis of the current internetwork can help with these predictions.

Analyzers have always done an amazing job of collecting reams of data. But what do you do with all that information? Early analyzers provided a hardcopy ASCII output of the captured data. Later analyzers could convert the data into a spreadsheet or database file format for further analysis. For example, the spreadsheet could sort traffic on a LAN by source address and bill the appropriate department for network usage.

Most products in the LAN market today integrate the LAN analyzer with a LAN simulation or modeling software tool such as BONeS (ComDisco Systems, Inc., Foster City, CA) or LANSIM (InternetiX, Inc., Upper Marlboro, MD). (In Table 2-1,

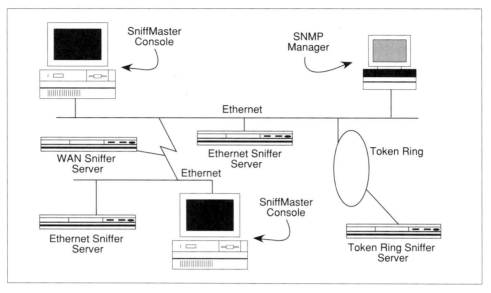

Figure 2-8a. Distributed Sniffer System Connected to a Network

(Courtesy Network General Corp.)

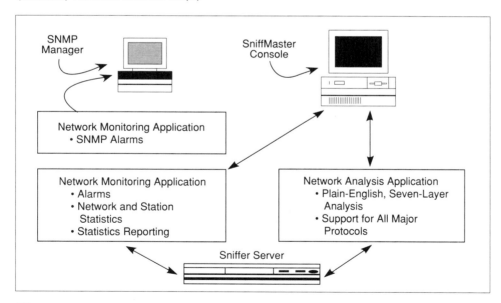

Figure 2-8b. Distributed Sniffer System Overview

(Courtesy Network General Corp.)

"SIM" indicates the ability to integrate the LAN analyzer data with either the ComDisco or LANSIM simulation/modeling tools.) Quintessential Solutions, Inc. (San Diego, CA), a developer of WAN simulation and modeling tools, offers products with the ability to input data from WAN analyzers. A typical application is modeling the response time of a polled SNA circuit. Given the actual polling or response time delays from the analyzer, the QSI software can then predict the changes in these variables resulting from increases in traffic, adding applications, and so on.

Simulation/modeling software is useful for a number of purposes, including initial network design, reconfiguration or re-design, and stress testing. Numerous variables (which can exceed 100, depending on the network under study) specifying the number and type of workstations, servers, protocols in use, traffic loads, and so on must be entered into the model. The value of these variables can change the outcome of the simulation significantly. For example, network response time is a function of the number of servers plus the number of users logically attached to each one. If response time degrades, the administrator might consider redistributing the users or adding servers. Rather than making an educated guess about the network's traffic measurements, using actual data from the analyzer allows the simulation to provide a much more accurate representation of the network's characteristics (Figure 2-9). This facilitates the interactive process of network design, growth, and redesign.

Bytex, Network General, and Spider Systems are among the LAN analyzer vendors that can export their data to one of the simulation/modeling tools mentioned. In the future, simulation/modeling software will be directly incorporated into LAN analyzers. Reference [2-11] explores the integration of analyzers and simulation/modeling tools.

2.4 Selecting Your Ultimate Analyzer

Managers of complex internetworks confront many challenges, not the least of which is selecting the correct test equipment for their configuration. An analytical approach, as outlined on the following page, can often help network administrators wade through the multitude of vendors, models, and options.

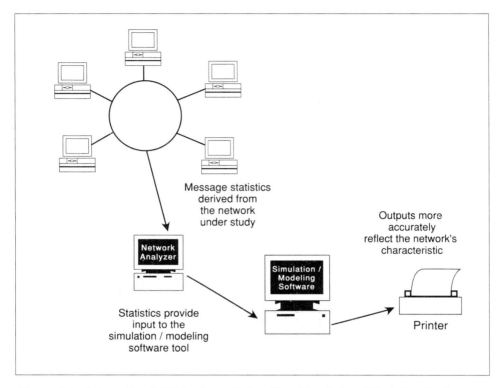

Message statistics
derived from
the network
under study

Outputs more
accurately
reflect the network's
characteristic

Statistics provide
input to the
simulation / modeling
software tool

Printer

Figure 2-9. Integrating LAN Analyzer Data with a Simulation / Modeling Tool

1. Define the requirements for the analyzer: Will it need to work with a LAN, MAN, WAN, or some combination? Don't neglect any future requirements, such as additional protocols that you may need in the future. Write a requirements document for use as an internal guide and for distribution to vendors. You can use the surveys shown in Tables 2-3 and 2-4 as a starting point for this document.

2. Determine an appropriate price range for the analyzer. Software or hardware/software kits run $2,000-$3,000, while turnkey systems can exceed $40,000. Include all relevant factors, such as the value of the PC that you supply. Don't invest in analysis capabilities you don't really need.

3. Set up an evaluation room where vendors can demonstrate their products. Provide access points to the LAN/MAN/WAN so that vendors can perform a live demonstration on your network, instead of using previously recorded data. Provide plenty of bench space for the analyzer, and ask each vendor to leave a unit for a few days.

4. Evaluate each demo unit vis a vis its competition. Be aware of any "specsmanship" that might bias your decision. In addition to the technical merits of each product, consider the ease of use, documentation, warranty, size and weight, and vendor support. For example, Frederick Engineering, Hewlett-Packard, and Network General offer a Bulletin Board System for analyzer support, and Network General has initiated a user group, known as the Network Analysis Users Group. These resources can be invaluable for ongoing support.

Tables 2-3 and 2-5 provide survey forms that you can use to evaluate LAN/WAN analyzers from various manufacturers, thus removing any bias associated with "specsmanship." Responses to this survey are given in Tables 2-4 and 2-6. Note that the responses reflect information on the vendor's product line; not every analyzer will support every interface and/or protocol option in the line. Since these specifications are frequently enhanced, contact the vendors at the time of purchase for current information. References [2-12], [2-13], and [2-14] are examples of recent evaluations of both LAN and WAN analyzers.

Table 2-3. Evaluating The Ultimate LAN Analyzer

Date _____

Vendor_____

Address _____

City, State, Zip_____

Phone_____

Fax_____

Contact person_____

Model number_____

Base price _____

Price as optioned_____

LAN Interfaces Supported

ARCNET _____

Apple LocalTalk_____

Ethernet V1 _____

Ethernet V2 _____

FDDI _____

IBM PC Network _____

IEEE 802.3 _____

IEEE 802.4 _____

IEEE 802.5 _____

StarLAN _____

Other _____

LAN Protocols Supported

    AppleTalk _____

    Banyan VINES _____

    DECnet _____

    IBM SNA _____

    ISO _____

    OS/2 LAN Manager _____

    NetBIOS _____

    Novell NetWare _____

    Sun _____

    TCP/IP _____

    XNS _____

    X Windows _____

    Other _____

Support for Emerging Trends

    Expert system _____

    Graphical User Interface _____

    LAN/WAN Combination _____

    Multiport/Multiprocessing _____

    Network management protocols _____

    PC-based _____

    Remote data gathering or analysis _____

    Simulation/Modeling software input _____

Analyzer Capabilities

Buffer size _____

Capture rate _____

Processing rate _____

Character Formats _____

Number of Triggers _____

BERT _____

Video Output _____

Printer Output _____

Custom Programming _____

Power Requirements _____

Data Storage _____

Other _____

Vendor Support

Documentation _____

Training _____

Warranty _____

BBS Access _____

Table 2-4. LAN Analyzer Interface and Protocol Support

Vendor	ARC	AT	EV1	EV2	FDDI	PCN	SL	802.3	802.4	802.5
AG		S						S		
BYTEX				S				S		S
CABLE				S				S		
CXR/DIGILOG			S	S	F			S		S
DIG TECH					S					
FTP			S	S			S	S		S
H-P			S	S	F			S		S
IDS			S	S				S		S
MICRO			S	S				S		
NET GEN	S	S	S	S	F	S	S	S		S
NOVELL			S	S			S	S		S
PROTOOL			S	S				S		S
SPIDER			S	S			S	S		S
TEKELEC			S	S	S			S		S
TTC/LP COM			S	S		S	S	S	S	S
W & G			S	S	F			S		S

Vendor	AT	BAN	DEC	ISO	LM	NB	NW	SNA	SUN	TCP	XNS	XWIN
AG	S	S	S				S			S	S	
BYTEX						S	S	S		S		
CABLE	S	S	S	S			S			S	S	
CXR/DIGI	S	S	S	F	S	S	S	S	F	S	S	F
DIG TECH	S		S	S								S
FTP	S	S	S	S	S	S	S		S	S	S	
H-P	S	F	S	F		S	S	S	F	S	S	F
IDS	S	S	S	S	S	S	S	S	S	S	S	
MICRO	S	S	S	S			S	S	S	S	S	S
NET GEN	S	S	S	S	S	S	S	S	S	S	S	S
NOVELL	S	S	S	S	S	S	S	S	S	S	S	F
PROTOOLS		S			S	S	S			S	S	
SPIDER	S	S	S	S	S	S	S	S	S	S	S	
TEKELEC	F		S	S				F	F	S	F	
TTC/LP COM			S	S		S	S	S	S	S	S	
W & G	S	S	S	S	F	S	S	S	F	S	S	F

Legend:

S: Currently supports

F: Committed future release

Abbreviations:

AG:	AG Group
ARC:	ARCNET
AT:	AppleTalk
BAN:	Banyan VINES
DEC:	DEC DECnet
EV1:	Ethernet V1
EV2:	Ethernet V2
FDDI:	ANSI FDDI
ISO:	ISO Protocols

LM:	OS/2 LAN Manager
NB:	NetBIOS
NW:	Novell NetWare
PCN:	IBM PC Network
SL:	StarLAN
SNA:	IBM SNA
SUN:	Sun Protocols
TCP:	TCP/IP
XNS:	Xerox XNS
XWIN:	X Windows
802.3:	IEEE 802.3
802.4:	IEEE 802.4
802.5:	IEEE 002.5
BYTEX:	Bytex Corporation
CABLE:	Cabletron Systems Inc.
CXR/DIGI:	CXR/Digilog Inc.
DIG TECH:	Digital Technology Inc.
FTP:	FTP Software Inc.
H-P:	Hewlett-Packard Company
IDS:	International Data Sciences, Inc.
NET GEN:	Network General Corporation
NOVELL:	Novell Inc.
PROTOOLS:	ProTools Inc.
SPIDER:	Spider Systems Inc.
TEKELEC:	Tekelec
TTC/LP COM:	Telecommunications Techniques Corporation (successors to LP/COM)
W&G:	Wandel & Goltermann Technologies, Inc.

Table 2-5. Evaluating the Ultimate WAN Analyzer

Date _____

Vendor_____

Address_____

City, State, Zip _____

Phone_____

Fax _____

Contact person_____

Model number _____

Base price _____

Price as optioned _____

WAN Interfaces Supported

Mil-188C _____

RS-232 _____

RS-422 _____

RS-423 _____

RS-449 _____

RS-485 _____

SONET _____

T1/E1 _____

Vendor Support

Documentation _____

Training _____

Warranty _____

BBS Access _____

Support for Emerging Trends

Graphical User Interface _____

LAN/WAN Combination _____

Multiport/Multiprocessing _____

Network management protocols _____

PC-based _____

Emerging MAN/WAN protocols _____

Remote data gathering or analysis _____

Table 2-6. WAN Analyzer Interface and Protocol Support

Vendor	188	232	422	423	449	485	SON	T1	FT1	V.35	X.21
ANDO	S	S			S		S			S	S
AR/TELENEX	S	S	S	S	S	S	S	S		S	S
CXR/DIGILOG		S	S	S	S					S	S
DIG TECH											
DIG IND			S					S	S	S	
FRED ENGR	S	S						S		S	
GN NAV	S	S	S	S	S			S	S	S	S
H-P	S	S	S	S	S			S		S	S
IDACOM		S	S		S			S	S	S	S
IDS		S	S	S	S					S	S
KAMPUTE		S			S			S		S	
NET COM	S	S	S	S	S			S	S	S	S
NET GEN		S								S	
PRO COMP	S	S	S	S	S			S		S	S
REALTIME	S	S			S			F		S	
TEKELEC	S	S	S	S	S			S		S	S
TTC/LP COM	S	S	S	S	S	S		S	S	S	S
TTC	S	S	S	S	S	S		S	S	S	S
W & G	S	S	S	S	S			S	S	S	S

Vendor	ASY	BSC	HDLC	SDLC	DEC	FR	802.6	ISDN	SS7	X.25
ANDO	S	S	S	S	S			S		S
AR/TELENEX	S	S	S	S	S	S		S	S	S
CXR/DIGILOG	S	S	S	S	S	F		S	S	S
DIG TECH										
DIG IND						S				
FRED ENGR	S	S	S	S	S			S		S
GN NAV	S	S	S		S	S		S	S	S
H-P	S	S	S	S	S	S		S	S	S
IDACOM	S	S	S	S		S		S	S	S
IDS	S	S	S	S						S
KAMPUTE			S	S				S	S	S
NET COM	S	S	S	S	S			S	S	S
NET GEN			S	S		F		F		S
PRO COMP	S	S	S		S			S	S	S
REALTIME	S	S	S	S				F	S	S
TEKELEC	S	S	S	S	S	S		S	S	S
TTC/LP COM	S	S	S	S	S	S	S	S	S	S
TTC	S	S	S	S				S		S
W & G	S	S	S	S	S	S		F	F	S

Legend:

S: Currently supports

F: Committed future release

Abbreviations:

188:	Mil-188C
232:	EIA-232
422:	EIA-422
423:	EIA-423
449:	EIA-449

485:	EIA-485
SON:	SONET
T1:	T1/E1
FT1:	Fractional T1
V.35:	CCITT V.35
X.21:	CCITT X.21
ASY:	Asynchronous
BSC:	Bisync
HDLC:	HDLC
SDLC:	SNA/SDLC
DEC:	DEC DDCMP
FR:	Frame Relay
802.6:	IEEE 802.6
ISDN:	ISDN
SS7:	SS7/SS#7
X.25:	X.25/X.75

ANDO:	Ando Electric Co., Ltd.
AR/TELENEX:	AR Division Telenex Corp.
CXR/DIGI:	CXR/Digilog Inc.
DIG IND:	Digitech Industries Inc.
DIG TECH:	Digital Technology Inc.
FRED ENG:	Frederick Engineering Inc.
GN NAV:	GN Navtel Inc.
H-P:	Hewlett-Packard Company
IDACOM:	Idacom Electronic Ltd.
IDS:	International Data Sciences, Inc.
KAMPUTE:	Kamputech Inc.
MICRO:	Micro Technology, Inc.
NET COMM:	Network Communications Corporation
NET GEN:	Network General Corporation
PRO COMP:	Progressive Computing Inc.

REALTIME: Realtime Techniques

TEKELEC: Tekelec

TTC/LP COM:Telecommunications Techniques Corporation (successors to LP/COM)

TTC: Telecommunications Techniques Corporation

W&G: Wandel & Goltermann Technologies, Inc.

So is there an Ultimate Analyzer? Yes. It's the tool that meets the requirements for your network testing today, while providing the capacity to grow with the increasing complexities of tomorrow.

2.5 Using Your Ultimate Analyzer

The numerous LAN/WAN analyzer features shown in Tables 2-1 through 2-6 might make these products seem dauntingly complex. Fortunately, the analyzer's user interface provides excellent insulation between the raw data and the user. In addition, analyzer manufacturers often supply quick-reference cards or on-screen help for further assistance.

Developing a standard troubleshooting methodology for internetworks can also bring order to the chaos of a complex problem. One method suggested by Digital Equipment Corporation (DEC) is shown in Figure 2-10. The analyst receives the problem report, and first develops a clear understanding of the type of problem involved (LAN, WAN, host, etc.). Information is then gathered, possibly from multiple sources such as a protocol analyzer, network management system, user hypotheses, etc. This information is analyzed in an attempt to isolate the problem. If the problem can be solved, the solution is verified and documented. If not, additional information (such as an overnight data capture with the analyzer) must be gathered. This iterative process continues until the solution is found. References [2-15] and [2-16] also provide useful information on troubleshooting methodology.

Most network managers would feel quite comfortable with six out of the seven steps shown in Figure 2-10. Step 3, Analyze, Interpret, and Classify Information, however, may cause some nervousness. This unease is due to the implication that protocols must be analyzed. The next five chapters will help clarify what analysis is all about. Separate chapters will discuss the protocols of AppleTalk, Banyan VINES,

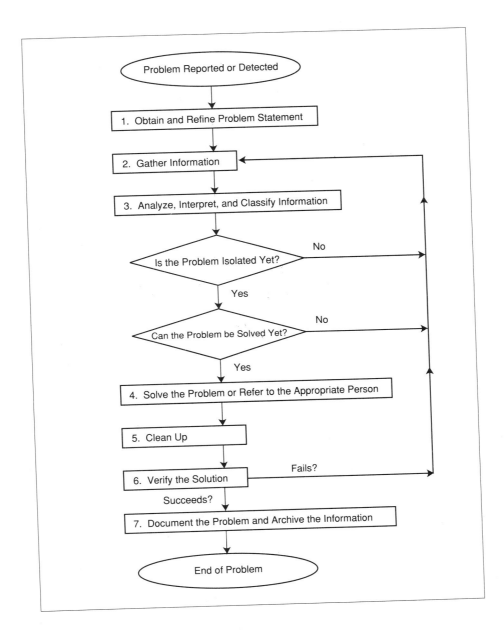

Figure 2-10. Internetwork Troubleshooting Methodology
(Courtesy Digital Equipment Corporation)

DECnet, Token Ring/SNA, Novell's NetWare, and TCP/IP. Each of these chapters begins with an overview of the internetwork protocols, then provides a number of in-depth analyses of typical internetwork problems. For consistency, all analyzer trace files have been captured with a Network General Corporation Sniffer protocol analyzer. Reference [2-17] discusses popular LAN protocols in depth. Now, turn on that Ultimate Analyzer and let's get started!

2.6 References

[2-1] This chapter is based upon "LAN/WAN Protocol Analyzers: Network Management's Overnight Sensation — 20 Years in the Making" by Steven S. King and Mark A. Miller. *Data Communications* (May 1991): 78-94. Copyright 5/91 McGraw-Hill, Inc. All rights reserved.

[2-2] "Data Communications 1991 Market Forecast." *Data Communications*, (December 1990): 95-98.

[2-3] *IEEE Network Magazine.* Special Issue on Expert Systems in Network Management, Volume 2, Number 5, September 1988.

[2-4] Pederson, Ken. *Expert Systems Programming.* New York: John Wiley & Sons, 1989.

[2-5] Kessler, Gary C. *ISDN.* New York: McGraw-Hill, Inc., 1990.

[2-6] Bellamy, John. *Digital Telephony.* 2nd ed., New York: John Wiley & Sons, 1991.

[2-7] Freeman, Roger L. *Telecommunication System Engineering.* 2nd ed., New York: John Wiley & Sons, 1989.

[2-8] Lindberg, Bertil C. *Troubleshooting Communications Facilities.* New York: John Wiley & Sons, 1990.

[2-9] Lippis, Nick. "Frame Relay Redraws the Map for Wide-Area Networks." *Data Communications* (July 1990): 80-94.

[2-10] AR/Telenex Corporation, "An Introduction to Useful Frame Relay Testing," 1991.

[2-11] Jander, Mary. "Picture Perfect Simulation." *Data Communications* (May 1991): 69-72.

[2-12] Mick, Colin and Dan Nagel. "Testing the LAN Testers." *Network World* (September 10, 1990): 1-74.

[2-13] Fratus, John, Al Graeff, and Don Preuss. "Five LAN Analyzers Meet Diverse Needs." *PC Week* (November 26, 1990): 105-111.

[2-14] Jander, Mary. "Users Rate WAN Protocol Analyzers." *Data Communications* (February 1991): 103-110.

[2-15] CrossComm Corporation. "How to Troubleshoot Your Enterprise-Wide Network, Quickly." *Internetworking Solutions*, May 1991.

[2-16] Smith, Mark. "Diagnosing Network Disorders." *LAN Technology* (October 1991): 20-36.

[2-17] Miller, Mark A. *LAN Protocol Handbook.* Redwood City, CA: M&T Books Inc., 1990.

CHAPTER 3

Troubleshooting AppleTalk Internetworks

First introduced in 1985, AppleTalk was designed in the tradition of the Apple Macintosh. It offered a straightforward user interface, a "plug-and-play" interconnection strategy, and a peer-to-peer architecture. In June of 1989, AppleTalk Phase 2 added enhancements, such as support for large internetworks and for token ring (IEEE 802.5). We'll begin this chapter with a brief overview of the AppleTalk protocols. References [3-1] through [3-4] provide specifics on the protocols; Chapter 7 of Reference [3-5] discusses AppleTalk troubleshooting from a LAN, rather than an internetwork, perspective.

3.1 AppleTalk Architecture and Protocols

AppleTalk is a seven-layer architecture that conforms closely to the OSI Reference Model, as shown in Figure 3-1. We'll begin our discussion of the AppleTalk architecture with the Physical and Data Link Layer options.

3.1.1 AppleTalk Physical and Data Link Layers

AppleTalk defines a number of implementations for the first two OSI layers, the Physical and Data Link. In Phase 1, the Data Link Layer included the LocalTalk Link Access Protocol (LLAP) operating at 230 Kbps and the EtherTalk Link Access Protocol (ELAP), which implemented an IEEE 802.3 (CSMA/CD bus network) frame operating at 10 Mbps. The Phase 1 version of EtherTalk supported the DEC, Intel, and Xerox Ethernet version 2.0 standards.

In Phase 2, Apple added the TokenTalk Link Access Protocol (TLAP), which implements the IEEE 802.5 (token passing ring network) frame operating at either 4 or 16 Mbps. Also in Phase 2, ELAP and TLAP frames were enhanced to incorporate

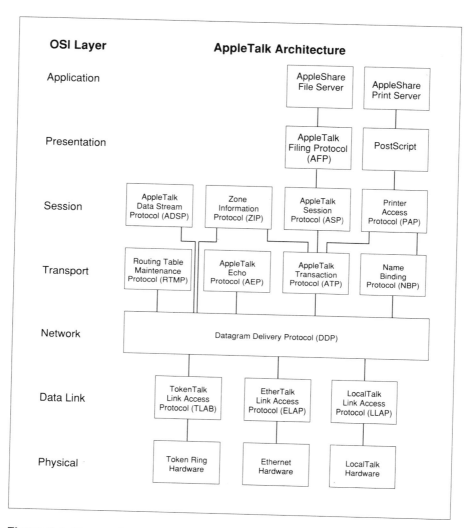

Figure 3-1. Comparing the AppleTalk Architecture with OSI
(Courtesy Apple Computer, Inc.)

the IEEE 802.2 Logical Link Control (LLC) header. The higher layers set Source and Destination Service Access Point addresses (SSAP and DSAP, respectively) to AAH, followed by the LLC Control Field (set to 03H). Immediately following the 802.2 header is the Sub-Network Access Protocol (SNAP) header. This header contains the value 080007809BH for AppleTalk data packets, or 00000080F3H for AppleTalk Address Resolution Protocol (AARP) packets. See Chapter 1 of Reference [3-5] for further information on LLC and SNAP. (Note that throughout this text we will use an "H" to designate hexadecimal notation.)

The ELAP or TLAP transmission may use multicast addresses to send the frame to more than one destination node. AppleTalk defines two types of multicast addresses. A Broadcast uses 090007FFFFFFH (ELAP) or C00040000000H (TLAP). Zone Multicast addresses range from 090007000000H to 0900070000FCH for ELAP; or 0C00000000800H to 0C0020000000H for TLAP.

It is not uncommon for a single AppleTalk node to contain multiple protocol stacks that encompass the Network through Application Layers. A 2-octet protocol address identifies these protocol stacks. Thus, a node would be assigned one hardware address (e.g. the 48-bit IEEE 802 address within a ROM), but its software might contain multiple protocols, each with a unique address. The AppleTalk Address Resolution Protocol (AARP) maps between the hardware and AppleTalk protocol addresses. Each node maintains a cache of its known mappings, called the *Address Mapping Table* (AMT). If a node needs a mapping that is not found in its AMT, it multicasts an AARP Request on the network cable segment (or broadcast on the data link for Phase 1 networks), seeking that information. When the mapping has been located, an AARP Response packet is returned. If no response is forthcoming, the node retransmits the AARP Request a limited number of times. Note that AARP is not required on LocalTalk data links since its hardware and protocol addresses are the same.

3.1.2 AppleTalk Network Layer

Just one AppleTalk protocol, the Datagram Delivery Protocol (DDP), implements the OSI Network Layer. The DDP delivers AppleTalk packets on an internetwork. The DDP header includes the network number and socket number required to route the packet via Internet Routers or IRs between source and destination networks. The routers can be connected via either LAN or WAN transmission facilities. Thus, using DDP, the IR takes a packet from a source socket in one node on the internetwork, and transfers it to the destination socket in another. (A socket is a logical entity having an address that identifies a specific higher-layer process or application needing AppleTalk services. Typically, multiple sockets are active within one machine.)

3.1.3 AppleTalk Transport Layer

AppleTalk uses four protocols to provide OSI Transport Layer functions: the Routing Table Maintenance Protocol (RTMP), the AppleTalk Echo Protocol (AEP), the AppleTalk Transaction Protocol (ATP), and the Name Binding Protocol (NBP).

The Internet Routers (IRs), such as the AppleTalk Internet Router, use the Routing Table Maintenance Protocol (RTMP). The architecture defines three types of routers: Local routers connect local area networks; half routers hook up networks via WAN links; and backbone routers tie a network to a backbone cable, such as an Ethernet. Routers frequently have multiple output connections or ports, though no two ports can attach to the same network. Each port has an associated Data Link Layer process (e.g. EtherTalk, TokenTalk, etc.). The maximum distance between nodes on distinct networks is 16 hops; i.e. through 16 different routers.

The IRs use RTMP to exchange and update their routing tables, thus determining the shortest path to each destination network. They send this routing information every 10 seconds. For large internetworks, however, transmitting the contents of large routing tables consumes a large percentage of the available bandwidth. AppleTalk Phase 2, therefore, added a technique called split horizon in which RTMP broadcasts only information that applies to the other networks.

The AppleTalk Echo Protocol (AEP) tests the transmission path between two nodes. The AEP listens at the Echoer Socket (socket number 4) for packets. When it receives one, it returns a copy to the sender. Troubleshooters use the AEP to determine whether a particular node exists on the internetwork and to measure the round trip transmission delay between source and destination nodes.

The AppleTalk Transaction Protocol (ATP) provides a reliable transport mechanism for Session Layer Protocols. ATP performs these tasks, called *transactions*, between one socket in the requesting node and another in the responding node. Thus, the ATP assures reliable transactions between clients.

The Name Binding Protocol (NBP) is a mechanism that translates between the entity names that users specify for network resources and those by the network itself. AppleTalk users employ an entity name containing three fields of up to 32 characters —object: type @ zone (e.g. File Server 1: AFP Server @ Marketing)—to request network services. AppleTalk protocols, however, require a 4-octet address, which specifies the socket number, network number, and node ID. Before the internetwork can access the entity name, it must be translated into an internet address. This translation process is known as *name binding*. Each AppleTalk node contains a names table to keep track of the name-to-address mappings within that node. The Names Information Socket, socket 02H, implements the NBP process. This socket also responds to requests from other nodes to look up a name within its table.

3.1.4 AppleTalk Higher Layers

As you can see in Figure 3-1, the OSI Session Layer implements four AppleTalk protocols: the AppleTalk Data Stream Protocol (ADSP), the Zone Information Protocol (ZIP), the AppleTalk Session Protocol (ASP), and the Printer Access Protocol (PAP).

The AppleTalk Data Stream Protocol (ADSP) communicates directly with the Network Layer DDP. ADSP assures that the data stream between two AppleTalk sockets is delivered full duplex, in sequence, and without duplications. ADSP also controls the data flow rate to assure that a fast sender won't overwhelm a slower receiver.

The Zone Information Protocol (ZIP) translates between network numbers and zone names within the internetwork. (As described in Section 3.1.5, a *zone* is a logical grouping of nodes that organize a large internetwork. A non-extended network has only one zone. The number of zones in an extended network depends on the implementation, although 255 is a popular choice.)

ZIP uses three processes to perform these translations. First, ZIP offers a mapping service within the routers. This is implemented via the Zone Information

Table (ZIT), which contains an entry for each network within the internetwork. New networks are added with information supplied by the RTMP. Second, ZIP distributes this mapping information to other nodes. This is handled through requests and replies sent to and from the router via the Zone Information Socket (ZIS), socket number 6. Third, ZIP informs the node of the valid network range number for this cable. (A cable is a collection of nodes on a network segment that are all on the same side of a router). Upon startup, ZIP then helps the new node select a zone name. To facilitate the process, newly added nodes pick a network number in the startup range (FF00-FFFEH), then ask the router for the actual network number they should use.

The AppleTalk Session Protocol (ASP) adds Session Layer services to the AppleTalk Transaction Protocol (ATP) in the Transport Layer. This service establishes and disconnects the logical connection or session between two communicating entities, such as a Macintosh and an AppleShare server. To facilitate this, the ASP header adds a 1-octet session identifier to the datastream. The ASP function maintains the session and it also may write blocks of data from a client workstation to a server. The Presentation Layer AppleTalk Filing Protocol (AFP) is an ASP client that workstations use to share files.

The Printer Access Protocol (PAP) is a connection-oriented protocol for communications between workstations and servers. Although PAP was originally developed for communication between the Macintosh and a LaserWriter, it can also be used for other types of servers. Note that the Presentation Layer dialogue for use with the Laser Writer is PostScript.

With that background into the various AppleTalk protocols, let's explore some analysis and troubleshooting techniques.

3.1.5 AppleTalk Addressing Conventions

When AppleTalk Phase 1 was first defined, no more than 254 nodes (Macintosh, printer, PC, and so on) could exist on a network cable segment. The node ID or address was defined as an 8-bit quantity ranging from 0 to 255, with Node ID = 0 reserved for unknown addresses and Node ID = 255 for broadcast addresses. Phase 1 networks also define a 16-bit network ID number that identifies all nodes on the same cable segment including bridges. (Nodes on Phase 1 networks also share the same zone name.) Thus, the effective address space is limited to that of the 8-bit node ID, or 254 addresses. Such networks, which include LocalTalk and Phase 1 EtherTalk networks, are referred to as non-extended addressing networks.

In Phase 2, AppleTalk introduced extended networks, such as EtherTalk Phase 2 and TokenTalk. Extended networks uniquely identify each node with a 16-bit network number, 8-bit node ID pair. This system can address up to 16 million nodes per cable segment, although no known Data Link hardware supports that many nodes. Each network number supports up to 253 nodes; node IDs 00, FEH, and FFH are reserved on extended networks. (Node 00 is for the support of the Name Binding Protocol (NBP), FE for use with certain data link implementations, and FF for cable-wide broadcasting.) Network numbers FF00H through FFFEH are referred to as the *startup range*, and are reserved for new nodes or for when an AppleTalk-capable router is absent. These network numbers are contained within the Datagram Delivery Protocol (DDP) header of the Network Layer (more on the DDP header in Section 3.1.6).

As noted earlier, a *socket* is an 8-bit quantity that identifies a software process within a node. Statically-assigned sockets range from 01-7FH. Examples of these sockets that are assigned and well-known include the Names Information Socket (NIS), socket number 02H; the Echoer Socket, number 04H; and the Zone Information Socket (ZIS), socket number 06H. Most AppleTalk traffic uses dynamically assigned sockets, which the operating system or protocol stack designate on request from an application program. These socket numbers range from 80-FFH. Socket numbers are also contained within the DDP packet of the Network Layer, and are located and/or identified for communications by NBP.

A *zone* is a logical grouping of nodes that organize a large internetwork. In Phase 1, each network could be associated with only one zone, although several networks could be included in the same zone. The Phase 2 protocols removed the strict zone-network relationship. Nodes on different Phase 2 networks can belong in the same zone, or nodes on the same network to different zones. Each node maintains a global variable called MyZone. Internetwork routers maintain lists of known zones and a Zone Information Table (ZIT) that associates network numbers and zone names on the internetwork.

With that background on AppleTalk node addressing, let's explore the packet formats.

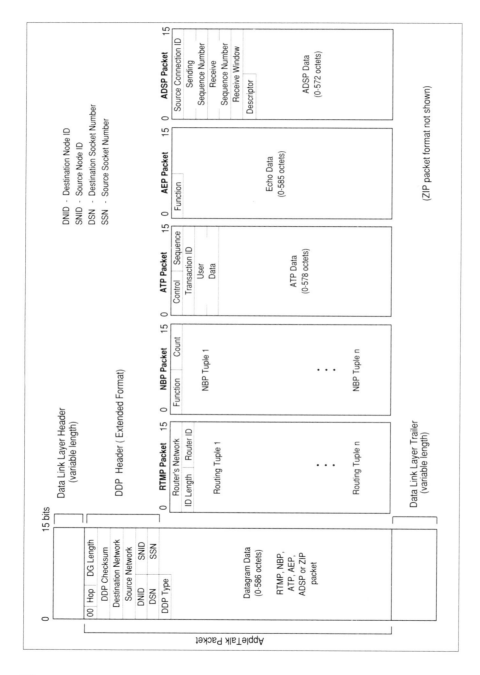

Figure 3-2. AppleTalk Packet Formats
(Courtesy Apple Computer, Inc.)

3.1.6 AppleTalk Packet Formats

The 19 protocols that comprise the AppleTalk architecture within one node must somehow communicate with their peer processes on another node. They do so by building a LocalTalk, EtherTalk, or TokenTalk frame into which they insert an AppleTalk packet that contains the appropriate higher layer protocols. Details of these packet formats are given in *Inside AppleTalk* [3-1]; general structures of the packets are shown in Figure 3-2.

The AppleTalk packet begins with a DDP header, which has two possible formats. The short DDP header is used on non-extended networks when the two communicating sockets have identical network numbers. The extended DDP header (shown in Figure 3-2) is used when those two sockets have different network numbers. The extended DDP header contains a number of fields including the Hop Count (4 bits), used by the Internet Routers; Datagram length (10 bits), which can be up to 586 octets; and DDP checksum (2 octets). Six address fields are transmitted next, identifying the Destination and Source network numbers (2 octets each); Destination and Source Node IDs (1 octet each); and the Destination and Source socket numbers (1 octet each.) The last field octet specifies the DDP packet type (1 octet).

The Datagram Data field can contain from 0-586 octets of information, coming from one of six higher layer protocols. RTMP packets update the router's tables. NBP packets transmit entity name-to-internet address associations, known as NBP name-address tuples. ATP packets contain an 8-octet ATP header plus up to 578 octets of sequenced data. AEP packets verify the path, or round-trip delay, to a particular node. ADSP packets provide a connection-oriented, full-duplex data stream service between two sockets. An ADSP packet includes a 13-octet ADSP header and up to 572 octets of ADSP data. ZIP packets transmit network-to-zone-name associations for the internet. (ZIP packets, which have many formats, are not shown in Figure 3-2.)

Note from Figure 3-1 that ATP packets can contain higher layer information within their respective data fields; for instance, ATP packets can contain ASP and AFP data.

Now that we have an understanding of the AppleTalk packet formats, let's look at some techniques for analyzing these packets.

3.2 AppleTalk Analysis Techniques

As with any of the LAN/WAN internetworks described in this book, trouble-shooting an AppleTalk internetwork is far from straightforward. Experts look for the following significant events [3-6]:

1. Verify that the Physical and Data Link Layers are stable. For instance, check for excessive collisions on an EtherTalk backbone, or examine the Medium Access Control (MAC) frames on a TokenTalk network. Section 3.3.1 will provide a benchmark analysis of TokenTalk.

2. Verify that nodes are caching their AARP information (AppleTalk protocol address to Data Link Layer address mapping). A stable network should have little AARP traffic. Section 3.3.5 will study AARP.

3. Identify the routers by noting the source address of the RTMP packets. Phase 1 routers broadcast to destination address FFFFFFFFFFFFH; Phase 2 routers to destination address 090007FFFFFFH (EtherTalk) or C00040000000H (TokenTalk). These broadcasts should occur every 10 seconds, with each router making a consistent number of routing entries. When the number of routing entries changes significantly, it means that additional routers have been added or deleted from the internet. Section 3.3.4 presents an example of these changes. Section 3.3.3 will discuss Phase 1 to Phase 2 transition routing.

4. Look for ZIP packets. Two types of ZIP packets can indicate significant changes in the internetwork topology. ZIP Query packets indicate that a router has discovered a new route (from RTMP packets) and doesn't know the zones associated with that route. Nodes use ZIP GetNetInfo packets at startup to determine their correct network number. Thus, GetNetInfo packets on the network might indicate an unexpected topology change. Section 3.3.6 will study ZIP in further detail.

5. Use NBP traffic to identify nodes. Recall that NBP provides a mapping between user-assigned entity names and the internet-designated internet address. You can easily identify intelligent devices, such as servers, gateways, and printers because they can respond to an NBP LookUp request packet. Section 3.3.2 will consider NBP transmissions.

6. Look for session or user application-related traffic. For instance, the server sends out ASP tickle packets every 30 seconds to maintain the AppleShare services. The server also transmits ATP tickle packets at server-defined intervals.

7. AppleTalk Phase 2 greatly enhanced the architecture's internetworking capabilities. These changes affected the AppleTalk Network and Transport Layer protocols (AARP, DDP, RTMP, NBP, and ZIP), which deal with addressing and moving packets around the internet. All other protocols within the architecture are unaffected by the enhancements.

With these guidelines in mind, let's examine AppleTalk troubleshooting.

3.3 AppleTalk Internetwork Troubleshooting

With so many protocols included within the AppleTalk architecture, trouble-shooting can often be a challenge. We'll begin with examples at the Physical and Data Link Layers, and add additional protocol examples as we proceed.

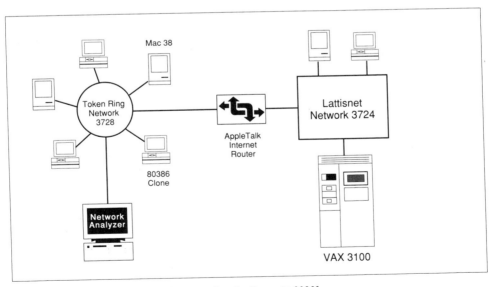

Figure 3-3. AppleTalk Node Connecting to Remote VAX

3.3.1 AppleTalk Nodes Entering a Token Ring Network

Our first AppleTalk example examines what happens when a Macintosh and an 80386 clone initialize on a token ring network (see the left side of Figure 3-3). This example will demonstrate that the token ring (IEEE 802.5) protocols require a specific sequence of events, and that these events remain the same whether the entering node is a PC, minicomputer, or mainframe communications controller. To see this, we'll look at the trace files from the Macintosh (shown as Mac 38 in Trace 3.3.1a) and the PC (shown as 80386 Clone in Trace 3.3.1b). We placed the network analyzer on the token ring for these tests.

Sniffer Network Analyzer data 2-Oct-90 at 06:40:26 file MACBOOT.TRC Pg 1

SUMMARY	Delta T	Destination	Source	Summary
M 1		Broadcast	AT Router	MAC Active Monitor Present
2	0.019	Broadcast	NwkGnl02096E	MAC Standby Monitor Present
4	6.907	Broadcast	AT Router	MAC Active Monitor Present
5	0.020	Broadcast	NwkGnl02096E	MAC Standby Monitor Present
7	6.906	Broadcast	AT Router	MAC Active Monitor Present
8	0.020	Broadcast	NwkGnl02096E	MAC Standby Monitor Present
9	6.905	Broadcast	AT Router	MAC Active Monitor Present
10	0.021	Broadcast	NwkGnl02096E	MAC Standby Monitor Present
12	2.056	Broadcast	AT Router	MAC Ring Purge
13	0.000	Mac 38	Mac 38	MAC Duplicate Address Test
14	0.001	Broadcast	AT Router	MAC Active Monitor Present
15	0.000	Mac 38	Mac 38	MAC Duplicate Address Test
16	0.018	Broadcast	NwkGnl02096E	MAC Standby Monitor Present
17	0.000	Config Srv	Mac 38	MAC Report SUA Change
18	0.015	Broadcast	Mac 38	MAC Standby Monitor Present
19	0.000	Config Srv	AT Router	MAC Report SUA Change
20	0.000	Param Server	Mac 38	MAC Request Initialization
21	0.001	Param Server	Mac 38	MAC Request Initialization
22	0.001	Param Server	Mac 38	MAC Request Initialization
23	0.001	Param Server	Mac 38	MAC Request Initialization

24	1.935	Error Mon.	AT Router	MAC Report Soft Error
25	4.948	Broadcast	AT Router	MAC Active Monitor Present
26	0.012	Broadcast	NwkGnl02096E	MAC Standby Monitor Present
27	0.015	Broadcast	Mac 38	MAC Standby Monitor Present
29	6.899	Broadcast	AT Router	MAC Active Monitor Present
30	0.013	Broadcast	NwkGnl02096E	MAC Standby Monitor Present
31	0.014	Broadcast	Mac 38	MAC Standby Monitor Present
33	6.913	Broadcast	AT Router	MAC Active Monitor Present
34	0.013	Broadcast	NwkGnl02096E	MAC Standby Monitor Present
35	0.013	Broadcast	Mac 38	MAC Standby Monitor Present
36	6.899	Broadcast	AT Router	MAC Active Monitor Present
37	0.014	Broadcast	NwkGnl02096E	MAC Standby Monitor Present
38	0.013	Broadcast	Mac 38	MAC Standby Monitor Present
40	6.899	Broadcast	AT Router	MAC Active Monitor Present
41	0.015	Broadcast	NwkGnl02096E	MAC Standby Monitor Present
42	0.012	Broadcast	Mac 38	MAC Standby Monitor Present
61	6.899	Broadcast	AT Router	MAC Active Monitor Present
62	0.015	Broadcast	NwkGnl02096E	MAC Standby Monitor Present
63	0.011	Broadcast	Mac 38	MAC Standby Monitor Present

Trace 3.3.1a. AppleTalk/token ring Macintosh initialization

Sniffer Network Analyzer data 2-Oct-90 at 06:40:26 PCBOOT.TRC Pg 1

SUMMARY	Delta T	Destination	Source	Summary
M 1		Broadcast	AT Router	MAC Active Monitor Present
2	0.019	Broadcast	NwkGnl02096E	MAC Standby Monitor Present
3	0.015	Broadcast	Mac 38	MAC Standby Monitor Present
5	4.447	Broadcast	AT Router	MAC Ring Purge
6	0.000	80386 Clone	80386 Clone	MAC Duplicate Address Test
7	0.001	Broadcast	AT Router	MAC Active Monitor Present
8	0.000	80386 Clone	80386 Clone	MAC Duplicate Address Test
9	0.001	Config Srv	80386 Clone	MAC Report SUA Change
10	0.016	Broadcast	80386 Clone	MAC Standby Monitor Present

11	0.000	Param Server	80386 Clone	MAC Request Initialization
12	0.000	Config Srv	NwkGnl02096E	MAC Report SUA Change
13	0.000	Param Server	80386 Clone	MAC Request Initialization
14	0.000	Param Server	80386 Clone	MAC Request Initialization
15	0.000	Param Server	80386 Clone	MAC Request Initialization
16	0.015	Broadcast	NwkGnl02096E	MAC Standby Monitor Present
17	0.014	Broadcast	Mac 38	MAC Standby Monitor Present
25	1.904	Error Mon.	NwkGnl02096E	MAC Report Soft Error
27	0.018	Error Mon.	AT Router	MAC Report Soft Error
44	4.948	Broadcast	AT Router	MAC Active Monitor Present
46	0.021	Broadcast	80386 Clone	MAC Standby Monitor Present
47	0.019	Broadcast	NwkGnl02096E	MAC Standby Monitor Present
48	0.013	Broadcast	Mac 38	MAC Standby Monitor Present
87	6.872	Broadcast	AT Router	MAC Active Monitor Present
88	0.013	Broadcast	80386 Clone	MAC Standby Monitor Present
89	0.018	Broadcast	NwkGnl02096E	MAC Standby Monitor Present
90	0.013	Broadcast	Mac 38	MAC Standby Monitor Present
100	6.882	Broadcast	AT Router	MAC Active Monitor Present
101	0.014	Broadcast	80386 Clone	MAC Standby Monitor Present
102	0.017	Broadcast	NwkGnl02096E	MAC Standby Monitor Present
103	0.012	Broadcast	Mac 38	MAC Standby Monitor Present

Trace 3.3.1b. AppleTalk/token ring PC initialization

To illustrate the process, we filtered the trace files to show only the MAC (Medium Access Control) frames. Both the Mac and the 80386 clone are nodes on network 3728, which is connected via an AppleTalk Internet Router (AT Router in Traces 3.3.1a and b) to several other networks.

In the case of the Macintosh, Frames 1 through 10 in Trace 3.3.1a indicate normal ring operation. The Active Monitor (AT Router) transmits an Active Monitor Present frame approximately every seven seconds, while the analyzer (NwkGnl 02096E), the only other node on the network, transmits a Standby Monitor Present frame in response. When the Macintosh (Mac 38) enters the ring, it opens the relay connected to its port on the Multi-Station Access Unit (MSAU), the token ring wiring hub. This contact opening causes a brief disruption in data transmission, so the Active Monitor tests the transmission path with a Ring Purge in Frame 12. Next, the Macintosh uses the Duplicate Address Test (DAT) in Frames 13 and 15 to test for any other node with an identical hardware (Medium Access Control or MAC-Layer) address. In Frame 17, Mac 38 reports a change in its Stored Upstream Address (SUA) register to the Configuration Report Server. The AT Router transmits a similar message in Frame 19.

Next, the new node requests its initialization parameters from the Ring Parameter Server (RPS). After four attempts (Frames 20 through 23) the node assumes that the RPS is inactive and uses its default parameters. The new node's downstream neighbor (AT Router) reports a Soft Error two seconds after the actuated relay disrupted the ring communications. The new node then participates in a Ring Poll (Frames 25 through 27) in which all nodes learn the current address of their Nearest Active Upstream Neighbor (NAUN). Now, the new node can become a fully functional member of the ring. The Active Monitor conducts Subsequent Ring Polls every seven seconds. These polls identify the ring topology as AT Router to Analyzer to Mac 38 and back to AT Router. (Remember that the 80386 Clone is not active yet.)

In summary, the node initialization sequence is:

Event 1— the relay actuation triggers the transmission of a Ring Purge frame.

Event 2— the new node transmits one or two Duplicate Address Test frames.

Event 3— the new node and its downstream neighbor report a Stored Upstream Address change to the Configuration Report Server.

Event 4— the new node requests Initialization Parameters from Ring Parameter Server (maximum four tries).

Event 5— the new node's downstream neighbor transmits a Report Error frame.

Event 6— the new node participates in a Ring Poll.

For comparison, consider Trace 3.3.1b, which shows a similar course of events when the 80386 Clone boots up:

Event 1—Ring Purge (Frame 5)

Event 2—Duplicate Address Test (Frames 6 and 8)

Event 3—Report SUA Change (Frames 9 and 12)

Event 4—Request Initialization (Frames 11 and 13 through 15)

Event 5—Report Error (Frames 25 and 27)

Event 6—Ring Poll (Frames 44 and 46 through 48)

Clearly, the MAC-level protocol process is identical for all token ring nodes— Macintosh or PC.

3.3.2 AppleTalk Node Accessing a Remote Host

Our second case study builds upon the example shown in Section 3.3.1, and demonstrates the higher layer protocols involved in establishing a connection from a Macintosh on the token ring to a remote DEC VAX host via the internet router (review Figure 3-3). The Macintosh user (Mac 38 in Trace files 3.3.2) opens the desk accessory, invokes the Chooser, and selects a server in the Engineering Zone.

Let's first summarize the process (Trace 3.3.2a). The internet router (IR), node 3728.31 in Frame 4 transmits an RTMP packet, which carries routing table information to the other routers on the internet. Frames 5 through 8 contain NBP packets, looking for the VAX server. Frames 9 and 10 use the Echo protocol to query the server in order to verify the communication path between Mac 38 and the VAX. Frames 11 and 12 begin to establish the session using ASP. The actual login is initiated in Frame 27 and confirmed in Frame 34. The server's available volumes can then be opened (Frames 36 through 49).

TROUBLESHOOTING APPLETALK INTERNETWORKS

Sniffer Network Analyzer data 2-Oct-90 at 06:40:26 file AFP2VAX.TRC Pg 1

SUMMARY	Delta T	Destination	Source	Summary
M 1		Broadcast	AT Router	MAC Active Monitor Present
2	0.015	Broadcast	NwkGnl02096E	MAC Standby Monitor Present
3	0.011	Broadcast	Mac 38	MAC Standby Monitor Present
4	1.213	C00040000000	AT Router	RTMP R Node=3728.31
				Rou ent=8
5	0.343	AT Router	Mac 38	NBP C Request ID=14
				(=:AFPServer@NVL-Engr)
6	0.013	Mac 38	AT Router	NBP R Lookup ID=14 N=1
				1=[3724.111;214;
				(VAXShare FileSvr:AFPSvr@*)]
7	0.917	AT Router	Mac 38	NBP C Request ID=14
				(=:AFPSvr@NVL-Engr)
8	0.012	Mac 38	AT Router	NBP R Lookup ID=14 N=1
				1=[3724.111;214;
				(VAXShare FileSvr:AFPSvr@*)]
9	0.699	AT Router	Mac 38	ECHO C LEN=585
10	0.015	Mac 38	AT Router	ECHO R LEN=585
11	0.009	AT Router	Mac 38	ASP C GetStat
12	0.012	Mac 38	AT Router	ASP R GetStat LEN=390
13	0.180	AT Router	Mac 38	NBP C Request ID=14
				(=:AFPSvr@NVL-Engr)
14	0.012	Mac 38	AT Router	NBP R Lookup ID=14 N=1
				1=[3724.111;214;
				(VAXShare FileSvr:AFPSvr@*)]
15	0.917	AT Router	Mac 38	NBP C Request ID=14
				(=:AFPSvr@NVL-Engr)
16	0.012	Mac 38	AT Router	NBP R Lookup ID=14 N=1
				1=[3724.111;214;
				(VAXShare FileSvr:AFPSvr@*)]

17	0.917	AT Router	Mac 38	NBP C Request ID=14
				(=:AFPSvr@NVL-Engr)
18	0.017	Mac 38	AT Router	NBP R Lookup ID=14 N=1
				1=[3724.111;214;
				(VAXShare FileSvr:AFPSvr@*)]
19	0.274	AT Router	Mac 38	ATP C ID=3557 LEN=6
20	0.016	Mac 38	AT Router	ATP R ID=3557 LEN=10 NS=0
				(Last)
21	0.007	AT Router	Mac 38	ATP D ID=3557
22	0.793	AT Router	Mac 38	ASP C OpenSess WSS=251
				Version=0100
23	0.009	Mac 38	AT Router	ASP R OpenSess SSS=196 ID=9
				ERR=0
24	0.001	Mac 38	AT Router	ASP C Tickle ID=9
25	0.005	AT Router	Mac 38	ATP D ID=3558
26	0.001	AT Router	Mac 38	ASP C Tickle ID=9
27	0.002	AT Router	Mac 38	AFP C Login AFPVersion 2.0
28	0.490	Broadcast	AT Router	MAC Active Monitor Present
29	0.016	Broadcast	NwkGnl02096E	MAC Standby Monitor Present
30	0.020	Broadcast	Mac 38	MAC Standby Monitor Present
31	0.869	AT Router	Mac 38	AFP C Login AFPVersion 2.0
32	0.019	Mac 38	AT Router	ECHO C LEN=585
33	0.010	AT Router	Mac 38	ECHO R LEN=585
34	0.162	Mac 38	AT Router	AFP R OK
35	0.006	AT Router	Mac 38	ATP D ID=3560
36	0.001	AT Router	Mac 38	AFP C GetSrvrParms
37	0.019	Mac 38	AT Router	AFP R OK 4 volumes
38	0.007	AT Router	Mac 38	ATP D ID=3561
39	0.152	AT Router	Mac 38	AFP C OpenVol Volume=
				"More LanWORKS Apps"
40	0.189	Mac 38	AT Router	AFP R OK
41	0.007	AT Router	Mac 38	ATP D ID=3562

42	0.001	AT Router	Mac 38	AFP C GetFileDirParms
				VolID=4 DirID=2 Obj=""
43	0.797	Mac 38	AT Router	AFP R OK
44	0.007	AT Router	Mac 38	ATP D ID=3563
45	0.001	AT Router	Mac 38	AFP C CloseVol VolID=4
46	0.092	Mac 38	AT Router	AFP R OK
47	0.007	AT Router	Mac 38	ATP D ID=3564
48	0.003	AT Router	Mac 38	AFP C OpenVol Volume=
				"MSA Apps T1.0-EFT2"
49	0.193	Mac 38	AT Router	AFP R OK

Trace 3.3.2a. AppleTalk node connecting to remote VAX server

Now, let's examine each step in detail. The internet router broadcasts the RTMP packet in Frame 4 to all other routers on that internetwork (the details of that frame are shown in Trace 3.3.2b). The IEEE 802.5 Data Link Control (DLC) header identifies the Destination address as C00040000000H (TokenTalk Broadcast). The Source Address (5000E0000022H) contains the address block that the IEEE assigned to Apple Computer (5000E0H) plus the serialized address (000022H) for that specific network interface card (NIC). The IEEE 802.5 frame also contains source routing information (more on this in Section 6.1). The Logical Link Control (LLC) and Sub-Network Access Protocol (SNAP) headers that come next identify Apple as the vendor (080007H) and AppleTalk as the protocol type (809BH).

```
Sniffer Network Analyzer data 2-Oct-90 at 06:40:26 AFP2VAX.TRC Pg 1

- - - - - - - - - - - - - - - Frame 4 - - - - - - - - - - - - - - - - -

DLC:        —— DLC Header ——
DLC:
DLC:        Frame 4 arrived at  06:47:02.340; frame size is 74 (004A hex) bytes.
DLC:        AC:    Frame priority 0,  Reservation priority 0,  Monitor count 0
DLC:        FC:    LLC frame,  PCF attention code: None
DLC:        FS:    Addr recognized indicators: 00, Frame copied indicators: 00
DLC:        Destination = Functional address C00040000000
```

```
DLC:        Source     = Station 5000E0000022, AT Router
DLC:

RI :               —— Routing Indicators ——
RI :

RI :        Routing control = E2
RI :                111. .... = Single-route broadcast, non-broadcast return
RI :                ...0 0010 = RI length is 2
RI :        Routing control = 78
RI :                0... .... = Forward direction
RI :                .111 .... = Largest frame is unspecified maximum value
RI :                .... 1000 = Reserved
RI :

LLC:        —— LLC Header ——
LLC:

LLC:        DSAP = AA, SSAP = AA, Command, Unnumbered frame: UI
LLC:

SNAP:       —— SNAP Header ——
SNAP:

SNAP:       Vendor ID = 080007 (Apple)
SNAP:       Type = 809B (AppleTalk)
SNAP:

DDP:        —— DDP header ——
DDP:

DDP:        Hop count      = 0
DDP:        Length     = 50
DDP:        Checksum       = 0000
DDP:        Destination Network Number = 0
DDP:        Destination Node      = 255
DDP:        Destination Socket       = 1 (RTMP)
DDP:        Source Network Number     = 3728
DDP:        Source Node        = 31
DDP:        Source Socket        = 1 (RTMP)
```

DDP:	DDP protocol type = 1 (RTMP data)
DDP:	
RTMP:	—— RTMP Data ——
RTMP:	
RTMP:	Net = 3728
RTMP:	Node ID length = 8 bits
RTMP:	Node ID = 31
RTMP:	Tuple 1 : Cable range = 3728 to 3728 (Version 2)
RTMP:	Tuple 2 : Net = 3732, Distance = 3
RTMP:	Tuple 3 : Net = 3731, Distance = 2
RTMP:	Tuple 4 : Net = 3730, Distance = 1
RTMP:	Tuple 5 : Net = 3722, Distance = 0
RTMP:	Tuple 6 : Net = 3723, Distance = 0
RTMP:	Tuple 7 : Cable range = 3724 to 3724 (Version 2)
RTMP:	Tuple 8 : Cable range = 3726 to 3726 (Version 2)
RTMP:	
RTMP:	[Normal end of "RTMP Data ".]
RTMP:	

Trace 3.3.2b. AppleTalk internet router RTMP broadcast details

The DDP header indicates a Destination Network Number of 0, Destination Node of 255 (network-wide broadcast), and Destination Socket of 1 (RTMP). The Source addresses define the token ring network (3728), the IR's node number for its token ring port (31), and the RTMP Socket (1).

The RTMP data has eight routing tuples that contain routing table information—a network number or range and the distance to that network in hops. The first tuple defines the cable range of the source network. (Looking for RTMP tuple 1 is a quick way to identify the network number.) Subsequent tuples indicate other networks and their distances in IR hops from this router. Note that networks 3722, 3723, 3724, and 3726 are directly connected to this IR (shown by a distance = 0 or a cable range specification). We can, therefore, determine that this IR has a total of five ports: network 3728 (this network) plus the four directly connected networks listed above.

Returning to Trace 3.3.2a, Frame 5 contains an NBP broadcast request from the Macintosh to locate AFPServer @ NVL-Engineering. Frame 6 contains the reply: Node 3724.111 is the server in question (see the NBP details in Trace 3.3.2c). Frame 9 contains a request from Mac 38's Echoer socket to the VAX's Echoer socket to test the destination network address (3724.111) previously obtained using NBP. Frame 10 contains details of the successful reply (Trace 3.3.2d).

Sniffer Network Analyzer data 2-Oct-90 06:40:26 AFP2VAX.TRC Pg 1

- - - - - - - - - - - - - - - - Frame 5 - - - - - - - - - - - - - - - -

```
NBP:—— NBP header ——
NBP:
NBP:          Control     = 1 (Broadcast Request)
NBP:          Tuple count   = 1
NBP:          Transaction id = 14
NBP:
NBP:          —— Entity # 1 ——
NBP:
NBP:          Node      = 3728.59,  Socket = 254
NBP:          Enumerator = 0
NBP:          Object    = "="
NBP:          Type      = "AFPServer"
NBP:          Zone      = "NVL-Engineering"
NBP:
NBP:          [Normal end of "NBP header".]
```

- - - - - - - - - - - - - - - - Frame 6 - - - - - - - - - - - - - - - -

```
NBP:—— NBP header ——
NBP:
NBP:          Control     = 3 (Reply)
NBP:          Tuple count   = 1
NBP:          Transaction id = 14
NBP:
```

```
NBP:            —— Entity # 1 ——
NBP:
NBP:            Node      = 3724.111,  Socket = 214
NBP:            Enumerator = 5
NBP:            Object    = "VAXShare FileServer"
NBP:            Type      = "AFPServer"
NBP:            Zone      = "*"
NBP:
NBP:            [Normal end of "NBP header".]
```

Trace 3.3.2c. AppleTalk node NBP broadcast details

```
Sniffer Network Analyzer data 2-Oct-90 06:40:26 AFP2VAX.TRC Pg 1

- - - - - - - - - - - - - - - Frame 9 - - - - - - - - - - - - - - - - -

DDP:—— DDP header ——
DDP:
DDP:            Hop count      = 0
DDP:            Length        = 599
DDP:            Checksum       = 0000
DDP:            Destination Network Number = 3724
DDP:            Destination Node        = 111
DDP:            Destination Socket      = 4 (Echo)
DDP:            Source Network Number    = 3728
DDP:            Source Node            = 59
DDP:            Source Socket          = 251 (Echo)
DDP:            DDP protocol type = 4 (Echo)
DDP:
ECHO:—— ECHO header ——
ECHO:
ECHO:           Function = 1 (Request)
ECHO:
ECHO:           [585 byte(s) of data]
ECHO:
```

```
ECHO:          [Normal end of "ECHO header".]


- - - - - - - - - - - - - - - - Frame 10 - - - - - - - - - - - - - - - - -
DDP:—— DDP header ——
DDP:
DDP:          Hop count      = 1
DDP:          Length         = 599
DDP:          Checksum       = 0000
DDP:          Destination Network Number = 3728
DDP:          Destination Node      = 59
DDP:          Destination Socket    = 251
DDP:          Source Network Number   = 3724
DDP:          Source Node           = 111
DDP:          Source Socket         = 4
DDP:          DDP protocol type = 4 (Echo)
DDP:

ECHO:—— ECHO header ——
ECHO:
ECHO:         Function = 2 (Reply)
ECHO:
ECHO:         [585 byte(s) of data]
ECHO:
ECHO:         [Normal end of "ECHO header".]
```

Trace 3.3.2d. AppleTalk node Echo to remote host

Establishment of the session between Mac 38 and the VAX begins in Frame 11. An ASP status request is transmitted as a client function of an ATP packet (Trace 3.3.2e). Details of the response in Frame 12 (contained within the 390 bytes of data) include information on the VMS and AFP versions running on the VAX. Note from Trace 3.3.3a that in Frames 22 and 23 ASP opens the session between Mac 38 and VAX.

Sniffer Network Analyzer data 2-Oct-90 06:40:26 AFP2VAX.TRC Pg 1

- - - - - - - - - - - - - - - Frame 11 - - - - - - - - - - - - - - - - -

ATP:—— ATP header ——

ATP:

ATP: Client   = (ASP)

ATP: Function = 1 (Request)

ATP: Control field = 0X

ATP: ..0. .... = At-least-once transaction

ATP: Request bitmap = 01

ATP: ....1 = Request bitmap

ATP: Transaction id = 3556

ATP: User data = 03000000

ATP:

ASP:—— ASP header ——

ASP:

ASP: SPCmdType   = 3 (Get Status)

ASP:

ASP: [Normal end of "ASP header".]

ASP:

- - - - - - - - - - - - - - - Frame 12 - - - - - - - - - - - - - - - - -

ATP:—— ATP header ——

ATP:

ATP: Client   = (ASP)

ATP: Function = 2 (Response)

ATP: Control field = 10

ATP: ...1 .... = Last reply for this transaction

ATP: Response sequence = 0

ATP: Transaction id = 3556

ATP: User data = 00000000

ATP:

ASP:—— ASP header ——

```
ASP:

ASP:            SPCmdType (reply)      = (Get Status)

ASP:

ASP:            [390 byte(s) of data]

ASP:

ASP:            [Normal end of "ASP header".]

ASP:
```

Trace 3.3.2e. AppleTalk node establishing session with remote host

Reviewing Trace 3.3.2a, the final step in the Mac to VAX connection process is to log in to the remote host. The AFP accomplishes the login in Frames 27 and 34. Note from Trace 3.3.3f that the AFP function = 18 specifies the login command; the AFP version denotes AFP version 2.0; and the User Authentication Method (UAM) indicates that authentication is not required. Frame 34 confirms Login. Subsequent frames (Trace 3.3.2a) obtain volume information from the remote server and transmit that information to Mac 38. The four volumes' names ("More LanWorks Apps", MSA Apps T1.0-EFT2," "LanWorks Test Volume," and "DEC LanWorks T1.0-EFT3") are displayed for user selection. The user of Mac 38 would then specify the volume(s) that should appear as icons on the desktop.

```
Sniffer Network Analyzer data 2-Oct-90 06:40:26 AFP2VAX.TRC Pg 1
- - - - - - - - - - - - - - - Frame 27 - - - - - - - - - - - - - - - - -
AFP:—— AFP ——

AFP:

AFP:    FP command      = 18 (Login)

AFP:    FP version    = "AFPVersion 2.0"

AFP:    UAM string    = "No User Authent"

AFP:

AFP:

AFP:    [Normal end of "AFP".]

AFP:
```

```
- - - - - - - - - - - - - - Frame 34 - - - - - - - - - - - - - - - -
AFP:—— AFP ——
AFP:
AFP:       FP reply      = (Login)
AFP:       Error         = 0 (NoErr)
AFP:
AFP:
AFP:       [Normal end of "AFP".]
AFP:
```

Trace 3.3.2f. AppleTalk node login to remote host

3.3.3 AppleTalk Phase 1 to Phase 2 Transition Services Impact

With the AppleTalk Phase 2 enhancements, the EtherTalk Data Link Layer Protocol changed from Ethernet version 2 to IEEE 802.3. When some nodes are running Phase 1 protocols and others are running Phase 2, an Internet Transition Router must make the conversion between these protocols.

Although the conversion is straightforward, it generates two frames on the cable for every transmission over the transition router. These extra frames can consume valuable bandwidth. Trace 3.3.3 demonstrates this situation.

In Figure 3-4, a Macintosh on the LocalTalk network 3722 sends an ADSP connect packet ("I'd like to talk") to the MicroVAX on another network via the Internet Router (shown as InterRoute in Trace 3.3.3). (We can't see this packet in Trace 3.3.3 because of the location of the analyzer on the EtherTalk network.) However, InterRoute is a Phase 2-only device, while the destination (MicroVAX) is a Phase 1-only device. So, a protocol conversion is required. This conversion occurs in Frame 85—InterRoute sends the ADSP packet to the Transition Router (TransRoute in Trace 3.3.3). TransRoute then performs the conversion and sends the ADSP packet to the MicroVAX in Frame 86. The second step in the connection process ("It's OK with me if its OK with you") occurs in Frame 87 when the Micro VAX acknowledges the connection request with an ADSP Conn & Ack packet. This packet uses Phase 1, and is sent from the Micro VAX to TransRoute, which forwards it to the originating Macintosh (again, not shown in Trace 3.3.3). The Macintosh

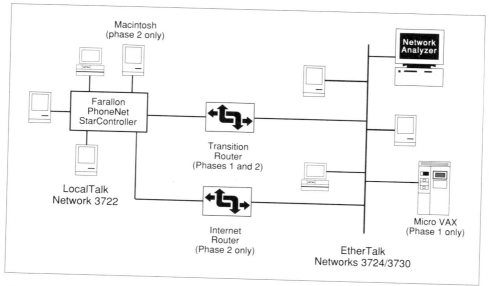

Figure 3-4. AppleTalk Transition Router Operation

transmits an ADSP ConnAck packet ("Fine, let's talk") that must also be converted (Frames 88 and 89). The connection is established after Frame 89. Subsequent frames (90 through 100) show data transfer between the Macintosh and MicroVAX.

Sniffer Network Analyzer data 17-Apr-90 14:13:38, ADSP.ENC, Pg 1

SUMMARY	Delta T	Destination	Source	Summary
70	0.0023	FFFFFFFFFFFF	MicroVAX	RTMP R Node=3730.254 Rou en=13
71	0.9685	InterRoute	DECnet006418	ATP C ID=1897 LEN=6
72	0.0108	DECnet006418	InterRoute	ATP R ID=1897 LEN=10 NS=0
73	0.0014	InterRoute	DECnet006418	ATP D ID=1897
74	0.2094	InterRoute	DECnet006418	ATP C ID=1898 LEN=24
75	0.0038	DECnet006418	InterRoute	ATP R ID=1898 LEN=24 NS=0
76	0.2453	FFFFFFFFFFFF	TransRoute	RTMP R Node=3730.148 Rou en=14
77	0.0034	090007FFFFFF	TransRoute	RTMP R Node=3724.152 Rou en=14
78	0.1346	090007FFFFFF	InterRoute	RTMP R Node=3724.39 Rou en=5
79	0.4392	TransRoute	MicroVAX	ADSP Probe
				CID=B7A0 WIN=4096

80	0.0085	TransRoute	InterRoute	ADSP Ack CID=1645 SEQ=20
				ACK=0 WIN=533
81	0.0027	MicroVAX	TransRoute	ADSP Ack CID=1645 SEQ=20
				ACK=0 WIN=533
82	0.0189	TransRoute	MicroVAX	ADSP Data CID=B7A0 SEQ=0
				ACK=20 WIN=4096
				LEN=21 [EOM]
83	0.0101	TransRoute	InterRoute	ADSP Close CID=1645 SEQ=20
				ACK=22
84	0.0027	MicroVAX	TransRoute	ADSP Close CID=1645 SEQ=20
				ACK=22
85	0.0010	TransRoute	InterRoute	ADSP Conn CID=1646 WIN=533
86	0.0027	MicroVAX	TransRoute	ADSP Conn CID=1646 WIN=533
87	0.0507	TransRoute	MicroVAX	ADSP Conn & Ack
				CID=BE01 WIN=4096 DCID=1646
88	0.0091	TransRoute	InterRoute	ADSP Conn Ack CID=1646
				WIN=533 DCID=BE01
89	0.0027	MicroVAX	TransRoute	ADSP Conn Ack CID=1646
				WIN=533 DCID=BE01
90	0.0037	TransRoute	InterRoute	ADSP Data CID=1646 SEQ=0
				ACK=0 WIN=533
				LEN=35 [EOM]
91	0.0027	MicroVAX	TransRoute	ADSP Data CID=1646 SEQ=0
				ACK=0 WIN=533
				LEN=35 [EOM]
92	0.9515	TransRoute	InterRoute	ADSP Probe CID=1646 WIN=533
93	0.0027	MicroVAX	TransRoute	ADSP Probe CID=1646 WIN=533
94	0.0327	TransRoute	MicroVAX	ADSP Ack CID=BE01 SEQ=0
				ACK=36 WIN=4060
95	0.8296	AB0000030000	MicroVAX	DRP ROUTER Hello
				S=6.68 BLKSZ=1498

96	0.2788	TransRoute	MicroVAX	ADSP Data CID=BE01 SEQ=0
				ACK=36 WIN=4096
				LEN=35 [EOM]
97	0.0147	TransRoute	InterRoute	ADSP Data CID=1646 SEQ=36
				ACK=36 WIN=533
				LEN=31 [EOM]
98	0.0027	MicroVAX	TransRoute	ADSP Data CID=1646 SEQ=36
				ACK=36 WIN=533
				LEN=31 [EOM]
99	0.1423	DECnet002F2C	InterRoute	ATP C ID=2452 LEN=0
100	0.0890	InterRoute	DECnet006418	ATP C ID=1899 LEN=24

Trace 3.3.3. AppleTalk packets with Transition Routing

Note that an extra packet is required for transmission from the Macintosh to MicroVAX:

Macintosh to InterRoute (Phase 2)

InterRoute to TransRoute(Phase 2 to Phase 1)

TransRoute to MicroVAX (Phase 1)

If all nodes were running Phase 2, InterRoute could communicate directly with the MicroVAX:

Macintosh to InterRoute

InterRoute to MicroVAX

The lesson is clear: By upgrading AppleTalk Phase 1 nodes to Phase 2, you eliminate the extra transmissions caused by the Transition Services.

3.3.4 AppleTalk Internetwork Additions

Routers maintain tables of information about the internet topology, which they transmit every 10 seconds. When a new router comes online or fails, the analyst can look for changes in this routing table information (the RTMP packets) to assist with troubleshooting.

Figure 3-5 illustrates the original topology of the internetwork we will discuss in this example. It includes a Shiva Corporation (Cambridge, MA) EtherGate half router connected to a second EtherGate at another location via a modem and dial-up telephone line. By examining a filtered trace file that contains only the RTMP and ZIP packets (Trace 3.3.4a), we were able to identify changes in internet topology. The number of routing entries (tuples, containing the network and distance information) changes as new networks are added to or deleted from the internet. Note that the time (Delta T) between broadcasts from a particular node is approximately 10 seconds (e.g. add the times from Frames 1 to 31).

Details of the initial configuration, Frames 1 and 2, (Trace 3.3.4b) show that a Phase 1 node (3730.148) transmits nine routing entities, while the Phase 2 node 3724.152 (within the same Phase 1 to Phase 2 transition router) transmits only five. The difference is the split horizon; the Phase 2 router does not transmit information about networks 3722, 3723, 3726, or 3728 because the Internet Router handles traffic to those networks.

In Frame 545 the telephone line connected to the EtherGate routers becomes active. Trace 3.3.4c indicates this change, since the number of routing entries (tuples) jumps from nine to 25. The additional 16 networks (7500, 7501, 7502, etc.) are at the remote location. Note that the Phase 1 RTMP data (Frame 545) contains 25 tuples, while the Phase 2 RTMP data (Frame 546) contains only five with the split horizon.

Because the routing table has changed in size, the Zone Information Table (ZIT) is now incomplete. A ZIP Query to the EtherGate router (InterRoute) remedies the problem in Frame 556. The responses come in Frames 607 through 609 (Trace 3.3.4d) giving one, one, and 13 zone mappings, respectively. Another query (Frame 636) accounts for the last network (Net 7501) in Frame 637.

Since the internetwork topology changes dynamically, a router's tables could easily fill up with obsolete information. To prevent this, bad routes are removed from

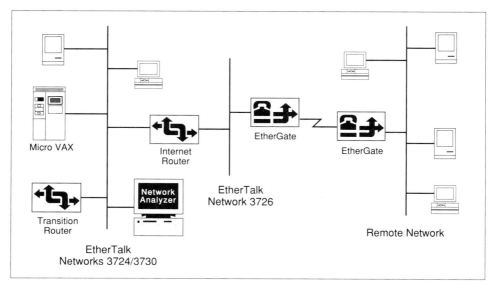

Figure 3-5. AppleTalk Remote Network Connections

a router's tables and routine RTMP update packets. The validity timer considers each router's RTMP data valid for 20 seconds. After 20 seconds, the validity timers in the adjacent routers expire, remove the bad routes from their tables, and stop including them in their updates. Each propagation of a bad route thus adds 20 seconds of delay.

AppleTalk Phase 2 introduced a more efficient way to remove (or poison) a route. Rather than simply omitting an invalid route, it includes the route in an update packet, but sets the RTMP distance to 31. Routers receiving a routing entry with distance = 31 must stop using that route immediately, thus saving up to 20 seconds of delay.

When the remote link attached to the EtherGate fails (or in this case was disconnected), the RTMP data specifies a poison route for the networks previously reached via that link. Frame 2652 (Trace 3.3.4e) shows this process. This RTMP packet contains a total of 21 tuples, 16 of which have distance = 31. The remaining five tuples (Net 3722, 3723, 3724, 3726, and 3728) are the networks on the local side of the EtherGate.

Sniffer Network Analyzer data 12-Oct-90 10:20:28 NEWNETS.ENC Pg 1

SUMMARY	Delta T	Destination	Source	Summary
M 1		Broadcast	TransRoute	RTMP R Node=3730.148 Rou en=9
2	0.0025	090007FFFFFF	TransRoute	RTMP R Node=3724.152 Rou en=5
23	5.5687	Broadcast	MicroVAX	RTMP R Node=3730.254 Rou en=8
24	1.5387	090007FFFFFF	InterRoute	RTMP R Node=3724.26 Rou en=5
31	3.0252	Broadcast	TransRoute	RTMP R Node=3730.148 Rou en=9
32	0.0025	090007FFFFFF	TransRoute	RTMP R Node=3724.152 Rou en=5
62	5.4337	Broadcast	MicroVAX	RTMP R Node=3730.254 Rou en=8
65	1.5509	090007FFFFFF	InterRoute	RTMP R Node=3724.26 Rou en=5
70	3.0549	Broadcast	TransRoute	RTMP R Node=3730.148 Rou en=9
71	0.0025	090007FFFFFF	TransRoute	RTMP R Node=3724.152 Rou en=5
.				
.				
.				
503	3.5425	Broadcast	TransRoute	RTMP R Node=3730.148 Rou en=9
504	0.0025	090007FFFFFF	TransRoute	RTMP R Node=3724.152 Rou en=5
531	4.8625	Broadcast	MicroVAX	RTMP R Node=3730.254 Rou en=8
534	1.5905	090007FFFFFF	InterRoute	RTMP R Node=3724.26 Rou en=21
545	3.6230	Broadcast	TransRoute	RTMP R Node=3730.148 Rou en=25
546	0.0037	090007FFFFFF	TransRoute	RTMP R Node=3724.152 Rou en=5
556	4.0141	InterRoute	TransRoute	ZIP C Query Network Count=16
563	0.7688	Broadcast	MicroVAX	RTMP R Node=3730.254 Rou en=24
564	0.0013	TransRoute	MicroVAX	ZIP C Query Network Count=16
572	1.6213	090007FFFFFF	InterRoute	RTMP R Node=3724.26 Rou en=21
582	3.7587	Broadcast	TransRoute	RTMP R Node=3730.148 Rou en=25
583	0.0037	090007FFFFFF	TransRoute	RTMP R Node=3724.152 Rou en=5
606	4.0612	InterRoute	TransRoute	ZIP C Query Network Count=16
607	0.0068	TransRoute	InterRoute	ZIP R Ext Reply Net Count=1
608	0.0082	TransRoute	InterRoute	ZIP R Ext Reply Net Count=1
609	0.0010	TransRoute	InterRoute	ZIP R Reply Network Count=13
611	0.5378	Broadcast	MicroVAX	RTMP R Node=3730.254 Rou en=24

612	0.0013	TransRoute	MicroVAX	ZIP C Query Network Count=16
613	0.0151	MicroVAX	TransRoute	ZIP R Reply Network Count=15
619	1.7563	090007FFFFFF	InterRoute	RTMP R Node=3724.26 Rou en=21
626	3.7674	Broadcast	TransRoute	RTMP R Node=3730.148 Rou en=25
627	0.0037	090007FFFFFF	TransRoute	RTMP R Node=3724.152 Rou en=5
636	4.0073	InterRoute	TransRoute	ZIP C Query Network Count=1
637	0.0017	TransRoute	InterRoute	ZIP R Reply Network Count=1

.
.
.

2610	1.1599	090007FFFFFF	InterRoute	RTMP R Node=3724.26 Rou en=21
2649	8.4381	Broadcast	TransRoute	RTMP R Node=3730.148 Rou en=25
2650	0.0037	090007FFFFFF	TransRoute	RTMP R Node=3724.152 Rou en=5
2651	0.3981	Broadcast	MicroVAX	RTMP R Node=3730.254 Rou en=24
2652	1.1923	090007FFFFFF	InterRoute	RTMP R Node=3724.26 Rou en=21
2675	8.4735	Broadcast	TransRoute	RTMP R Node=3730.148 Rou en=9
2676	0.0037	090007FFFFFF	TransRoute	RTMP R Node=3724.152 Rou en=5
2677	0.3306	Broadcast	MicroVAX	RTMP R Node=3730.254 Rou en=24
2682	1.2105	090007FFFFFF	InterRoute	RTMP R Node=3724.26 Rou en=21
2706	8.6426	Broadcast	TransRoute	RTMP R Node=3730.148 Rou en=25
2707	0.0044	090007FFFFFF	TransRoute	RTMP R Node=3724.152 Rou en=21
2708	0.1423	Broadcast	MicroVAX	RTMP R Node=3730.254 Rou en=24
2712	1.2431	090007FFFFFF	InterRoute	RTMP R Node=3724.26 Rou en=21
2735	8.6749	Broadcast	TransRoute	RTMP R Node=3730.148 Rou en=25
2736	0.0044	090007FFFFFF	TransRoute	RTMP R Node=3724.152 Rou en=21
2737	0.0777	Broadcast	MicroVAX	RTMP R Node=3730.254 Rou en=24
2740	1.2457	090007FFFFFF	InterRoute	RTMP R Node=3724.26 Rou en=21
2761	8.7301	Broadcast	TransRoute	RTMP R Node=3730.148 Rou en=24
2762	0.0044	090007FFFFFF	TransRoute	RTMP R Node=3724.152 Rou en=20
2763	0.0196	Broadcast	MicroVAX	RTMP R Node=3730.254 Rou en=24
2769	1.2769	090007FFFFFF	InterRoute	RTMP R Node=3724.26 Rou en=5
2788	8.7234	Broadcast	MicroVAX	RTMP R Node=3730.254 Rou en=23

2791	0.0751	Broadcast	TransRoute	RTMP R Node=3730.148 Rou en=19
2792	0.0039	090007FFFFFF	TransRoute	RTMP R Node=3724.152 Rou en=15
2796	1.1999	090007FFFFFF	InterRoute	RTMP R Node=3724.26 Rou en=5
2818	8.7209	Broadcast	MicroVAX	RTMP R Node=3730.254 Rou en=23
2819	0.1751	Broadcast	TransRoute	RTMP R Node=3730.148 Rou en=19
2820	0.0039	090007FFFFFF	TransRoute	RTMP R Node=3724.152 Rou en=15
2826	1.1206	090007FFFFFF	InterRoute	RTMP R Node=3724.26 Rou en=5
2827	0.0460	TransRoute	InterRoute	ZIP C Query Network Count=10
2828	0.0075	InterRoute	TransRoute	ZIP R Reply Network Count=10

Trace 3.3.4a. AppleTalk topology revisions transmitted with RTMP and ZIP

Sniffer Network Analyzer data 12-Oct-90 10:20:28 NEWNETS.ENC Pg 1

- - - - - - - - - - - - - - - Frame 1 - - - - - - - - - - - - - - - - -

RTMP:───── RTMP Data ─────

RTMP:

RTMP: Net   = 3730

RTMP: Node ID length = 8 bits

RTMP: Node ID   = 148

RTMP: Tuple 1 : Version 2

RTMP: Tuple 2 : Net = 3722, Distance = 1

RTMP: Tuple 3 : Net = 3723, Distance = 1

RTMP: Tuple 4 : Net = 3724, Distance = 0

RTMP: Tuple 5 : Net = 3726, Distance = 1

RTMP: Tuple 6 : Net = 3728, Distance = 1

RTMP: Tuple 7 : Net = 3730, Distance = 0

RTMP: Tuple 8 : Net = 3731, Distance = 1

RTMP: Tuple 9 : Net = 3732, Distance = 2

RTMP:

RTMP:[Normal end of "RTMP Data ".]

```
- - - - - - - - - - - - - - - - Frame 2 - - - - - - - - - - - - - - - - -
RTMP:—— RTMP Data ——
RTMP:
RTMP:        Net        = 3724
RTMP:        Node ID length = 8 bits
RTMP:        Node ID      = 152
RTMP:        Tuple 1 :  Cable range = 3724 to 3724 (Version 2)
RTMP:        Tuple 2 :  Cable range = 3724 to 3724 (Version 2)
RTMP:        Tuple 3 :  Net = 3730, Distance = 0
RTMP:        Tuple 4 :  Net = 3731, Distance = 1
RTMP:        Tuple 5 :  Net = 3732, Distance = 2
RTMP:
RTMP:[Normal end of "RTMP Data ".]
```

Trace 3.3.4b. AppleTalk RTMP data (initial internet topology)

```
Sniffer Network Analyzer data 12-Oct-90 10:20:28 NEWNETS.ENC Pg 1
- - - - - - - - - - - - - - - Frame 545 - - - - - - - - - - - - - - - - -
RTMP:—— RTMP Data ——-
RTMP:
RTMP: Net        = 3730
RTMP: Node ID length = 8 bits
RTMP: Node ID      = 148
RTMP: Tuple 1 : Version 2
RTMP: Tuple 2 : Net = 3722, Distance = 1
RTMP: Tuple 3 : Net = 3723, Distance = 1
RTMP: Tuple 4 : Net = 3724, Distance = 0
RTMP: Tuple 5 : Net = 7500, Distance = 4
RTMP: Tuple 6 : Net = 140, Distance = 7
RTMP: Tuple 7 : Net = 7501, Distance = 4
RTMP: Tuple 8 : Net = 3726, Distance = 1
RTMP: Tuple 9 : Net = 7502, Distance = 4
RTMP: Tuple 10 : Net = 7503, Distance = 4
RTMP: Tuple 11 : Net = 3728, Distance = 1
RTMP: Tuple 12 : Net = 7504, Distance = 4
RTMP: Tuple 13 : Net = 7505, Distance = 4
RTMP: Tuple 14 : Net = 3730, Distance = 0
```

RTMP: Tuple 15 : Net = 7506, Distance = 4
RTMP: Tuple 16 : Net = 3731, Distance = 1
RTMP: Tuple 17 : Net = 7507, Distance = 3
RTMP: Tuple 18 : Net = 3732, Distance = 2
RTMP: Tuple 19 : Net = 7508, Distance = 4
RTMP: Tuple 20 : Net = 7510, Distance = 4
RTMP: Tuple 21 : Net = 150, Distance = 9
RTMP: Tuple 22 : Net = 160, Distance = 8
RTMP: Tuple 23 : Net = 170, Distance = 8
RTMP: Tuple 24 : Net = 120, Distance = 8
RTMP: Tuple 25 : Net = 190, Distance = 7
RTMP:
RTMP:[Normal end of "RTMP Data ".]

- - - - - - - - - - - - - - - Frame 546 - - - - - - - - - - - - - - - - -
RTMP:—— RTMP Data ——-
RTMP:
RTMP: Net   = 3724
RTMP: Node ID length = 8 bits
RTMP: Node ID   = 152
RTMP: Tuple 1 : Cable range = 3724 to 3724 (Version 2)
RTMP: Tuple 2 : Cable range = 3724 to 3724 (Version 2)
RTMP: Tuple 3 : Net = 3730, Distance = 0
RTMP: Tuple 4 : Net = 3731, Distance = 1
RTMP: Tuple 5 : Net = 3732, Distance = 2
RTMP:
RTMP:[Normal end of "RTMP Data ".]

Trace 3.3.4c. AppleTalk RTMP data (revised internet topology)

Sniffer Network Analyzer data 12-Oct-90 10:20:28 NEWNETS.ENC Pg 1
- - - - - - - - - - - - - - - Frame 606 - - - - - - - - - - - - - - - - -

ZIP:—— ZIP header ——

ZIP:

ZIP: ZIP command = 1 (Query)

ZIP: Network count = 16

ZIP:

ZIP: — Networks being queried: —

ZIP: #1: Net = 120

ZIP: #2: Net = 140

ZIP: #3: Net = 150

ZIP: #4: Net = 160

ZIP: #5: Net = 170

ZIP: #6: Net = 190

ZIP: #7: Net = 7500

ZIP: #8: Net = 7501

ZIP: #9: Net = 7502

ZIP: #10: Net = 7503

ZIP: #11: Net = 7504

ZIP: #12: Net = 7505

ZIP: #13: Net = 7506

ZIP: #14: Net = 7507

ZIP: #15: Net = 7508

ZIP: #16: Net = 7510

ZIP:

ZIP:

ZIP:[Normal end of "ZIP header".]

- - - - - - - - - - - - - - - - Frame 607 - - - - - - - - - - - - - - - - -

ZIP:—— ZIP header ——

ZIP:

ZIP: ZIP command   = 8 (Extended Reply)

ZIP: Network count = 1

ZIP:

ZIP: — Network-zone list —

ZIP: #1: Net = 7500, Zone = AMC-Token Ring

ZIP:

ZIP:[Normal end of "ZIP header".]

- - - - - - - - - - - - - - Frame 608 - - - - - - - - - - - - - - - - -

ZIP:—— ZIP header ——

ZIP:

ZIP: ZIP command   = 8 (Extended Reply)

ZIP: Network count = 1

ZIP:

ZIP: — Network-zone list —

ZIP: #1: Net = 7507, Zone = AMC-Ethernet

ZIP:

ZIP:[Normal end of "ZIP header".]

- - - - - - - - - - - - - - Frame 609 - - - - - - - - - - - - - - - - -

ZIP:—— ZIP header ——

ZIP:

ZIP: ZIP command   = 2 (Reply)

ZIP: Network count = 13

ZIP:

ZIP: — Network-zone list —

ZIP: #1: Net = 120, Zone = Engineer Drive

ZIP: #2: Net = 140, Zone = Stebbins Street

ZIP: #3: Net = 150, Zone = Fenn Way

ZIP: #4: Net = 160, Zone = Tullo Lane

ZIP: #5: Net = 170, Zone = Seifert Blvd.

ZIP: #6: Net = 190, Zone = Gotham City

ZIP: #7: Net = 7502, Zone = AMC-Networking

ZIP: #8: Net = 7503, Zone = AMC-Publishing/Engineering

ZIP: #9: Net = 7504, Zone = AMC-Staff

ZIP: #10: Net = 7505, Zone = AMC-The Classroom

ZIP: #11: Net = 7506, Zone = AMC-The Office

ZIP: #12: Net = 7508, Zone = AMC-Ethernet

ZIP: #13: Net = 7510, Zone = AMC-Ethernet

ZIP:

ZIP:[Normal end of "ZIP header".]

ZIP:

- - - - - - - - - - - - - - - - Frame 612 - - - - - - - - - - - - - - - - -

ZIP:—— ZIP header ——

ZIP:

ZIP: ZIP command   = 1 (Query)

ZIP: Network count = 16

ZIP:

ZIP: — Networks being queried: —

ZIP: #1: Net = 7500

ZIP: #2: Net = 140

ZIP: #3: Net = 7501

ZIP: #4: Net = 7502

ZIP: #5: Net = 7503

ZIP: #6: Net = 7504

ZIP: #7: Net = 7505

ZIP: #8: Net = 7506

ZIP: #9: Net = 7507

ZIP: #10: Net = 7508

ZIP: #11: Net = 7510

ZIP: #12: Net = 150

ZIP: #13: Net = 160

ZIP: #14: Net = 170

ZIP: #15: Net = 120

ZIP: #16: Net = 190

ZIP:

ZIP:

ZIP:[Normal end of "ZIP header".]

- - - - - - - - - - - - - - - Frame 613 - - - - - - - - - - - - - - - - - -

ZIP:—— ZIP header ——

ZIP:

ZIP: ZIP command   = 2 (Reply)

ZIP: Network count = 15

ZIP:

ZIP: —— Network-zone list ——

ZIP: #1: Net = 7500, Zone = AMC-Token Ring

ZIP: #2: Net = 140, Zone = Stebbins Street

ZIP: #3: Net = 7502, Zone = AMC-Networking

ZIP: #4: Net = 7503, Zone = AMC-Publishing/Engineering

ZIP: #5: Net = 7504, Zone = AMC-Staff

ZIP: #6: Net = 7505, Zone = AMC-The Classroom

ZIP: #7: Net = 7506, Zone = AMC-The Office

ZIP: #8: Net = 7507, Zone = AMC-Ethernet

ZIP: #9: Net = 7508, Zone = AMC-Ethernet

ZIP: #10: Net = 7510, Zone = AMC-Ethernet

ZIP: #11: Net = 150, Zone = Fenn Way

ZIP: #12: Net = 160, Zone = Tullo Lane

ZIP: #13: Net = 170, Zone = Seifert Blvd.

ZIP: #14: Net = 120, Zone = Engineer Drive

ZIP: #15: Net = 190, Zone = Gotham City

ZIP:

ZIP:[Normal end of "ZIP header".]

- - - - - - - - - - - - - - - Frame 636 - - - - - - - - - - - - - - - - - -

ZIP:—— ZIP header ——

ZIP:

ZIP: ZIP command   = 1 (Query)

ZIP: Network count = 1

ZIP:

ZIP: —— Networks being queried: ——

```
ZIP:            #1: Net = 7501
ZIP:
ZIP:
ZIP:[Normal end of "ZIP header".]
ZIP:


- - - - - - - - - - - - - - - - Frame 637 - - - - - - - - - - - - - - - - -
ZIP:—— ZIP header ——
ZIP:
ZIP:            ZIP command   = 2 (Reply)
ZIP:            Network count = 1
ZIP:
ZIP:            — Network-zone list —
ZIP:            #1: Net = 7501, Zone = AMC-Conference
ZIP:
ZIP:[Normal end of "ZIP header".]
ZIP:
```

Trace 3.3.4d. AppleTalk ZIP data (revised internet topology)

```
Sniffer Network Analyzer data 12-Oct-90 10:20:28 NEWNETS.ENC Pg 1

- - - - - - - - - - - - - - - Frame 2652 - - - - - - - - - - - - - - - - -
RTMP:—— RTMP Data ——
RTMP:
RTMP:       Net        = 3724
RTMP:       Node ID length = 8 bits
RTMP:       Node ID    = 26
RTMP:       Tuple 1 :  Cable range = 3724 to 3724 (Version 2)
RTMP:       Tuple 2 :  Net = 7510, Distance = 31
RTMP:       Tuple 3 :  Net = 7508, Distance = 31
RTMP:       Tuple 4 :  Range = 7507 to 7507, Distance = 31 (Version 2)
RTMP:       Tuple 5 :  Net = 7506, Distance = 31
RTMP:       Tuple 6 :  Net = 7505, Distance = 31
```

RTMP:	Tuple 7 : Net = 7504, Distance = 31
RTMP:	Tuple 8 : Net = 7503, Distance = 31
RTMP:	Tuple 9 : Net = 7502, Distance = 31
RTMP:	Tuple 10 : Net = 7501, Distance = 31
RTMP:	Tuple 11 : Range = 7500 to 7500, Distance = 31 (Version 2)
RTMP:	Tuple 12 : Net = 190, Distance = 31
RTMP:	Tuple 13 : Net = 170, Distance = 31
RTMP:	Tuple 14 : Net = 160, Distance = 31
RTMP:	Tuple 15 : Net = 150, Distance = 31
RTMP:	Tuple 16 : Net = 140, Distance = 31
RTMP:	Tuple 17 : Net = 120, Distance = 31
RTMP:	Tuple 18 : Cable range = 3728 to 3728 (Version 2)
RTMP:	Tuple 19 : Net = 3722, Distance = 0
RTMP:	Tuple 20 : Net = 3723, Distance = 0
RTMP:	Tuple 21 : Cable range = 3726 to 3726 (Version 2)
RTMP:	
RTMP:[Normal end of "RTMP Data ".]	

Trace 3.3.4e. AppleTalk RTMP data with poison routes

3.3.5 AppleTalk and the IBM 8209 Bridge

The IBM 8209 is one of the few bridges available to connect token ring and Ethernet LANs. Unfortunately, connecting AppleTalk nodes across this bridge can be challenging. In this example, users on the token ring side complained of an inability to attach to any AppleTalk device on the Ethernet side (see Figure 3-6).

To isolate the problem, we first obtained a trace of the Macintosh workstation (Mac FF2) initializing on the token ring (Trace 3.3.5 a). The token ring MAC Layer (beginning in Frame 278) indicated normal operation, following the sequence discussed in Section 3.3.1 : Duplicate Address Test, Ring Poll, Report SUA Change, Request Initialization, and so on. However, the AppleTalk initialization beginning in Frame 290 was unusual. Mac FF2 broadcasts 10 AARP Probes, identifying a tentative address of 65362.26. The AARP probes go unanswered, i.e. no other node objects to the use of address 65362.26.

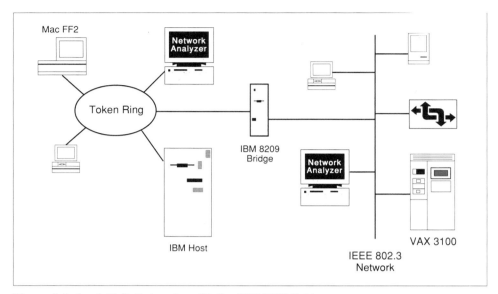

Figure 3-6. AppleTalk Networks with the IBM 8209 Bridge

In Frames 344 through 365, the initializing node attempts to contact a router on the cable segment by multicasting the ZIP GetNetInfo packets. These packets include a request to test the zone name (WB.Backbone II) for validity in this network environment. No routers answer. In Frames 373 through 392, the node assumes that there is no router, and continues its normal boot sequence. Next, the node registers its name on the AppleTalk internetwork. To insure the uniqueness of the name, the node tries to contact itself before adding the name (Buehler:Macintosh IIcx@*) to its local table. Again, it hears no response, so it adopts the name.

Because the network has no router, it can have no zones. Thus, the node registers itself in the "*" zone (No Zone), instead of the "WB.Backbone II" zone. But, in reality, several routers were up and running on the Ethernet side of the bridge.

As a second step, we attached the analyzer to the Ethernet side of the bridge and monitored it. AARP, ZIP, and NBP traffic was present on that link. The source address of Mac FF2 (5000E0000FF2H), however, did not match the source address

(0A000700F04FH) of any packets on the Ethernet side (Trace 3.3.5b), and the destination address of 030020000000H is not a standard or valid EtherTalk multicast address. We suspected a problem with the AARP driver on the Macintosh.

Returning to the token ring side of the bridge, we studied the AARP packet in detail (Trace 3.3.5c). The Data Link Layer addresses were correct, with Destination = C00040000000H (TokenTalk broadcast) and Source = 5000E0000FF2H. Routing information, LLC, and SNAP data (Type = 80F3H, AppleTalk ARP) was also correct. The AARP probe packet also contained the proper source hardware address (5000E 0000FF2H). Thus, everything on the token ring side appeared normal.

Going back to the Ethernet side, we obtained another trace of an AARP packet (Trace 3.3.5d) and noted two differences. First, the Source and Destination protocol addresses were different: 65362.26 (token ring) versus 65483.34 (Ethernet). We attributed this difference to the random choices for a startup address that the node had made between the two trace files (token ring side and Ethernet side). However, the source hardware address (5000E0000FF2H) within both AARP frames was consistent.

The second problem was that the transmitted addresses in the Data Link Layer did not match those received:

	TX Address (802.5)	RX Address (802.3)
Source	C00040000000H	030002000000H
Destination	5000E0000FF2H	0A000700F04FH

A binary expansion of these addresses provided a clue:

Address	Binary Expansion	After Bit Reversal	Result
C000..H	11000000 00000000..	00000011 00000000..	0300...H
5000..H	01010000 00000000..	00001010 00000000..	0A00...H

Sniffer Network Analyzer data 13-Nov-90 14:43:50 WB8209.TRC Pg 1

SUMMARY	Delta T	Destination	Source	Summary
278		Mac FF2	Mac FF2	MAC Duplicate Address Test
279	0.000	Mac FF2	Mac FF2	MAC Duplicate Address Test
282	0.019	Config Srv	Mac FF2	MAC Report SUA Change
284	0.002	Broadcast	Mac FF2	MAC Standby Monitor Present
285	0.000	Param Server	Mac FF2	MAC Request Initialization
286	0.002	Mac FF2	IBM 4D00A8	MAC Initialize Ring Station
287	0.001	IBM 4D00A8	Mac FF2	MAC Response
290	0.026	C00040000000	Mac FF2	AARP Probe Node=65362.26
299	0.172	C00040000000	Mac FF2	AARP Probe Node=65362.26
305	0.209	C00040000000	Mac FF2	AARP Probe Node=65362.26
310	0.209	C00040000000	Mac FF2	AARP Probe Node=65362.26
312	0.209	C00040000000	Mac FF2	AARP Probe Node=65362.26
320	0.209	C00040000000	Mac FF2	AARP Probe Node=65362.26
325	0.209	C00040000000	Mac FF2	AARP Probe Node=65362.26
329	0.209	C00040000000	Mac FF2	AARP Probe Node=65362.26
333	0.210	C00040000000	Mac FF2	AARP Probe Node=65362.26
337	0.209	C00040000000	Mac FF2	AARP Probe Node=65362.26
344	0.215	C00040000000	Mac FF2	ZIP C GetNetInfo
				ZONE=WB.BackboneII
358	0.489	C00040000000	Mac FF2	ZIP C GetNetInfo
				ZONE=WB.BackboneII
365	0.498	C00040000000	Mac FF2	ZIP C GetNetInfo
				ZONE=WB.BackboneII
373	0.523	C00040000000	Mac FF2	NBP C Lookup ID=1
				(Buehler:Macintosh IIcx@*)
382	0.523	C00040000000	Mac FF2	NBP C Lookup ID=1
				(Buehler:Macintosh IIcx@*)
392	0.531	C00040000000	Mac FF2	NBP C Lookup ID=1
				(Buehler:Macintosh IIcx@*)

430	2.250	Broadcast	Mac FF2	MAC Standby Monitor Present
576	6.926	Broadcast	Mac FF2	MAC Standby Monitor Present
698	6.926	Broadcast	Mac FF2	MAC Standby Monitor Present
822	6.926	Broadcast	Mac FF2	MAC Standby Monitor Present
935	6.936	Broadcast	Mac FF2	MAC Standby Monitor Present
1062	6.926	Broadcast	Mac FF2	MAC Standby Monitor Present
1189	6.941	Broadcast	Mac FF2	MAC Standby Monitor Present
1312	6.926	Broadcast	Mac FF2	MAC Standby Monitor Present
1448	6.926	Broadcast	Mac FF2	MAC Standby Monitor Present

Trace 3.3.5a. AppleTalk Macintosh startup (IEEE 802.5 side of IBM 8209)

Sniffer Network Analyzer data 13-Nov-90 15:05:58 WB8209.ENC Pg 1

SUMMARY	Delta T	Destination	Source	Summary
132		030002000000	0A000700F04F	AARP Probe Node=65483.34
133	0.0002	030002000000	0A000700F04F	AARP Probe Node=65483.34
136	0.1719	030002000000	0A000700F04F	AARP Probe Node=65483.34
137	0.0002	030002000000	0A000700F04F	AARP Probe Node=65483.34
138	0.2095	030002000000	0A000700F04F	AARP Probe Node=65483.34
139	0.0002	030002000000	0A000700F04F	AARP Probe Node=65483.34
140	0.2096	030002000000	0A000700F04F	AARP Probe Node=65483.34
141	0.0002	030002000000	0A000700F04F	AARP Probe Node=65483.34
142	0.2092	030002000000	0A000700F04F	AARP Probe Node=65483.34
143	0.0002	030002000000	0A000700F04F	AARP Probe Node=65483.34
144	0.2095	030002000000	0A000700F04F	AARP Probe Node=65483.34
145	0.0002	030002000000	0A000700F04F	AARP Probe Node=65483.34
149	0.2094	030002000000	0A000700F04F	AARP Probe Node=65483.34
150	0.0002	030002000000	0A000700F04F	AARP Probe Node=65483.34
151	0.2095	030002000000	0A000700F04F	AARP Probe Node=65483.34
152	0.0002	030002000000	0A000700F04F	AARP Probe Node=65483.34
154	0.2094	030002000000	0A000700F04F	AARP Probe Node=65483.34
155	0.0002	030002000000	0A000700F04F	AARP Probe Node=65483.34
160	0.2109	030002000000	0A000700F04F	AARP Probe Node=65483.34

161	0.0002	030002000000	0A000700F04F	AARP Probe Node=65483.34
164	0.2137	030002000000	0A000700F04F	ZIP C GetNetInfo
				ZONE=WB.BackboneII
165	0.0002	030002000000	0A000700F04F	LAP D=0 S=33 Type=0
167	0.4945	030002000000	0A000700F04F	ZIP C GetNetInfo
				ZONE=WB.BackboneII
168	0.0002	030002000000	0A000700F04F	LAP D=0 S=33 Type=0
170	0.4986	030002000000	0A000700F04F	ZIP C GetNetInfo
				ZONE=WB.BackboneII
.				
.				
.				
268	1.2106	030000800000	0A000700F04F	NBP C Lookup ID=2
				(Buehler:AppleRouter
				@WB.BackboneII)
269	0.0002	030000800000	0A000700F04F	LAP D=0 S=54 Type=0
274	0.5220	030000800000	0A000700F04F	NBP C Lookup ID=2
				(Buehler:AppleRouter
				@WB.BackboneII)
275	0.0002	030000800000	0A000700F04F	LAP D=0 S=54 Type=0
278	0.5314	030000800000	0A000700F04F	NBP C Lookup ID=2
				(Buehler:AppleRouter
				@WB.BackboneII)
279	0.0002	030000800000	0A000700F04F	LAP D=0 S=54 Type=0
329	8.0017	030000800000	0A000700F04F	NBP C Lookup ID=3
				(Buehler:Public
				Folder<A0>@WB.BackboneII)
330	0.0002	030000800000	0A000700F04F	LAP D=0 S=57 Type=0

Trace 3.3.5b. AppleTalk Macintosh startup (IEEE 802.3 side of IBM 8209)

Sniffer Network Analyzer data 13-Nov-90 14:43:50 WB8209.TRC Pg 1

- - - - - - - - - - - - - - - Frame 290 - - - - - - - - - - - - - - - -

DLC: —— DLC Header ——-

DLC:

DLC: Frame 290 arrived at 14:45:15.621; frame size is 52 (0034 hex) bytes.

DLC: AC: Frame priority 0, Reservation priority 0, Monitor count 0

DLC: FC: LLC frame, PCF attention code: None

DLC: FS: Addr recognized indicators: 11, Frame copied indicators: 11

DLC: Destination = Functional address C00040000000

DLC: Source   = Station 5000E0000FF2

DLC:

RI : —— Routing Indicators ——-

RI :

RI : Routing control = 82

RI :   100. .... = All-routes broadcast, non-broadcast return

RI :   ...0 0010 = RI length is 2

RI : Routing control = 78

RI :   0... .... = Forward direction

RI :   .111 .... = Largest frame is unspecified maximum value

RI :   .... 1000 = Reserved

RI :

LLC: —— LLC Header ——-

LLC:

LLC: DSAP = AA, SSAP = AA, Command, Unnumbered frame: UI

LLC:

SNAP: —— SNAP Header ——-

SNAP:

SNAP: Type = 80F3 (AppleTalk ARP)

SNAP:

AARP:—— AARP ——-

AARP:

AARP: Hardware type   = 2 (3Mb Ethernet)

AARP: Protocol type   = 809B (AppleTalk)

AARP: Hardware length   = 6 bytes

AARP: Protocol length   = 4 bytes

AARP: Command   = 3 (Probe)

AARP: Source hardware address   = 5000E0000FF2

AARP: Source protocol address   = 65362.26

AARP: Destination hardware address = 000000000000

AARP: Destination protocol address = 65362.26

AARP:

AARP:[Normal end of "AARP".]

AARP:

Trace 3.3.5c. AppleTalk AARP packet (IEEE 802.5 side of IBM 8209)

Sniffer Network Analyzer data 13-Nov-90 15:05:58 WB8209.ENC Pg 1

- - - - - - - - - - - - - - - Frame 132 - - - - - - - - - - - - - - - - -

DLC: —— DLC Header ——

DLC:

DLC: Frame 132 arrived at 15:06:19.7373; frame size is 60 (003C hex) bytes.

DLC: Destination = Multicast 030002000000

DLC: Source   = Station 0A000700F04F

DLC: 802.3 length = 36

DLC:

LLC: —— LLC Header ——-

LLC:

LLC: DSAP = AA, SSAP = AA, Command, Unnumbered frame: UI

LLC:

SNAP: —— SNAP Header ——

SNAP:

SNAP: Type = 80F3 (AppleTalk ARP)

SNAP:

AARP:—— AARP ——

AARP:

AARP:	Hardware type	= 2 (3Mb Ethernet)
AARP:	Protocol type	= 809B (AppleTalk)
AARP:	Hardware length	= 6 bytes
AARP:	Protocol length	= 4 bytes
AARP:	Command	= 3 (Probe)
AARP:	Source hardware address	= 5000E0000FF2
AARP:	Source protocol address	= 65483.34
AARP:	Destination hardware address	= 000000000000
AARP:	Destination protocol address	= 65483.34
AARP:		
AARP:	[Normal end of "AARP".]	
AARP:		
DLC:	Frame padding= 10 bytes	

Trace 3.3.5d. AppleTalk AARP packet (IEEE 802.3 side of IBM 8209)

The reason for these bit reversals was the difference in the way IEEE 802.3 and IEEE 802.5 transmit addresses. For 802.3, "each octet of each address field shall be transmitted least significant bit first" (IEEE 802.3, Section 3.2.3). For 802.5 the "left-most bit (most significant) or symbol transmitted first" (IEEE 802.5, Section 3.1).

To verify that the routers were working on the Ethernet side, we compared two RTMP frames. On the Ethernet side, a Kinetics Router (Kinetx A18597) transmitted an RTMP packet in Frame 81 (Trace 3.3.5e). It came from Node 20400.241 and contained 19 tuples. The token ring side received this packet as Frame 93. Note in Trace 3.3.5f that the same Node (20400.241) transmitted the RTMP packet, and that the routing tuples in both frames are identical. The only differences were in the DLC addresses. The Kinetics router (08008 9A1A597H) multicasts the frame to address 090007FFFFFFH. The IBM 8209 bridge does a bit reversal of the addresses and claims the source is 10009185A1E9H with destination 9000E0FFFFFFH.

Since the destination (9000E0FFFFFFH) is not a valid multicast address on the TokenTalk side (it wants to see C00040000000H), the AppleTalk nodes ignore the packet. The problem is not just the bit reversal, but a failure of the 8209 to remap the multicast address required by one data link to the multicast address required by the other. Without meaningful RTMP information, the nodes assume that no routers exist.

115

TROUBLESHOOTING INTERNETWORKS

As Reference [3-7] details, using the IBM 8209 bridge on AppleTalk networks can be daunting. The only solution to this problem is for the path between AppleTalk nodes to contain an even number of IBM 8209 bridges. This will remove the effects of the address bit reversals and properly map the multicast addresses.

```
Sniffer Network Analyzer data 13-Nov-90 15:05:58 WB8209.ENC Pg 1
- - - - - - - - - - - - - - - - Frame 81 - - - - - - - - - - - - - - - - -
DLC:          —— DLC Header ——
DLC:
DLC:          Frame 81 arrived at  15:06:11.4464; frame size is 102 (0066 hex) bytes.
DLC:          Destination       = Multicast 090007FFFFFF
DLC:          Source            = Station KinetxA18597
DLC:          802.3 length      = 88
DLC:
LLC:          —— LLC Header ——
LLC:
LLC:          DSAP = AA, SSAP = AA, Command, Unnumbered frame: UI
LLC:
SNAP:         —— SNAP Header ——
SNAP:
SNAP:         Vendor ID = 080007 (Apple)
SNAP:         Type = 809B (AppleTalk)
SNAP:
DDP:—— DDP header ——
DDP:
DDP:          Hop count       = 0
DDP:          Length          = 80
DDP:          Checksum        = 0000
DDP:          Destination Network Number  = 0
DDP:          Destination Node            = 255
DDP:          Destination Socket          = 1 (RTMP)
DDP:          Source Network Number       = 20400
```

DDP:	Source Node	= 241
DDP:	Source Socket	= 1 (RTMP)
DDP:	DDP protocol type	= 1 (RTMP data)
DDP:		

RTMP:—— RTMP Data ——

RTMP:

RTMP:	Net	= 20400
RTMP:	Node ID length	= 8 bits
RTMP:	Node ID	= 241

RTMP: Tuple 1 : Cable range = 20400 to 20400 (Version 2)

RTMP: Tuple 2 : Net = 20300, Distance = 0

RTMP: Tuple 3 : Net = 8338, Distance = 2

RTMP: Tuple 4 : Net = 20116, Distance = 1

RTMP: Tuple 5 : Net = 20321, Distance = 1

RTMP: Tuple 6 : Net = 20322, Distance = 1

RTMP: Tuple 7 : Net = 20323, Distance = 1

RTMP: Tuple 8 : Net = 20325, Distance = 1

RTMP: Tuple 9 : Net = 20326, Distance = 1

RTMP: Tuple 10 : Net = 20327, Distance = 1

RTMP: Tuple 11 : Net = 20331, Distance = 1

RTMP: Tuple 12 : Net = 20332, Distance = 1

RTMP: Tuple 13 : Net = 20398, Distance = 0

RTMP: Tuple 14 : Cable range = 20400 to 20400 (Version 2)

RTMP: Tuple 15 : Net = 20086, Distance = 1

RTMP: Tuple 16 : Net = 20087, Distance = 1

RTMP: Tuple 17 : Net = 20023, Distance = 1

RTMP: Tuple 18 : Net = 20028, Distance = 1

RTMP: Tuple 19 : Net = 20094, Distance = 1

RTMP:

RTMP:[Normal end of "RTMP Data ".]

RTMP:

Trace 3.3.5e. AppleTalk RTMP packet (IEEE 802.3 side of IBM 8209)

Sniffer Network Analyzer data 13-Nov-90 14:43:50 WB8209.TRC Pg 1
- - - - - - - - - - - - - - - Frame 93 - - - - - - - - - - - - - - - -

```
DLC:    —— DLC Header ——
DLC:
DLC:    Frame 93 arrived at  14:45:04.283; frame size is 108 (006C hex) bytes.
DLC:    AC: Frame priority 0,  Reservation priority 0,  Monitor count 0
DLC:    FC: LLC frame,  PCF attention code: None
DLC:    FS: Addr recognized indicators: 00, Frame copied indicators: 00
DLC:    Destination       = Group address 9000E0FFFFFF
DLC:    Source            = Station 10009185A1E9
DLC:
RI :    —— Routing Indicators ——
RI :
RI :    Routing control      = C6
RI :           110. ....  = Single-route broadcast, all-routes broadcast return
RI :           ...0 0110  = RI length is 6
RI :    Routing control      = 10
RI :           0... ....  = Forward direction
RI :           .001 ....  = Largest frame is 1470
RI :           .... 0000  = Reserved
RI :    Ring number FFF0 via bridge 0
RI :    Ring number 001
RI :
LLC:    —— LLC Header ——
LLC:
LLC:    DSAP = AA, SSAP = AA, Command, Unnumbered frame: UI
LLC:
SNAP:   —— SNAP Header ——
SNAP:
SNAP:   Vendor ID = 080007 (Apple)
SNAP:   Type = 809B (AppleTalk)
SNAP:
```

```
DDP:———— DDP header ————
DDP:
DDP:        Hop count           = 0
DDP:        Length              = 80
DDP:        Checksum            = 0000
DDP:        Destination Network Number = 0
DDP:        Destination Node    = 255
DDP:        Destination Socket  = 1 (RTMP)
DDP:        Source Network Number = 20400
DDP:        Source Node         = 241
DDP:        Source Socket       = 1 (RTMP)
DDP:        DDP protocol type   = 1 (RTMP data)
DDP:
RTMP:———— RTMP Data ————
RTMP:
RTMP:       Net                 = 20400
RTMP:       Node ID length      = 8 bits
RTMP:       Node ID             = 241
RTMP:       Tuple 1 : Cable range = 20400 to 20400 (Version 2)
RTMP:       Tuple 2 : Net = 20300, Distance = 0
RTMP:       Tuple 3 : Net = 8338, Distance = 2
RTMP:       Tuple 4 : Net = 20116, Distance = 1
RTMP:       Tuple 5 : Net = 20321, Distance = 1
RTMP:       Tuple 6 : Net = 20322, Distance = 1
RTMP:       Tuple 7 : Net = 20323, Distance = 1
RTMP:       Tuple 8 : Net = 20325, Distance = 1
RTMP:       Tuple 9 : Net = 20326, Distance = 1
RTMP:       Tuple 10 : Net = 20327, Distance = 1
RTMP:       Tuple 11 : Net = 20331, Distance = 1
RTMP:       Tuple 12 : Net = 20332, Distance = 1
RTMP:       Tuple 13 : Net = 20398, Distance = 0
RTMP:       Tuple 14 : Cable range = 20400 to 20400 (Version 2)
```

RTMP:	Tuple 15 : Net = 20086, Distance = 1
RTMP:	Tuple 16 : Net = 20087, Distance = 1
RTMP:	Tuple 17 : Net = 20023, Distance = 1
RTMP:	Tuple 18 : Net = 20028, Distance = 1
RTMP:	Tuple 19 : Net = 20094, Distance = 1
RTMP:	
RTMP:	[Normal end of "RTMP Data ".]

Trace 3.3.5f. AppleTalk RTMP packet (IEEE 802.5 side of IBM 8209)

3.3.6 AppleTalk with an SNA Gateway

Internet routers use the Zone Information Protocol (ZIP) to maintain a table known as the *Zone Information Table* (ZIT). As discussed in Section 3.1.4, this table associates the network ranges that the internet uses with zone names that users deal with. The ZIP process keeps track of any routing changes by listening for RTMP packets, and comparing their data with the current contents of the ZIT. Should it discover a route that is not in the ZIT, the router transmits a ZIP Query packet to the Zone Information Socket (ZIS) of the other router (the source of the recent RTMP information) asking for further details. The response is a ZIP reply packet.

Another ZIP function is to assure that the node's protocol address falls within the network number ranges valid for that cable segment. When the node initializes, it randomly picks a node number from the range FF00 to FFFEH (65,280 to 65,535 decimal). It then sends a multicast ZIP packet, known as a ZIP GetNetInfo Request, to all AppleTalk routers on the same cable segment asking if the selected range is valid. Each router responds with a ZIP GetNetInfo Reply packet stating whether the zone is valid or invalid. If the zone is invalid, the router returns a valid range.

In this example, users connecting to an SNA gateway on a Phase 2 AppleTalk network were experiencing intermittent operation. Sometimes, the SNA gateway was accessible, allowing users to establish a 3270 session to the host via the gateway (see Figure 3-7). At other times, the network returned a message indicating that the user could not access the requested network resource. We traced the problem to the addition of a router on the internet: The gateway was accessible when the router was not installed, access failed when it was. An analysis of the ZIP packets provided the solution.

When initialized, the SNA gateway sends the ZIP GetNetInfo Request, and four routers respond (Trace 3.3.6a). Following the four ZIP GetNetInfo Reply packets, the gateway transmits multiple AARP Probe packets testing the tentative protocol address. No responses came back, which indicated that no other nodes were using the tentative address (50.171).

Sniffer Network Analyzer data 11-Jun-91 at 16:37:06 BEFORE.ENC Pg 1

SUMMARY	Delta T	Destination	Source	Summary
392	0.2202	090007FFFFFF	SNA Gateway	ZIP C GetNetInfo
393	0.0006	090007FFFFFF	OCCB1 Router	ZIP R NetInfoReply RANGE=50-60
394	0.0001	090007FFFFFF	OCCA1 Router	ZIP R NetInfoReply RANGE=50-60
395	0.0011	090007FFFFFF	Mac Router	ZIP R NetInfoReply RANGE=50-60
396	0.0002	090007FFFFFF	ADMIN 1	ZIP R NetInfoReply RANGE=50-60
397	0.0015	090007FFFFFF	SNA Gateway	AARP Probe Node=50.171
398	0.2152	090007FFFFFF	SNA Gateway	AARP Probe Node=50.171
399	0.0961	090007FFFFFF	3E469C	AARP Locate Node=52.172
400	0.1235	090007FFFFFF	SNA Gateway	AARP Probe Node=50.171
401	0.2197	090007FFFFFF	SNA Gateway	AARP Probe Node=50.171
402	0.2196	090007FFFFFF	SNA Gateway	AARP Probe Node=50.171
403	0.2196	090007FFFFFF	SNA Gateway	AARP Probe Node=50.171
404	0.2198	090007FFFFFF	SNA Gateway	AARP Probe Node=50.171

Trace 3.3.6a. AppleTalk ZIP GetNetInfo and AARP Probe packets

Details of the ZIP packets (Trace 3.3.6b) show disagreement between the routers. The first two routers indicate that the requested zone ("" —no zone) is valid, while the last two claim an invalid zone. All four routers specify a cable range of 50-60, indicating that the SNA gateway should be using a network range of 50-60, rather than the tentative range of 65280. At this point, we can determine that the problem is with routers OCCA1 and OCCB1. The SNA Gateway had requested to be in "no zone," and routers OCCA1 and OCCB1 (on an extended-address network, with multiple zones in their lists) just said OK.

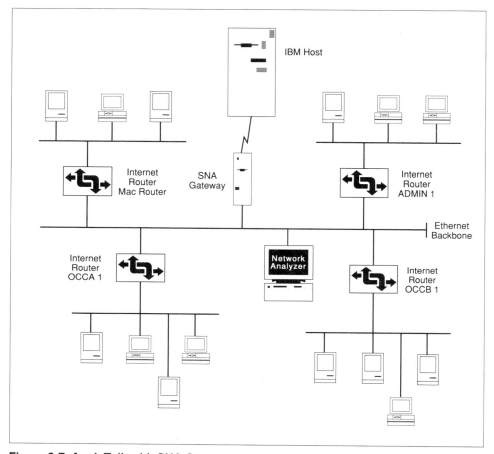

Figure 3-7. AppleTalk with SNA Gateway

When the zone invalid flag bit is set, it indicates that the zone requested in the node's ZIP GetNetInfo packet was not a valid choice for the node in this environment. In other words, the requested zone is not in the router's ZIT for this cable. If the zone invalid flag bit is not sent, the sender's tentative zone may be used. In this example the routers could not agree—two said that the range was valid; two said it was not. All four returned a cable range (50-60) that was different from the tentative range. Since the first two routers (OCCA1 and OCCB1) were from the same manufacturer and the other routers were from different vendors, we suspected a software bug in routers OCCA1 and OCCB1.

Sniffer Network Analyzer data 11-Jun-91 at 16:37:06, file BEFORE.ENC Pg 1

`- - - - - - - - - - - - - - - Frame 392 - - - - - - - - - - - - - - - - -`

```
DDP:—— DDP header ——
DDP:
DDP:    Hop count                   = 0
DDP:    Length                      = 20
DDP:    Checksum                    = 0000
DDP:    Destination Network Number  = 0
DDP:    Destination Node            = 255
DDP:    Destination Socket          = 6 (Zone)
DDP:    Source Network Number       = 65280
DDP:    Source Node                 = 171
DDP:    Source Socket               = 6 (Zone)
DDP:    DDP protocol type           = 6 (Zone)
DDP:
ZIP:—— ZIP header ——
ZIP:
ZIP:    ZIP command                 = 5 (GetNetInfo)
ZIP:    Zone                        = ""
ZIP:
ZIP:[Normal end of "ZIP header".]
ZIP:
```

`- - - - - - - - - - - - - - - Frame 393 - - - - - - - - - - - - - - - - -`

```
ZIP:—— ZIP header ——
ZIP:
ZIP:    ZIP command                 = 6 (NetInfoReply)
ZIP:    Flags                       = 0X
ZIP:        0... ....               = Zone valid
ZIP:        .0.. ....               = Use multicast
ZIP:        ..0. ....               = More than one zone
ZIP:    Cable range                 = 50 to 60
```

```
ZIP:          Zone              = ""
ZIP:          Multicast         = 090007000004
ZIP:
ZIP:*** 10 byte(s) of additional data present ***
ZIP:
ZIP:[Abnormal end of "ZIP header".]
ZIP:
```

- - - - - - - - - - - - - - - Frame 394 - - - - - - - - - - - - - - - -

```
ZIP:—— ZIP header ——
ZIP:
ZIP:          ZIP command       = 6 (NetInfoReply)
ZIP:          Flags             = 0X
ZIP:                  0... ....  = Zone valid
ZIP:                  .0.. ....  = Use multicast
ZIP:                  ..0. ....  = More than one zone
ZIP:          Cable range       = 50 to 60
ZIP:          Zone              = ""
ZIP:          Multicast         = 090007000004
ZIP:
ZIP:*** 10 byte(s) of additional data present ***
ZIP:
ZIP:[Abnormal end of "ZIP header".]
ZIP:
```

- - - - - - - - - - - - - - - Frame 395 - - - - - - - - - - - - - - - -

```
ZIP:—— ZIP header ——
ZIP:
ZIP:          ZIP command       = 6 (NetInfoReply)
ZIP:          Flags             = AX
ZIP:                  1... ....  = Zone invalid
ZIP:                  .0.. ....  = Use multicast
```

```
ZIP:                        ..1. ....     = Only one zone
ZIP:          Cable range                 = 50 to 60
ZIP:          Zone                         = ""
ZIP:          Multicast                    = 090007000004
ZIP:          Default zone                 = "EtherTalk"
ZIP:
ZIP:[Normal end of "ZIP header".]
ZIP:


- - - - - - - - - - - - - - - Frame 396 - - - - - - - - - - - - - - - -

ZIP:—— ZIP header ——
ZIP:
ZIP:          ZIP command                  = 6 (NetInfoReply)
ZIP:          Flags                        = AX
ZIP:                        1... ....      = Zone invalid
ZIP:                        .0.. ....      = Use multicast
ZIP:                        ..1. ....      = Only one zone
ZIP:          Cable range                  = 50 to 60
ZIP:          Zone                         = ""
ZIP:          Multicast                    = 090007000004
ZIP:          Default zone                 = "EtherTalk"
ZIP:
ZIP:[Normal end of "ZIP header".]
ZIP:
```

Trace 3.3.6b. AppleTalk ZIP GetNetInfo packet details

That hunch proved to be correct. Discussions with the manufacturer indicated that the zone invalid bit was not being set properly. If the zone was invalid, the flag bit would indicate otherwise. As a result, the SNA gateway would take the first response (zone invalid in Frame 393) as the truth and proceed to bind its name in "no zone." Although the node had a valid protocol address (50.17 1), users couldn't even "see" this resource because its name had been improperly bound.

When we obtained a software patch for the first two routers from the manufacturer, all four routers responded to the ZIP GetNetInfo packet in identical fashion (Trace 3.3.6c). The subsequent AARP transmissions (Trace 3.3.6d) verified that the tentative SNA gateway address had been corrected to 50.171. Users could then access the SNA gateway without difficulty.

Sniffer Network Analyzer data 12-Jun-91 11:21:46 AFTER.ENC Pg 1

SUMMARY	Delta T	Destination	Source	Summary
38	0.0992	090007FFFFFF	SNA Gateway	ZIP C GetNetInfo
39	0.0006	090007FFFFFF	OCCB1 Router	ZIP R NetInfoReply RANGE=50-60
40	0.0002	090007FFFFFF	OCCA1 Router	ZIP R NetInfoReply RANGE=50-60
41	0.0013	090007FFFFFF	Mac Router	ZIP R NetInfoReply RANGE=50-60
42	0.0012	090007FFFFFF	SNA Gateway	AARP Probe Node=50.102
43	0.2158	090007FFFFFF	SNA Gateway	AARP Probe Node=50.102
44	0.2196	090007FFFFFF	SNA Gateway	AARP Probe Node=50.102
45	0.2197	090007FFFFFF	SNA Gateway	AARP Probe Node=50.102
46	0.2196	090007FFFFFF	SNA Gateway	AARP Probe Node=50.102
47	0.2197	090007FFFFFF	SNA Gateway	AARP Probe Node=50.102
48	0.2198	090007FFFFFF	SNA Gateway	AARP Probe Node=50.102
49	0.2195	090007FFFFFF	SNA Gateway	AARP Probe Node=50.102
50	0.2197	090007FFFFFF	SNA Gateway	AARP Probe Node=50.102
51	0.2199	090007FFFFFF	SNA Gateway	AARP Probe Node=50.102
52	5.8103	090007FFFFFF	Mac Router	RTMP R Node=51.109 Rou ent=2
53	1.9591	090007FFFFFF	OCCA1 Router	RTMP R Node=50.242 Rou ent=13
54	0.3121	090007FFFFFF	OCCB1 Router	RTMP R Node=50.183 Rou ent=13

Trace 3.3.6c. AppleTalk ZIP and AARP packets (revised ZIP software)

Sniffer Network Analyzer data 12-Jun-91 at 11:21:46, file AFTER.ENC Pg 1

- - - - - - - - - - - - - - - Frame 38 - - - - - - - - - - - - - - - - -

DDP:—— DDP header ——

DDP:

DDP:	Hop count	= 0
DDP:	Length	= 20
DDP:	Checksum	= 0000
DDP:	Destination Network Number	= 0
DDP:	Destination Node	= 255
DDP:	Destination Socket	= 6 (Zone)
DDP:	Source Network Number	= 65280
DDP:	Source Node	= 102
DDP:	Source Socket	= 6 (Zone)
DDP:	DDP protocol type	= 6 (Zone)

DDP:

ZIP:—— ZIP header ——

ZIP:

| ZIP: | ZIP command | = 5 (GetNetInfo) |
| ZIP: | Zone | = "" |

ZIP:

ZIP:[Normal end of "ZIP header".]

ZIP:

- - - - - - - - - - - - - - - Frame 39 - - - - - - - - - - - - - - - - -

ZIP:—— ZIP header ——

ZIP:

ZIP:	ZIP command	= 6 (NetInfoReply)
ZIP:	Flags	= AX
ZIP:	1...	= Zone invalid
ZIP:	0..	= Use multicast
ZIP:	..1.	= Only one zone
ZIP:	Cable range	= 50 to 60

```
ZIP:            Zone                = ""
ZIP:            Multicast           = 090007000004
ZIP:            Default zone        = "EtherTalk"
ZIP:
ZIP:[Normal end of "ZIP header".]
ZIP:
```

```
- - - - - - - - - - - - - - - Frame 40 - - - - - - - - - - - - - - - -
ZIP:—— ZIP header ——
ZIP:
ZIP:            ZIP command         = 6 (NetInfoReply)
ZIP:            Flags               = AX
ZIP:                      1... ....  = Zone invalid
ZIP:                      .0.. ....  = Use multicast
ZIP:                      ..1. ....  = Only one zone
ZIP:            Cable range         = 50 to 60
ZIP:            Zone                = ""
ZIP:            Multicast           = 090007000004
ZIP:            Default zone        = "EtherTalk"
ZIP:
ZIP:[Normal end of "ZIP header".]
ZIP:
```

```
- - - - - - - - - - - - - - - Frame 41 - - - - - - - - - - - - - - - -
ZIP:—— ZIP header ——
ZIP:
ZIP:            ZIP command         = 6 (NetInfoReply)
ZIP:            Flags               = AX
ZIP:                      1... ....  = Zone invalid
ZIP:                      .0.. ....  = Use multicast
ZIP:                      ..1. ....  = Only one zone
ZIP:            Cable range         = 50 to 60
```

ZIP: Zone   = ""

ZIP: Multicast   = 090007000004

ZIP: Default zone   = "EtherTalk"

ZIP:

ZIP:[Normal end of "ZIP header".]

ZIP:

- - - - - - - - - - - - - - - Frame 42 - - - - - - - - - - - - - - - - -

AARP:——— AARP ———

AARP:

AARP: Hardware type   = 1 (10Mb Ethernet)

AARP: Protocol type   = 809B (AppleTalk)

AARP: Hardware length   = 6 bytes

AARP: Protocol length   = 4 bytes

AARP: Command   = 3 (Probe)

AARP: Source hardware address = 3Com 3D9DCD (SNA Gateway)

AARP: Source protocol address   = 50.102

AARP: Destination hardware address = 000000000000 (000000000000)

AARP: Destination protocol address = 50.102

AARP:

AARP:[Normal end of "AARP".]

AARP:

Trace 6.3.6d. AppleTalk ZIP GetNetInfo and AARP Probe packet details (revised ZIP software)

3.3.7 EtherTalk to LocalTalk Wiring Problems

In many cases, we can be fooled into thinking that a problem is more difficult than it really is. In this final example, the user complained of slow response time for print jobs.

In this scenario, a Macintosh was submitting the print job over a LocalTalk network (node 3A) to a LaserWriter attached to a fileserver on a thick Ethernet backbone (see Figure 3-8). We placed the network analyzer on the LocalTalk side of the internetwork. Between the LocalTalk and the Ethernet was a Fastpath 4 gateway manufactured by Shiva Corporation (Cambridge, MA). The Fastpath hardware has two ports: one for LocalTalk and one for Ethernet/IEEE 802.3. It supports AppleTalk Phases 1 and 2, TCP/IP, DECnet, and Simple Network Management Protocol (SNMP). The Fastpath 4 is also an AppleTalk internet router. The typical path for a print job was from the Macintosh to the Fastpath to the Sun fileserver and LaserWriter. Because this path contained four hardware devices and two networks, we could generate a number of failure hypotheses.

To study the problem, we attached a network analyzer to the LocalTalk network and monitored the traffic. We filtered the analyzer data (Trace 3.3.7) to display only the frames between the Macintosh (Mac 3A) and the LaserWriter. From the captured data, we observed that Mac 3A frequently retransmitted Printer Access Protocol (PAP) packets sent to the LaserWriter.

In Frames 89 through 92, it took three tries before the response in Frame 93. In Frames 101 through 107, it took six tries before the response (Frame 108). These PAP packets are transmitted at two second intervals (subtract the relative timestamps between frames from the Delta T column). A similar situation occurs in Frames 112 through 121. Given the number of retransmissions, it's no wonder that the user complained of poor printer response time.

One of PAP's functions is to transmit/receive Tickle packets every 60 seconds. These packets verify that the printer is still operational. The first tickle packet is transmitted in Frame 69 (Mac to LaserWriter), and the LaserWriter replies in Frame 71. About 60 seconds later, the Mac tickles the LaserWriter again (Frame 128). This time, the printer does not respond. Three seconds later the Mac detects a half-open connection and closes the session (Frame 134). The LaserWriter (via the Fast Path) responds in Frame 135. All four hardware devices (Mac, Fast Path, Server, and LaserWriter) appear to be working properly because the PAP Close Connection command received a response. This conclusion lead the analyst to suspect LocalTalk and EtherTalk cabling.

The solution was not a software problem. We discovered that the physical specifications of the backbone cable had been violated, permitting nodes to be too close together. As a result, collisions on the transmission line prohibited the print job from completing the first time. Once the backbone was re-wired, the print jobs

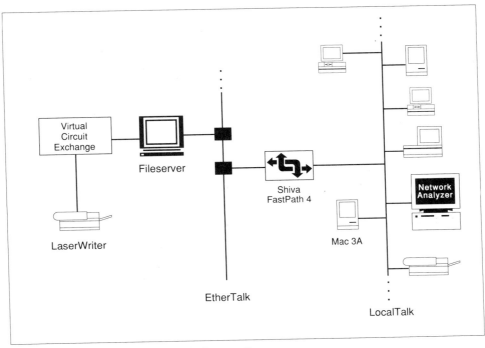

Figure 3-8. EtherTalk to LocalTalk Connections

operated successfully. The protocol analyzer had, thus, identified a Physical layer problem: improper wiring.

AppleTalk is an interesting architecture that is gaining momentum in both the PC and minicomputer arenas. References [3-8] through [3-13] detail some of the interest in AppleTalk internetworks since Phase 2. There's clearly tremendous growth potential for these protocols, considering the strength of AppleTalk advocates such as DEC and Novell. Apple's addition of token ring support further signals that they're preparing the architecture to tackle the mainframe big leagues. Will we soon see ZIP packets traversing an SNA WAN link? Stay tuned.

Sniffer Network Analyzer data 9-Apr-91 at 06:39:40 file TEST1.LTC, Pg 1

SUMMARY Rel Time From Laser (via FastPath)   From Mac 3A

63   -0.0110   NBP R Lookup ID=17 N=1

1=[Laser;152;(2200:LaserWriter@*)]

M	64	0.0000		PAP C OpenConn ID=110 RW=253
				Q=8 T=0
	66	1.3477		PAP C OpenConn ID=110 RW=253
				Q=8 T=0
	67	2.0727	PAP R OpenConnRepl	
			ID=110 RS=173 Q=8	
			OK STATUS="status: idle"	
	68	2.0774		ATP D ID=4374
	69	2.0822		PAP C Tickle ID=110
	70	2.1130		PAP C SendData ID=110 SEQ=1
	71	2.5409	PAP C Tickle ID=110	
	72	2.5474	PAP C SendData ID=110 SEQ=1	
	73	2.5595		PAP R Data ID=110 LEN=228
	83	12.8283	NBP R Lookup ID=18 N=1	
			1=[Laser;152;(2200:LaserWriter@*)]	
	84	12.8337		PAP C SendStatus
	85	12.8522	PAP R Status	
			STATUS="status: idle"	
	86	16.3389		PAP C SendData ID=110 SEQ=1
	87	17.5419	PAP C SendData ID=110 SEQ=1	
	88	17.5547		PAP R Data ID=110 LEN=228
	89	17.8882		PAP C SendStatus
	90	19.3308		PAP C SendStatus
	92	21.3254		PAP C SendStatus
	93	21.3398	PAP R Status	
			STATUS="status: idle"	
	94	26.3647		PAP C SendStatus
	95	28.3067		PAP C SendStatus
	96	28.3248	PAP R Status	
			STATUS="status: idle"	
	98	31.2986		PAP C SendData ID=110 SEQ=1
	99	32.5404	PAP C SendData ID=110 SEQ=1	

100	32.5517		PAP R Data ID=110 LEN=228
101	33.3625		PAP C SendStatus
102	35.2879		PAP C SendStatus
103	37.2825		PAP C SendStatus
104	39.2772		PAP C SendStatus
106	41.2718		PAP C SendStatus
107	43.2665		PAP C SendStatus
108	43.2879	PAP R Status	
		STATUS="status: idle"	
109	46.2584		PAP C SendData ID=110 SEQ=1
110	47.5375	PAP C SendData ID=110 SEQ=1	
111	47.5489		PAP R Data ID=110 LEN=228
112	48.3222		PAP C SendStatus
114	50.2508		PAP C SendStatus
118	52.2423		PAP C SendStatus
120	54.2370		PAP C SendStatus
121	54.2555	PAP R Status	
		STATUS="status: idle"	
125	59.2924		PAP C SendStatus
126	59.3163	PAP R Status	
		STATUS="status: idle"	
128	61.2196		PAP C Tickle ID=110
129	61.2230		PAP C SendData ID=110 SEQ=1
130	62.0768	PAP C SendData ID=110 SEQ=1	
131	62.0881		PAP R Data ID=110 LEN=228
132	62.5322	PAP C SendData ID=110 SEQ=1	
133	62.5435		PAP R Data ID=110 LEN=228
134	64.0366		PAP C CloseConn ID=110
136	65.2242		PAP C CloseConn ID=110
137	65.2385	PAP R CloseConnRepl ID=110	

Trace 3.3.7. LocalTalk packets between Macintosh and LaserWriter

3.4 References

[3-1] Sidhu, Gursharan S., Richard F. Andrews and Alan B. Oppenheimer, *Inside AppleTalk*. 2nd ed., Reading, MA: Addison-Wesley, 1991.

[3-2] Apple Compter, Inc., "AppleTalk Phase 2 Protocol Specification, an Addendum to Inside AppleTalk." document ADPA #C0144LL/A, 1989.

[3-3] Apple Computer, Inc., "The Advantages of AppleTalk Phase 2." document M0785LL/A,1990.

[3-4] Apple Computer, Inc., "Macintosh AppleTalk Connections Programmer's Guide." document ADPA M7056A, 1990.

[3-5] Miller, Mark A. *LAN Protocol Handbook*. Redwood City, CA: M&T Books, 1990.

[3-6] Hornbuckle, Garry. "AppleTalk Protocols." Sniffcon III Tutorial Notes, 1991.

[3-7] Hornbuckle, Garry. "AppleTalk and MacTCP Interoperability with the IBM 8209 Ethernet Token Ring Bridge." SniffCon III Application Note, 1991.

[3-8] Sanz, Steve. "AppleTalk Grows Up." *LAN Technology* (April 1990): 63-68.

[3-9] Kosiur, Dave. "File Services: How to Move and Share Files Over an AppleTalk Network." *MacWorld* (August 1990):160-167.

[3-10] Hafernik, Rob. "Tips for Appletalk Design." *LAN Technology* (February 1991): 69-75.

[3-11] Wylie, Margie. "New Standards to Extend AppleTalk." *Mac Week* (July 30, 1991): 1-124.

[3-12] Wittman, Art. "Choosing Between AppleTalk Phase 1 and Phase 2." *Network Computing* (August 1991): 93-96.

[3-13] Grehan, Rick. "Apple Sharing." *Byte* (October 1991): 247-328.

CHAPTER 4

Troubleshooting Banyan VINES Internetworks

VINES from Banyan Systems Inc. (Westboro, MA) is the only internetwork architecture explored in this book that is based on the UNIX operating system. VINES, which stands for VIrtual NEtworking System, takes advantage of UNIX's multi-user, multitasking characteristics to internetwork LANs and WANs. The VINES architecture is also noteworthy for being the first to incorporate industry-standard protocols, such as TCP/IP and X.25, as well as support for the popular SNA gateway service and its own proprietary protocols. (References [4-1] through [4-4] provide user application and implementation information on VINES.)

We'll begin by exploring this architecture and its protocols.

4.1 VINES Architecture and Protocols

While the VINES server uses the UNIX Kernel, workstations can run under DOS, OS/2, or the Macintosh Operating System (See Figure 4 -1). Despite the use of different operating systems, VINES software for both the workstations and the server conforms to the layers of the OSI model. This software incorporates both proprietary and many well-known protocols that support both LAN and WAN connections.

Let's study these layers in more depth; for additional details on the VINES architecture, see References [4-5] through [4-8].

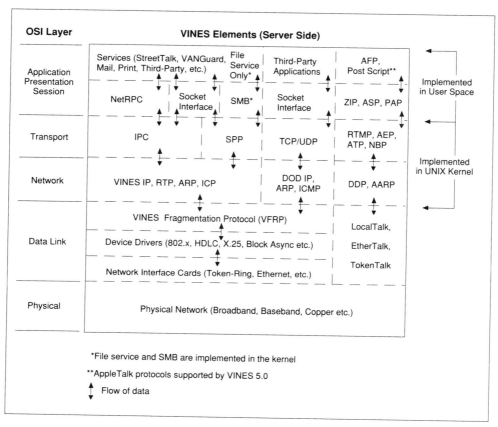

Figure 4-1. VINES Elements and the OSI Model (Server Side)
(Courtesy Banyan Systems Inc.)

4.1.1 VINES Physical and Data Link Layers

VINES' Physical and Data Link layers support nearly every conceivable type of WAN and LAN hardware. VINES offers WAN connections, such as block asynchronous, bisynchronous, High-level Data Link Control (HDLC) and Link Access Procedure-Balanced (LAPB), which is used with X.25. LAN options include ARCNET, Ethernet, IEEE 802.x, and broadband implementations. The DOS and OS/2 workstations also support the Network Driver Interface Standard (NDIS) from Microsoft Corporation (Redmond, WA) and 3Com Corporation (Santa Clara, CA). The NDIS provides a standard interface between the network hardware and the higher-layer (Network Layer and above) protocols.

To support such a wide range of LAN and WAN hardware, VINES adds a protocol layer called the VINES Fragmentation Protocol (VFRP). VFRP resides at the top of the Data Link Layer, and segments and reassembles Network Layer packets into Data Link Layer frames. In this way, VFRP allows the VINES protocols to communicate over hardware that uses short frames, such as ARCNET, or long frames, such as token ring. When transmitting, VFRP divides the VINES Internet Protocol (VIP) packets into the frame size defined by the hardware. At the receiver, VFRP reassembles the frames into the VIP packet, maintaining the correct data sequence. VFRP assumes that the media is reliable and that frames will arrive in sequence. Therefore, VFRP does not resequence frames that are out of order, but instead probes for a retransmission.

4.1.2 VINES Network Layer

The VINES Network Layer protocols can be divided into three groups of protocols based on the applications they support.

The first group of protocols is proprietary to the VINES architecture. These include the VINES Internet Protocol (VIP), the VINES Routing Update Protocol (VRTP), the VINES Address Resolution Protocol (VARP), and the VINES Internet Control Protocol (VICP).

The VINES Internet Protocol (VIP) routes packets through a VINES network using the destination address included in VIP header. We will discuss the VINES addressing scheme further in Section 4.1.5.

The VINES Routing Update Protocol (VRTP) distributes network topology information among the VINES servers. VRTP defines four types of packets. Both network and service nodes transmit Routing Update packets every 90 seconds to inform neighbors of their existence and type of node (client or service). Network nodes send out Routing Request packets when they need to learn the internetwork topology quickly. In response to the Routing Request packets, the service nodes issue Routing Response packets that contain the full topological information. Finally, servers send Routing Redirect packets to inform other nodes on the internetwork of an optimized path between two nodes.

A node must have an internet address before it can communicate with other nodes on the VINES internetwork. Routing servers use the VINES Address Resolution Protocol (VARP) to assign these addresses. The process defines two protocol entities: The address resolution client seeks an address; and the address resolution service assigns it.

Finally, the VINES Internet Control Protocol (VICP) conveys metric information (about the final transmission used to reach a particular client node) and exception information (address mismatches) within the VINES internetwork to the VINES Transport Layer protocols.

All of VINES' proprietary Network Layer packets are limited to 1,450 octets of higher-layer information. This limit assures that the complete VINES packet, including the Network and Transport Layer headers, does not exceed the 1,500 octet length of an Ethernet/802.3 frame. For WAN connections, the maximum packet size is constrained by the Data Link Layer in use, e.g., a link to a PSPDN using the X.25 protocol.

The second and third groups of VINES Network Layer protocols support industry standard protocols. One group is the X.25 protocols for access to Packet Switched Public Data Networks (PSPDNs). Built-in support for this popular protocol gives VINES administrators an alternative to dial-up or leased WAN connections. The other group supports the Department of Defense (DOD)-related Internet protocols. These include the Internet Protocol (IP), the Internet Control Message Protocol (ICMP), and the DOD Address Resolution Protocol (ARP). (Note that the VINES VIP and VARP are distinct protocols from the DOD IP and ARP. The DOD IP and ARP will be studied in Chapter 8.)

138

4.1.3 VINES Transport Layer

The VINES Transport Layer also contains proprietary and industry-standard protocols. The VINES Sequenced Packet Protocol (VSPP) acts as a data pipe between two processes, thus providing a virtual connection between any two Transport Layer ports within the VINES internetwork. The length of VSPP messages is unlimited. The VINES Interprocess Communications Protocol (VIPC) provides unreliable datagram and reliable message data transmission service. VINES defines an unreliable datagram as a single data packet transmitted between Transport Layer ports. A reliable message is a set of one to four data packets sent between Transport Layer ports. A reliable message can be up to 5,800 octets in length (4 * 1,450 octets/packet). Both VSPP and VIPC are based upon XNS protocols.

VINES supports such industry-standard transport protocols as the DOD Transmission Control Protocol (TCP) and User Datagram Protocol (UDP), as well as the TCP/IP protocols. (TCP and UDP will also be discussed in Chapter 8.)

4.1.4 VINES Higher Layers

Like the Transport Layer, the VINES Session, Presentation, and Application layers divide into proprietary and industry-standard implementations. The VINES-proprietary protocols include NetRPC (Remote Procedure Calls) and various VINES Services that support file, print, and mail services. Industry-standard higher layer services include support for DOS, UNIX, and NetBIOS applications. One of the most frequently used protocols for client/server applications is Microsoft's Server Message Block (SMB)/Redirector, used to establish connections between DOS or OS/2 workstations and VINES servers.

4.1.5 VINES 5.0

VINES 5.0, announced in October of 1991, added support for AppleTalk Protocols at the server (see Figure 4-1). Known as the VINES Option For Macintosh, this server option allows an unlimited number of Macintosh clients to be connected into the VINES LAN/WAN internetwork. Depending upon the internetwork design, the AppleTalk packets can be encapsulated within a VINES packet for transmission via the VINES internetwork, or the AppleTalk protocols may be transmitted without encapsulation. Macintosh protocols that are supported include: LocalTalk, EtherTalk, and TokenTalk at the Data Link Layer; DDP and AARP at the Network Layer; RTMP, AEP, ATP, and ABP at the Transport Layer; ZIP, ASP, and PAP at the Session Layer, plus AFP and Postscript at the higher layers. Chapter 3 provides further details on these AppleTalk Protocols.

4.1.6 Addressing the VINES User Process

Another way to look at the VINES architecture is from the perspective of the application (from the top down) rather than from that of the various protocol stacks (from the bottom up) (see Reference [4-9]). In Figure 4-2 note that the user process interacts with a socket interface, which then communicates with a specific protocol family, such as VINES, SNA, X.25, DOD, AppleTalk, and Virtual Terminal (VT). After the user process accesses a particular socket, the protocols resident within that protocol family complete the communication. For example, when the user process wants to interact with the VINES family, shown in greater detail on the left side of Figure 4-2, the socket interface chooses either the VSPP or VIPC protocols at the Transport Layer. Subsequent actions involve the VINES Internet Protocol (VIP) and Data Link Layer device drivers.

All of these processes and protocols have a unique address, which may consist of several elements. The first element is the VINES Data Link Layer address, which is assigned by the network hardware. For example, it might be set to 7DH for an ARCNET board (which uses 8-bit addresses) or 10005A123456H for a token ring board (which uses 48-bit addresses).

The VINES Network Layer defines a two-part, 48-bit internet address. This address is displayed in the format: Network Number:Subnetwork Number. The Network Number is the 32-bit serial number of the VINES server. This number is extracted from a hardware key that must be installed on the server's parallel port then coded into the server software. Network number FFFFFFFFH is used for broadcasts to all networks. The Subnetwork number is a 16-bit quantity that uniquely identifies a client node within the service node's network. The service nodes assign subnetwork numbers in the range f 8000 to FFFEH (from 32,768 to 65,534 decimal). Subnetwork number 1 indicates the server itself, and number FFFFH is used for broadcasts within that network.

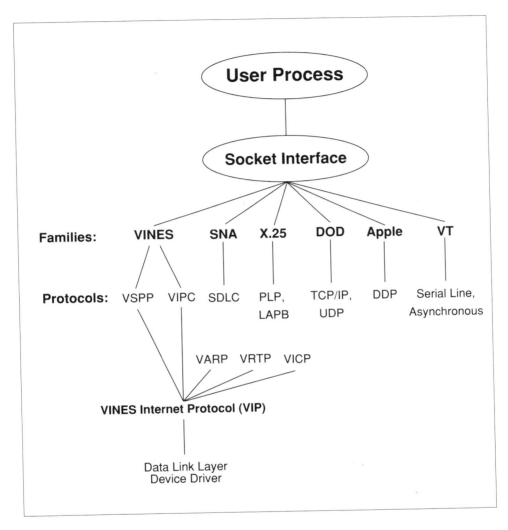

Figure 4-2. VINES Protocol Families
(Courtesy Banyan Systems Inc.)

The complete VINES address for the Transport Layer consists of a 64-bit port address, containing two subfields. The high-order 48 bits contain the VINES internet address of the node in question. The low-order 16 bits, called the *local port number*, defines a socket through which higher layer processes communicate. One Transport Layer entity (such as VSPP) might support a number of ports within a specific node. Local port numbers can be either well-known (reserved for a particular VINES process, such as StreetTalk) or transient. Well-known ports use addresses 0001-01FFH. Transient ports are given values of 0200-FFFEH and are assigned on a rotating basis by the Transport Layer entity.

To summarize, let's assume that a VINES server has a serial number of 2,107,480 (decimal). Therefore, it would have a VINES internet address of 00202858:0001H. (The 2,107,480 decimal converts to 00202858 hexadecimal, and the subnetwork number 0001H indicates a server.) A workstation on that network could have an address of 00202858:801BH. The Transport Layer entity within that workstation would have a socket address of 00202858:801B:0200H. A Banyan Systems Technical note "How VINES Adapts to Changes on the Network" [4-10] elaborates on the VINES addressing scheme in greater detail.

4.1.7 VINES Packet Formats

Because of all the protocols defined within the VINES family, the architecture requires a standard format for the transmission of information. This format is known as the *VINES packet*, and it can take on a number of configurations depending on the protocols in use (see Figure 4-3). Details of the VINES packet formats are described in References [4-11] and [4-12].

The VINES packet is carried within the Data Link Layer frame. The frame's configuration depends upon the network topology (Ethernet, token ring, and so on). The packet begins with the VINES Fragmentation Protocol (VFRP) header and ends with the user data being transmitted. The VINES Internet Protocol (VIP) header follows the VFRP header, and is used with all packet types. The VINES Network/Transport header is transmitted next, and can be one of five types, depending upon the application. Three Network/Transport header protocols (VICP, VRTP, and VARP) are used for network control purposes only, and, therefore, include no user

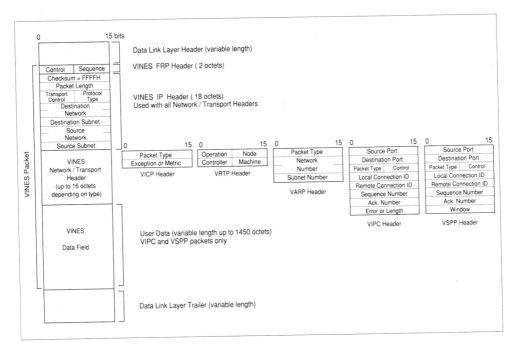

Figure 4-3. VINES Packet Formats
(Courtesy Banyan Systems Inc.)

data. As a result, these headers are also shorter (4 octets for VICP and VRTP, 8 octets for VARP). The two remaining protocols, VIPC and VSPP, require a 16-octet header because they control the communication of user data. Note that the VIPC and VSPP headers are identical except for the last 2 octets. Notice also that the short VIPC header only uses the first 6 octets and does not contain the connection ID or numbering provisions of the longer VIPC header. This short version is used for unreliable datagram service.

4.2 VINES Protocol Analysis Techniques

VINES' unique mix of proprietary and industry-standard protocols makes the analysis of these internetworks quite challenging. Standard protocol analyzers are sufficient for the industry-standard protocols, such as X.25, HDLC, and TCP/IP. But

143

you'll need an analyzer with protocol interpreters for VINES for VINES-specific protocols such as SPP, IPC, NetRPC, and StreetTalk. As of this writing, products with those capabilities include AG Group's (Walnut Creek, CA) EtherPeek, Network General's (Menlo Park, CA) Sniffer, and Novell's (San Jose, CA) LANalyzer. Listed below are some hints for analyzing the VINES protocols.

1. Check the operation of the VINES hardware layers. More options (e.g. ARCNET, Ethernet, token ring, asynchronous lines, Bisync connections, etc.) are available here than for other internetwork software, so a stability check of all subsystems is a must. On ARCNET LANs, look for excessive reconfigurations, which would indicate a workstation NIC with a faulty receiver. For Ethernets, check for excessive collisions or errored (CRC failing) frames. If you find them, check to see if the maximum cable length for that particular topology (thick cable, thin cable, or unshielded twisted pair) has been exceeded. For token ring networks, verify that the MAC-layer operation is stable (review Section 3.4.1). On VINES internetworks using WAN links, verify that the transmission facility has no excessive noise or other analog or digital transmission impairments. Many of the WAN analyzers discussed in Chapter 2 can test for these situations.

2. Become familiar with the VINES hardware diagnostic utilities: DIAGARC (for ARCNET hardware) and DIAGETHER (for Ethernet hardware).

3. Identify the servers on the VINES internetwork. Recall that the VINES internet addressing is of the form "network address:subnet address" (32 bits:16 bits), and that a server is always assigned a subnet address = 1. Thus, if you find a VINES Internet Protocol (VIP) packet with a subnet address = 1, you've identified a server. If the 1 is in the Source subnetwork number, the packet is coming from the server, if the 1 is in the Destination subnetwork number, the packet is going to the server. See Section 4.3.2 for a more detailed discussion of VINES server operation.

4. Each server and workstation node maintains two internal routing tables. The first is the table of networks, which identifies the logical networks according

to the server's serial number (the network number) plus an estimated round trip delay (given in 200 millisecond ticks) associated with the route to that network. The second routing table is the table of neighbors, which identifies the network and subnetwork number, the transmission medium (Ethernet, HDLC, etc.), the LAN (or WAN) address, plus an estimated round-trip delay time (also given in 200 millisecond ticks).

These two tables are updated periodically. For nodes that are neighbors on a LAN, this information is sent in VINES Routing Update Protocol (VRTP) packets every 90 seconds. To minimize the bandwidth overhead, nodes that are neighbors on serial lines, X.25 virtual circuits, or TCP/IP server-to-server connections broadcast VRTP packets only when changes are made to the internetwork topology. Neighbors that are not heard from within six minutes are removed from the table of neighbors and/or table of networks. (TCP/IP entries in the neighbor table are static and never removed.)

5. Nodes that wish to maintain their end of a VINES Sequenced Packet Protocol (VSPP) connection will transmit a VSPP Ack packet every 30 seconds. This packet will identify the current source and destination port numbers, the local and remote connection IDs, sequence, and acknowledgement numbers. If a node receives no packet on a given connection for 120 seconds plus the rounded cost metric to this destination, the connection will be dropped with a Disconnect error.

6. Verify that the StreetTalk directory database updates are transmitted periodically. These should occur as changes are made or every 12 hours, whichever is more frequent.

With these general VINES troubleshooting hints in mind, let's look at some case studies of VINES internetwork analysis.

4.3 VINES Internetwork Troubleshooting

The key to analyzing a VINES internetwork successfully is understanding how the servers route packets from source to destination, possibly over a number of dissimilar physical links. We'll begin our study by demonstrating a workstation login to a file server within a multiserver VINES internetwork.

4.3.1 VINES Internetwork Login Sequence

Consider the processes by which a workstation logs in to the VINES Server. Trace 4.3.1 illustrates the login sequence of a workstation (designated Network Control) to a VINES server. Both the workstation and server are on the same network (see Figure 4-4).

Sniffer Network Analyzer data 1-Aug-91 at 16:19:34, file LOGIN2.TRC Pg 1

SUMMARY	Delta T	Destination	Source	Summary
8	0.750	Broadcast	VINES SVR 2	MAC Standby Monitor Present
9	6.869	Broadcast	VINES SVR 2	MAC Standby Monitor Present
10	6.999	Broadcast	VINES SVR 2	MAC Standby Monitor Present
11	1.395	NTWK CONTR	NTWK CONTR	MAC Duplicate Address Test
12	0.001	NTWK CONTR	NTWK CONTR	MAC Duplicate Address Test
13	0.375	Config Srv	NTWK CONTR	MAC Report SUA Change
14	0.016	Broadcast	NTWK CONTR	MAC Standby Monitor Present
15	0.001	Param Server	NTWK CONTR	MAC Request Initialization
16	0.000	Param Server	NTWK CONTR	MAC Request Initialization
17	0.000	Param Server	NTWK CONTR	MAC Request Initialization
18	0.000	Param Server	NTWK CONTR	MAC Request Initialization
19	0.016	Broadcast	VINES SVR 2	MAC Standby Monitor Present
20	0.167	Broadcast	NTWK CONTR	VARP C ARP service locate
21	0.002	NTWK CONTR	VINES SVR 3	VARP R ARP service located
22	0.000	NTWK CONTR	VINES SVR1	VARP R ARP service located
23	0.000	NTWK CONTR	VINES SVR 2	VARP R ARP service located
24	0.004	VINES SVR 3	NTWK CONTR	VARP C Address assign req
25	0.002	NTWK CONTR	VINES SVR 3	VARP R Address Assigned

26	0.003	Broadcast	NTWK CONTR	VRTP C Endnode Hello
27	0.003	Broadcast	NTWK CONTR	VRTP C Endnode update req
28	0.002	NTWK CONTR	VINES SVR 3	VRTP ILLEGAL OPERATION
29	0.000	NTWK CONTR	VINES SVR1	VRTP ILLEGAL OPERATION
30	0.000	NTWK CONTR	VINES SVR 2	VRTP ILLEGAL OPERATION
31	0.000	NTWK CONTR	VINES SVR 3	VRTP R Router update
				(2 nets, cost=2,0,0,0,0,>>0)
32	0.000	NTWK CONTR	VINES SVR 2	VRTP R Router update
				(2 nets, cost=2,0,0,0,0,>>0)
33	0.000	NTWK CONTR	VINES SVR1	VRTP R Router update
				(2 nets, cost=2,0,0,0,0,>>0)
34	0.262	Broadcast	NTWK CONTR	VIPC Datagram D=0006 S=0200
35	0.004	NTWK CONTR	VINES SVR 2	VIPC Datagram D=0200 S=0006
36	0.000	NTWK CONTR	VINES SVR 3	VIPC Datagram D=0200 S=0006
37	0.000	NTWK CONTR	VINES SVR1	VIPC Datagram D=0200 S=0006
38	0.008	VINES SVR 2	NTWK CONTR	VFILE C Report Port Number
39	0.005	NTWK CONTR	VINES SVR 2	VFILE R OK
40	0.006	VINES SVR 2	NTWK CONTR	VSPP Data NS=1 NR=0
				Win=4 DID=0000 SID=0002
				D=0237 S=0202
41	0.002	NTWK CONTR	VINES SVR 2	VSPP Ack NS=0 NR=1
				Win=5 DID=0002 SID=0053
42	0.001	NTWK CONTR	VINES SVR 2	VSPP Ack NS=0 NR=1
				Win=5 DID=0002 SID=0053
43	0.004	VINES SVR 2	NTWK CONTR	SMB C VINES 4.00 (more)
44	0.002	NTWK CONTR	VINES SVR 2	SMB R Negotiated Protocol 0
45	0.005	VINES SVR 2	NTWK CONTR	SMB C Connect [Missing]
46	0.093	NTWK CONTR	VINES SVR 2	SMB R T=25 Connected
47	0.019	Broadcast	NTWK CONTR	VRTP C Endnode Hello
48	0.025	VINES SVR 2	NTWK CONTR	SMB C Search \\LOGIN.???
49	0.069	NTWK CONTR	VINES SVR 2	SMB R 1 entry found
50	0.007	VINES SVR 2	NTWK CONTR	SMB C Open \\LOGIN.EXE

51	0.006	NTWK CONTR	VINES SVR 2	SMB R F=0001 Opened
52	0.006	VINES SVR 2	NTWK CONTR	SMB C F=0001 Read 2048 at 0
53	0.026	NTWK CONTR	VINES SVR 2	SMB R OK
54	0.002	NTWK CONTR	VINES SVR 2	VSPP Data NS=6 NR=6
				Win=10 DID=0002 SID=0053
				D=0202 S=0237
55	0.008	VINES SVR 2	NTWK CONTR	SMB C F=0001 Read 32768
				at 5632
56	0.014	NTWK CONTR	VINES SVR 2	SMB R OK
57	0.036	NTWK CONTR	VINES SVR 2	VSPP Data NS=8 NR=7
				Win=11 DID=0002 SID=0053
				D=0202 S=0237
58	0.005	NTWK CONTR	VINES SVR 2	VSPP Data NS=9 NR=7
				Win=11 DID=0002 SID=0053
				D=0202 S=0237
59	0.005	NTWK CONTR	VINES SVR 2	VSPP Data NS=10 NR=7
				Win=11 DID=0002 SID=0053
				D=0202 S=0237
60	0.004	VINES SVR 2	NTWK CONTR	VSPP Ack NS=7 NR=10
				Win=14 DID=0053 SID=0002

Trace 4.3.1. VINES Workstation Login Sequence

When executing the BAN.EXE file, the workstation (designated in Trace 4.3.1 as CONTR) must establish both a physical and a logical connection to the network. Figure 4-5 summarizes the process of making these connections in graphical form. For a token ring network, the usual MAC-layer station initialization sequence establishes the physical connection. The analyst should note the significant events detailed in the Section 3.3.1. Because VINES was running on a token ring in this example, the MAC-layer functions associated with station initialization are present. These include the Duplicate Address Test (DAT) in Frames 11 and 12; Report Stored Upstream Address (SUA) Change in Frame 13; and Request Initialization in Frames 15 through 18. Since no Ring Parameter Server is present, (i.e., no response is

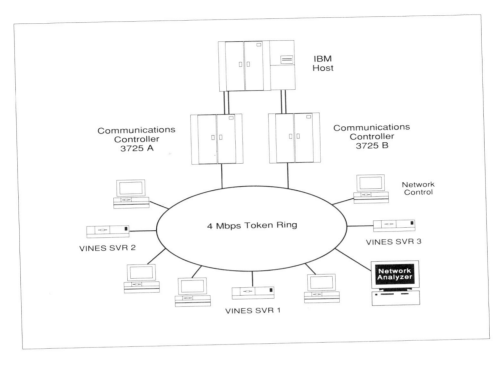

Figure 4-4. VINES Login and SNA Gateway

received from the Request Initialization frames), the workstation (CONTR) uses its default parameters. After Frame 18, it is physically connected into the token ring network.

Next, the new workstation uses a three-step VINES process to make the logical connection to the VINES internetwork. First, the workstation transmits VARP query request packets to all neighbor servers. (A neighbor is any node that is directly connected to the same LAN or serial line as the workstation and can, therefore, be reached without forwarding the data via a routing server.) The ARP Service Locate packet (Frame 20) requests the service of a server that can assign internet addresses to clients. This packet is transmitted as a 0 hop broadcast. The first response received (from VINES SVR 3 in Frame 21) defines which server will be that workstation's routing server. Two other servers (VINES SRV 1 and VINES SVR 2) responded later

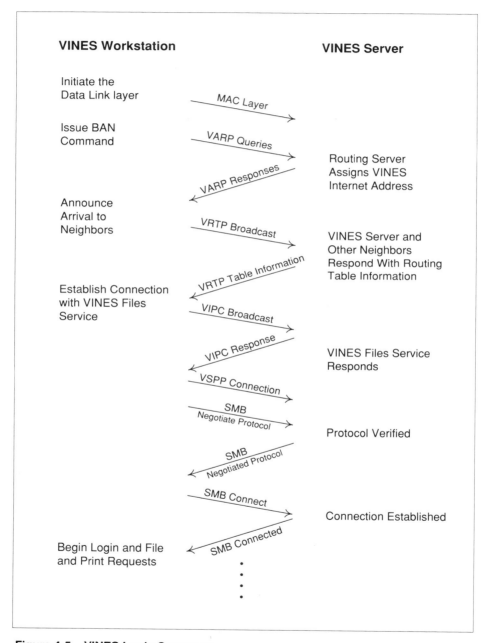

Figure 4-5. VINES Login Sequence

(Frames 22 and 23) but were not selected as the routing server. The workstation then sends a VARP Address Assignment Request packet (Frame 24) directly to the routing server. The VARP Address Assignment Response packet (Frame 25) containing the sought-for internet address (00262CB6.8201) acknowledges the request.

The second step to making the logical connection is when the workstation announces its arrival to its neighbors. The workstation broadcasts A VINES RTP Request packet (Frame 27) so that its neighbors can add it to their routing tables. The new workstation uses the VRTP response packets that it receives (Frames 31 through 33) to build its own table of neighbors.

The third step is establishing the connection with the VINES file server, known as *VINES Files*. (Note that one server can act as the workstation's routing server while another server can be that workstation's file server). The workstation redirector broadcasts a VINES IPC packet (Frame 34) to all neighbor servers at a well-known destination port address (0006H). (VIPC locates the VINES FILE service that matches the revision running on the client. The first broadcast is specified at 0 hops. If no response is heard, another broadcast is made at 1 hop. VIPC is used because VSPP does not support broadcast messages.) The workstation then reports a port number to the first responding server (VINES SVR 2 in Frame 38), and that server assigns a destination connection number (Frame 39). Next, the workstation uses the Server Message Block (SMB) protocol to establish a VSPP connection with the redirector-server (Frame 40). (As discussed in [4-13] and [4-14], Microsoft developed the SMB Protocol, shown in Figure 4-1, as part of the Microsoft Networks program implemented by a number of OEMs, including IBM (PC LAN Program), 3Com Corporation (3+), and Banyan (SMB).) SMB verifies the dialect (VINES 4.0 in Frames 43 and 44), starts the connection (Frames 45 and 46), then issues any file or print service commands. In this case, the first file accessed is LOGIN.EXE (beginning in Frame 48). Then the BAN program invokes the LOGIN.EXE program displaying the VINES user menu screen. Once the user logs in, SMB validates the user's password (using the VINES Security Service, formerly known as VANGUARD), disconnects the original VINES Files connection (in the PCINIT directory), and re-connects with the user's name. The second VINES Files connection allows access to all VINES commands in the DOS\USA directory. This process is shown in Frames 55 through 60. Our client is now logged in to the VINES internetwork.

In summary, VINES has defined the following protocol processes for establishing and disconnecting Workstation-to-Server connections:

1. Establish MAC-Layer physical connection

2. Establish VINES logical connection

    a. Find the routing server (using VARP)

    b. Announce workstation arrival to neighbors (using VRTP)

    c. Establish session with a VINES Files Service (using VIPC and VSPP/SMB)

3. Perform required functions—file, print, etc.

4. Disconnect VINES logical connection

5. Disconnect MAC-Layer physical connection

As the next example illustrates, if the connection to VINES Files is lost, the workstation redirector will repeat the above algorithm (VIPC Findsvc, VSPP connection with SMB data, and so on).

4.3.2 VINES Intermittent Server Operation

What happens if the server does not perform as expected? In this example, an intermittent token ring card in the server triggered the following sequence of events, which demonstrate how VINES protocols attempt to recover from a failure on the internetwork.

In this example (see Figure 4-6) two 4 Mbps token ring networks are connected via bridges to a 4 Mbps backbone. The intermittent server resides on the ring on Floor 72. Let's look at the communication between one user (Chuck) and the server in question (VINES SVR), shown in Trace 4.3.2a. (All other network traffic was filtered out.)

The trace begins with the workstation (Chuck) attempting to run the network version of Word Perfect 5.1. Frames 1through 8 show the SMB Protocol searching, opening, and closing the user's profile (\WPCRD}.SET). All of these frames appear normal.

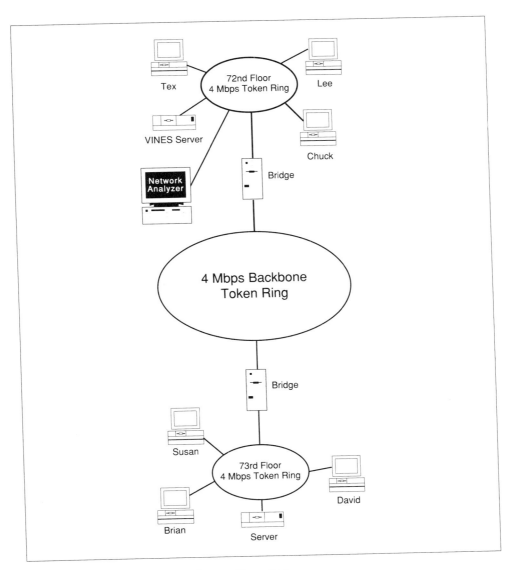

Figure 4-6. VINES Intermittent Server Operation

A number of VSPP packets appear next. Recall that the Sequenced Packet Protocol provides a flow-controlled virtual connection between two Transport Layer ports. This connection supports two communicating processes. If one of the communicating ports closes, the virtual connection terminates. Reviewing Figure 4-3, you can see that the VSPP header includes 16 octets of control information, including the 2-octet Source and Destination ports, a 1-octet Packet Type (Data, Ack, Disconnect, and so on), a 1-octet Control byte (end of message, beginning of message, etc.), the 2-octet Local and Remote Connection IDs, a 2-octet Sequence number (the first packet has sequence = 1), a 2-octet Acknowledgement number (the last packet that was accepted, not next expected), and concludes with a 2-octet window field for flow control (the highest sequence number that the receiver can accept).

Sniffer Network Analyzer data 9-May-91 at 07:23:50 file CRDVINES.TRC, Pg 1

SUMMARY	Delta T	From Chuck	From VINES Svr
M 1		SMB C Search \WPCRD}.SET	
2	0.002		SMB R 1 entry found
3	0.004	SMB C Open \WPCRD}.SET	
4	0.001		SMB R F=0081 Opened
5	0.004	SMB C F=0081 Seek to end	
6	0.001		SMB R Seek to 2426
7	0.005	SMB C F=0081 Close	
8	0.001		SMB R Closed
9	0.117	VSPP Ack NS=35 NR=34 Window=38 DID=0051 SID=000A	
10	0.001	VSPP Ack NS=3261 NR=8977 Window=8981 DID=0045 SID=0008	
11	0.002	VSPP Ack NS=2411 NR=3260 Window=3264 DID=0039 SID=0006	
12	0.014	VSPP Ack NS=664 NR=711 Window=715 DID=003B SID=0009	
13	0.100	VSPP Ack NS=10 NR=9 Window=13 DID=003D SID=000C	
14	0.001	VSPP Ack NS=4 NR=3 Window=7 DID=004F SID=0007	
15	0.002	VSPP Ack NS=4 NR=3 Window=7 DID=0043 SID=0005	
16	0.001	VSPP Ack NS=4 NR=3 Window=7 DID=004D SID=0004	
20	1.444	SMB C F=0093 Read 6992 at 434816	
21	0.005		SMB R OK
22	0.003		VSPP Data NS=8979 NR=3262

		Window=3266 DID=0008
		SID=0045 D=0202 S=0227
23	0.003	VSPP Data NS=8980 NR=3262
		Window=3266 DID=0008
		SID=0045 D=0202 S=0227
24	0.003	VSPP Data NS=8981 NR=3262
		Window=3266 DID=0008
		SID=0045 D=0202 S=0227
25	0.003	VSPP Ack NS=3262 NR=8981 Window=8985 DID=0045 SID=0008
26	0.005	VSPP Data NS=8982 NR=3262
		Window=3266 DID=0008
		SID=0045 D=0202 S=0227
27	0.007	SMB CF=0093 Read 324 at 434480
28	0.002	SMB R OK
29	0.010	SMB C F=0093 Read 9808 at 421584
30	0.006	SMB R OK
31	0.003	VSPP Data NS=8985 NR=3264
		Window=3268 DID=0008
		SID=0045 D=0202 S=0227
32	0.003	VSPP Data NS=8986 NR=3264
		Window=3268 DID=0008
		SID=0045 D=0202 S=0227
33	0.003	VSPP Data NS=8987 NR=3264
		Window=3268 DID=0008
		SID=0045 D=0202 S=0227
34	0.002	VSPP Ack NS=3264 NR=8987 Window=8991 DID=0045 SID=0008
35	0.005	VSPP Data NS=8988 NR=3264
		Window=3268 DID=0008
		SID=0045 D=0202 S=0227
36	0.003	VSPP Data NS=8989 NR=3264
		Window=3268 DID=0008
		SID=0045 D=0202 S=0227
37	0.002	VSPP Data NS=8990 NR=3264

		Window=3268 DID=0008
		SID=0045 D=0202 S=0227
38	0.008	SMB C F=0093 Read 660 at 420912
39	0.003	SMB R OK
40	0.032	VSPP Ack NS=3265 NR=8991 Window=8995 DID=0045 SID=0008
44	1.328	VSPP Ack NS=35 NR=34 Window=38 DID=0051 SID=000A
45	0.001	VSPP Ack NS=2411 NR=3260 Window=3264 DID=0039 SID=0006
46	0.018	VSPP Ack NS=664 NR=711 Window=715 DID=003B SID=0009
47	0.120	VSPP Ack NS=10 NR=9 Window=13 DID=003D SID=000C
48	0.001	VSPP Ack NS=4 NR=3 Window=7 DID=004F SID=0007
49	0.001	VSPP Ack NS=4 NR=3 Window=7 DID=0043 SID=0005
50	0.001	VSPP Ack NS=4 NR=3 Window=7 DID=004D SID=0004
52	1.543	VSPP Ack NS=3265 NR=8991 Window=8995 DID=0045 SID=0008
57	1.349	VSPP Ack NS=35 NR=34 Window=38 DID=0051 SID=000A
58	0.001	VSPP Ack NS=2411 NR=3260 Window=3264 DID=0039 SID=0006
59	0.017	VSPP Ack NS=664 NR=711 Window=715 DID=003B SID=0009
60	0.119	VSPP Ack NS=10 NR=9 Window=13 DID=003D SID=000C
61	0.001	VSPP Ack NS=4 NR=3 Window=7 DID=004F SID=0007
62	0.002	VSPP Ack NS=4 NR=3 Window=7 DID=0043 SID=0005
63	0.001	VSPP Ack NS=4 NR=3 Window=7 DID=004D SID=0004
71	1.543	VSPP Ack NS=3265 NR=8991 Window=8995 DID=0045 SID=0008
77	0.699	VRTP C Endnode Hello
81	0.640	VSPP Ack NS=35 NR=34 Window=38 DID=0051 SID=000A
82	0.001	VSPP Ack NS=2411 NR=3260 Window=3264 DID=0039 SID=0006
83	0.018	VSPP Ack NS=664 NR=711 Window=715 DID=003B SID=0009
84	0.119	VSPP Ack NS=10 NR=9 Window=13 DID=003D SID=000C
85	0.001	VSPP Ack NS=4 NR=3 Window=7 DID=004F SID=0007
86	0.001	VSPP Ack NS=4 NR=3 Window=7 DID=0043 SID=0005
87	0.001	VSPP Ack NS=4 NR=3 Window=7 DID=004D SID=0004
93	1.544	VSPP Ack NS=3265 NR=8991 Window=8995 DID=0045 SID=0008
96	0.179	VSPP Disconnect D=0227 S=0202
97	0.001	VSPP Disconnect D=0227 S=0202
98	0.001	VSPP Disconnect D=0227 S=0202

99	0.276	VSPP Disconnect D=0227 S=0202			
103	0.889	VSPP Ack NS=35 NR=34	Window=38	DID=0051 SID=000A	
104	0.001	VSPP Ack NS=2411 NR=3260	Window=3264	DID=0039 SID=0006	
105	0.018	VSPP Disconnect D=0217 S=0202			
106	0.001	VSPP Ack NS=664 NR=711	Window=715	DID=003B SID=0009	
107	0.002	VSPP Disconnect D=0227 S=0202			
108	0.015	VSPP Disconnect D=0227 S=0202			
111	1.649	VSPP Ack NS=3265 NR=8991	Window=8995	DID=0045 SID=0008	
112	0.019	VSPP Disconnect D=0227 S=0202			
128	3.698	VRTP C Endnode Hello			
135	2.531	STRTK C *** UNDOCUMENTED STREET TALK FUNCTION ***			
136	0.005	STRTK R OK *** UNDOCUMENTED STREET TALK FUNCTION ***			
137	0.004	VSPP Data NS=1 NR=0 Window=4 DID=0000 SID=000E			
138	0.001		D=0227 S=0202 VSPP Ack NS=0 NR= Window=5 DID=000E SID=0049		
139	0.000		VSPP Ack NS=0 NR=1 Window=5 DID=000E SID=0049		
140	0.004	SMB C VINES 4.00 (more)			
141	0.001		SMB R Negotiated Protocol 0		
142	0.004	SMB C Connect [Missing]Chuck@INFO_SERVICES@DENVER			
143	0.010	VIPC Ack NS=1 NR=1	DID=0053 SID=000D		
144	0.006		SMB R T=AD Connected		
145	0.004	SMB C F=0093 Read 13504 at 66912			
146	0.001		SMB R Invalid file handle		
147	0.027	VSPP Ack NS=4 NR=3	Window=7	DID=0049 SID=000E	
156	3.018	VSPP Ack NS=4 NR=3	Window=7	DID=0049 SID=000E	
160	3.038	VSPP Ack NS=4 NR=3	Window=7	DID=0049 SID=000E	
164	0.439	VRTP C Endnode Hello			
173	2.589	VSPP Ack NS=4 NR=3	Window=7	DID=0049 SID=000E	
191	3.038	VSPP Ack NS=4 NR=3	Window=7	DID=0049 SID=000E	
192	0.020	VSPP Disconnect D=0227 S=0202			

Trace 4.3.2a VINES Intermittent Server Summary

Let's dissect one of these VSPP connections. Frame 20 is an SMB request from Chuck to read 6,992 octets of data from file handle 93 (F = 0093). The server acknowledges the request in Frame 21 (SMB Response = OK), and transmits the data in Frames 22 through 24. Note that the Source Connection ID = 0045H, Destination ID = 0008H, Source Port = 0227H and Destination Port = 0202H. The send sequence counter increments in Frames 22 to 24 from NS = 8979 to NS = 8981. Chuck acknowledges this data in Frame 25 with NR = 8981 indicating normal reception.

Another read data request (Frame 38) is ignored, however. The server acknowledges the SMB packet (Frame 39), but transfers no data via the VSPP connection. This confuses Chuck's workstation. He wants to keep his half of the VSPP connection active, so he transmits a VSPP Ack as a "keep alive." These Acks can be seen in Frames 40, 52, 71, 93, and 111. In the meantime, a number of other VSPP connections have been acknowledged and disconnected in Frames 81 through 112; however, the connection from SID = 0008H to DID = 0045H is still active, using file handle 93. When the analyzer is set to display only the SMB information (Trace 4.3.2b), all appears normal until Frame 140. After some delay (18.424 seconds), Chuck's workstation re-negotiates the protocol with the server.

Sniffer Network Analyzer data 9-May-91 at 07:23:50, CRDVINES.TRC, Pg 1

SUMMARY	Delta T	From Chuck	From VINES Svr
M 1		SMB C Search \WPCRD}.SET	
2	0.002		SMB R 1 entry found
3	0.004	SMB C Open \WPCRD}.SET	
4	0.001		SMB R F=0081 Opened
5	0.004	SMB C F=0081 Seek to end	
6	0.001		SMB R Seek to 2426
7	0.005	SMB C F=0081 Close	
8	0.001		SMB R Closed
20	1.688	SMB C F=0093 Read 6992 at 434816	
21	0.005		SMB R OK
27	0.025	SMB C F=0093 Read 324 at 434480	
28	0.002		SMB R OK

29	0.010	SMB C F=0093 Read 9808 at 421584
30	0.006	SMB R OK
38	0.032	SMB C F=0093 Read 660 at 420912
39	0.003	SMB R OK
140	18.424	SMB C VINES 4.00 (more)
141	0.001	SMB R Negotiated Protocol 0
142	0.004	SMB C Connect [Missing]Chuck@INFO_SERVICES@DENVER
144	0.016	SMB R T=AD Connected
145	0.004	SMB C F=0093 Read 13504 at 66912
146	0.001	SMB R Invalid file handle

Trace 4.3.2b. VINES Intermittent Server SMB information

Looking back a few frames (Trace 4.3.2a), Chuck's workstation decided to open a new connection in Frame 137. Note that VSPP re-initializes the counters (NS = 1, NR = 0), sets the Window = 4, and transmits to an unknown connection number (DID = 0000) from source connection SID = 000EH. The server acknowledges this request in Frame 138, replacing the unknown connection number with SID = 0049. Chuck now attempts to re-initialize the SMB connection (Frame 140), which is acknowledged in Frame 144.

The problem is identified in the details of Frames 145 and 146 (Trace 4.3.2c). Chuck has been under the assumption that file handle = 0093 is still active since he transmitted the ACKs periodically (Frames 40, 52, 71, 93, 111). Unfortunately, the server does not agree. It rejects the SMB read with an "Invalid file handle" response in Frame 146. Apparently, the intermittent token ring card in the server went to sleep just when Chuck needed it.

```
Sniffer Network Analyzer data from 9-May-91 at 07:23:50 CRDVINES.TRC, Pg 1
SUMMARY Rel Time     From Chuck          From VINES Svr
    145   18.537     DLC    AC=10, FC=40, FS=14
                     LLC C  D=BC S=BC UI
                     VIP    D=002DC739.0001
                            S=002DC739.801D
                            LEN=82 HopsLeft=15
                     VSPP   Data  NS=4    NR=2
```

159

```
                    Window=6    DID=0049
                    SID=000E D=0227 S=0202
            SMB C  F=0093 Read 13504 at 66912



146   18.538                          DLC    AC=10, FC=40, FS=14
                                      LLC C  D=BC S=BC UI
                                      VIP    D=002DC739.801D
                                             S=002DC739.0001
                                             LEN=69 HopsLeft=15
                                      VSPP   Data NS=3   NR=4
                                             Window=8   DID=000E
                                             SID=0049 D=0202 S=0227
                                      SMB R  Invalid file handle
```

Trace 4.3.2c. VINES Intermittent Server File Handles

Reviewing the summary trace (4.3.2a), you'll notice that Chuck sends several more ACKs for the new connection in Frames 147, 156, 160, 173, and 191, then disconnects in Frame 192. Replacing the defective token ring card solved the problem of the intermittent server.

4.3.3 VINES SMTP Gateway Service

One of VINES' strengths is the number of gateway services that a VINES server can incorporate. In this example, we will study the TCP/IP and SMTP (Simple Mail Transfer Protocol) gateway service (see References [4-15] and [4-16]). In the next example, we will consider an SNA gateway.

SMTP is a standard (see Reference [4-17]) for the *way* electronic messages are transmitted, not for their contents. As its name implies, the protocol is designed for simplicity, not necessarily for reliability. Therefore, the dependability of message delivery depends on factors, such as the network, the host, and so forth. (We will consider these factors in Chapter 9.) Therefore, an underlying protocol, such as the Transmission Control Protocol (TCP), is used to provide the reliable message transfer as well as functions such as acknowledgements, flow control, etc.

SMTP commands consist of one line of text. All SMTP hosts must implement a basic set of these commands, including HELO (Hello, initiating the mail session), MAIL (the source of the message), DATA (the text of the message), RCPT (the recipient of the message), RSET (reset, to abort the current transaction), NOOP (no operation, for diagnostic purposes), and QUIT (terminating the mail session). SMTP replies consist of a three-digit code plus text. (The SMTP standard defines a number of these unique codes. Consult Reference [4-18], *The Handbook of Computer Communications Standards*, Volume III for further details.)

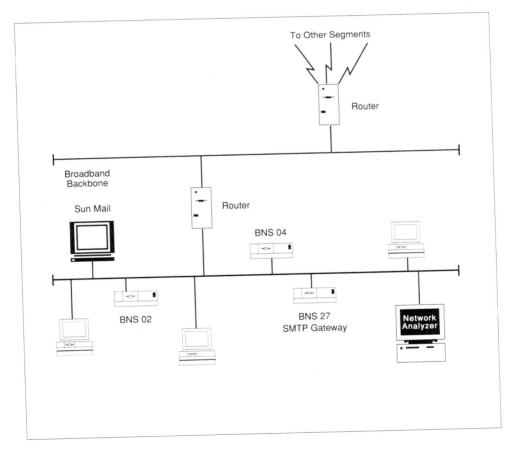

Figure 4-7. VINES SMTP Gateway Service

TROUBLESHOOTING INTERNETWORKS

The SMTP gateway in Figure 4-7 resides within a VINES server. Let's look at the interaction between that server (BNS 27) and a UNIX mail host (Sun Mail) shown in Trace 4.3.3. First, we initiate the TCP connection between SMTP sender (Sun Mail) and SMTP receiver (BNS 27) with a three-way handshake. This handshake, which verifies operation at both ends of the connection, occurs in Frames 1 through 3. Frame 1 identifies the Sun Mail TCP sequence number (1473856000); Frame 2 provides an ACK (1473856001) plus the BNS 27 sequence number (1434458625); and Frame 3 transmits the confirming ACK (1434458626) from Sun Mail.

Sniffer Network Analyzer data from 8-May-91 at 15:05:24, SMTP.ENC, Pg 1

SUMMARY	Delta T	From Sun Mail	From BNS 27
M 1		TCP D=25 S=1252 SYN	
		SEQ=1473856000	
		LEN=0 WIN=4096	
2	0.0024		TCP D=1252 S=25 SYN
			ACK=1473856001
			SEQ=1434458625
			LEN=0 WIN=4096
3	0.0007	TCP D=25 S=1252	
		ACK=1434458626 WIN=4096	
4	0.0056		SMTP R PORT=1252
			220 cts27.cs.pge.com
			SMTP Mail Transfer Service
5	0.0031	SMTP C PORT=1252	
		HELO csd01.cs.pge.com<0D><0A>	
6	0.0032		TCP D=1252 S=25
			ACK=1473856024
			WIN=4096
7	0.0032		SMTP R PORT=1252
			250 OK<0D><0A>
8	0.0022	SMTP C PORT=1252	
		MAIL From:<root@csd01><0D><0A>	

9	0.0033		TCP D=1252 S=25
			ACK=1473856048
			WIN=4096
10	0.1291		SMTP R PORT=1252
			250 OK<0D><0A>
11	0.0046	SMTP C PORT=1252	
		RCPT To:<lch4%csdsi%cts@testx>	
		<0D><0A>	
12	0.0031		TCP D=1252 S=25
			ACK=1473856080
			WIN=4096
13	0.0046		SMTP R PORT=1252
			250 OK<0D><0A>
14	0.0022	SMTP C PORT=1252	
		DATA<0D><0A>	
15	0.0031		TCP D=1252 S=25
			ACK=1473856086
			WIN=4096
16	0.0065		SMTP R PORT=1252
			354 Start mail input,
			end data with
			<CRLF>.<CRLF><0D>...
17	0.0052	SMTP C PORT=1252	
		Received: by csd01.cs.pge.com	
		(4.1/SMI-4.1)<0D><0A>...	
18	0.0036		TCP D=1252 S=25
			ACK=1473856341
			WIN=4096
19	0.0007	SMTP C PORT=1252	
		<0D><0A>	
20	0.0065		TCP D=1252 S=25
			ACK=1473856344 WIN=4096

21	0.0035		SMTP R PORT=1252
			250 OK<0D><0A>
22	0.0022	SMTP C PORT=1252	
		QUIT<0D><0A>	
23	0.0031		TCP D=1252 S=25
			ACK=1473856350 WIN=4096
24	0.0796		SMTP R PORT=1252
			221 cts27.cs.pge.com
			Service closing transmission
25	0.0020	TCP D=25 S=1252 FIN	
		ACK=1434458823	
		SEQ=1473856350	
		LEN=0 WIN=4096	
26	0.0010		TCP D=1252 S=25 FIN
			ACK=1473856350
			SEQ=1434458823
			LEN=0 WIN=4096
27	0.0007	TCP D=25 S=1252 FIN	
		ACK=1434458824	
		SEQ=1473856350	
		LEN=0 WIN=4096	
28	0.0024		TCP D=1252 S=25 FIN
			ACK=1473856351
			SEQ=1434458823
			LEN=0 WIN=4096
29	0.0007	TCP D=25 S=1252	
		ACK=1434458824	
		WIN=4096	
30	0.0014		TCP D=1252 S=25
			ACK=1473856351
			WIN=4096

Trace 4.3.3. VINES SMTP packet details

Next, the SMTP sender and receiver identify themselves. Frame 4 identifies the SMTP receiver (with address cts27.cs.pge.com). Frame 5 identifies the sender (csd01.cs.pge.com) with an SMTP HELO command. Frames 6 and 7 provide TCP and SMTP acknowledgements, respectively. Note the three digit SMTP reply code in Frame 4 (220) and in Frame 7 (250).

Message transfer from Sun Mail to BNS 27 commences in Frame 8 with a MAIL command identifying the source (root@csd01). Frame 11 identifies the intended recipient (lch4%csdsi%cts@testx). In Frame 16 the Banyan Server (BNS 27) asks for mail input and states that the message text should be terminated with the five-character sequence <CRLF>.<CRLF>. Both TCP and SMTP processes acknowledge the message transfer in Frames 20 and 21, respectively.

After finishing its task, the Sun Mail server issues a SMTP QUIT command in Frame 22. The server agrees to close in Frame 24 (service closing transmission). The final step requires both sender and receiver to close their respective TCP connections. The message initiator (Sun Mail) terminates its connection in Frame 25, the message recipient (BNS 27) acknowledges this termination request in Frame 28, and the initiator confirms the connection close in Frame 29. Frame 30 provides a final acknowledgement from the VINES server.

While this trace does not reveal any specific protocol problems, it does illustrate an important troubleshooting concept: Electronic mail applications can be used very effectively to isolate internetwork problems. They are usually easy to use and quick to implement, and they test a variety of systems along the way. Again referring to Figure 4-7, note that a single electronic mail message verified the operation of all the hardware between the VINES server (BNS 27) and the UNIX mail host (Sun Mail). It also verified the application processes of these two systems, including the general health of the server, its hard disk, and so on. Remember to isolate the internetwork problems one at a time, and use an electronic mail application as a convenient means to speed your troubleshooting process.

4.3.4 VINES SNA Gateway

Another gateway function that can be incorporated into a VINES internetwork server is the 3270/SNA option. This function, in effect, enables the VINES server to emulate an IBM 3174, 3274, or 3276 cluster controller in order to access an IBM host computer, such as a 3090. The 3270/SNA option also allows a VINES workstation to emulate an IBM 327X terminal. With this gateway in place, workstations can access the IBM host via the VINES internetwork, rather than a separate dedicated path. Reference [4-19] provides details on SNA in general, and Reference [4-20] discusses Banyan's 3270/SNA option in particular.

Not surprisingly, the interactions between emulations at the workstation, server, and host can be quite complex. Reviewing Figure 4- 4, recall that all of these devices are physically attached to a token ring network, which implies a physical connection via the token ring hardware. But a logical connection is necessary as well. Figure 4-8 summarizes the process.

When the user invokes the 3270/SNA service, that service issues a command (known as DLC_OPEN_STATION) that instructs the server's token ring card to establish a logical link station. The server then transmits a Logical Link Control (LLC) Test Command (C), and receives an LLC Test Response (R) when the remote host (or, in this example, the remote 3725 communications controller) is inserted into the ring. Next, the server transmits two exchange station identification (XID) frames. These frames allow the Network Control Program (NCP) within the host to allocate a Physical Unit (PU) for this communication session. When this is complete, the host activates the data link to the server using an LLC Set Asynchronous Balanced Mode Extended (SABME) command. The link is established when the server responds with an LLC Unnumbered Acknowledgement (UA) frame. The host then issues the Activate Physical Unit (ACTPU) and Activate Logical Unit (ACTLU) commands. When these are acknowledged, the server-to-host session is established.

During the process of establishing the workstation-to-server-to-host connection and the ensuing communication, the system makes a number of parameter assumptions. One of these parameters is the maximum amount of data that can be transmitted from the server to the host. This parameter is known as the *maximum transmit buffer size* (a software parameter within the server) and must be no greater than the

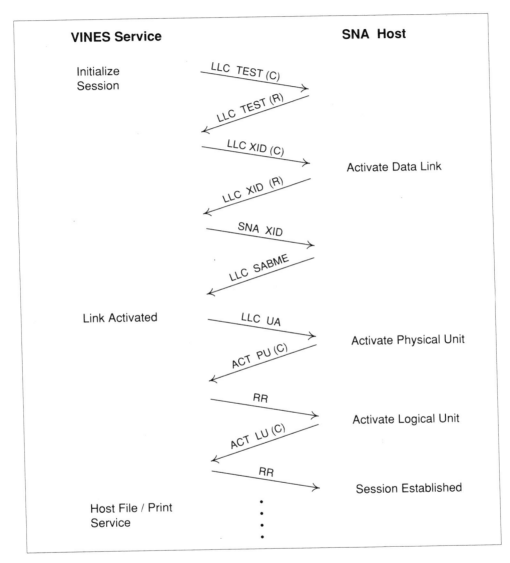

Figure 4-8. VINES SNA Gateway Access Sequence

maximum allowable frame size of the server's token ring card or the transmit buffer size coded in the Network Control Program (NCP) of the 3725 communication controller. In other words, all of the links in this chain must agree to the maximum amount of data and the window size to be communicated at one time. When disagreements exist, communication errors can result.

In this example, the engineering group had attempted to tune the 3270/SNA service for the fastest response time and the minimum file transfer time. To do so, they set the buffers for the 3725 to 2K octets/frame, and both the transmit and receive buffers on the VINES server to that same value. In addition, they increased the transmit and receive window size from 2 to 7 so that more frames could be sent before an acknowledgement was required. Unfortunately, the 3725 would only support 1K octet transmit buffers. Let's see what happened.

The problem occurred when the VINES workstation user tried to retrieve a NetView screen from the host. The workstation began to receive the screen without error, but suddenly locked up. An analyzer was set to capture the data from the workstation (shown as CONTROL), the server (VINES SVR 1), and the host communication controller (IBM 3725B). As shown in Trace 4.3.4a, all communication appeared normal. In Frame 1, CONTR requested the screen, and VINES SVR 1 passed this request to the host (Frame 2). The host's response was contained in Frames 8 through 14. The server then retransmitted the screen data to the workstation in Frames 15 through 19. NTWK CONTR acknowledged this transmission in Frame 20.

Sniffer Network Analyzer data 16-May-91 at 12:22:30 LOCK.TRC, Pg 1

SUMMARY	Delta T	Destination	Source	Summary
M 1		VINES SVR 1	CONTR..	VSPP Data NS=283 NR=588
				Window=592 DID=004F
				SID=0009 D=23AB S=0209
2	0.006	IBM 3725B ..	VINES SVR 1	SNA C FMD user data
3	0.003	VINES SVR 1	IBM 3725B ..	LLC R D=04 S=04 RR NR=93
4	0.403	CONTR..	VINES SVR 1	VSPP Ack NS=588 NR=283
				Window=287 DID=0009
				SID=004F

5	2.002	CONTR..	VINES SVR 2	VBG C Get User Name
6	0.005	VINES SVR 2	CONTR..	VBG R OK
7	0.411	CONTR..	VINES SVR 2	VIPC Ack NS=1 NR=1
				DID=000A SID=003F
8	0.005	VINES SVR 1	IBM 3725B ..	SNA C FMD user data
9	0.003	VINES SVR 1	IBM 3725B ..	SNA FID Type 2 continuation
10	0.003	VINES SVR 1	IBM 3725B ..	SNA FID Type 2 continuation
11	0.003	VINES SVR 1	IBM 3725B ..	SNA FID Type 2 continuation
12	0.003	VINES SVR 1	IBM 3725B ..	SNA FID Type 2 continuation
13	0.003	VINES SVR 1	IBM 3725B ..	SNA FID Type 2 continuation
14	0.002	VINES SVR 1	IBM 3725B ..	SNA FID Type 2 continuation
15	0.001	IBM 3725B ..	VINES SVR 1	LLC R D=04 S=04 RR NR=19
16	0.006	CONTR..	VINES SVR 1	VSPP Data NS=589 NR=283
				Window=287 DID=0009
				SID=004F D=0209 S=23AB
17	0.003	CONTR..	VINES SVR 1	VSPP Data NS=590 NR=283
				Window=287 DID=0009
				SID=004F D=0209 S=23AB
18	0.003	CONTR..	VINES SVR 1	VSPP Data NS=591 NR=283
				Window=287 DID=0009
				SID=004F D=0209 S=23AB
19	0.003	CONTR..	VINES SVR 1	VSPP Data NS=592 NR=283
				Window=287 DID=0009
				SID=004F D=0209 S=23AB
20	0.021	VINES SVR 1	CONTR..	VSPP Ack NS=283 NR=592
				Window=596 DID=004F
				SID=0009

Trace 4.3.4a. VINES SNA Gateway Screen Lock Summary

Unfortunately, the entire screen was not transmitted because the transmit buffer size was set too high in the 3725 NCP. The 3725 at the host could only handle a 1K transmit buffer size. As a result, the screen appeared to lock up mid-transmission. The engineer discovered this problem because he was unable to receive the bottom line of the NetView screen as expected:

1=HELP 2=END 3=RET 5=BOT 6=ROLL 8=FWD 9=RPTFND 12=CURSOR

Looking at the hexadecimal data and its EBCDIC values within the last frame sent from the host (Frame 14), we would expect to see "12=CURSOR." Instead some data from the middle of the screen (L.S. 0018) was sent instead (see the EBCDIC decode in the lower right-hand corner of Trace 4.3.4b).

```
Sniffer Network Analyzer data from 16-May-91 at 12:22:30, LOCK.TRC, Pg 1
- - - - - - - - - - - - - - - Frame 14 - - - - - - - - - - - - - - - -
SUMMARY  Delta T    Destination  Source      Summary
14   0.002   VINES SVR 1  IBM 3725B ..  DLC AC=18, FC=40, FS=14
LLC C D=04 S=04 I  NR=93 NS=18
SNA FID Type 2 continuation
DLC: —— DLC Header ——
DLC:
DLC: Frame 14 arrived at  12:50:38.459; frame size is 71 (0047 hex) bytes.
DLC: AC: Frame priority 0,  Reservation priority 0,  Monitor count 1
DLC: FC: LLC frame,  PCF attention code: None
DLC: FS: Addr recognized indicators: 00, Frame copied indicators: 01
DLC: Destination = Station IBM   SVR1, VINES SVR 1
DLC: Source     = Station 400020000001, IBM 3725B TIC 2
DLC:
LLC: —— LLC Header ——
LLC:
```

LLC: DSAP = 04, SSAP = 04, Command, I frame, N(R) = 93, N(S) = 18

LLC:

SNA: ——— SNA Transmission Header ———

SNA:

SNA: Format identification (FID) = 2

SNA:

SNA: Header flags = 24

SNA: 0010 .... = Format identification

SNA: .... 01.. = Last segment

SNA: .... ..0. = Address field negotiation flag

SNA: ....0 = Normal flow

SNA: Destination address = 03

SNA: Origin   address = 01

SNA: Sequence number = 190

SNA:

SNA: ——— SNA FID Type 2 continuation ———

SNA:

SNA: [47 bytes of data in last segment]

SNA:

ADDR	HEX		EBCDIC
0000	18 40 10 00 5A 1E 8C A7	40 00 20 00 00 01 04 04	. ..!..x ....
0010	24 BA 24 00 03 01 00 BE	40 40 40 40 40 40 40 40	....
0020	40 40 40 40 40 40 40 40	40 40 40 40 40 40 40 40	
0030	40 40 40 40 40 40 40 40	40 40 40 40 40 40 D3 4B	L.
0040	E2 4B 40 F0 F0 F1 F8		S. 0018

Trace 4.3.4b. VINES SNA Gateway Screen Lock Details

Sniffer Network Analyzer data 24-May-91 at 09:39:18, PCSULOCK.TRC, Pg 1

SUMMARY	Delta T	Destination	Source	Summary
64	0.312	VINES SVR 1	NTWK CONTR..	VSPP Data NS=254 NR=847 Window=851 DID=0050 SID=000B D=068C S=0209
65	0.005	IBM 3725B ..	VINES SVR 1	SNA C FMD user data
66	0.003	VINES SVR 1	IBM 3725B ..	LLC R D=04 S=04 RR NR=112
67	0.167	VINES SVR 1	IBM 3725B ..	SNA C FMD user data
68	0.003	VINES SVR 1	IBM 3725B ..	SNA FID Type 2 continuation
69	0.003	VINES SVR 1	IBM 3725B ..	SNA FID Type 2 continuation
70	0.003	VINES SVR 1	IBM 3725B ..	SNA FID Type 2 continuation
71	0.002	VINES SVR 1	IBM 3725B ..	SNA FID Type 2 continuation
72	0.009	NTWK CONTR..	VINES SVR 1	VSPP Data NS=848 NR=254 Window=258 DID=000B SID=0050 D=0209 S=068C
73	0.003	NTWK CONTR..	VINES SVR 1	VSPP Data NS=849 NR=254 Window=258 DID=000B SID=0050 D=0209 S=068C
74	0.003	NTWK CONTR..	VINES SVR 1	VSPP Data NS=850 NR=254 Window=258 DID=000B SID=0050 D=0209 S=068C
75	0.003	NTWK CONTR..	VINES SVR 1	VSPP Data NS=851 NR=254 Window=258 DID=000B SID=0050 D=0209 S=068C
76	0.020	VINES SVR 1	NTWK CONTR..	VSPP Ack NS=254 NR=851 Window=855 DID=0050 SID=000B

Trace 4.3.4c. VINES SNA Gateway Correct Screen Transmission Summary

TROUBLESHOOTING BANYAN VINES INTERNETWORKS

Sniffer Network Analyzer data 24-May-91 at 09:39:18, PCSULOCK.TRC, Pg 1

- - - - - - - - - - - - - - - Frame 71 - - - - - - - - - - - - - - - -

SUMMARY Delta T   Destination Source   Summary

71   0.002   VINES SVR 1 IBM 3725B .. SNA FID Type 2 continuation

SNA: —— SNA Transmission Header ——

SNA:

SNA: Format identification (FID) = 2

SNA:

SNA: Header flags = 24

SNA: 0010 .... = Format identification

SNA: .... 01.. = Last segment

SNA: .... ..0. = Address field negotiation flag

SNA: ....0 = Normal flow

SNA: Destination address = 05

SNA: Origin   address = 01

SNA: Sequence number = 134

SNA:

SNA: —— SNA FID Type 2 continuation ——

SNA:

SNA: [50 bytes of data in last segment]

SNA:

ADDR	HEX		EBCDIC
0000	18 40 10 00 5A 1E 8C A7	40 00 20 00 00 01 04 04	. ..!..x ....
0010	CE E0 24 00 05 01 00 86	D6 E3 40 40 F6 7E D9 D6	.\\.....fOT 6=RO
0020	D3 D3 40 40 F7 7E C2 C1	C3 D2 40 40 F8 7E C6 E6	LL 7=BACK 8=FW
0030	C4 40 40 F9 7E D9 D7 E3	C6 D5 C4 40 40 F1 F2 7E	D 9=RPTFND 12=
0040	C3 E4 D9 E2 D6 D9 11 5B	E8 13	CURSOR.$Y.

Trace 4.3.4d. VINES SNA Gateway Correct Screen Transmission Details

The solution was to reconfigure the 3725 and server buffers for a maximum size of 1K. After this adjustment, the screen transfer didn't lock up. Trace 4.3.4c, shows what happened when we performed a new request for the Netview screen. In Frame 64 the workstation requested the screen. Frame 65 shows the server's request to the host. The host's transmission of data occurred in Frames 67 through 71. The server then transferred the data to the workstation (Frames 72 through 76). The workstation received the expected line of screen information (1=HELP 2=END ...), as shown in the detail of the last host transmission (Frame 71 in Trace 4.3.4d). Note that you can now see the screen information for the lower right-hand corner (6=ROLL 7=BACK 8=FWD . . .).

As we have seen, Banyan VINES provides an interesting mixture of proprietary and industry-standard protocols for LAN and WAN internetworking. The strength of this operating system also makes it a challenge for the analyst. All these protocols make for a lot of information to digest! In Chapter 6 (Token Ring/SNA) and Chapter 8 (TCP/IP), you'll find additional case studies that are relevant to these protocols.

4.4 References

[4-1] Wong, William. "VINES 4.0: Small Changes Add Up." *LAN Technology* (August 1990): 45-52.

[4-2] Penzias, Bonnie. "Authorization Is Basic to VINES Security." *LAN Times* (December 10, 1990): 20-22.

[4-3] Schnaidt, Patricia. "Make the Leap: Multiprocessing NOSs are the Next Step." *LAN Magazine* (February 1991): 38-44.

[4-4] Penzias, Bonnie. "The Hows and Whys of VINES Applications." *LAN Times* (March 18, 1991): 25-28.

[4-5] Banyan Systems Inc. *VINES Architecture Definition*, document number 092015-001, 1988.

[4-6] Banyan Systems Inc. *An Introduction to Symmetric Multiprocessing Technology*, August 16, 1990.

[4-7] Banyan Systems Inc. *Application Directory*, document number 092012-003, April 1989.

[4-8] Banyan Systems Inc. *VINES Application Developer's Guide*, document number 092044-000, 1989.

[4-9] Banyan Systems Inc. *Advanced Communications and Protocols* Vol. I-III, document number 092-152-000ED, 1989.

[4-10] Banyan Systems Inc. "How VINES Adapts to Changes on the Network." *Tech Note Bulletin* Number 204, February 1, 1991.

[4-11] Banyan Systems Inc. *VINES Protocol Definition*, document number DA254-00, 1989.

[4-12] Miller, Mark A. *LAN Protocol Handbook*. Redwood City, CA: M&T Books, 1990.

[4-13] IBM. "IBM PC Network SMB Protocol." *IBM Personal Computer Seminar Proceedings*, Volume 2, Number 8-1, May 1985, document number G320-9319-00.

[4-14] Microsoft Corporation. "Microsoft Networks SMB File Sharing Protocol Extensions." document version 1.10, March 14, 1990.

[4-15] Banyan Systems Inc. *VINES TCP/IP Option Guide*, document number 092050-000, February 1988.

[4-16] Banyan Systems Inc. *SMTP Gateway Option Guide*, document number 092127-000, June 1989.

[4-17] DDN Network Information Center. *Simple Mail Transfer Protocol (SMTP)*. RFC 821, August 1982.

[4-18] Stallings, William, et.al. *Handbook of Computer-Communications Standards*, volume 3. Indianapolis, IN: Howard W. Sams & Co., 1987.

[4-19] Martin, James and Kathleen Kavanagh Chapman. *SNA: IBM's Networking Solution*. Englewood Cliffs, NJ: Prentice-Hall, Inc., 1987.

[4-20] Banyan Systems Inc. *3270/SNA Option Guide*, document number 092042-001, November 1989.

CHAPTER 5

Troubleshooting DECnet Phase IV Internetworks

Digital Equipment Corporation's (Maynard, MA) DECnet has undergone several upgrades since its introduction in 1976. The first release, DECnet Phase I, permitted file transfers between two directly-connected PDP-11 minicomputers running the Realtime resource-Sharing eXecutive (RSX) operating system. DECnet Phase II (1978) integrated additional DEC hosts, such as the DEC-10, DEC-20, and VAX, into the network environment. However, the system still required point-to-point configurations, which meant that it did not allow routing between hosts. DECnet Phase III (1980) added routing and distributed network management; but it could accommodate only 255 nodes.

DECnet Phase IV (1982) offered significant internetworking enhancements. These included Ethernet LAN connectivity, WAN connections using the X.25 protocol, SNA gateways, and expanded addressing to accommodate larger networks. DECnet Phase V, also known as Advantage-Networks (1991), incorporates the OSI protocols. To accomplish this, DEC has defined a dual protocol stack, one for backward compatibility with DECnet protocols, and a second for OSI-compliance. Since DECnet Phase IV networks have a much larger installed base than DECnet Phase V as of this writing, this chapter will concentrate its analysis on the Phase IV protocols. However, we will consider the Phase V enhancements that impact internetworking. We'll begin by looking inside these two protocol stacks.

5.1 DECnet Architecture and Protocols

The installed base of DECnet systems is currently in transition between the proprietary DECnet Phase IV and the OSI-compliant Phase V. As a result, the DECnet architecture must incorporate a number of proprietary and OSI-compliant protocols. These protocols are summarized in Figure 5-1 (Phase IV) and Figure 5-2 (Phase V). We will examine these figures in detail in the following sections, beginning with the hardware layers of DECnet Phase IV.

For further information about the DECnet protocols, consult DEC's excellent system reference documents. The DECnet Phase IV General Description [5-1] is an overview of the protocol architectures. References [5-2] and [5-3] provide examples of Phase IV network design and configuration. If you're interested in following DEC developments, check out the DEC catalog [5-4], which is published several times a year, or review some of the recent articles describing the DECnet Phase IV implementation ([5-5] through [5-7].) Reference [5-8] presents an excellent history of DECnet's development.

5.1.1 DECnet Phase IV Physical Link and Data Link Layers

DECnet network nodes connect to LANs and WANs via separate physical line controllers. As shown in Figure 5-1, these connections include telephone lines and modems, Packet Switched Public Data Networks (PSPDNs) using the X.25 protocol, and Ethernet connections.

Data is transferred to the DECnet Physical Link Layer via one of three available Data Link Layer modules, each of which uses different protocols. The first module incorporates the Digital Data Communications Message Protocol (DDCMP), designed specifically for DECnet Phase I. The flexible DDCMP can operate in either point-to-point or multipoint network configurations over synchronous or asynchronous lines. DDCMP is a character-count (or byte-count) oriented protocol, which means that it counts every octet of data within a frame, and transmits that count along with the data. The receiver interprets the count to determine the amount of data to expect. DDCMP's flexibility makes it extremely practical for use on high-speed WAN communication facilities, such as satellite circuits.

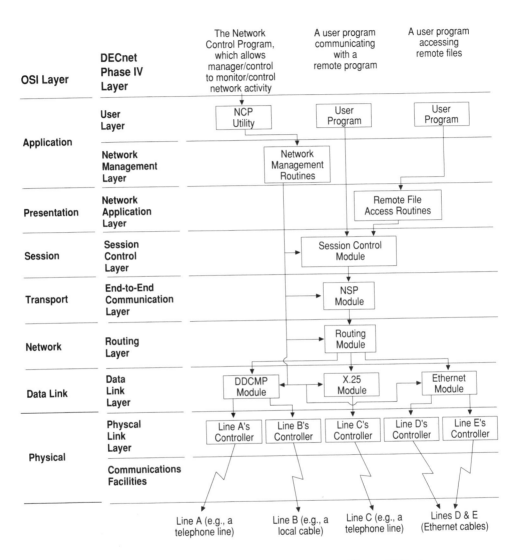

Figure 5-1. DNA Modules Resident in a Typical DECnet Phase IV Node

(Courtesy Digital Equipment Corporation)

The second Data Link Layer module supports the X.25 protocol known as Link Access Procedure Balanced (LAPB), described in the ISO 7776 standard. LAPB is a subset of the ISO High-level Data Link Control (HDLC) protocol, ISO 7809. HDLC and LAPB are bit-oriented protocols that operate over synchronous communication facilities. HDLC is also closely related to IBM's Synchronous Data Link Control (SDLC) protocol used within SNA environments. Thus, DECnet's support of HDLC allows natural extensions to Packet Switched Public Data Networks (PSPDNs) using X.25, and IBM SNA systems using SDLC.

The third module supports the Ethernet frame format. Note that Phase IV supports the DEC, Intel, and Xerox (DIX) version of Ethernet (known as Ethernet version 2) [5-9], not IEEE 802.3.

5.1.2 DECnet Phase IV Routing Layer

In Phase III, DECnet incorporated routing capabilities with the DECnet Routing Layer, which is equivalent to the OSI Network Layer. The DECnet Routing Layer is implemented by the DECnet Routing Module, which includes the DECnet Routing Protocol (DRP). This layer performs three functions. First, it determines the best path for a packet to take from its source to its intended destination. If the destination is the local node, the Routing Layer forwards the packet to the next highest layer within that node; if it is another node, the Routing Layer finds a path to that node. Second, the Routing Layer keeps track of changes in the network topology so that alternate routes are available when necessary. Third, it advises other nodes of changes to the network topology.

Before we can explain the functions of the Routing Layer in more depth, you need to understand how a packet moves from one node to another. For this, you need to know how the DECnet architecture is designed. To ease the administration of large networks, DECnet organizes nodes into a hierarchical structure. A network managed by a single authority is known as an *Administrative Domain*. The Administrative domain may be divided into multiple *Routing Domains*. Each Routing Domain may be partitioned into a maximum of 63 *areas*. Each area may contain up to 1,023 nodes; though each node may belong to only one area. Thus, a DECnet Phase IV network can have a maximum of 64,449 (63 x 1023) nodes. (Phase V effectively removes this limitation by using an address space with 20 octets per node. More on DECnet addressing in Section 5.1.7.)

DECnet defines two types of nodes. End nodes can support only one active DECnet physical line (e.g. Ethernet) at a time. Routing nodes can support multiple active physical lines (e.g. Ethernet, X.25, and synchronous DDCMP) simultaneously. Routing nodes are also designated based on the domain in which they operate. A Level 1 router handles packets traveling from one node to another node within the same area. A Level 2 router can also route a packet to other areas.

The DECnet Routing Module makes its determination of the optimum path for each packet (review Figure 5-1) based on the network topology and on the costs unique to each internetwork. The objective is to find the least-cost, not necessarily the shortest path. The DECnet Phase IV Routing specification [5-10] suggests a method by which a network administrator can assign path costs based upon the bandwidth of each available path (or circuit). Typically, the path cost is inversely proportional to the link speed.

The DECnet Routing Protocol (DRP) supplies two types of routing messages: Data packets and Routing Control messages. Data Packets originate at a higher layer process, such as a user application program. Control messages originate in the routing modules of adjacent nodes, and initialize, maintain, and monitor the Routing layer functions.

DRP defines six types of Routing Control messages. The first type, the Routing Message, is used with all communication circuits and updates the routing tables of adjacent nodes. Two of the Routing Control messages, the Ethernet Router Hello and the Ethernet End Node Hello, are used only by Ethernet circuits to transmit internetwork status information between Ethernet nodes. The Ethernet router periodically sends Ethernet Router Hello to other nodes on the Ethernet. End nodes periodically send the Ethernet End Node Hello message to routers on the Ethernet.

Non-Ethernet (DDCMP or X.25 WAN) circuits use the remaining three Routing Control messages. The Initialization message initializes the link to an adjacent node. Network nodes use the Verification message as needed during the initialization process. Nodes transmit the Hello and Test message periodically to determine whether an adjacent node is still operational. The formats of these DRP packets will be discussed in Section 5.1.6. DEC's Phase IV architecture overview [5-3] and the Routing Layer Specification [5-10] provide further details on DRP.

5.1.3 DECnet Phase IV End Communication Layer

The DECnet End Communication Layer (or ECL) is equivalent to the OSI Transport Layer and controls the flow of data between two DECnet nodes. The path for the data is known as a *logical link*; thus, the ECL establishes, maintains, and disconnects these logical links. The protocol used at the ECL is known as the *Network Services Protocol* (NSP). The architecture defines three types of NSP messages: Data, Acknowledgement, and Control. Data messages carry higher layer (i.e. Session Layer) information, Interrupt (urgent) data, Data Request (data flow control), or Interrupt Request (interrupt flow control) messages. Acknowledgement messages confirm the data or control messages. Control messages initiate and disconnect the logical link. Consult the NSP Specification [5-11] for further details.

5.1.4 DECnet Phase IV Session Control Layer

The DECnet Session Control Layer supports sessions between various user processes. The functions of this OSI Session Layer equivalent include initiating/ disconnecting logical links on behalf of user processes; validating (or authenticating) access to node resources; and creating and activating processes to handle incoming connect requests. We will study the Session connection process in detail in Section 5.3.3. Reference [5-12] provides the detailed specification on the Session Control Layer.

5.1.5 DECnet Phase IV Higher Layers

As shown in Figure 5-1, the DECnet Network Application, Network Management, and User Layers provide OSI Presentation and Application Layer services. Note that the Network Management routines logically connect to the lower layers.

The DECnet upper layers contain a number of higher layer services. The Data Access Protocol (DAP) [5-13] resides in the DECnet Network Application Layer and supports remote file transfers between heterogeneous systems. Two higher layer protocols, the Terminal Communication Protocol and the Command Terminal

OSI Layer

Application	**M**	User Applications	DNA Application Layer Protocols	OSI Application Layer Protocols	User Applications	**M**
Presentation	**A**			Naming Service	OSI Presentation (ASN.1)	**A**
Session	**N**	DNA Session Control		OSI Session (X.225)		**N**
Transport	**A** **G** **E**	Common Transport Interface				**A** **G** **E**
		NSP		OSI Transport (X.224)		
Network	**M** **E**	OSI CLNS ISO 8473 CLNP ISO 9542 ES-IS Protocol ISO 10584 IS-IS Protocol		OSI CONS	X.25	**M** **E**
Data Link	**N**	DDCMP	Ethernet	FDDI	8802-2,3,5 (LLC 1&2)	HDLC	**N**
Physical	**T**						**T**

Figure 5-2. DECnet /OSI Architecture

(Courtesy Digital Equipment Corporation)

Protocol (CTERM) allow a terminal in one location to connect to a host node in another: The Terminal Communication Protocol establishes and disconnects the terminal-to-application connection; CTERM supports various terminal input/output functions. Network management functions use the Network Information and Control Exchange (NICE) protocol [5-14] for local or remote testing, to change system parameters, or to log network events.

Two additional protocols, the Local Area Transport (LAT) and the Maintenance Operations Protocols (MOP), operate directly within the Data Link Layer (e.g. Ethernet) frame, bypassing the DRP, NSP, and Session Control services. The LAT protocol [5-15] supports terminals that communicate with Ethernet-attached hosts. The protocol is implemented within a terminal server that connects to host via

Ethernet on one side and to several terminals (e.g. VT-100) on the other. A complementary LAT module resides in the host. LAT increases the efficiency of the Ethernet backbone by multiplexing together messages from several terminals, thus reducing the number of shorter messages going to that host. Users also see benefits, since LAT allows users to maintain simultaneous sessions to different host processes.

The MOP [5-16] manages remote or unattended nodes. Many of these devices, such as diskless CPUs, don't have the capacity to store their own operating system and, therefore, operate in a client/server relationship with the host. The client's book ROM contains the MOP protocols that ask the server (host) for its booting information. In response, the host downloads the operating system and parameters. Both LAT and MOP will be studied in the troubleshooting examples in Section 5.3.

5.1.6 DECnet Phase IV Packet Formats

Given the many internetworking options available within DECnet Phase IV, it should come as no surprise that the DECnet packet format can be complex (see Figures 5-3a and 5-3b).

The packet is encapsulated within a Data Link Layer header and trailer. The composition of the header and trailer depends on the particular LAN/WAN configuration, and would include Ethernet (LAN), DDCMP (serial lines), and X.25 (WAN).

Within the DECnet Phase IV packet, the DECnet Routing information is transmitted first, and can be either a Routing Data Packet (one of two types) or a Routing Control Packet (one of six types). The structures of the Routing Data and Routing Control packets are illustrated in the top and bottom of Figure 5-3b, respectively.

The Phase IV Data Packet uses a 16-bit DECnet address (described in detail in Section 5.1.7) for both Destination and Source ID. The Ethernet Endnode Data packets use 48-bit addresses for both Destination and Source node IDs, and also include Reserved fields, which are not currently implemented. Both Data packets contain a Forward field that indicates the number of nodes the packet is allowed to visit.

Routing Control Packets have six formats; their use depends on the application. These include Routing Messages, Ethernet Router Hello, Ethernet Endnode Hello, Hello and Test Messages, Initialization Messages, and Verification Messages.

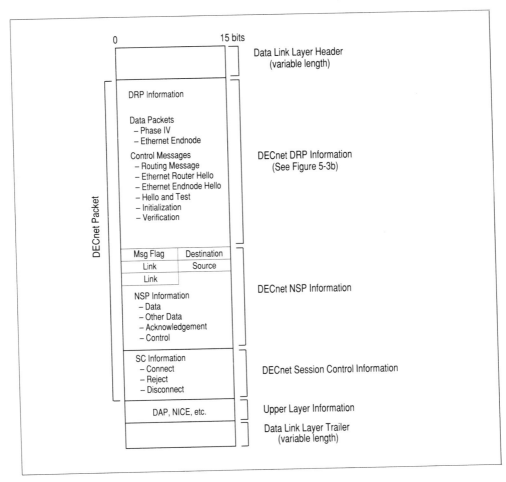

Figure 5-3a. DECnet Phase IV Packet Formats
(Courtesy Digital Equipment Corporation)

All data links use Routing Messages to distribute routing information. Ethernet data links use the Ethernet Router Hello and the Ethernet Endnode Hello packets. The Ethernet Router Hello performs device initialization and transmits status information regarding Ethernet routers. Ethernet End nodes periodically broadcast the Endnode Hello packet to inform the Ethernet routers of their status. Both of these Ethernet-specific control packets identify the transmitter with a 48-bit address.

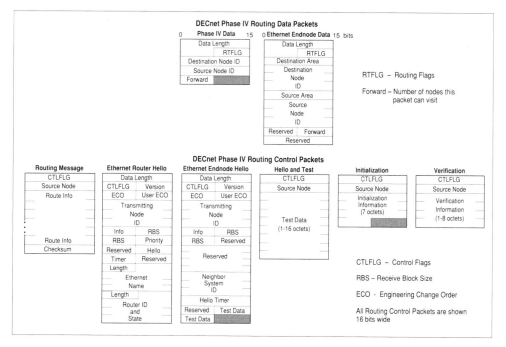

Figure 5-3b. DECnet Phase IV Routing Information Details
(Courtesy Digital Equipment Corporation)

Non-Ethernet circuits use three other types of routing control packets. The Hello and Test packet tests an adjacent node. The Initialization and Verification packets are both used during circuit initialization. All of these packets use a DECnet 16-bit address to identify their source.

DECnet Routing Data Packets also contain End Communication Layer (ECL) information (Section 5.1.3 describes ECLs in more detail). The Network Services Protocol (NSP) conveys the ECL information. The NSP header includes a Message Flag (1 octet) identifying the message type, as well as Destination and Source Logical Link Addresses (2 octets each). Information from one of the four NSP message types (Data, Other Data, Acknowledgement, or Control) would follow. The NSP information field would contain Session Control Protocol (SCP) data. Three types of messages are defined: Connect Data, Reject Data, and Disconnect Data. The

Connect Data message contains a number of identification, authentication, and accounting-related fields. The Reject and Disconnect Data messages provide reasons for terminating the session.

Any upper layer protocol information (e.g. DAP, NICE, etc.) would conclude the DECnet packet, and the Data Link Layer trailer would conclude the frame.

5.1.7 DECnet Phase IV Internetwork Addressing

Each node within a DECnet Phase IV internetwork contains a unique 16-bit address, which is read by the Network layer processes. This address is divided into two parts: a 6-bit area address plus a 10-bit node address. The address is usually expressed in decimal format, such as 32.250. The first number (the area) can range from 0 to 63, and the second number (the node) from 0 to 1,023. Thus, the maximum number of nodes within a unique Phase IV DECnet can be 64,449 [5-17].

Both Ethernet version 2.0 (used with DECnet Phase IV) [5-9] and IEEE 802.3 (used with DECnet Phase V) [5-18] use 48-bit addresses, which are read by the Data Link Layer processes. These addresses are divided into one 24-bit block assigned to a particular manufacturer, such as DEC, and a second 24-bit portion that the manufacturer itself assigns. For both the Ethernet and IEEE 802.3 standards, the block address assigned to DEC is 08002BH. Thus, every Ethernet/802.3 board contains an address ROM with the contents 08002BXXXXXXH where the Xs represent hexadecimal characters assigned by DEC. Together, these 16-bit and 48-bit addresses uniquely define the network nodes.

When a DECnet Phase IV Ethernet/802.3-based device becomes active within a DECnet network, the 48-bit local address in ROM is replaced with an address that indicates that DECnet is active. This DECnet address is also 48 bits in length, but is made up of a 32-bit DECnet prefix (AA000400H) and the 16-bit DECnet address (defined below). For example, an Ethernet/802.3 board with address 08002B 12 3456 would be known as DEC-manufactured board, number 123456. When DECnet was loaded on the node (e.g. node 32.466) containing this board, it would be addressed as AA000400D281. (Note that the DECnet address 32.466 is represented as 100000.0011111010 in binary, or 81D2 in hexadecimal. The transmitted address would be AA000400D281.)

DEC has defined other addresses as multicast addresses, which are received by more than one destination. These include:

Multicast Address (hex)	Usage
09002B00000F	LAT
09002B010000	All Bridges
09002B010001	All Local Bridges
09002B020000	DECnet Level 2 Routers
AB0000010000	MOP Dump/Load Assistance
AB0000020000	MOP Remote Console
AB0000030000	DECnet Level 1 Routers
AB0000040000	DECnet End Node
FFFFFFFFFFFF	Broadcast

5.1.8 DECnet Phase V Protocols

DECnet Phase V (formerly known as DECnet/OSI) was announced in 1987 and began shipping in 1991. As its name implies, Phase V represents DEC's commitment to integrating the emerging OSI protocols into DECnet. Thus, DECnet Phase V manages two concurrent protocol stacks: OSI and DECnet Phase IV. The June 1991 announcement of Advantage Networks added TCP/IP connectivity to DECnet Phase V. References [5-19] through [5-21] are excellent sources of information on these enhancements.

DECnet Phases IV and V are made compatible via common protocols at the OSI Physical through Transport Layers (review Figure 5-2). At the OSI Physical and Data Link Layers, Phase V incorporates support for DDCMP and Ethernet. Phase V also supports Fiber Data Distributed Interface (FDDI), HDLC, and IEEE 802.2, 802.3, and 802.5. An important note for LAN administrators is DEC's transition from the DIX version of Ethernet to the IEEE 802.3 CSMA/CD LAN. The frame formats of these standards are similar but not identical (see the frame format figures in Appendix G).

The Phase V Network Layer provides Connectionless-mode Network Service (CLNS) using the ISO Internetwork Protocol, described in standard ISO 8473. CLNS defines a datagram service that transmits and receives packets up to 65,535 octets in size. Support for ISO Connection-mode Network Services (CONS), described in ISO 8348, is also available.

One of the significant advantages of the ISO Network Layer protocols is their use of a larger and more flexible addressing scheme. While Phase IV uses 16-bit or 2 octet addressing, Phase V addresses can be up to 20 octets in length. The address structure can also use other numbering plan standards, such as CCITT X.121 for X.25 protocols, CCITT E.163 for telephone networks, and E.164 for Integrated Services Digital Networks (ISDNs). To ease the transition from Phase IV to V, Phase V routers can handle Phase IV traffic. When the Phase IV router is ready for the upgrade, you simply reload the software. Reference [5-22] examines the differences between DECnet Phases IV and V in detail.

At the Transport Layer, DECnet Phase V uses the OSI Transport Protocol (TP), standard ISO 8073. Of the five classes of protocol defined by the standard (TP0 through TP4), Phase V supports TP0, TP2, and TP4. TP0 offers minimal overhead and features, and must be used on a very reliable subnetwork (Physical through Network Layers), such as a LAN. TP2 adds multiplexing capabilities. Both TP0 and TP2 require a connection-oriented subnetwork. TP4 provides enhanced capabilities and overhead; and it can be used with either connectionless (CLNS) or connection-oriented (CONS) modes. The Network Services Protocol (NSP) may be used for communication with Phase IV and Phase V nodes. Communication with non-DECnet systems always requires ISO Transport protocols.

Above the Transport Layer foundation, the Phase V user can choose between two upper layer protocol stacks, depending on their application. The Session Control Protocol and other higher layer DECnet protocols are used with DECnet Phase IV applications. A second protocol stack (illustrated in the upper right hand corner of Figure 5-2) provides compatibility with OSI protocols. Since many of these OSI protocols are still under development, DEC has committed itself to continued support as these standards become finalized. The initial release of Phase V includes File Transfer Access and Management (FTAM), X.400 electronic messaging, and the Common Management Information Protocol (CMIP).

DECnet Phase V demonstrates DEC's strong commitment to OSI standards. As of this writing, the product has received a good deal of favorable press, as recent journal articles (References [5-23] through [5-27]) indicate. However, as with all new product announcements, network managers will vote on DEC's multiprotocol implementation with their wallets.

5.2 DECnet Phase IV Protocol Analysis Techniques

In its *Network Troubleshooting Guide* [5-28], DEC does a good job of providing network managers with network analysis and troubleshooting techniques. The following is a summary of some of the DECnet Phase IV analysis tips found in this reference:

1. The highly-distributed nature of DECnet makes it important to pinpoint the cause of the problem clearly. Determine whether a node, LAN, or WAN is the most likely culprit. If possible, obtain a drawing of the network topology to assist with this step. In addition, gather sufficient information from users to develop an informed hypothesis about the problem. For example, if one node is unable to establish communication with another, determine whether the path to that node is via a LAN or WAN connection, and proceed with troubleshooting accordingly.

2. Verify that the DECnet hardware layers (Physical Link and Data Link) are operating normally. To define "normal," compile a benchmark of statistics during a period of stable internetwork operation. Sample statistics include the typical number of collisions or CRC errors for Ethernet links; connect or response times for WAN links. Compare the benchmark statistics with current statistics for clues regarding possible hardware failures.

3. Take advantage of DECnet's many built-in network monitoring and management capabilities. Examples include the LAN Traffic Monitor (a VMS product), the LAT Control Program (included with the VMS operating system), the Network Control Program—NCP (included with DECnet-VAX software) and NMCC/VAX ETHERnim (a VMS-based system for Ethernet

Management). Each of these utilities provides an internal view of the network's operation.

4. Identify the source and interpretation of any messages presented at the system console. Chapter 5 of Reference [5-28] enumerates possible causes for various messages. Also, become familiar with the DECnet diagnostics, such as loopback tests, that are available within the system.

5. Use the flowcharts and troubleshooting guides that DEC has published. Become familiar with these documents before a problem occurs.

6. Confirm that DECnet has been initialized on each DECnet node. When this occurs, the node address will change from a DEC address prefix (08002BH) to a DECnet address prefix (AA0004H). Section 5.3.2 will illustrate these address changes.

7. Analyze the DECnet Routing Layer and identify all of the internetwork routers. To determine the function of each device (Routing or End node) on the internetwork, set the analyzer to capture Router Hello and End Node Hello packets. Also check that the broadcasts from these devices are occurring within the time period set by the network manager. (The default routing update period is 40 seconds, and the default hello timer is 15 seconds.)

8. Verify that all virtual connections between nodes have been properly established. The examples in Sections 5.3.3 and 5.3.4 will illustrate this.

With these guidelines for DECnet analysis in mind, let's look at four case studies of DECnet problems.

5.3 DECnet Phase IV Internetwork Troubleshooting

A DECnet node-to-node connection involves a number of elements: Ethernet hardware, DECnet Routing Protocol (DRP), End Communication Layer (ECL), and Session Control Protocol (SCP) software modules, as well as the desired upper layer applications. In our discussion of internetwork analysis, we will concentrate on the connection and the underlying protocols that facilitate that connection, i.e. the Physical Link through Session Control Layers. We'll begin by looking at an elusive and very frustrating problem, a jabbering Ethernet node.

5.3.1 DECnet Ethernet Frame Errors

The Ethernet network uses a mechanism known as a Carrier Sense Multiple Access Bus with Collision Detection (CSMA/CD) to provide a best-effort, though not error-free, local communications link for workstations, hosts, routers, and other DECnet devices. As an Ethernet network becomes more heavily loaded, the probability that two nodes' transmissions will collide increases. The collisions are a self-perpetuating phenomenon that generates fragmented frames and CRC errors. However, when a collision occurs, the transmitting node sends a jam signal to alert other transmitting nodes. The other stations then temporarily stop transmitting to prevent further collisions. In most cases, the network quickly recovers, and proper transmissions resume.

Erroneous signals, however, don't always result from collisions. In this case study, consultations with DEC and observations that the erroneous signals occurred only sporadically led the network administrator to conclude that the cause was not excessive traffic, but rather a problem with a device on the network. The task for the administrator, then, became tracking down the source of the problem. This was difficult because the collisions eradicated information in the packets that might have lead to the source or intended destination of the data.

In this example, the internetwork was rather complex, with various devices and hosts connected to a backbone (Figure 5-4). A number of protocols were in operation, including DECnet, X.25, and TCP/IP. The network manager kept a network analyzer on the backbone to monitor traffic levels. Seemingly out of the blue, an errant signal would generate a number of network errors and degrade the response time for a while, then normal operation would resume. Later, the errant signal would re-appear.

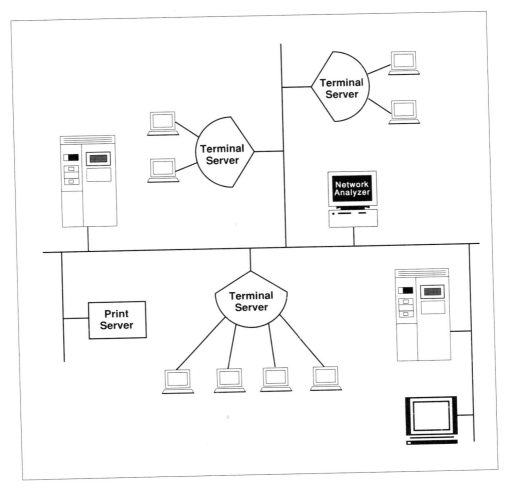

Figure 5-4. DECnet Erroneous Signal Analysis

Sniffer Network Analyzer data 20-Jun-91 at 08:07:04, FRAGTRIG.ENC, Pg 1

SUMMARY		Delta T	Size	Destination	Source	Summary
	88	0.0040	64	Novell1002E0	0080C7CCBBBD	NCP C F=B88D
						Read 1024 at 17408
	89	0.0137	1078	0080C7CCBBBD	Novell1002E0	NCP R OK
						1024 bytes read
	90	0.0104	64	Novell1002E0	0080C7CCBBBD	NCP C F=B88D
						Read 1024 at 18432
	91	0.0150	1078	0080C7CCBBBD	Novell1002E0	NCP R OK
						1024 bytes read
T	92	0.0103	11	???????????	???????????	DLC, BAD FRAME
						size=11 bytes
	93	0.0003	11	???????????	???????????	DLC, BAD FRAME
						size=11 bytes
	94	0.0001	119	AB0000020000	DEC 0A2860	MOP RC System ID
						Receipt=0
	95	0.0001	64	Novell1002E0	0080C7CBBBD	NCP C F=B88D
						Read 1024 at 19456
	96	0.0170	60	DECnet000314	DEC 0DDD3D	LAT C Data D=1E06
						S=1401 NR=80 NS=E4
	97	0.0008	1078	0080C7CCBBBD	Novell1002E0	NCP R OK
						1024 bytes read
	98	0.0028	60	DEC0DDD3D	DECnet000314	LAT R Data D=1401
						S=1E06 NR=E4 NS=81

Trace 5.3.1a. DECnet Ethernet Fragments Summary

To troubleshoot this network, we set the network analyzer to trigger on the errant signal (101010. . .) and capture the frames immediately before and after the error (Trace 5.3.1a). The errant signal was very similar to the Ethernet frame preamble and appeared in two frames (92 and 93). Both of these 11-octet frames were labeled as bad frames. (Recall that the minimum valid Ethernet frame size is 64 octets.) An examination of the details of the frame (Trace 5.3.1b) yielded no additional clues.

Since we could not identify the Source address of the bad frame, we could not identify the defective node.

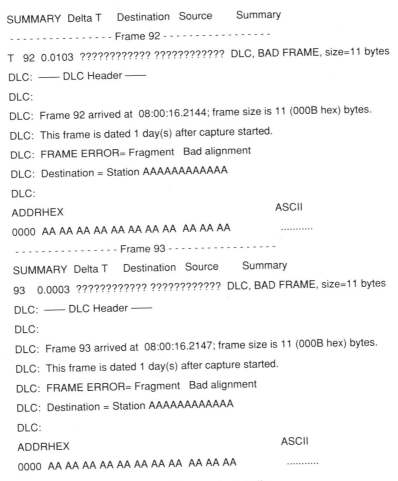

```
SUMMARY  Delta T    Destination  Source      Summary
- - - - - - - - - - - - - - - Frame 92 - - - - - - - - - - - - - - - -
T  92  0.0103  ???????????? ????????????  DLC, BAD FRAME, size=11 bytes

DLC: —— DLC Header ——
DLC:
DLC: Frame 92 arrived at  08:00:16.2144; frame size is 11 (000B hex) bytes.
DLC: This frame is dated 1 day(s) after capture started.
DLC: FRAME ERROR= Fragment   Bad alignment
DLC: Destination = Station AAAAAAAAAAAA
DLC:
ADDRHEX                                      ASCII
0000  AA AA AA AA AA AA AA AA  AA AA AA         ...........
- - - - - - - - - - - - - - Frame 93 - - - - - - - - - - - - - - - -
SUMMARY  Delta T    Destination  Source      Summary
93   0.0003  ???????????? ????????????  DLC, BAD FRAME, size=11 bytes

DLC: —— DLC Header ——
DLC:
DLC: Frame 93 arrived at  08:00:16.2147; frame size is 11 (000B hex) bytes.
DLC: This frame is dated 1 day(s) after capture started.
DLC: FRAME ERROR= Fragment   Bad alignment
DLC: Destination = Station AAAAAAAAAAAA
DLC:
ADDRHEX                                      ASCII
0000  AA AA AA AA AA AA AA AA  AA AA AA         ...........
```

Trace 5.3.1b. DECnet Ethernet Fragments Details

By examining the internetwork topology (Figure 5-4), we were able to form three hypotheses. All Ethernet segments were connected to a DEC Multiport Repeater (DEMPR), shown as a backbone cable in Figure 5-4. Therefore, one cause could be a defective port in the DEMPR. A second possibility was that a thin wire segment to the terminal servers exceeded the length specification (185 meters maximum). A third scenario was a kink in the segment going to a print server. Any of these occurrences could have violated the CSMA/CD algorithm, thus causing the collision that generated the fragmented frames.

To isolate the cause, we disconnected these three components from the backbone one at a time while the network continued to operate overnight. We configured the network analyzer to trigger on any erroneous signals. Through a process of elimination, we found that the culprit was the segment that connected the print server to the DEMPR. Further examination showed a severe kink in the cable close to the server. When the cable was repaired, print server operation returned to normal.

The technique we used to identify the defective Ethernet nodes, known as a *binary search*, is very time-consuming. The name is derived from the technique of disconnecting half of the network, testing, then cutting the remaining defective portion in half again, and so on, until the problem is completely isolated. While this internetwork troubleshooting technique isn't particularly elegant, given the clues available (Trace 5.3.1b) it was certainly effective.

5.3.2 DECnet Erroneous LAT Packets

The Local Area Transport (LAT) protocol connects dumb terminals to a DECnet host via an Ethernet. LAT does not use the DECnet internetwork protocols (DRP, NSP, and SCP) for connection; rather, it uses a client/server architecture. The client is a terminal server that implements LAT. The server is any VAX/VMS host that is running the host side of the LAT protocol. With Ethernet as the physical channel between the two, LAT is sufficient to make this terminal-to-host link. The terminal user requests the link, which causes a connect request to the host. When the user receives the host's response, the connection is activated.

In this example, two Ethernet segments were connected to a common broadband backbone (see Figure 5-5). Asynchronous terminals attached to the Terminal Server

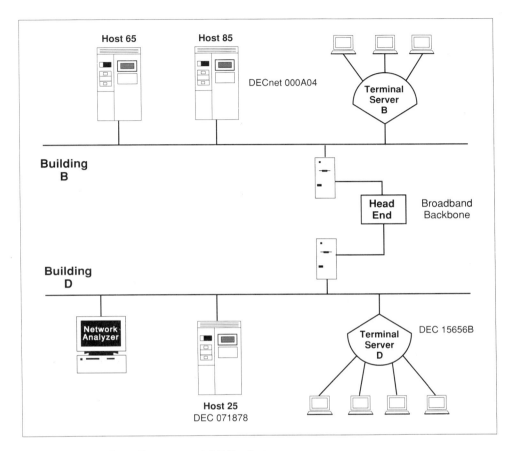

Figure 5-5. DECnet Erroneous LAT Packets

in Building D could then access one of two hosts in Building B. After several weeks of successful operation, both buildings suffered a major power outage. The VAX hosts crashed and had to be restarted from backup tapes. All terminals in Building B were again able to access Hosts 65 and 85 successfully, but the users in Building D were unable to complete a session successfully. The Building D terminals could log on to a host, but the session would lock up after logon. Both buildings had identical terminal server configurations, leading the network managers to suspect a problem with the internetwork link (broadband backbone) between the two buildings.

Sniffer Network Analyzer data 28-Sep-90 at 10:16:00, TERMINAL.ENC, Pg 1

SUMMARY	Delta T	Size	Destination	Source	Summary
2	1.5720	60	DECnet000A04	DEC 15656B	LAT C Connect
					D=0000 S=0001
					Node=DOE85
					Master=
					LAT_08002B15656B
3	0.0058	60	DEC 15656B	DEC 071878	LAT R Connect
					D=0001 S=0B01
					Node= Master=
4	0.0014	84	DEC 15656B	DECnet000A04	LAT R Connect
					D=0001 S=0119
					Node=DOE85
					Master=LAT_08002B15656B
5	0.0722	274	DECnet000A04	DEC 15656B	LAT C
					Start, Start, Start
					D=0B01 S=0001
					NR=00 NS=01

Trace 5.3.2a. DEC LAT Packet Summary

To isolate the problem, we attached a network analyzer to the Ethernet in Building D and set it to capture only LAT packets to and from Terminal Server D (address 08002B15656BH). The terminal server was initially turned off, and then powered on. The resulting packets are shown in Trace 5.3.2a. Frame 2 is a LAT connect addressed to Host 85 (address AA0004000A04H). Surprisingly, two responses are received. The first (Frame 3) came from a host on the same segment, Host 25 (address 08002B071878H). The second response (Frame 4) came from Host 85 (AA0004000A04H) as expected. The two responses were separated in time by 1.4 milliseconds (see the Delta T column in Frame 4). Since Host 25 resided on the same physical cable as the terminal server, the electrical propagation of its response to the LAT Connect command beat the response from the proper host by a fraction of a second. When the terminal server received the two responses, it became confused and locked up.

After studying the LAT connect commands and responses in detail (Trace 5.3.2b), the solution became apparent. The unwelcome host (Host 25) had also gone through the power outage. Since it was used infrequently, no one had remembered to re-initialize the DECnet protocols. When power was restored, the operating system was in an unknown state. This can be verified from the Data Link Layer addresses. Recall that a DEC address begins with 08002BH and is half of the 48-bit Ethernet address. When DECnet is initialized, these address characters are logically replaced with AA0004H. Thus, in Frame 2, Host 85 (AA0004000A04H0 is currently running DECnet, while Terminal Server D (08002B15656BH) is not. Frame 3 shows a response from a DEC (not DECnet) host, address 08002B071878H. Since Host 25 is still using a DEC hardware address, it has not initialized DECnet. Host 85 is running DECnet, but the imposter (Host 25) beat its LAT response by 1.4 milliseconds. Therefore, the terminal server did not know which host to believe.

Sniffer Network Analyzer data 28-Sep-90 at 10:16:00, TERMINAL.ENC, Pg 1

- - - - - - - - - - - Frame 2 - - - - - - - - - - - - - - - - - -

SUMMARY	Delta T	Size	Destination	Source		Summary
2	1.5720	60	DECnet000A04	DEC	15656B	LAT C Connect

```
LAT:    —— Local Area Transport ——
LAT:
LAT:    Message type / flags = 06
LAT:       0000 01.. = Connect
LAT:       .... ..1. = To host
LAT:       .... ...0 = No response requested
LAT:    Number of slots = 0
LAT:       Destination link ID = 0000
LAT:          Source link ID = 0001
LAT:          Sequence number = 00
LAT:    Acknowlegement number = FF
LAT:    Maximum receive datagram size = 1518 bytes
LAT:    Version number = 5
LAT:    ECO level = 1
```

LAT: Maximum simultaneous sessions = 64

LAT: Extra data link buffers queued = 0

LAT: Server circuit timer = 8 x 10msec

LAT: Server keep alive timer = 20 seconds

LAT: Facility number = 0

LAT: Product type = 17

LAT: Product version number = 2

LAT: Node name = "DOE85"

LAT: Master node name = "LAT_08002B15656B" \

LAT: Location = "" \

LAT:


```
- - - - - - - - - - - - - - - - Frame 3 - - - - - - - - - - - - - - - - -
```

SUMMARY	Delta T	Size	Destination	Source	Summary
3	0.0058	60	DEC 15656B	DEC 071878	LAT R Connect

LAT: —— Local Area Transport ——

LAT:

LAT: Message type / flags = 04

LAT: 0000 01.. = Connect

LAT: .... ..0. = From host

LAT: ....0 = No response requested

LAT: Number of slots = 0

LAT: Destination link ID = 0001

LAT: Source link ID = 0B01

LAT: Sequence number = 00

LAT: Acknowlegement number = 00

LAT: Maximum receive datagram size = 1500 bytes

LAT: Version number = 5

LAT: ECO level = 1

LAT: Maximum simultaneous sessions = 255

LAT: Extra data link buffers queued = 0

LAT: Server circuit timer = 8 x 10msec

LAT: Server keep alive timer = 0 seconds

LAT: Facility number = 0

LAT: Product type = 11

LAT: Product version number = 2

LAT: Node name = ""

LAT: Master node name = ""

LAT: Location = ""

LAT:

- - - - - - - - - - - - - - - Frame 4 - - - - - - - - - - - - - - - - -

SUMMARY	Delta T	Size	Destination	Source		Summary
4	0.0014	84	DEC 15656B	DECnet	000A04	LAT R Connect

LAT: ⸺ Local Area Transport ⸺

LAT:

LAT: Message type / flags = 04

LAT: 0000 01.. = Connect

LAT: .... ..0. = From host

LAT: ....0 = No response requested

LAT: Number of slots = 0

LAT: Destination link ID = 0001

LAT: Source link ID = 0119

LAT: Sequence number = 00

LAT: Acknowlegement number = 00

LAT: Maximum receive datagram size = 1500 bytes

LAT: Version number = 5

LAT: ECO level = 1

LAT: Maximum simultaneous sessions = 64

LAT: Extra data link buffers queued = 0

LAT: Server circuit timer = 0 x 10msec

LAT: Server keep alive timer = 0 seconds

```
LAT:    Facility number = 0
LAT:    Product type = 3
LAT:    Product version number = 1
LAT:    Node name = "DOE85"
LAT:    Master node name = "LAT_08002B15656B"
LAT:    Location = "Welcome to VAX/VMS V5.3-1"
LAT:
```

Trace 5.3.2b. DEC LAT Packet Details

The solution was straightforward. The administrator restarted Host 25 to re-initialize DECnet. When the protocols re-initialized, the hardware address was changed to a DECnet (not DEC) address. The host's LAT process restarted at the same time and no longer responded to every LAT connection request. What appeared to be an internetwork problem was actually a simple problem caused by the power failure.

5.3.3 DECnet Lost Connection

Because of DECnet's distributed nature, a connection between two DECnet nodes may involve LAN and WAN hardware, as well as multiple layers of the DECnet software. The connection sequence begins with a higher layer (User, Network Management, or Network Application) process requesting a session with another DECnet node. After the Session Control Module (review Figure 5-1) receives this request, it performs several tasks: It identifies the destination node address from the node-name mapping table, formats and issues a Connect Request to the ECL, and may also start an outgoing connection timer that monitors the connection request/acceptance process [5-3]. Next, the Session Control Module and the NSP and Routing modules work successively to establish the end-to-end path, which may be over various data links, such as X.25 (WAN) or Ethernet (LAN). A failure at any of these layers (Session Control through Physical Link) would cause a failure of the end-user session.

Since DECnet provides such a variety of internetworking options, it is essential to recognize the connection establishment process when it occurs. The process is illustrated in Figure 5-6. It begins when the Session Control Module issues a command to the ECL to initiate the session between Node A and Node B. This generates an NSP Connect Initiate Message. If the remote node agrees, its Session Control module tells the ECL to return an NSP Connect Confirm packet. Data can then be transferred and acknowledged. When Node A finishes its business, the Session Control module requests termination, which prompts an NSP Disconnect Initiate packet to signal the formal termination of the session.

To illustrate this process, consider the internetwork shown in Figure 5-7. Two Ethernet segments are connected via a leased line, modems, and bridges. Users complained of problems with intermittent connections across the WAN link. In some cases, a connection would appear normal, but in others it would abruptly fail. Let's see why.

In our first scenario, Host 4 on Segment B wishes to access Host 1 on Segment A. To get there, Host 4 must traverse the WAN link. A successful connection is illustrated in Trace 5.3.3a, beginning with Frame 144. Host 4 issues an SCP Connect message which is passed as an NSP Connect Initiate Message to Host 1, the File Access Listener process (or FAL, object 17). (FAL is a VAX/VMS process/network object that provides file access to remote users. It maintains a unique process number (17) across all operating systems on a DECnet network. Host 1 returns a Connect Confirm (Frame 146) and then a file transfer begins (Frame 149). When Host 4 is finished, it issues an SCP Disconnect (Frame 162), which is confirmed from the remote end (Host 1). Note that the disconnection reason (Reason = 0 in Frame 162) indicates a normal end of process. The details of the SCP initiation and termination message are shown in Trace 5.3.3b. Note the various parameters such as the User ID and the Access Password that must be included within the SCP End User Connect Message.

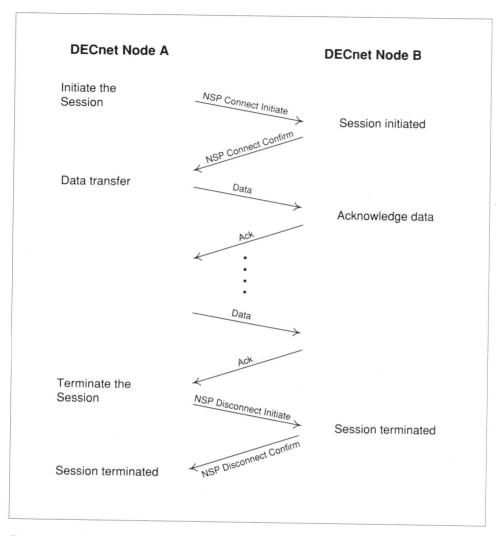

Figure 5-6. DECnet Session Establishment
(Courtesy Digital Equipment Corporation)

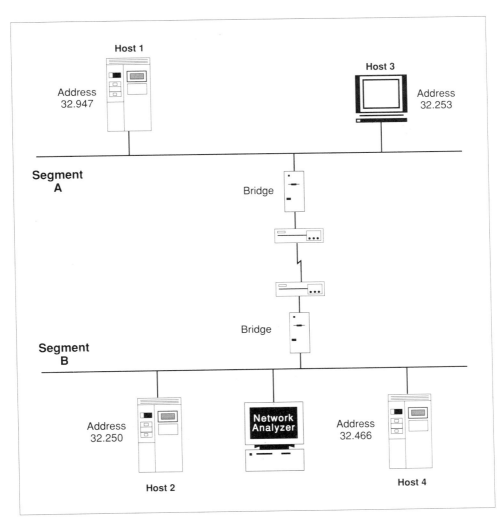

Figure 5-7. DECnet Lost Connection

Sniffer Network Analyzer data 30-Mar-91 at 09:57:06 file LOST_CON.ENC Pg 1

SUMMARY	Delta T	Destination	Source	Summary
143	0.2547	DEC 059AF7	DECnet003980	LAT R Data
				D=0C01 S=1204 NR=74
				NS=7D
144	0.0661	Host 1	Host 4	SCP CONN
				D=17 (FAL) S=BUSTER
145	0.0045	Host 4	Host 1	NSP ACK Connect D=82A7
146	0.4655	Host 4	Host 1	NSP CTRL Connect Confirm
				D=82A7 S=205D
147	0.1042	Host 1	Host 4	NSP DATA Link D=205D
				S=82A7
				LACK=0 LSEG=1 CRED=0
148	0.0030	Host 4	Host 1	NSP DATA Link D=82A7
				S=205D
				LACK=1 LSEG=1 CRED=0
149	0.0118	Host 1	Host 4	DAP OS=VAX/VMS
				FILSYS=RMS-32
150	0.0083	Host 4	Host 1	DAP OS=VAX/VMS
				FILSYS=RMS-32
151	0.0438	Host 1	Host 4	NSP ACK Oth-Data D=205D
				S=82A7 LACK=1
152	0.0395	Host 1	Host 4	DAP (File Attr) (Alloc Attr)
				(Created datetime)
				Open new file HOLDIT.COM;8
153	0.2020	Host 4	Host 1	DAP (File Attr) (Alloc Attr)
				(Created/Updated datetime)
				Spec=DISK$USER:
				[BUSTER]HOLDIT.COM;
				10 (Ack)
154	0.0921	Host 1	Host 4	DAP Display
155	0.0389	Host 4	Host 1	DAP (File Attr) (Alloc Attr)
				(Created/Updated datetime)

				(Group/World Prot Attr)
				Spec=DISK$USER:
				[BUSTER]HOLDIT.COM;
				10 (Ack)
156	0.0907	Host 1	Host 4	DAP Connect
157	0.0070	Host 4	Host 1	DAP (Ack)
158	0.2858	Host 1	Host 4	DAP Write Data,
				140 bytes End-of-stream
159	0.0592	Host 4	Host 1	DAP Response
160	0.0623	Host 1	Host 4	DAP Change-begin
				(Updated datetime)
				Terminate
161	0.0892	Host 4	Host 1	DAP Response
162	0.0749	Host 1	Host 4	SCP DISC Reason=0
163	0.0034	Host 4	Host 1	NSP CTRL Disconn Confirm
				D=82A7 S=205D

Trace 5.3.3a. DECnet Lost Connection Summary

Sniffer Network Analyzer data 30-Mar-91 at 09:57:06 file LOST_CON.ENC Pg 1

- - - - - - - - - - - - - - - - Frame 144 - - - - - - - - - - - - - - - - - -

NSP: —— Network Services Protocol ——

NSP:

NSP: Message Identifier = 18

NSP: 0... .... = Non-extensible field

NSP: .001 .... = Connect Initiate Message

NSP: .... 10.. = Control Message

NSP: .... ..00 = always zero

NSP: Type   = 2 (Control Message)

NSP: Sub-type = 1 (Connect Initiate Message)

NSP: Logical Link Destination = 0000

NSP: Logical Link Source   = 82A7

NSP: Requested Services = 01

NSP: 0000 ..0. = always zero

NSP: .... 00.. = none

NSP: ....1 = always one

NSP: Version Information = 03

NSP: 0000 00.. = always zero

NSP: .... ..11 = reserved

NSP: Segment Size (bytes)   = 1459

NSP: [44 data bytes] \par NSP:

SCP: —— Session Control Protocol ——

SCP:

SCP: Destination Name:

SCP: Name Format Type = 0

SCP: Object Type   = 17 (File Access FAL/DAP-Version 4 and later)

SCP: Source Name:

SCP: Name Format Type = 2

SCP: Object Type   = 0 (General Task, User Process)

SCP: Group Code   = 066E

SCP: User Code   = 2020

SCP: Descriptor Length = 8

SCP: Descriptor   = "BUSTER"

SCP: Menu Version = 27

SCP: 0... .... = non-extensible field

SCP: .01. .... = reserved

SCP: ...0 01.. = should be zero

SCP: .... ..1. = USRDATA field included

SCP: ....1 = RQSTRID, PASSWRD and ACCOUNT fields included

SCP: Destination User Identification = "buster"

SCP: Access Verification Password = "rufus"

SCP: Account Data Length   = 0

SCP: End User Connect Data Length = 0

SCP:

Trace 5.3.3b. DECnet Lost Connection Details

Later in the day, a connection is again needed between Host 4 and Host 1 (review Figure 5-7). This time it fails, with the Host 4 displaying the message:

SYSTEM-F-LINKEXIT, NETWORK PARTNER EXITED

A similar analysis (Trace 5.3.3c) shows what occurred. Host 4 requests the connection as before (SCP Connect, Frame 540); however, the other host (Host 1) returns an SCP disconnect in Frame 542. The reason was an invalid user process. Examining the NSP and SCP details of Frame 540 (Trace 5.3.3d) revealed the culprit: The Access Verification was incorrect. The remote host assumed that Host 4 did not have permission to access that process, so it returned the SCP Disconnect message. The WAN link was not the culprit, the end user was. Only with a detailed analysis of the DECnet Session Layer protocol was the true failure source (the user) identified.

Sniffer Network Analyzer data 30-Mar-91 at 09:57:06, LOST_CON.ENC Pg 1

SUMMARY	Delta T	Destination	Source	Summary
540	0.2058	Host 1	Host 4	DLC Ethertype=6003
				size=91 bytes
				DRP DATA D=32.947
				S=32.466 Visits=2
				NSP CTRL Connect Initiate
				D=0000 S=8345
				SCP CONN D=17 (FAL)
				S=BUSTER
541	0.0045	Host 4	Host 1	DLC Ethertype=6003
				size=60 bytes
				DRP DATA D=32.466
				S=32.947 Visits=0
				NSP ACK Connect D=8345
542	3.7756	Host 4	Host 1	DLC Ethertype=6003
				size=60 bytes
				DRP DATA D=32.466
				S=32.947 Visits=0

				NSP CTRL Disconn Initiate
				D=8345 S=2062
				SCP DISC Reason=38
543	0.0569	Host 1	Host 4	DLC Ethertype=6003
				size=64 bytes
				DRP DATA D=32.947
				S=32.466 Visits=2
				NSP CTRL Disconn Confirm
				D=2062 S=8345

Trace 5.3.3c. DECnet Subsequent Connection Attempt Summary

Sniffer Network Analyzer data 30-Mar-91 at 09:57:06 file LOST_CON.ENC Pg 1

- - - - - - - - - - - - - - - - Frame 540 - - - - - - - - - - - - - - - - -

DLC: ──── DLC Header ────

DLC:

DLC: Frame 540 arrived at 10:20:09.4456; frame size is 91 (005B hex) bytes.

DLC: Destination = Station DECnet00B383, Host 1

DLC: Source   = Station DECnet00D281, Host 4

DLC: Ethertype = 6003 (DECNET)

DLC:

DRP: ──── DECNET Routing Protocol ────

DRP:

DRP: Data Length = 75, Optional Padding Length = 1

DRP: Data Packet Format = 0E

DRP: 0... .... = no padding

DRP: .0.. .... = version

DRP: ..0. .... = Inter-Ethernet packet

DRP: ...0 .... = not return packet

DRP: .... 1... = try to return

DRP: .... .110 = Long Data Packet Format

DRP: Data Packet Type = 6

DRP: Destination Area   = 00

DRP: Destination Subarea = 00

DRP: Destination ID   = 32.947

DRP: Source Area   = 00

DRP: Source Subarea   = 00

DRP: Source ID   = 32.466

DRP: Next Level 2 Router = 00

DRP: Visit Count   = 2

DRP: Service Class   = 00

DRP: Protocol Type   = 00

DRP:

NSP: —— Network Services Protocol ——

NSP:

NSP: Message Identifier = 18

NSP: 0... .... = Non-extensible field

NSP: .001 .... = Connect Initiate Message

NSP: .... 10.. = Control Message

NSP: .... ..00 = always zero

NSP: Type   = 2 (Control Message)

NSP: Sub-type = 1 (Connect Initiate Message)

NSP: Logical Link Destination = 0000

NSP: Logical Link Source   = 8345

NSP: Requested Services = 01

NSP: 0000 ..0. = always zero

NSP: .... 00.. = none

NSP: ....1 = always one

NSP: Version Information = 03

NSP: 0000 00.. = always zero

NSP: .... ..11 = reserved

NSP: Segment Size (bytes)   = 1459

NSP: [44 data bytes]

NSP:

SCP: —— Session Control Protocol ——

SCP:

SCP: Destination Name:

```
SCP:    Name Format Type = 0
SCP:    Object Type      = 17  (File Access FAL/DAP-Version 4 and later)
SCP: Source Name:
SCP:    Name Format Type = 2
SCP:    Object Type      = 0  (General Task, User Process)
SCP:    Group Code       = 066E
SCP:    User Code        = 2020
SCP:    Descriptor Length = 8
SCP:    Descriptor       = "BUSTER"
SCP:       Menu Version = 27
SCP:        0... .... = non-extensible field
SCP:        .01. .... = reserved
SCP:        ...0 01.. = should be zero
SCP:        .... ..1. = USRDATA field included
SCP:        .... ...1 = RQSTRID, PASSWRD and ACCOUNT fields included
SCP: Destination User Identification  = "buster"
SCP: Access Verification Password = "rufus"
SCP: Account Data Length       = 0
SCP: End User Connect Data Length = 0
SCP:
```

Trace 5.3.3d. DECnet Subsequent Connection Attempt Details

5.3.4 DECnet Invisible Connection

To increase cost effectiveness, many internetwork devices are designed with a minimum of input/output peripherals. One example would be a diskless workstation that receives its operating system from a server via the network, rather than from its own internal disk drive. DEC's Maintenance Operation Protocol (MOP) accommodates these configurations by providing a mechanism for downline loads from a host to a designated target device. If the target device resides on an Ethernet, it transmits a MOP Program Request message to a designated MOP multicast address. Hosts that can respond return an Assistance Volunteer message. The target then selects a volunteer, requests the necessary program, and waits for the volunteer to transmit the memory load. In most cases, the entire process only takes a few seconds.

212

In the internetwork shown in Figure 5-8, two Ethernet segments were connected by a fiber optic bridge. The top segment contained three VAX hosts that made up a Local Area VAX Cluster-LAVC. (A *LAVC* is a group of nodes that communicate via Ethernet, but use DEC's System Communication Services (SCS) instead of the DECnet protocols for node-to-node communication. DECnet, SCS, and LAT protocols can coexist on the same Ethernet. Applications for LAVCs include desktop publishing and graphics.) In this example, all three LAVC nodes (VAXs 3, 4, and 7) were able to communicate without difficulty.

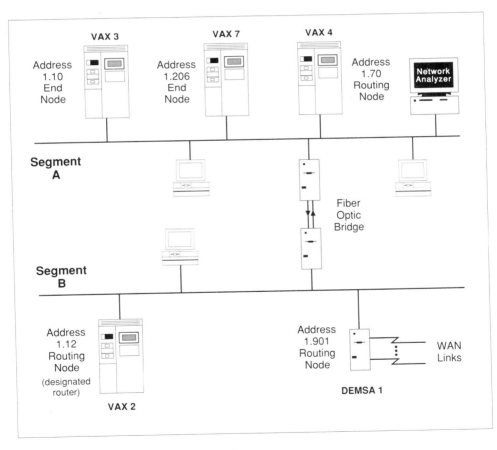

Figure 5-8. DECnet Invisible Connection

The bottom segment contained one routing node (designated VAX 2) plus a DEC Micro Server (DEMSA) router. The DEMSA required assistance from a host to load its image file (operating system). VAX 2 was the designated router for the internetwork.

The problem was described to the analyst as a complex internetwork communications failure. VAX 4 (a routing node) could communicate with VAX 3 (an end node) using DECnet, but VAX 3 could not communicate with VAX 4. Likewise, VAX 3 could not communicate with either VAXs 2 or 7 (using DECnet), but could communicate (using LAVC) with VAXs 4 and 7 on its same segment. In addition, the DEMSA (Router 1) could not properly receive loads requested from VAX 4.

Therefore, we attached a network analyzer to the top segment and set it to capture the load request from DEMSA 1 (Trace 5.3.4a). DEMSA 1 would issue a MOP Request Program service type (Frame 9) and receive a response (Assistance Volunteer in Frame 10) from the remote host. Seemingly unsatisfied, the router would repeat the request (Frames 11 and 12, 14 and 15, 17 and 18) and receive identical responses. Thus, the MOP assistance request was sent and acknowledged, but the router never began the memory download process.

Sniffer Network Analyzer data 18-Mar-91 at 14:58:36,INVIS_4.ENC, Pg 1

SUMMARY		Delta T	Destination	Source	Summary
M	1		VAX 4	DEMSA 1	MOP DL Request Memory Load
					Load No=129 Error=No Error
	2	4.9999	VAX 4	DEMSA 1	MOP DL Request Memory Load
					Load No=129 Error=No Error
	3	4.7999	VAX 4	DEMSA 1	MOP DL Request Memory Load
					Load No=129 Error=No Error
	4	5.1128	VAX 4	DEMSA 1	MOP DL Request Memory Load
					Load No=129 Error=No Error
	5	4.9572	VAX 4	DEMSA 1	MOP DL Request Memory Load
					Load No=129 Error=No Error
	6	4.7399	VAX 4	DEMSA 1	MOP DL Request Memory Load
					Load No=129 Error=No Error
	7	4.8799	VAX 4	DEMSA 1	MOP DL Request Memory Load
					Load No=129 Error=No Error

8	4.9800	VAX 4	DEMSA 1	MOP DL Request Memory Load
				Load No=129 Error=No Error
9	5.1816	AB0000010000	DEMSA 1	MOP DL Request Program
				Device Type=DLV
				Program Type=System
10	2.0426	DEMSA 1	VAX 4	MOP DL Assistance Volunteer
11	3.3058	AB0000010000	DEMSA 1	MOP DL Request Program
				Device Type=DLV
				Program Type=System
12	4.6198	AB0000010000	DEMSA 1	MOP DL Request Program
				Device Type=DLV
				Program Type=System
13	3.1393	DEMSA 1	VAX 4	MOP DL Assistance Volunteer
14	1.6806	AB0000010000	DEMSA 1	MOP DL Request Program
				Device Type=DLV
				Program Type=System
15	5.1000	AB0000010000	DEMSA 1	MOP DL Request Program
				Device Type=DLV
				Program Type=System
16	2.0724	DEMSA 1	VAX 4	MOP DL Assistance Volunteer
17	2.7576	AB0000010000	DEMSA 1	MOP DL Request Program
				Device Type=DLV
				Program Type=System
18	5.5500	AB0000010000	DEMSA 1	MOP DL Request Program
				Device Type=DLV
				Program Type=System
19	1.9935	DEMSA 1	VAX 4	MOP DL Assistance Volunteer

Trace 5.3.4a. DECnet Invisible Connection MOP Packets

Next, we allowed the analyzer to capture traffic on the top segment to determine the health of that segment. Our first conclusion was that routing nodes were properly transmitting their DRP Routing packets (see Trace 5.3.4b). DEMSA 1 multicast three DRP Router Hello packets (Frames 10-12) to the DECnet End Nodes, MOP

Remote Console, and DECnet level 1 Routers. VAX 3 multicast an Endnode Hello to the level 1 Routers (Frame 498); VAX 2 multicast a DRP Router Hello to the other level 1 Routers (Frame 680); and VAX 4 multicast a DRP Router Hello to the MOP Remote Console (Frame 730). All routing nodes were thus accounted for and could be heard on the top segment. Therefore, we identified no routing problems at that time.

Sniffer Network Analyzer data 18-Mar-91 at 14:17:12, INVIS_1.ENC, Pg 1

SUMMARY	Delta T	Destination	Source	Summary
10		AB0000040000	DEMSA 1	DRP ROUTER Hello
				S=1.901 BLKSZ=1498
11	0.0002	09002B020000	DEMSA 1	DRP ROUTER Hello
				S=1.901 BLKSZ=1498
12	0.0006	AB0000030000	DEMSA 1	DRP ROUTER Hello
				S=1.901 BLKSZ=1498
13	0.6116	VAX 4	DECnet003605	DRP DATA
				D=1.7 S=1.310 Visits=0
14	0.0038	DECnet003605	VAX 4	DRP DATA
				D=1.310 S=1.7 Visits=0
28	0.9336	DEMSA 1	DECnet00F505	DRP DATA
				D=1.7 S=1.501 Visits=0
29	0.0004	VAX 4	DEMSA 1	DRP DATA
				D=1.7 S=1.501 Visits=1
30	0.0051	DECnet00F505	VAX 4	DRP DATA
				D=1.501 S=1.7 Visits=0
31	0.1846	VAX 4	DECnet003D05	DRP DATA
				D=1.7 S=1.317 Visits=0
32	0.0039	DECnet003D05	VAX 4	DRP DATA
				D=1.317 S=1.7 Visits=0
428	0.9135	DECnet00F505	VAX 4	DRP DATA
				D=1.501 S=1.7 Visits=0
432	0.0077	VAX 4	DECnet00F505	DRP DATA
				D=1.7 S=1.501 Visits=0

433	0.0045	DECnet00F505	VAX 4	DRP DATA
				D=1.501 S=1.7 Visits=0
498	0.7122	AB0000030000	VAX 3	DRP ENDNODE Hello
				S=1.10 BLKSZ=1498
526	0.2734	VAX 4	DECnet002C05	DRP DATA
				D=1.7 S=1.300 Visits=0
528	0.0082	DECnet002C05	VAX 4	DRP DATA
				D=1.300 S=1.7 Visits=0
530	0.0061	VAX 4	DECnet002C05	DRP DATA
				D=1.7 S=1.300 Visits=0
536	0.0532	DECnet002C05	VAX 4	DRP DATA
				D=1.300 S=1.7 Visits=0
537	0.0210	VAX 4	DECnet002C05	DRP DATA
				D=1.7 S=1.300 Visits=0
680	0.9613	AB0000030000	VAX 2	DRP ROUTER Hello
				S=1.12 BLKSZ=1498
730	0.3719	09002B020000	VAX 4	DRP ROUTER Hello
				S=1.7 BLKSZ=1498

Trace 5.3.4b. DECnet Invisible Connection DRP Packets

The third step in the analysis was to see whether the downline load of the router image file from VAX 4 was being transmitted properly. Again, placing the analyzer on the top segment, we filtered the data to include only the MOP information between DEMSA 1 and VAX 4 (Trace 5.3.4c). The RC Boot Message is sent from VAX 4 to DEMSA 1 (Frame 60), and the router requests its program (Frame 62). The memory download begins in Frame 71 (Load number = 0) and continues to increment in Frames 73, 78, 84, 86, and so on. After each load, the router responds and asks for more data (Frames 72, 77, 83, 85, and so on.). We concluded that the host was operating normally. But the question still remained: Why didn't the router get the downline load? A second question was also unanswered: Why was Host 3 unable to communicate with Host 4 or 7 using DECnet?

Sniffer Network Analyzer data 18-Mar-91 at 14:17:12, INVIS_1.ENC, Pg 1

SUMMARY	Delta T	Destination	Source	Summary
60		DEMSA 1	VAX 4	MOP RC Boot Message
				Verif Code=0000000000000000
61	0.0031	DEC 11FD4D	VAX 4	MOP RC Boot Message
				Verif Code=0000000000000000
62	0.1083	VAX 4	DEMSA 1	MOP DL Request Program
				Device Type=DLV
				Program Type=System
71	0.2261	DEMSA 1	VAX 4	MOP DL Memory Load
				Load No=0
				Load Addr=00000000
72	0.0640	VAX 4	DEMSA 1	MOP DL Request Memory Load
				Load No=1
				Error=No Error
73	0.0166	DEMSA 1	VAX 4	MOP DL Memory Load
				Load No=1
				Load Addr=000005D4
74	0.0221	VAX 7	VAX 3	Ethertype=6007 (DEC LAVC)
75	0.0026	VAX 3	VAX 7	Ethertype=6007 (DEC LAVC)
77	0.0634	VAX 4	DEMSA 1	MOP DL Request Memory Load
				Load No=2
				Error=No Error
78	0.0090	DEMSA 1	VAX 4	MOP DL Memory Load
				Load No=2
				Load Addr=00000BA8
83	0.0726	VAX 4	DEMSA 1	MOP DL Request Memory Load
				Load No=3
				Error=No Error
84	0.0087	DEMSA 1	VAX 4	MOP DL Memory Load
				Load No=3
				Load Addr=0000117C

85	0.0713	VAX 4	DEMSA 1	MOP DL Request Memory Load
				Load No=4
				Error=No Error
86	0.0095	DEMSA 1	VAX 4	MOP DL Memory Load
				Load No=4
				Load Addr=00001750

Trace 5.3.4c. DECnet Invisible Connection MOP Download

The engineer finally discovered the answer through thoughtful consideration of the topology in question coupled with knowledge of the DECnet routing algorithms. VAX 3 was designated as an end node. Therefore, in order to communicate with another DECnet node, it needed to get its routing information from a designated router. VAX 3's designated router was VAX 2, on the other side of the fiber optic bridge. Thus, the path from VAX 3 to VAX 4 was VAX 3 to VAX 2 to VAX 4. It crossed the bridge twice. Because VAX 4 was a routing node, it didn't require the assistance of VAX 2 or the bridge to communicate with VAX 3. Since VAX 2 was properly sending out DRP Router Hello packets (review Frame 680 of Trace 5.3.4b), it appeared to be functioning properly.

The only internetwork element left was the bridge. Recall that the MOP requests from DEMSA 1 were received on the top segment, indicating that the bridge path from the bottom to the top segment was in place. Fiber optic bridges have two paths, however: transmit and receive. The transmit path (i.e. bottom segment to top segment) functioned properly—Trace 5.3.4a proved that. The only thing left to check was the bridge's receive path. After checking the fiber optic cable, we found a bad connector on the bridge's receive lead. This explained why the top segment could not communicate with the bottom segment, i.e. why the VAX 3 to VAX 2 to VAX 4 connection failed, and also why the VAX 4 to DEMSA 1 download failed. After replacing the fiber optic connector, the internetwork functioned properly. Although the DECnet connection had been there all along, the bad connector had made it invisible.

In this chapter, we have studied the internetwork capabilities of DECnet Phase IV, with a brief glimpse into the future of DECnet Phase V. References [5-29] through [5-33] provide further insight into what the future holds for this multiprotocol distributed architecture. With all of DECnet's features, it's not surprising that one of DEC's marketing themes is Connectivity!

5.4 References

[5-1] Digital Equipment Corporation. *DECnet Phase IV General Description*, order number AA-N149A-TC, May 1982.

[5-2] Malamud, Carl. *DEC Networks and Architectures*. New York: McGraw-Hill, 1989.

[5-3] Digital Equipment Corporation. *Digital's Networks: An Architecture With A Future*, order number EB-26013-42, 1984.

[5-4] Digital Equipment Corporation. *Telecommunications and Networks Buyer's Guide*, January-June 1991.

[5-5] Buss, Dennis. "The DECnet Architecture and the OSI Model." *LAN Times* (December 1989): 115-116.

[5-6] Harrison, Bradford T. "Multiprotocol Bridging and Routing." *DEC Professional* (June 1991): 112-117.

[5-7] Snellen, David M. "Making the DEC Connection to an IBM Environment." *Journal of Network Management*, Vol. 2 No. 1 (Spring 1990): 5-15.

[5-8] Lauck, Anthony G., David R. Oran, and Radia J. Perlman. "A Digital Network Architecture Overview." *Digital Technical Journal* (September 1986): 10-24.

[5-9] *The Ethernet: A Local Area Network Data Link Layer and Physical Layer Specification*, version 2.0. Published by DEC, Intel, and Xerox, DEC order number AA-K759B-TK, November 1982.

[5-10] Digital Equipment Corporation. *DECnet Phase IV Routing Layer Functional Specification*, order number AA-X435-TK, December 1983.

[5-11] Digital Equipment Corporation. *DECnet-DNA NSP Functional Specification*, version 4.0, order number AA-X439A-TK.

[5-12] Digital Equipment Corporation. *DNA Session Control Functional Specification*, order number AA-K182A-TK.

[5-13] Digital Equipment Corporation. *DNA Data Access Protocol Functional Specification*, version 5.6.0, order number AA-K177A-TK.

[5-14] Digital Equipment Corporation. *DNA Phase IV Network Management Functional Specification*, order number AA-X437A-TK, December 1983.

[5-15] Mann, Bruce E., Colin Strutt, and Mark F. Kempf. "Terminal Servers on Ethernet Local Area Networks." *Digital Technical Journal* (September 1986):73-87.

[5-16] Digital Equipment Corporation. *DECnet Phase IV Maintenance Operations Functional Specification*, order number AA-X436A-TK, December 1983.

[5-17] Buss, Dennis. "DECnet Address and Routing Functions." *LAN Times* (December 1989): 131-134.

[5-18] Institute of Electrical and Electronics Engineers. "Carrier Sense Multiple Access with Collision Detection (CSMA/CD) Access Method and Physical Layer Specifications." ISO 8802-3, ANSI/IEEE Std 802.3, 1988.

[5-19] Digital Equipment Corporation. *DECnet Digital Network Architecture (Phase V) General Description*, order number EK-DNAPV-GD, September 1987.

[5-20] Malamud, Carl. *Analyzing DECnet/OSI Phase V*. New York: Van Nostrand Reinhold, 1991.

[5-21] Bartee, Thomas C. *ISDN, DECnet, and SNA Communications*. Indianapolis, IN: Howard W. Sams & Company, 1989.

[5-22] Demar, Phil and Linda Porter. "Getting to Phase V." *Digital News Extra* (September 30, 1991): 14-18.

[5-23] Cox, John. "Getting Set for the Next DECnet." *Digital News* (January 8, 1990): 10,15,67.

[5-24] Brown, Jim. "Users Tackle Concepts of DECnet Phase V." *Network World* (March 4, 1991): 17-18.

[5-25] Malamud, Carl. "DEC set to Haul in DECnet V." *Network World* (April 29, 1991): 45,49-54.

[5-26] Harrison, Bradford T. "OSIing With DECnet Phase V." *DEC Professional* (April 1991): 130-134.

[5-27] Birkhead, Evan. "DECnet Outfitted With OSI Apparel." *LAN Computing* (July 1991): 1,9.

[5-28] Digital Equipment Corporation. *Network Troubleshooting Guide*, order number EK-339AA-GD-001, July 1989.

[5-29] King, Steven S. and Eric M. Hindin. "DECnet, A Peaceable Kingdom." *Data Communications* (September 1990): 79-96.

[5-30] Leben, Joe. "DEC's Naming Service: Directory Assistance for DECnet." *Data Communications* (September 1990): 99-102.

[5-31] Gillooly, Caryn. "Users Face Obstacles to Net Integration." *Network World* (March 4, 1991): 19-20.

[5-32] Clyde, Roberta. "DECnet Security," *DEC Professional* (April 1991):38-43.

[5-33] Hindin, Eric M. "It's Official: DEC and IBM Endorse Multivendor Networks." *Data Communications* (August 1991): 50-54.

CHAPTER 6

Troubleshooting IBM Token Ring/SNA Internetworks

Many organizations have selected IBM's System Network Architecture (SNA) as their predominate internetworking architecture for linking LANs and WANs worldwide. IBM's strong influence on, and support for, the IEEE 802.5 token ring LAN standard has resulted in a strong interest in that architecture as well. Just as Ethernet LANs and DECnet protocols are often used together, token ring and SNA protocols are closely associated through IBM's interest in both technologies. Like Ethernet, token ring workstations can extend their connectivity across multiple LANs via bridges. The IEEE 802.1d MAC Bridges standard provides a transparent bridge that connects multiple LANs into one large LAN. It also offers a source routing option that allows the workstation to define the path of transmitted frames through the bridged LAN. We'll begin our study by looking at the token ring protocols and the SNA architecture.

6.1 Token Ring/SNA Architecture and Protocols

This chapter will explore the internetworking capabilities of both token ring and SNA. The troubleshooting case studies will focus on the protocols and architectures of both of these areas as well. Let's begin by examining the token ring architecture and protocols.

6.1.1 Token Ring Architecture and Protocols

As its name implies, the token ring architecture connects stations into an electrical ring. A 24-bit token circulates around that ring, passing control of the network from one station to the next (see Figure G-5a in Appendix G). A station wishing to transmit attaches its data to the token, thereby changing the transmission into a frame (see Figure G-5b). After this frame travels around the ring to its desired destination, it returns to the sending station, which removes the frame and releases a new token. The next downstream station is then given the opportunity to play (i.e. attach data to a token making it a frame) or pass (repeat the token without sending data.) (For the purposes of this discussion, we will not consider the effects of other token ring mechanisms, such as token priorities or early token release.)

Volumes have been written about the IEEE 802.5 standard known as token ring [6-1]. *Inside the Token Ring* explores the architecture in depth [6-2]; *The IBM Token Ring Network* [6-3] considers market size and vendor directions; and *A C Programmer's Guide to the IBM Token Ring* [6-4] provides bit-level details. For information about mechanisms, such as token priorities and early token release, consult Chapter 6 of the *LAN Troubleshooting Handbook* [6-5] or Chapter 5 of the *LAN Protocol Handbook* [6-6].

6.1.2 Source Routing Protocol

Like Ethernet, all token ring networks have size limitations that determine the number of station attachments, the total ring length, the distances between repeaters, and so forth. What distinguishes the token ring architecture from Ethernet is the Source Routing protocol, defined by the 802.1 standard, that logically connects stations on different rings. The protocol gets its name from the fact that the source of the data (i.e. the sending station) supplies the route that the frame must take. The route may include multiple bridges and rings. When the source routing information is present in the frame, a bit, known as the *Route Information Indicator* (RII), is turned on. This bit alerts all the other stations and bridges to decode the route included in the frame.

The question is, "How does the sending station determine the path to its intended receiver, especially when that receiver may be several rings away?" The answer can be found within the source routing standard itself [6-7].

224

The sending station first attempts to locate its intended destination by transmitting at least one and perhaps more TEST or XID frames on the local ring. If no response is heard, the sending station concludes that the desired destination is not on the same ring. To discover the correct route to that remote destination, the originating station enters the Route Discovery process.

IBM's implementation of the Source Routing protocol, which is the defacto standard, uses two techniques, the All Routes Explorer (ARE) and the Spanning Tree Explorer (STE), to discover the correct route from source to destination stations. Consult IBM's *Token-Ring Network Architecture Reference* [6-8] for further details. Both techniques use a Logical Link Control (LLC) TEST or an Exchange ID (XID) frame. The two methods differ in the manner in which they transmit the discovery frame.

The All Routes Explorer (ARE) method, used by SNA, sends a TEST or XID frame to all rings. (In Figure 6-1a, the Routing Type (RT) bits within the Routing Control (RC) field are set to 10X, where X can be either a 0 or 1.) As the frame traverses the internetwork, it accumulates routing information from the bridges. It stores this information as Route Descriptors (review Figure 6-1a) that are 2 octets in length. Each descriptor contains a 12-bit LAN or ring ID and a 4-bit Bridge number, as shown in Figure 6-1b. When the destination station receives the frame, it returns a TEST or XID frame, including the accumulated routing information, to the originating station. The originating station chooses one of the returned routes as the preferred path. (The application determines the algorithm used to choose the preferred route, but it usually chooses the first returned path based on the assumption that the first path returned is the shortest.) The disadvantage of this method of route determination is that multiple copies of the TEST or XID frame can appear on the same ring coming from parallel bridges. As a result, the discovery process consumes additional internetwork resources.

The second technique, used by NetBIOS, is known as a *Spanning Tree Explorer* (STE) or single route broadcast frame. The frame transmits the TEST or XID frame in such a way that only one copy of the frame appears on each ring. The Routing Type bits are set to 11X, where X can be either a 0 or 1. The destination station receives one copy of the TEST or XID frame, then responds using the all-routes broadcast method. The frame's Routing Information (RI) field collects the routing information

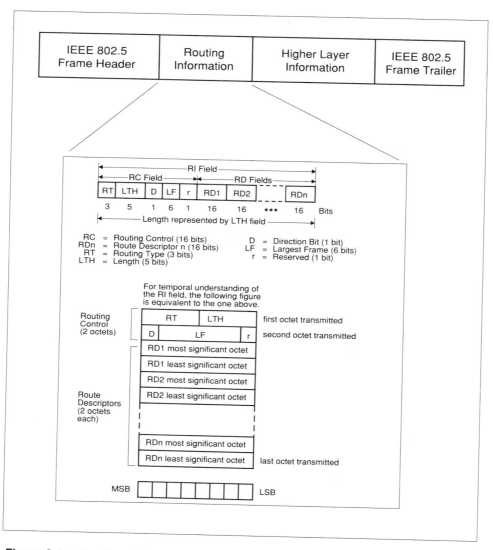

Figure 6-1a. Routing Information Within an IEEE 802.5 Frame

Reproduced from IEEE Draft Standard P802.5M/D5, IEEE Source Routing Supplement to IEEE MAC Bridges, copyright © 1991 by the Institute of Electrical and Electronics Engineers, Inc. with the permission of the IEEE. This is an unapproved draft and subject to change. Conformance to information contained in this document is at your own risk.

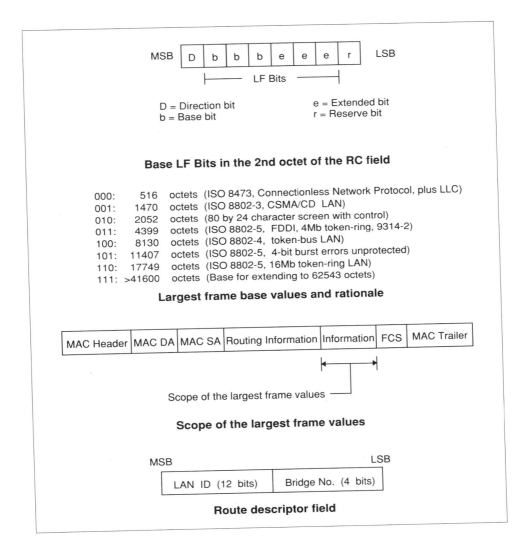

Figure 6-1b. Routing Information Field Details

Reproduced from IEEE Draft Standard P802.5M/D5, IEEE Source Routing Supplement to IEEE MAC Bridges, copyright © 1991 by the Institute of Electrical and Electronics Engineers, Inc. with the permission of the IEEE. This is an unapproved draft and subject to change. Conformance to information contained in this document is at your own risk.

along the return path. Depending on the internetwork topology, several responses are possible. The originating station chooses one of these responses as the preferred route.

For the next step in the discovery process, the originating station informs the destination of its selected path using a non-broadcast Specifically-Routed Frame (SRF) with Routing Type bits = 0XX, transmitted from the source to destination. When the destination responds, both ends are aware of the route.

Reviewing Figures 6-1a and 6-1b, you can see that other fields within the RC Field define other routing parameters. The Length (LTH) bits define the length of the RI field, and must be an even number between 2 and 30, inclusive. A maximum of 14 Route Descriptors (RDs) or 13 bridge hops is possible, though most of the current bridge implementations allow for a maximum of eight Route Descriptors, or seven bridge hops. Non-broadcast frames use the Direction (D) bit to determine how the Route Descriptors are interpreted. If D = 0 the Descriptors are interpreted by any entity that looks at the routing information field, such as a bridge, in the forward direction (i.e. RD1 to RD2 to . . . RDn). If D = 1 they are interpreted in the reverse direction (i.e. RDn to . . . RD2 to RD1). The D-bit is meaningful only for the Specifically-Routed Frames (SRF).

The Largest Frame (LF) bits determine the maximum size of the MAC information field that can be passed between source and destination stations. The LF bits are meaningful only to the ARE and STE frames. Coding of the base values is shown in Figure 6-1b; the extended values are further described in the standard.

For internetworks that include both source-routed (i.e. token ring) and non-source routed (i.e. Ethernet) bridging techniques, a method known as *Source Routing Transparent* (SRT) has been defined. This technique combines two algorithms: It performs Source Routing when the Routing Information is present (RII = 1) and Transparent Bridging as used in Ethernet when it is not (RII = 0). Further details on the SRT method are available in Chapter 1 of [6-9] and in the standard itself [6-7].

6.1.3 SNA Architecture

The SNA Architectural Model (see Figure 6-2) is a seven-layer model that is similar, though not identical, to the OSI Reference Model 7498. One reason for the differences is that SNA was first announced in 1974 and preceded the OSI Reference Model by several years. Although work began on the OSI Reference model in the late

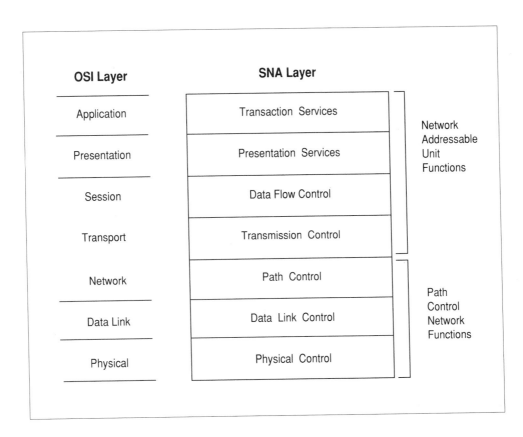

Figure 6-2. Comparing SNA with the OSI Reference Model

(Reprinted by permission from Systems Network Architecture Technical Overview GC30-3073-2 © by International Business Machines Corporation)

1970s, it wasn't published until 1984. A second reason was that IBM developed SNA as part of its proprietary networking architecture; the International Organization for Standardization designed the OSI Reference Model as an open standard for connecting multivendor networks. Since the two models came from different perspectives, it's not surprising that they would diverge somewhat. *Communications Architecture for Distributed Systems* [6-10] is considered the classic reference on SNA; IBM's documents [6-11] and [6-12] also provide substantial insights.

The SNA architecture divides its functional layers as follows. The lower three layers (Physical, Data Link Control, and Path Control) enable the end-user processes to transmit and receive data. For this reason, these layers are called the *Path Control Network Services*. The upper four layers (Transmission Control, Data Flow Control, Presentation Services, and Transaction Services) define the functions that the Network Addressable Units (NAUs) perform within a specific node. (There are three types of NAUs. The *System Service Control Point* (SSCP) resides within the host and manages the network. A *Physical Unit* (PU) represents an actual hardware or software device in the network. A *Logical Unit* (LU) is a logical addition through which end users can exchange data.)

For a more in-depth look, let's consider each layer separately. Further details can be found in *SNA: IBM's Networking Solution* [6-13].

6.1.4 SNA Physical and Data Link Layers

The SNA Physical and Data Link Layers perform the same functions as their OSI counterparts. They make the physical connection over point-to-point, multipoint, or token ring links, and they manage the reliable transfer of data across that link. IBM host-based internetworks typically use the Synchronous Data Link Control (SDLC) protocol on the link [6-14]. SDLC is the bit-oriented protocol from which the ISO High-level Data Link Control (HDLC) was derived. Current implementations of HDLC include the Link Access Procedure Balanced (LAPB) used with X.25 and the Link Access Procedure for the D-channel (LAPD) for ISDN. For LAN-based SNA internetworks, the IEEE 802.2 LLC becomes the Data Link Layer. (Readers interested in the integration of SNA hardware into token ring networks should consult References [6-15] through [6-18].) Other options include the S/370 channel for direct host connection and X.25 for access to Packet Switched Public Data Networks (PSPDNs).

6.1.5 SNA Path Control Layer

The SNA Path Control includes OSI Network Layer functions and also capabilities that extend into the Transport Layer. Path Control's primary job is routing; it establishes the path from the source to the destination of the data. The path through the internetwork is known as a *virtual route*. Path Control also controls the transmission of that data—for example, by providing flow control. The flow control on the path is called *virtual route pacing* and it prevents data traffic on a particular virtual route from becoming overly congested. The Path Control layer appends the Transmission Header (TH) onto the higher layer information. The transmitted package of data is then called the *Basic Transmission Unit* (BTU). Path Control also extends its reach into the OSI Transport Layer by providing end-to-end message-oriented services, such as multiplexing of higher layer messages called *Basic Information Units* (BIU) into the BTUs that traverse the internetwork. BTUs, in turn, are transported within SDLC, token ring, or some other Data Link Layer frame.

6.1.6 SNA Transmission Control Layer

The SNA Transmission Control Layer completes the OSI Transport Layer responsibilities and also extends into the OSI Session Layer. The Transmission Control Layer performs two primary functions. First, it controls the flow of messages between two end-user sessions. Thus, it assures that the Network Addressable Unit (NAU) process does not overwhelm the receiving NAU with more data than it can accommodate. A second function is to encrypt the data communicated in the session. These session-related control mechanisms are contained in a Request/Response header (RH) that is appended to the higher-layer data. The Transmission Control data entity is known as the Basic Information Unit (BIU).

6.1.7 SNA Data Flow Control Layer

The Data Flow Control completes the OSI Session Layer functions. The Data Flow Control Layer generates the Request/Response Unit (RU), which is the basic element of information transmitted between NAUs. It then synchronizes the dialogue between the two NAUs during a particular session. Examples of this layer's functions include correlating requests and responses, coordinating the send and receive modes of each NAU, and grouping RUs into "chains" and related chains into "brackets." A *chain* is a group of RUs that are grouped together to facilitate error control. A *bracket* is a series of related chains and the responses associated with those chains. An example of bracketing would be the transmission of a screen-full of data as a single entity.

6.1.8 SNA Presentation Services and Transaction Services Layers

The SNA Presentation Services and Transaction Services Layers are equivalent to the OSI Presentation and Application Layers, respectively, and support user applications. The Presentation Services are concerned with the format of data and provide protocols for program-to-program communication. The Transaction Services implement specific user applications, such as electronic mail and distributed databases.

6.1.9 The SNA Packet Format

Associated with each layer of the SNA architecture is Protocol Control Information (PCI) that provides the control information specific to that layer. For example, when the Transmission Control Layer of node A communicates with the Transmission Control Layer of node B, it is the Transmission Control Layer's PCI that makes the communication work. The PCI at each layer has a specific header, and each header has a defined place within the frame (see Figure 6-3).

The frame construction begins with a Request/Response Unit (RU), which originates at one of the higher layer SNA processes. RUs can be divided into four categories: Function Management, Data Flow Control, Session Control, and Network Control. Function Management Data (FMD) RUs either transfer user data or perform network services, such as initiating and terminating sessions. Data Flow Control RUs and Session Control RUs perform layer-specific functions. Network Control RUs are used for intra-network management and testing.

An RU category field within the Request/Response header designates the four types of RUs. When the RU is carrying FMD data, it includes a Function Management (FM) header specific to that data. A number of FM headers are defined: They control the flow of data within an LU; perform a management activity on that data, such as create or delete; or further describe the data that is to follow. IBM reference [6-19] provides details on the FM headers. To summarize, the RU and FM header are sent from the Data Flow Control Layer to the Transmission Control Layer where the Request/Response Header is added. The RU plus RH is known as a Basic Information Unit (BIU).

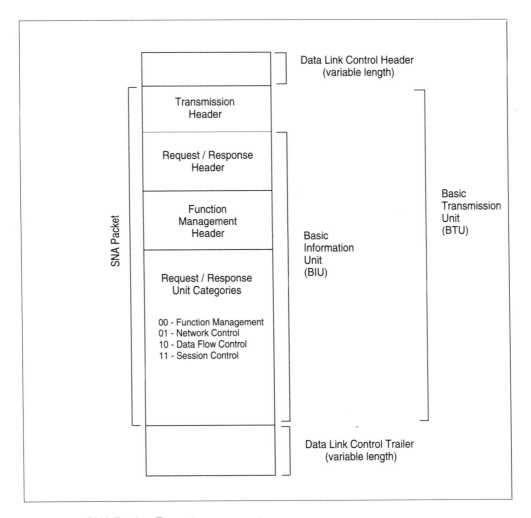

Figure 6-3. SNA Packet Format
(Reprinted by permission from Systems Network Architecture Reference Summary
(Document number GA27-3136-4) © by International Business Machines Corporation)

The next layer to process the information, the Path Control Layer, adds a Transmission Header (TH). The TH can take on one of several formats, each of which is uniquely identified with a Format Identifier (FID) number. These formats identify the type of machines (SNA, non-SNA, and so on), the type of nodes (PU type 1, 2, and so on), and other addressing and routing information necessary to get the data from its source to destination node. IBM references [6-20] and [6-21] describe FIDs in detail. Thus, an SNA packet would consist of the TH, RH, FMH, and RU. In SNA nomenclature, this data entity is called a Basic Transmission Unit (BTU). The Data Link Control Header and Trailer would then be appended to the BTU, and the complete frame would be ready for transmission.

6.2 Token Ring/SNA Protocol Analysis Techniques

As discussed in the previous section, Token Ring/SNA environments have a number of protocols that must be analyzed. When approaching an internetwork problem, consider the following analysis strategy:

1. Check the token ring Physical Layer for obvious problems. The trend in LAN architectures today is for most of the wiring to be concentrated at an intelligent hub located in a wiring closet. The advantage of a centralized hub is that you can diagnose much of the cable plant from a single location. The disadvantage is that all of the network's "eggs" are in one basket—the wiring closet. A power outage at a wiring closet or a failed fiber optic link between two closets can cause significant problems. So as you start the troubleshooting process, obtain the network documentation and consider any central points of vulnerability. References [6-22] through [6-24] present token ring configuration and troubleshooting guidelines.

2. If the internetwork includes SDLC links (WAN connections), check the status of those links. Many problems, such as slow response times, can be traced to retransmissions caused by noisy communication lines. Consider the WAN analyzers discussed in Chapter 2, and make sure to choose one that can test all your SDLC WAN links. Proteon, Inc. (Westborough, MA) and CrossComm Corporation (Marlboro, MA) discuss their WAN perspectives on SNA in References [6-25] and [6-26], respectively.

3. When troubleshooting token ring connections, look for significant MAC-layer events, which were detailed in Section 3.1.1. You should also be aware that the token ring architecture contains 25 MAC frames designed specifically for built-in token ring management. For example, a Duplicate Address Test frame indicates that a station wishes to join the ring. When this test fails it means that another station with the same address is already active. The Report Error frame reports routine and out of character events, such as retransmitted frames, to the Ring Error Monitor. Establish a benchmark for the Report Error Frames under normal conditions in order to identify abnormalities quickly. Other frames point to a clear problem; the Beacon, for instance, indicates a faulty transmitter or receiver at a node. For further details, consult the standard [6-1], Chapter 5 of Reference [6-6], or Chapter 2 of Reference [6-27]. Some of these MAC frames will be discussed in Section 6.3.1.

4. Many network administrators use Locally-Administered Addresses (LAAs) rather than the built-in ROM address for token ring network boards. If a particular workstation cannot enter the ring, a duplicate LAA is a possible culprit.

5. Identify significant events at the Logical Link Control (LLC) layer. These would include the route discovery process, which uses the TEST or XID frames, and host polling frames, which use the Receive Ready (RR) frames. Also look for LLC events that don't make sense, such as retransmitted frames or excessive times between frames. The lower layers (MAC and LLC) must be stable for the upper layers to function properly.

6. Identify the stations that are failing or somehow participating in the LLC or MAC-Layer significant events. Set the network analyzer to capture data to/from these workstations to further isolate the problem.

7. Look for significant SNA events that indicate communication to or from the host. Know how to recognize commands such as SNA Exchange ID (XID), Activate Physical Unit (ACTPU), Activate Logical Unit (ACTLU), and so on. The IBM reference [6-21] is a valuable guide to SNA protocols. If an SNA gateway connects the SNA host and a LAN, verify that the workstation-to-gateway and gateway-to-host communication is working.

8. Look for a negative SNA response from the host to a workstation request. A response such as "Function Not Supported" would indicate a workstation configuration error. Remember that the host is in charge, and workstations must obey the host's rules.

9. Utilize IBM's network management system, NetView, to monitor the overall health of the SNA environment, including rings, bridges, and SDLC links.

10. Take advantage of IBM's troubleshooting documentation. References [6-24], [6-28], [6-29], and [6-30] are excellent examples of the available resources.

With this outline for Token Ring/SNA analysis, let's put our techniques to use. We'll begin with some problems with source routing bridges.

6.3 Token Ring/SNA Internetwork Troubleshooting

Since SNA has been around for nearly two decades, we would expect the protocols to have developed a fair amount of complexity. IBM has not disappointed us, as you can see in Reference [6-20]. Since it would be impossible for this book to present an exhaustive tutorial, we will instead focus on several problems that can occur on token ring/SNA internetworks. The first example, however, provides an introduction to the protocols' operation by illustrating the process by which a PC emulates a host terminal.

6.3.1 Token Ring/SNA Terminal Emulation

Applications must use the Route Discovery process to make a connection to a station that is not on the local ring. Two types of discovery processes are available. The first sends a single route broadcast with an all routes broadcast return, as illustrated below. The second method, which will be discussed further in the next section, uses an all routes broadcast with a non-broadcast return. Either way, the sending station discovers all possible routes to its intended destination.

In this example, a workstation (designated Ray) wishes to attach to a remote SNA host. An extensive internetwork of token rings and bridges connects the two devices (see Figure 6-4). Before the workstation can make the connection, it must enter its local ring and become active on that ring. Next, it must discover the route

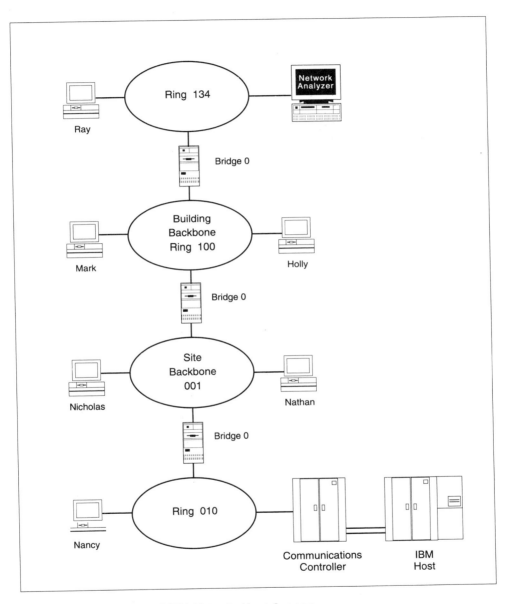

Figure 6-4. Token Ring / SNA Remote Host Access

to the remote host if it doesn't already know it. Third, it must establish a logical SNA session with the host. Now the workstation is prepared to access the desired host application.

The internetwork in question consists of four rings connected by three bridges. The workstation is attached to a departmental ring, designated Ring 134H. This ring connects via a bridge to the building backbone, Ring 100H. A third ring is the designated site backbone, Ring 001H. The host is connected to Ring 010H through an IBM 3745 communications controller. Since only one bridge connects each ring, all bridges are designated Bridge 0. (This configuration won't cause any addressing problems because each ring-bridge-ring path is unique, e.g. 134-0-100 is different from 100-0-001.) Let's trace the steps required to establish the connection to the remote host (Trace 6.3.1a). The SNA connection process discussed in this section is shown schematically in Figure 6-5.

Sniffer Network Analyzer data 22-Apr-91 at 13:03:32 file HOSTCONN.TRC Pg 1

SUMMARY		Delta T	Destination	Source	Summary
M	1		Ray	Ray	MAC Duplicate Address Test
	2	0.001	Ray	Ray	MAC Duplicate Address Test
	3	0.027	Config Srv	Ray	MAC Report SUA Change
	4	0.012	Broadcast	Ray	MAC Standby Monitor Present
	5	0.001	Param Server	Ray	MAC Request Initialization
	6	0.006	Ray	40007FF134F1	MAC Initialize Ring Station
	7	0.001	40007FF134F1	Ray	MAC Response
	8	0.096	Host	Ray	LLC C D=00 S=04 XID P
	9	0.001	Host	Ray	LLC C D=00 S=04 XID P
	10	0.001	Host	Ray	LLC C D=00 S=04 XID P
	11	0.001	Host	Ray	LLC C D=00 S=04 XID P
	12	0.010	Ray	Host	LLC R D=04 S=00 XID F
	13	0.001	Host	Ray	LLC C D=04 S=04 XID P
	14	0.025	Ray	Host	LLC R D=04 S=04 XID F
	15	0.001	Host	Ray	SNA XID Fmt 0 T2
	16	0.436	Ray	Host	LLC C D=04 S=04 SABME P

17	0.001	Host	Ray	LLC R D=04 S=04 UA F
18	0.009	Ray	Host	LLC C D=04 S=04 RR NR=0 P
19	0.000	Host	Ray	LLC R D=04 S=04 RR NR=0 F
20	0.079	Ray	Host	SNA C ACTPU PU5
21	0.001	Host	Ray	LLC R D=04 S=04 RR NR=1
22	0.002	Host	Ray	SNA R ACTPU
23	0.010	Ray	Host	LLC R D=04 S=04 RR NR=1
24	0.178	Ray	Host	SNA C NMVT Request RTM
25	0.001	Host	Ray	LLC R D=04 S=04 RR NR=2
26	0.001	Host	Ray	SNA R NMVT, Request err:
				Fct not supported
27	0.013	Ray	Host	LLC R D=04 S=04 RR NR=2
28	0.074	Ray	Host	SNA C ACTLU
29	0.001	Host	Ray	LLC R D=04 S=04 RR NR=3
30	0.002	Host	Ray	SNA R ACTLU
31	0.007	Ray	Host	LLC R D=04 S=04 RR NR=3
32	0.001	Host	Ray	SNA C NOTIFY
33	0.009	Ray	Host	LLC R D=04 S=04 RR NR=4
34	0.013	Ray	Host	SNA C ACTLU
35	0.001	Host	Ray	LLC R D=04 S=04 RR NR=4
36	0.001	Host	Ray	SNA R ACTLU
37	0.011	Ray	Host	SNA C ACTLU
38	0.001	Host	Ray	LLC R D=04 S=04 RR NR=5
39	0.001	Host	Ray	SNA R ACTLU, Path err:
				Unrecognzd dest.
40	0.010	Ray	Host	LLC R D=04 S=04 RR NR=6
41	0.122	Ray	Host	SNA R NOTIFY
42	0.001	Host	Ray	LLC R D=04 S=04 RR NR=6
43	0.007	Ray	Host	SNA C FMD user data
44	0.001	Host	Ray	LLC R D=04 S=04 RR NR=7
45	0.001	Host	Ray	SNA R FMD, Request err:
				Category not spprtd

46	0.009	Ray	Host	SNA C FMD user data
47	0.001	Host	Ray	LLC R D=04 S=04 RR NR=8
48	0.085	Host	Ray	SNA R FMD
49	0.007	Ray	Host	LLC R D=04 S=04 RR NR=8
50	5.741	Broadcast	Ray	MAC Standby Monitor Present
51	7.009	Broadcast	Ray	MAC Standby Monitor Present
52	6.999	Broadcast	Ray	MAC Standby Monitor Present
53	1.961	Host	Ray	LLC C D=04 S=04 DISC P
54	0.012	Ray	Host	LLC R D=04 S=04 UA F
55	5.015	Broadcast	Ray	MAC Standby Monitor Present

Trace 6.3.1a. SNA/Token Ring Terminal Emulation Summary

The trace begins with seven Medium Access Control (MAC) frames that result from the workstation's (Ray's) initialization onto Ring 134. In the first two frames, Ray sends a Duplicate Address Test (DAT) frame to look for any other workstation that might have an identical hardware address. The DAT frame (or frames) is sent with identical source and destination addresses, i.e. from Ray to Ray on the local ring (ring number 134H). After the frame travels around the ring, Ray's workstation examines the Address Recognized Indicator (ARI) bits within the Frame Status field. If ARI = 1, the initialization process halts to avoid the confusion that would result from two identically-addressed workstations being on the same network segment. Presumably a higher lay application would determine what to do should the initialization halt. If ARI = 0, no duplicate workstations exist and the initialization proceeds. In this example, the initialization procedes and Ray reports a change to his Stored Upstream Address (SUA) register to the Configuration Report Server (CRS). The CRS is a functional address that maintains a database of workstations currently active on the network. (This trace only captures the frames to/from Ray's workstation. If we had captured traffic from all workstations, you would see that a second Report SUA Change frame was sent to the CRS from Ray's downstream neighbor. In other words, Ray reports the existence of his new upstream neighbor, and Ray's downstream neighbor reports Ray.) Next, the workstation participates in a Ring Poll, indicated by the transmission of the Standby Monitor Present (SMP) frame. (Again, the Active Monitor workstation's and other Standby Monitor workstations' transmissions are not shown.) Ray then requests his initialization parameters (e.g. Local Ring Number = 134) from the Ring Parameter Server in Frame 5, and the response is returned in Frame 6. Ray's acknowledgement is sent in Frame 7, indicating that he is now a functioning member of Ring 134.

Ray must now establish communication with the remote host. To discover the route to the host, the workstation begins by sending at least one (in this case, three) Logical Link Control (LLC) Exchange Identification (XID) frames (see Trace 6.3.1b, Frames 8 through 10). In each of these frames, the poll bit is set, which indicates that a response is necessary. In addition, the routing information for Frames 8 through 10 is set to non-broadcast (a specific route through the internetwork), but without any route designators within the Routing Information field. The LLC header specifies a DSAP = 00H (null SAP) and an SSAP = 04H (SNA Path Control-Individual). (Appendix F lists commonly used SAPs.) Unfortunately, no response comes back, which indicates to Ray's workstation that the desired host is not on the same ring.

Sniffer Network Analyzer data 22-Apr-91 at 13:03:32 file HOSTCONN.TRC Pg 1

- - - - - - - - - - - - - - - Frame 8 - - - - - - - - - - - - - - - - -

DLC: —— DLC Header ——

DLC:

DLC: Frame 8 arrived at 13:04:10.253; frame size is 22 (0016 hex) bytes.

DLC: AC: Frame priority 0, Reservation priority 0, Monitor count 1

DLC: FC: LLC frame, PCF attention code: None

DLC: FS: Addr recognized indicators: 00, Frame copied indicators: 00

DLC: Destination = Station 400020600209, Host

DLC: Source   = Station 400004002320, Ray

DLC:

RI : —— Routing Indicators ——

RI :

RI : Routing control = 02

RI :   000. .... = Non-broadcast

the Active Monitor workstation's and other Standby Monitor workstations' transmissions are not shown.) Ray then requests his initialization parameters (e.g. Local Ring Number = 134) from the Ring Parameter Server in Frame 5, and the response is returned in Frame 6. Ray's acknowledgement is sent in Frame 7, indicating that he is now a functioning member of Ring 134.

Ray must now establish communication with the remote host. To discover the route to the host, the workstation begins by sending at least one (in this case, three) Logical Link Control (LLC) Exchange Identification (XID) frames (see Trace 6.3.1b, Frames 8 through 10). In each of these frames, the poll bit is set, which indicates that a response is necessary. In addition, the routing information for Frames 8 through 10 is set to non-broadcast (a specific route through the internetwork), but without any route designators within the Routing Information field. The LLC header specifies a DSAP = 00H (null SAP) and an SSAP = 04H (SNA Path Control-Individual). (Appendix F lists commonly used SAPs.) Unfortunately, no response comes back, which indicates to Ray's workstation that the desired host is not on the same ring.

```
Sniffer Network Analyzer data 22-Apr-91 at 13:03:32 file HOSTCONN.TRC Pg 1
- - - - - - - - - - - - - - - - Frame 8 - - - - - - - - - - - - - - - - -
DLC: —— DLC Header ——
DLC:
DLC:  Frame 8 arrived at  13:04:10.253; frame size is 22 (0016 hex) bytes.
DLC:  AC: Frame priority 0,  Reservation priority 0,  Monitor count 1
DLC:  FC: LLC frame,  PCF attention code: None
DLC:  FS: Addr recognized indicators: 00, Frame copied indicators: 00
DLC:  Destination = Station 400020600209, Host
DLC:  Source     = Station 400004002320, Ray
DLC:
RI :  —— Routing Indicators ——
RI :
RI :  Routing control = 02
RI :      000. .... = Non-broadcast
```

RI :   ...0 0010 = RI length is 2

RI : Routing control = 00

RI :   0... .... = Forward direction

RI :   .000 .... = Largest frame is 516

RI :   .... 0000 = Reserved

RI :

LLC: —— LLC Header ——

LLC:

LLC: DSAP = 00, SSAP = 04, Command, Unnumbered frame: XID, POLL

LLC:

LLC: IEEE 802.2 Basic Format ID = 81

LLC: Class of service = 03

LLC: ....1 = Class I (connectionless)

LLC: .... ..1. = Class II (connection-oriented)

LLC: Window size = 127

- - - - - - - - - - - - - - - - Frame 9 - - - - - - - - - - - - - - - - -

DLC: —— DLC Header ——

DLC:

DLC: Frame 9 arrived at 13:04:10.254; frame size is 22 (0016 hex) bytes.

DLC: AC: Frame priority 0, Reservation priority 0, Monitor count 1

DLC: FC: LLC frame, PCF attention code: None

DLC: FS: Addr recognized indicators: 00, Frame copied indicators: 00

DLC: Destination = Station 400020600209, Host

DLC: Source   = Station 400004002320, Ray

DLC:

RI : —— Routing Indicators ——

RI :

RI : Routing control = 02

RI :   000. .... = Non-broadcast

RI :   ...0 0010 = RI length is 2

RI : Routing control = 00

RI : 0... .... = Forward direction

RI : .000 .... = Largest frame is 516

RI : .... 0000 = Reserved

RI :

LLC: —— LLC Header ——

LLC:

LLC: DSAP = 00, SSAP = 04, Command, Unnumbered frame: XID, POLL

LLC:

LLC: IEEE 802.2 Basic Format ID = 81

LLC: Class of service = 03

LLC: ....1 = Class I (connectionless)

LLC: .... ..1. = Class II (connection-oriented)

LLC: Window size = 127

- - - - - - - - - - - - - - - - Frame 10 - - - - - - - - - - - - - - - -

DLC: —— DLC Header ——

DLC:

DLC: Frame 10 arrived at 13:04:10.255; frame size is 22 (0016 hex) bytes.

DLC: AC: Frame priority 0, Reservation priority 0, Monitor count 1

DLC: FC: LLC frame, PCF attention code: None

DLC: FS: Addr recognized indicators: 00, Frame copied indicators: 00

DLC: Destination = Station 400020600209, Host

DLC: Source = Station 400004002320, Ray

DLC:

RI : —— Routing Indicators ——

RI :

RI : Routing control = 02

RI : 000. .... = Non-broadcast

RI : ...0 0010 = RI length is 2

RI : Routing control = 00

RI : 0... .... = Forward direction

RI : .000 .... = Largest frame is 516

RI : .... 0000 = Reserved

RI :

LLC: ——— LLC Header ———

LLC:

LLC: DSAP = 00, SSAP = 04, Command, Unnumbered frame: XID, POLL

LLC:

LLC: IEEE 802.2 Basic Format ID = 81

LLC: Class of service = 03

LLC: ....1 = Class I (connectionless)

LLC: .... ..1. = Class II (connection-oriented)

LLC: Window size = 127

- - - - - - - - - - - - - - - Frame 11 - - - - - - - - - - - - - - - - -

DLC: ——— DLC Header ———

DLC:

DLC: Frame 11 arrived at 13:04:10.256; frame size is 22 (0016 hex) bytes.

DLC: AC: Frame priority 0, Reservation priority 0, Monitor count 1

DLC: FC: LLC frame, PCF attention code: None

DLC: FS: Addr recognized indicators: 11, Frame copied indicators: 11

DLC: Destination = Station 400020600209, Host

DLC: Source   = Station 400004002320, Ray

DLC:

RI : ——— Routing Indicators ———

RI :

RI : Routing control = C2

RI :   110. .... = Single-route broadcast, all-routes broadcast return

RI :   ...0 0010 = RI length is 2

RI : Routing control = 00

RI :   0... .... = Forward direction

RI :   .000 .... = Largest frame is 516

RI :   .... 0000 = Reserved

RI :

LLC: ——— LLC Header ———

LLC:

LLC: DSAP = 00, SSAP = 04, Command, Unnumbered frame: XID, POLL

LLC:

LLC: IEEE 802.2 Basic Format ID = 81

LLC: Class of service = 03

LLC: ....1 = Class I (connectionless)

LLC: .... ..1. = Class II (connection-oriented)

LLC: Window size = 127

- - - - - - - - - - - - - - - Frame 12 - - - - - - - - - - - - - - - -

DLC: ——— DLC Header ———

DLC:

DLC: Frame 12 arrived at 13:04:10.266; frame size is 30 (001E hex) bytes.

DLC: AC: Frame priority 0, Reservation priority 0, Monitor count 0

DLC: FC: LLC frame, PCF attention code: None

DLC: FS: Addr recognized indicators: 00, Frame copied indicators: 00

DLC: Destination = Station 400004002320, Ray

DLC: Source   = Station 400020600209, Host

DLC:

RI : ——— Routing Indicators ———

RI :

RI : Routing control = 0A

RI :   000. .... = Non-broadcast

RI :   ...0 1010 = RI length is 10

RI : Routing control = 80

RI :   1... .... = Backward direction

RI :   .000 .... = Largest frame is 516

RI :   .... 0000 = Reserved

RI : Ring number 134 via bridge 0

RI : Ring number 100 via bridge 0

RI : Ring number 001 via bridge 0

RI : Ring number 010

RI :

LLC: —— LLC Header ——

LLC:

LLC: DSAP = 04, SSAP = 00, Response, Unnumbered frame: XID, FINAL

LLC:

LLC: IEEE 802.2 Basic Format ID = 81

LLC: Class of service = 03

LLC: ....1 = Class I (connectionless)

LLC: .... ..1. = Class II (connection-oriented)

LLC: Window size = 127

- - - - - - - - - - - - - - - Frame 13 - - - - - - - - - - - - - - - -

DLC: —— DLC Header ——

DLC:

DLC: Frame 13 arrived at 13:04:10.268; frame size is 27 (001B hex) bytes.

DLC: AC: Frame priority 0, Reservation priority 0, Monitor count 1

DLC: FC: LLC frame, PCF attention code: None

DLC: FS: Addr recognized indicators: 11, Frame copied indicators: 11

DLC: Destination = Station 400020600209, Host

DLC: Source   = Station 400004002320, Ray

DLC:

RI : —— Routing Indicators ——

RI :

RI : Routing control = 0A

RI :   000. .... = Non-broadcast

RI :   ...0 1010 = RI length is 10

RI : Routing control = 00

RI :   0... .... = Forward direction

RI :   .000 .... = Largest frame is 516

RI :   .... 0000 = Reserved

RI : Ring number 134 via bridge 0

RI : Ring number 100 via bridge 0

RI : Ring number 001 via bridge 0

RI : Ring number 010

RI :

LLC: —— LLC Header ——

LLC:

LLC: DSAP = 04, SSAP = 04, Command, Unnumbered frame: XID, POLL

LLC:

- - - - - - - - - - - - - - - - Frame 14 - - - - - - - - - - - - - - - - - -

DLC: —— DLC Header ——

DLC:

DLC: Frame 14 arrived at 13:04:10.294; frame size is 27 (001B hex) bytes.

DLC: AC: Frame priority 0, Reservation priority 0, Monitor count 0

DLC: FC: LLC frame, PCF attention code: None

DLC: FS: Addr recognized indicators: 00, Frame copied indicators: 00

DLC: Destination = Station 400004002320, Ray

DLC: Source   = Station 400020600209, Host

DLC:

RI : —— Routing Indicators ——

RI :

RI : Routing control = 0A

RI :   000. .... = Non-broadcast

RI :   ...0 1010 = RI length is 10

RI : Routing control = 80

RI :   1... .... = Backward direction

RI :   .000 .... = Largest frame is 516

RI :   .... 0000 = Reserved

RI : Ring number 134 via bridge 0

RI : Ring number 100 via bridge 0

RI : Ring number 001 via bridge 0

RI : Ring number 010

RI :

LLC: —— LLC Header ——

LLC:

LLC: DSAP = 04, SSAP = 04, Response, Unnumbered frame: XID, FINAL

LLC:

Trace 6.3.1b. SNA/Token Ring Terminal Emulation Routing Details

In Frame 11 the workstation initiates the route discovery process by transmitting a single-route LLC XID broadcast (one copy of the XID frame per ring) and requesting an all-routes broadcast return. The host responds in Frame 12 with the route information that was collected along the way. (Note that if multiple paths had existed the workstation could have received multiple responses, and the originating station would choose one of them as the desired route. With this internetwork, however (review Figure 6-4), only one path between Ray and the host is possible.) The resulting route is:

Ring number 134 via bridge 0
Ring number 100 via bridge 0
Ring number 001 via bridge 0
Ring number 010

Ray's workstation tests the route in Frame 13 (LLC XID, P) and receives a confirmation of its correctness (XID, F) in Frame 14. Note that the DSAP = 04H (SNA Path Control-Individual) is specified. The route discovery process is now complete. The Source Routing standard has created a great deal of interest among network designers and managers. Those readers desiring additional information on this subject should check out recent journal articles, References [6-30] through [6-40].

The only remaining issue is the establishment of the workstation to host session. The workstation initiates this process in Frame 15 (Trace 6.3.1a) with an SNA XID frame. The host sends a Set Asynchronous Balanced Mode Extended (SABME) command in Frame 16, which Ray's workstation acknowledges in Frame 17. The host then activates the Physical Unit (ACTPU in Frame 20); sends a Network Management Vector Transport request that is not supported at the workstation

(Frames 24 and 26); and then activates one LU (Frame 30) and a second LU (Frame 34). The host attempts to open a third LU (Frame 37), but the workstation cannot support it. The session initiation is completed when the function management data (FMD) is sent from the host to the workstation (Frames 43 and 46—see Trace 6. 3.1c) and the message "TERMINAL R4002322—WELCOME TO CORPORATE COMPUTING" appears on the workstation screen. The path to the host is now established physically and logically, and the workstation and host are communicating. Note the order of the data within the SNA packet sent from the host: Token ring header, Routing Information, Transmission Header, Request Header, Function Management Data.

In the next two examples, we will study what happens when the source routing options are not properly used.

Sniffer Network Analyzer data 22-Apr-91 at 13:03:32, HOSTCONN.TRC, Pg 1

- - - - - - - - - - - - - - - - Frame 43 - - - - - - - - - - - - - - - - -

SUMMARY	Delta T	Destination	Source	Summary
43	0.007	Ray	Host	DLC AC=10, FC=40, FS=00
				RI Back (134)-0-(100)-0-
				(001)-0-(010)
				LLC C D=04 S=04 I NR=6 NS=6
				SNA C FMD user data

DLC: —— DLC Header ——

DLC:

DLC: Frame 43 arrived at 13:04:11.299; frame size is 90 (005A hex) bytes.

DLC: AC: Frame priority 0, Reservation priority 0, Monitor count 0

DLC: FC: LLC frame, PCF attention code: None

DLC: FS: Addr recognized indicators: 00, Frame copied indicators: 00

DLC: Destination = Station 400004002320, Ray

DLC: Source   = Station 400020600209, Host

DLC:

RI : —— Routing Indicators ——

RI :

RI : Routing control = 0A

RI :   000. .... = Non-broadcast

RI :   ...0 1010 = RI length is 10

RI : Routing control = 80

RI :   1... .... = Backward direction

RI :   .000 .... = Largest frame is 516

RI :   .... 0000 = Reserved

RI : Ring number 134 via bridge 0

RI : Ring number 100 via bridge 0

RI : Ring number 001 via bridge 0

RI : Ring number 010

RI :

LLC: —— LLC Header ——

LLC:

LLC: DSAP = 04, SSAP = 04, Command, I frame, N(R) = 6, N(S) = 6

LLC:

SNA: —— SNA Transmission Header ——

SNA:

SNA: Format identification (FID) = 2

SNA:

SNA: Header flags = 2C

SNA: 0010 .... = Format identification

SNA: .... 11.. = Only segment

SNA: .... ..0. = Address field negotiation flag

SNA: ....0 = Normal flow

SNA: Destination address = 03

SNA: Origin   address = 00

SNA: Sequence number = 1

SNA:

SNA: —— SNA Request Header (RH) ——

SNA:

```
SNA:  RH byte 0       = 03
SNA:        0... .... = Command
SNA:        .00. .... = RU category is 'function management data'
SNA:        .... 0... = No header follows
SNA:        .... .0.. = Sense data not included
SNA:        .... ..11 = Only RU in chain
SNA:  RH byte 1       = 80
SNA:        1.00 .... = Definite response requested
SNA:        .... ..0. = Response bypasses TC queues
SNA:        .... ...0 = Pacing indicator
SNA:  RH byte 2       = 00
SNA:        0... .... = Begin bracket indicator
SNA:        .0.. .... = End bracket indicator
SNA:        .... ...0 = Conditional end bracket indicator
SNA:        ..0. .... = Change direction indicator
SNA:        .... 0... = Character code selection indicator
SNA:        .... .0.. = Enciphered data indicator
SNA:        .... ..0. = Padded data indicator
SNA:
SNA:  —— SNA FMD-RU (Function Management Data) ——
SNA:
SNA:  [53 bytes of FMD character-coded data]
SNA:
```

```
ADDR  HEX                                              EBCDIC
0000  10 40 40 00 04 00 23 20 C0 00 20 60 02 09 0A 80  . ......{..-....
0010  13 40 10 00 00 10 01 00 04 04 0C 0C 2C 00 03 00  . .............
0020  00 01 03 80 00 15 E3 C5 D9 D4 C9 D5 C1 D3 40 D9  ......TERMINAL R
0030  F4 F0 F0 F2 F3 F2 F2 40 60 60 40 E6 C5 D3 C3 D6  4002322 — WELCO
0040  D4 C5 40 E3 D6 40 C3 D6 D9 D7 D6 D9 C1 E3 C5 40  ME TO CORPORATE
0050  C3 D6 D4 D7 E4 E3 C9 D5 C7 15                    COMPUTING.
```

Trace 6.3.1c. SNA/Token Ring Connection Details

6.3.2 Token Ring/SNA Source (mis)routed Frames

The previous section discussed the type of route discovery process in which a single route is broadcast with an all routes broadcast return. This section looks at an all routes broadcast with a non-broadcast return. Specifically, this case study deals with what happens when more routes are returned than the sending station can handle.

In this case, a workstation running a 3270 emulation program wishes to connect to a remote host (see Figure 6-6). Between the workstation and host are a number of rings, some of which are connected with parallel bridges. When the workstation attempts to access the host, it receives no response, i.e. the CRT is still blank. When the analyzer was placed on the workstation ring (ring number 221), the MAC-Layer station initialization frame (Duplicate Address Test, Request Initialization, etc.) appeared normal (Frames 172 through 178 in Trace 6.3.2a). NetBIOS frames are transmitted next, looking for a particular name (BL01636) in Frames 180 through 193. In Frame 196 the Discovery Process begins, with a total of eight responses returned (Frames 197 through 204). According to Figure 6-5, the SNA connection should be initialized next, but that step never occurs. Instead, the Route Discovery Process starts over (Frames 213 through 221). A route is selected in Frame 222, but the host never confirms this chosen route.

Sniffer Network Analyzer data 3-Apr-91 at 08:45:58, GRUB221B.TRC, Pg 1

SUMMARY	Delta T	Destination	Source	Summary
172	7.201	Workstation	Workstation	MAC Duplicate Address Test
173	0.001	Workstation	Workstation	MAC Duplicate Address Test
174	0.355	Config Srv	Workstation	MAC Report SUA Change
175	0.011	Broadcast	Workstation	MAC Standby Monitor Present
176	0.002	Param Server	Workstation	MAC Request Initialization
177	0.009	Workstation	40007FF221F1	MAC Initialize Ring Station
178	0.002	40007FF221F1	Workstation	MAC Response
179	6.933	Broadcast	Workstation	MAC Standby Monitor Present
180	4.771	NetBIOS	Workstation	NETB Check name BL01636
181	1.312	NetBIOS	Workstation	NETB Check name BL01636

253

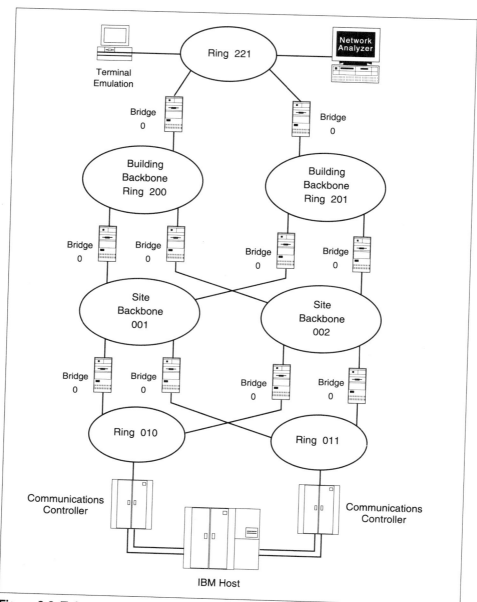

Figure 6-6. Token Ring/SNA Remote Terminal Emulation

182	0.904	Broadcast	Workstation	MAC Standby Monitor Present
183	0.095	NetBIOS	Workstation	NETB Check name BL01636
184	1.504	NetBIOS	Workstation	NETB Check name BL01636<03>
185	1.494	NetBIOS	Workstation	NETB Check name BL01636<03>
186	0.999	NetBIOS	Workstation	NETB Check name BL01636<03>
187	1.504	NetBIOS	Workstation	NETB Check name BL01636<00>
188	1.409	Broadcast	Workstation	MAC Standby Monitor Present
189	0.100	NetBIOS	Workstation	NETB Check name BL01636<00>
190	0.999	NetBIOS	Workstation	NETB Check name BL01636<00>
191	1.504	NetBIOS	Workstation	NETB Check name BL01636<05>
192	1.495	NetBIOS	Workstation	NETB Check name BL01636<05>
193	0.999	NetBIOS	Workstation	NETB Check name BL01636<05>
194	1.913	Broadcast	Workstation	MAC Standby Monitor Present
195	6.998	Broadcast	Workstation	MAC Standby Monitor Present
196	6.566	Host	Workstation	LLC C D=00 S=04 XID P
197	0.014	Workstation	Host	LLC R D=04 S=00 XID F
198	0.001	Workstation	Host	LLC R D=04 S=00 XID F
199	0.001	Workstation	Host	LLC R D=04 S=00 XID F
200	0.001	Workstation	Host	LLC R D=04 S=00 XID F
201	0.001	Workstation	Host	LLC R D=04 S=00 XID F
202	0.001	Workstation	Host	LLC R D=04 S=00 XID F
203	0.000	Workstation	Host	LLC R D=04 S=00 XID F
204	0.000	Workstation	Host	LLC R D=04 S=00 XID F
205	0.420	Broadcast	Workstation	MAC Standby Monitor Present
206	0.437	Host	Workstation	LLC C D=04 S=04 XID P
207	0.029	Workstation	Host	LLC R D=04 S=04 XID F
208	0.029	Host	Workstation	LLC C D=04 S=04 XID P
209	0.016	Workstation	Host	LLC R D=04 S=04 XID F
210	0.037	Host	Workstation	LLC C D=04 S=04 XID P
211	6.428	Broadcast	Workstation	MAC Standby Monitor Present
212	7.018	Broadcast	Workstation	MAC Standby Monitor Present
213	4.212	Host	Workstation	LLC C D=00 S=04 XID P

214	0.012	Workstation	Host	LLC R D=04 S=00 XID F
215	0.001	Workstation	Host	LLC R D=04 S=00 XID F
216	0.001	Workstation	Host	LLC R D=04 S=00 XID F
217	0.001	Workstation	Host	LLC R D=04 S=00 XID F
218	0.000	Workstation	Host	LLC R D=04 S=00 XID F
219	0.000	Workstation	Host	LLC R D=04 S=00 XID F
220	0.000	Workstation	Host	LLC R D=04 S=00 XID F
221	0.004	Workstation	Host	LLC R D=04 S=00 XID F
222	0.853	Host	Workstation	LLC C D=04 S=04 XID P
223	0.051	Host	Workstation	LLC C D=04 S=04 XID P
224	0.052	Host	Workstation	LLC C D=04 S=04 XID P
225	0.055	Host	Workstation	LLC C D=04 S=04 XID P
226	0.059	Host	Workstation	LLC C D=04 S=04 XID P
227	0.055	Host	Workstation	LLC C D=04 S=04 XID P
228	0.054	Host	Workstation	LLC C D=04 S=04 XID P
229	0.052	Host	Workstation	LLC C D=04 S=04 XID P
230	1.534	Broadcast	Workstation	MAC Standby Monitor Present
231	6.998	Broadcast	Workstation	MAC Standby Monitor Present
232	6.998	Broadcast	Workstation	MAC Standby Monitor Present
233	7.013	Broadcast	Workstation	MAC Standby Monitor Present

Trace 6.3.2a. Token Ring/SNA Failed Host Connection

The details of the Routing Information field indicate a total of eight paths between workstation and host (see Trace 6.3.2b):

frame 197:	221-0-200-0-002-0-011
frame 198:	221-0-200-0-002-0-010
frame 199:	221-0-201-0-001-0-011
frame 200:	221-0-201-0-001-0-010
frame 201:	221-0-201-0-002-0-011
frame 202:	221-0-201-0-002-0-010
frame 203:	221-0-200-0-001-0-010
frame 204:	221-0-200-0-001-0-011

Sniffer Network Analyzer data 3-Apr-90 at 8:45:58, file GRUB221B.TRC, Pg 1

- - - - - - - - - - - - - - - - Frame 196 - - - - - - - - - - - - - - - - -

RI : —— Routing Indicators ——

RI :

RI : Routing control = 82

RI :   100. .... = All-routes broadcast, non-broadcast return

RI :   ...0 0010 = RI length is 2

RI : Routing control = 00

RI :   0... .... = Forward direction

RI :   .000 .... = Largest frame is 516

RI :   .... 0000 = Reserved

RI :

- - - - - - - - - - - - - - - Frame 197 - - - - - - - - - - - - - - - - -

RI : —— Routing Indicators ——

RI :

RI : Routing control = 0A

RI :   000. .... = Non-broadcast

RI :   ...0 1010 = RI length is 10

RI : Routing control = 80

RI :   1... .... = Backward direction

RI :   .000 .... = Largest frame is 516

RI :   .... 0000 = Reserved

RI : Ring number 221 via bridge 0

RI : Ring number 200 via bridge 0

RI : Ring number 002 via bridge 0

RI : Ring number 011

RI :

- - - - - - - - - - - - - - - Frame 198 - - - - - - - - - - - - - - - -

RI : —— Routing Indicators ——

RI :

RI : Routing control = 0A

RI :   000. .... = Non-broadcast

RI :   ...0 1010 = RI length is 10

RI : Routing control = 80

RI :   1... .... = Backward direction

RI :   .000 .... = Largest frame is 516

RI :   .... 0000 = Reserved

RI : Ring number 221 via bridge 0

RI : Ring number 200 via bridge 0

RI : Ring number 002 via bridge 0

RI : Ring number 010

RI :

- - - - - - - - - - - - - - Frame 199 - - - - - - - - - - - - - - - -

RI : —— Routing Indicators ——

RI :

RI : Routing control = 0A

RI :   000. .... = Non-broadcast

RI :   ...0 1010 = RI length is 10

RI : Routing control = 80

RI :   1... .... = Backward direction

RI :   .000 .... = Largest frame is 516

RI :   .... 0000 = Reserved

RI : Ring number 221 via bridge 0

RI : Ring number 201 via bridge 0

RI : Ring number 001 via bridge 0

RI : Ring number 011

RI :

- - - - - - - - - - - - - - - Frame 200 - - - - - - - - - - - - - - - - -

RI : —— Routing Indicators ——

RI :

RI : Routing control = 0A

RI :   000. .... = Non-broadcast

RI :   ...0 1010 = RI length is 10

RI : Routing control = 80

RI :   1... .... = Backward direction

RI :   .000 .... = Largest frame is 516

RI :   .... 0000 = Reserved

RI : Ring number 221 via bridge 0

RI : Ring number 201 via bridge 0

RI : Ring number 001 via bridge 0

RI : Ring number 010

RI :

- - - - - - - - - - - - - - - Frame 201 - - - - - - - - - - - - - - - - -

RI : —— Routing Indicators ——

RI :

RI : Routing control = 0A

RI :   000. .... = Non-broadcast

RI :   ...0 1010 = RI length is 10

RI : Routing control = 80

RI :   1... .... = Backward direction

RI :   .000 .... = Largest frame is 516

RI :   .... 0000 = Reserved

RI : Ring number 221 via bridge 0

RI : Ring number 201 via bridge 0

RI : Ring number 002 via bridge 0

RI : Ring number 011

RI :

- - - - - - - - - - - - - - - Frame 202 - - - - - - - - - - - - - - - -

RI : —— Routing Indicators ——

RI :

RI : Routing control = 0A

RI :   000. .... = Non-broadcast

RI :   ...0 1010 = RI length is 10

RI : Routing control = 80

RI :   1... .... = Backward direction

RI :   .000 .... = Largest frame is 516

RI :   .... 0000 = Reserved

RI : Ring number 221 via bridge 0

RI : Ring number 201 via bridge 0

RI : Ring number 002 via bridge 0

RI : Ring number 010

RI :

- - - - - - - - - - - - - - Frame 203 - - - - - - - - - - - - - - - -

RI : —— Routing Indicators ——

RI :

RI : Routing control = 0A

RI :   000. .... = Non-broadcast

RI :   ...0 1010 = RI length is 10

RI : Routing control = 80

RI :   1... .... = Backward direction

RI :   .000 .... = Largest frame is 516

RI :   .... 0000 = Reserved

RI : Ring number 221 via bridge 0

RI : Ring number 200 via bridge 0

RI : Ring number 001 via bridge 0

RI : Ring number 010

RI :

```
- - - - - - - - - - - - - Frame 204 - - - - - - - - - - - - - - - -

RI :  ——— Routing Indicators ———

RI :

RI :  Routing control = 0A

RI :      000. .... = Non-broadcast

RI :      ...0 1010 = RI length is 10

RI :  Routing control = 80

RI :      1... .... = Backward direction

RI :      .000 .... = Largest frame is 516

RI :      .... 0000 = Reserved

RI :  Ring number 221 via bridge 0

RI :  Ring number 200 via bridge 0

RI :  Ring number 001 via bridge 0

RI :  Ring number 011

RI :
```

Trace 6.3.2b. Token Ring/SNA Discovered Routes (first result)

In Frame 197 the route is from Ring 221 to Bridge 0, Ring 200 to Bridge 0, Ring 002 to Bridge 0, and finally Ring 011 to the Host. All other routes are also plausible. The second try at the discovery (Frames 213 through 221 in Trace 6.3.2c) reveals the same routes, but in a different order:

frame 214:	221-0-200-0-001-0-010
frame 215:	221-0-200-0-002-0-011
frame 216:	221-0-200-0-002-0-010
frame 217:	221-0-200-0-001-0-011
frame 218:	221-0-201-0-002-0-010
frame 219:	221-0-201-0-002-0-011
frame 220:	221-0-201-0-001-0-010
frame 221:	221-0-201-0-001-0-011

Sniffer Network Analyzer data 3-Apr-90 at 8:45:58, GRUB221B.TRC, Pg 1

- - - - - - - - - - - - - - - - Frame 213 - - - - - - - - - - - - - - - - -

RI : —— Routing Indicators ——

RI :

RI : Routing control = 82

RI :   100. .... = All-routes broadcast, non-broadcast return

RI :   ...0 0010 = RI length is 2

RI : Routing control = 00

RI :   0... .... = Forward direction

RI :   .000 .... = Largest frame is 516

RI :   .... 0000 = Reserved

RI :

- - - - - - - - - - - - - - - - Frame 214 - - - - - - - - - - - - - - - - -

RI : —— Routing Indicators ——

RI :

RI : Routing control = 0A

RI :   000. .... = Non-broadcast

RI :   ...0 1010 = RI length is 10

RI : Routing control = 80

RI :   1... .... = Backward direction

RI :   .000 .... = Largest frame is 516

RI :   .... 0000 = Reserved

RI : Ring number 221 via bridge 0

RI : Ring number 200 via bridge 0

RI : Ring number 001 via bridge 0

RI : Ring number 010

RI :

- - - - - - - - - - - - - - - Frame 215 - - - - - - - - - - - - - - - - -

RI : —— Routing Indicators ——

RI :

RI : Routing control = 0A

RI :   000. .... = Non-broadcast

RI :   ...0 1010 = RI length is 10

RI : Routing control = 80

RI :   1... .... = Backward direction

RI :   .000 .... = Largest frame is 516

RI :   .... 0000 = Reserved

RI : Ring number 221 via bridge 0

RI : Ring number 200 via bridge 0

RI : Ring number 002 via bridge 0

RI : Ring number 011

RI :

- - - - - - - - - - - - - - Frame 216 - - - - - - - - - - - - - - - - -

RI : —— Routing Indicators ——

RI :

RI : Routing control = 0A

RI :   000. .... = Non-broadcast

RI :   ...0 1010 = RI length is 10

RI : Routing control = 80

RI :   1... .... = Backward direction

RI :   .000 .... = Largest frame is 516

RI :   .... 0000 = Reserved

RI : Ring number 221 via bridge 0

RI : Ring number 200 via bridge 0

RI : Ring number 002 via bridge 0

RI : Ring number 010

RI :

263

- - - - - - - - - - - - - - - - Frame 217 - - - - - - - - - - - - - - - -

RI : —— Routing Indicators ——

RI :

RI : Routing control = 0A

RI :   000. .... = Non-broadcast

RI :   ...0 1010 = RI length is 10

RI : Routing control = 80

RI :   1... .... = Backward direction

RI :   .000 .... = Largest frame is 516

RI :   .... 0000 = Reserved

RI : Ring number 221 via bridge 0

RI : Ring number 200 via bridge 0

RI : Ring number 001 via bridge 0

RI : Ring number 011

RI :

- - - - - - - - - - - - - - - Frame 218 - - - - - - - - - - - - - - - -

RI : —— Routing Indicators ——

RI :

RI : Routing control = 0A

RI :   000. .... = Non-broadcast

RI :   ...0 1010 = RI length is 10

RI : Routing control = 80

RI :   1... .... = Backward direction

RI :   .000 .... = Largest frame is 516

RI :   .... 0000 = Reserved

RI : Ring number 221 via bridge 0

RI : Ring number 201 via bridge 0

RI : Ring number 002 via bridge 0

RI : Ring number 010

RI :

- - - - - - - - - - - - - - - Frame 219 - - - - - - - - - - - - - - - - -

RI : —— Routing Indicators ——

RI :

RI : Routing control = 0A

RI :   000. .... = Non-broadcast

RI :   ...0 1010 = RI length is 10

RI : Routing control = 80

RI :   1... .... = Backward direction

RI :   .000 .... = Largest frame is 516

RI :   .... 0000 = Reserved

RI : Ring number 221 via bridge 0

RI : Ring number 201 via bridge 0

RI : Ring number 002 via bridge 0

RI : Ring number 011

RI :

- - - - - - - - - - - - - - Frame 220 - - - - - - - - - - - - - - - - -

RI : —— Routing Indicators ——

RI :

RI : Routing control = 0A

RI :   000. .... = Non-broadcast

RI :   ...0 1010 = RI length is 10

RI : Routing control = 80

RI :   1... .... = Backward direction

RI :   .000 .... = Largest frame is 516

RI :   .... 0000 = Reserved

RI : Ring number 221 via bridge 0

RI : Ring number 201 via bridge 0

RI : Ring number 001 via bridge 0

RI : Ring number 010

RI :

```
- - - - - - - - - - - - - - Frame 221 - - - - - - - - - - - - - - - -
RI :  ──── Routing Indicators ────
RI :
RI :  Routing control = 0A
RI :      000. .... = Non-broadcast
RI :      ...0 1010 = RI length is 10
RI :  Routing control = 80
RI :      1... .... = Backward direction
RI :      .000 .... = Largest frame is 516
RI :      .... 0000 = Reserved
RI :  Ring number 221 via bridge 0
RI :  Ring number 201 via bridge 0
RI :  Ring number 001 via bridge 0
RI :  Ring number 011
RI :
```

Trace 6.3.2c. Token Ring/SNA Discovered Routes (second result)

For example, the first response to the first discovery process (Frame 197) is the same as the second response to the second discovery process (Frame 215). All of these routes were also plausible; however, this still did not answer the question of why the host connection is never made.

The solution was found through experimentation. The analyst theorized that the large number of route responses (eight total) might be overwhelming the PC's terminal emulation software. To test this theory, he logically disconnected one of the bridges (Bridge 0 between Ring 221 and Ring 201 in Figure 6-6). He did this manually, setting the Frame Forwarding option to "NO." This allowed only one initial path from Ring 221 to the Host—the path via Ring 200. In doing so, he also reduced the number of route responses from eight to four.

He then re-initialized the station, and redid the route discovery process. This time, the host connected successfully (Trace 6.3.2d). The SNA session is initiated in Frame 228, the Physical Units are activated beginning in Frame 234, and the Logical Units are activated beginning in Frame 242. The workstation then received the expected host response, "WELCOME TO CORPORATE COMPUTING."

Sniffer Network Analyzer data 14-May-90 at 14:36:02 file OFF202_1.TRC, Pg 1

SUMMARY	Delta T	Destination	Source	Summary
217	1.603	Host	Workstation	LLC C D=00 S=04 XID P
218	0.009	Workstation	Host	LLC R D=04 S=00 XID F
219	0.000	Workstation	Host	LLC R D=04 S=00 XID F
220	0.000	Workstation	Host	LLC R D=04 S=00 XID F
221	0.000	Workstation	Host	LLC R D=04 S=00 XID F
222	0.859	Host	Workstation	LLC C D=04 S=04 XID P
223	0.019	Workstation	Host	LLC R D=04 S=04 XID F
224	0.035	Host	Workstation	LLC C D=04 S=04 XID P
225	0.022	Workstation	Host	LLC R D=04 S=04 XID F
226	0.039	Host	Workstation	LLC C D=04 S=04 XID P
227	0.057	Host	Workstation	LLC C D=04 S=04 XID P
228	0.055	Host	Workstation	SNA XID Fmt 0 T2
229	0.046	Host	Workstation	SNA XID Fmt 0 T2
230	0.345	Workstation	Host	LLC C D=04 S=04 SABME P
231	0.031	Host	Workstation	LLC R D=04 S=04 UA F
232	0.028	Workstation	Host	LLC C D=04 S=04 RR NR=0 P
233	0.001	Host	Workstation	LLC R D=04 S=04 RR NR=0 F
234	0.162	Workstation	Host	SNA C ACTPU PU5
235	0.002	Host	Workstation	LLC R D=04 S=04 RR NR=1
236	0.139	Host	Workstation	SNA R ACTPU
237	0.008	Workstation	Host	LLC R D=04 S=04 RR NR=1
238	0.134	Workstation	Host	SNA C NMVT Request RTM
239	0.002	Host	Workstation	LLC R D=04 S=04 RR NR=2
240	0.110	Host	Workstation	SNA R NMVT, Request err: Fct not supported
241	0.007	Workstation	Host	LLC R D=04 S=04 RR NR=2
242	0.030	Workstation	Host	SNA C ACTLU
243	0.002	Host	Workstation	LLC R D=04 S=04 RR NR=3
244	0.011	Workstation	Host	SNA C ACTLU
245	0.002	Host	Workstation	LLC R D=04 S=04 RR NR=4

246	0.008	Workstation	Host	SNA C ACTLU
247	0.002	Host	Workstation	LLC R D=04 S=04 RR NR=5
248	0.115	Host	Workstation	SNA R ACTLU
249	0.009	Workstation	Host	LLC R D=04 S=04 RR NR=3
250	0.079	Workstation	Host	SNA C FMD user data
251	0.002	Host	Workstation	LLC R D=04 S=04 RR NR=6
252	0.022	Host	Workstation	SNA R ACTLU
253	0.008	Workstation	Host	LLC R D=04 S=04 RR NR=4
254	0.040	Workstation	Host	SNA C FMD user data
255	0.002	Host	Workstation	LLC R D=04 S=04 RR NR=7
256	0.076	Host	Workstation	SNA R ACTLU
257	0.008	Workstation	Host	LLC R D=04 S=04 RR NR=5
258	0.109	Workstation	Host	SNA C FMD user data
259	0.002	Host	Workstation	LLC R D=04 S=04 RR NR=8
260	0.101	Host	Workstation	SNA R FMD
261	0.009	Workstation	Host	LLC R D=04 S=04 RR NR=6
262	0.094	Host	Workstation	SNA R FMD
263	0.010	Workstation	Host	LLC R D=04 S=04 RR NR=7
264	0.095	Host	Workstation	SNA R FMD
265	0.007	Workstation	Host	LLC R D=04 S=04 RR NR=8
266	2.344	Broadcast	Workstation	MAC Standby Monitor Present
267	6.928	Broadcast	Workstation	MAC Standby Monitor Present
268	6.928	Broadcast	Workstation	MAC Standby Monitor Present
269	6.918	Broadcast	Workstation	MAC Standby Monitor Present
270	3.598	Host	Workstation	LLC C D=04 S=04 RR NR=8 P
271	0.007	Workstation	Host	LLC R D=04 S=04 RR NR=8 F
272	3.312	Broadcast	Workstation	MAC Standby Monitor Present
273	6.918	Broadcast	Workstation	MAC Standby Monitor Present
274	6.928	Broadcast	Workstation	MAC Standby Monitor Present
275	6.953	Broadcast	Workstation	MAC Standby Monitor Present
276	5.887	Host	Workstation	LLC C D=04 S=04 RR NR=8 P
277	0.007	Workstation	Host	LLC R D=04 S=04 RR NR=8 F

278	1.023	Broadcast	Workstation	MAC Standby Monitor Present
279	6.928	Broadcast	Workstation	MAC Standby Monitor Present
280	6.928	Broadcast	Workstation	MAC Standby Monitor Present
281	6.918	Broadcast	Workstation	MAC Standby Monitor Present
282	6.927	Broadcast	Workstation	MAC Standby Monitor Present
283	1.259	Host	Workstation	LLC C D=04 S=04 RR NR=8 P
284	0.008	Workstation	Host	LLC R D=04 S=04 RR NR=8 F
285	5.661	Broadcast	Workstation	MAC Standby Monitor Present
286	6.928	Broadcast	Workstation	MAC Standby Monitor Present

Trace 6.3.2d. Token Ring/SNA Operational Host Connection

With the bridge between Ring 221 and Ring 201 logically off, the route discovery process only returned four possible routes (Trace 6.3.2e):

frame 218:	221-0-200-0-001-0-010
frame 219:	221-0-200-0-002-0-011
frame 220:	221-0-200-0-002-0-010
frame 221:	221-0-200-0-001-0-011

Sniffer Network Analyzer data 14-May-90 14:36:02, file OFF202_1.TRC, Pg 1

- - - - - - - - - - - - - - - - Frame 217 - - - - - - - - - - - - - - - - -

RI : —— Routing Indicators ——

RI :

RI : Routing control = 82

RI :   100. .... = All-routes broadcast, non-broadcast return

RI :   ...0 0010 = RI length is 2

RI : Routing control = 00

RI :   0... .... = Forward direction

RI :   .000 .... = Largest frame is 516

RI :   .... 0000 = Reserved

RI :

```
- - - - - - - - - - - - - - - - Frame 218 - - - - - - - - - - - - - - - - -
RI : —— Routing Indicators ——
RI :
RI :  Routing control = 0A
RI :     000. .... = Non-broadcast
RI :     ...0 1010 = RI length is 10
RI :  Routing control = 80
RI :     1... .... = Backward direction
RI :     .000 .... = Largest frame is 516
RI :     .... 0000 = Reserved
RI :  Ring number 221 via bridge 0
RI :  Ring number 200 via bridge 0
RI :  Ring number 001 via bridge 0
RI :  Ring number 010
RI :
```

```
- - - - - - - - - - - - - - - Frame 219 - - - - - - - - - - - - - - - -
RI : —— Routing Indicators ——
RI :
RI :  Routing control = 0A
RI :     000. .... = Non-broadcast
RI :     ...0 1010 = RI length is 10
RI :  Routing control = 80
RI :     1... .... = Backward direction
RI :     .000 .... = Largest frame is 516
RI :     .... 0000 = Reserved
RI :  Ring number 221 via bridge 0
RI :  Ring number 200 via bridge 0
RI :  Ring number 002 via bridge 0
RI :  Ring number 011
RI :
```

```
- - - - - - - - - - - - - - - Frame 220 - - - - - - - - - - - - - - - -
RI :  ——— Routing Indicators ———
RI :
RI :  Routing control = 0A
RI :      000. .... = Non-broadcast
RI :      ...0 1010 = RI length is 10
RI :  Routing control = 80
RI :      1... .... = Backward direction
RI :      .000 .... = Largest frame is 516
RI :      .... 0000 = Reserved
RI :  Ring number 221 via bridge 0
RI :  Ring number 200 via bridge 0
RI :  Ring number 002 via bridge 0
RI :  Ring number 010
RI :


- - - - - - - - - - - - - - - Frame 221 - - - - - - - - - - - - - - - -
RI :  ——— Routing Indicators ———
RI :
RI :  Routing control = 0A
RI :      000. .... = Non-broadcast
RI :      ...0 1010 = RI length is 10
RI :  Routing control = 80
RI :      1... .... = Backward direction
RI :      .000 .... = Largest frame is 516
RI :      .... 0000 = Reserved
RI :  Ring number 221 via bridge 0
RI :  Ring number 200 via bridge 0
RI :  Ring number 001 via bridge 0
RI :  Ring number 011
RI :
```

Trace 6.3.2e. Token Ring/SNA Stabilized Route Details

Note that Frames 222 and 223 (Trace 6.3.2d) confirm the first choice route: 221-0-200-0-001-0-010. Subsequent transmissions (Trace 6.3.2f) consistently use this route. The path from workstation to host is now stabilized.

Sniffer Network Analyzer data 14-May-90 at 14:36:02, file OFF202_1.TRC, Pg 1

SUMMARY	Delta T	Destination	Source	Summary
230	0.345	Workstation	Host	RI Back (221)-0-(200)-0-(001)-0-(010)
231	0.031	Host	Workstation	RI Fwrd (221)-0-(200)-0-(001)-0-(010)
232	0.028	Workstation	Host	RI Back (221)-0-(200)-0-(001)-0-(010)
233	0.001	Host	Workstation	RI Fwrd (221)-0-(200)-0-(001)-0-(010)
234	0.162	Workstation	Host	RI Back (221)-0-(200)-0-(001)-0-(010)
235	0.002	Host	Workstation	RI Fwrd (221)-0-(200)-0-(001)-0-(010)
236	0.139	Host	Workstation	RI Fwrd (221)-0-(200)-0-(001)-0-(010)
237	0.008	Workstation	Host	RI Back (221)-0-(200)-0-(001)-0-(010)
238	0.134	Workstation	Host	RI Back (221)-0-(200)-0-(001)-0-(010)
239	0.002	Host	Workstation	RI Fwrd (221)-0-(200)-0-(001)-0-(010)
240	0.110	Host	Workstation	RI Fwrd (221)-0-(200)-0-(001)-0-(010)
241	0.007	Workstation	Host	RI Back (221)-0-(200)-0-(001)-0-(010)
242	0.030	Workstation	Host	RI Back (221)-0-(200)-0-(001)-0-(010)

243	0.002	Host	Workstation	RI Fwrd (221)-0-(200)-0-(001)-0-(010)
244	0.011	Workstation	Host	RI Back (221)-0-(200)-0-(001)-0-(010)
245	0.002	Host	Workstation	RI Fwrd (221)-0-(200)-0-(001)-0-(010)
246	0.008	Workstation	Host	RI Back (221)-0-(200)-0-(001)-0-(010)
247	0.002	Host	Workstation	RI Fwrd (221)-0-(200)-0-(001)-0-(010)

Trace 6.3.2f. Token Ring/SNA Stabilized Route Operation

As a postscript to the story, the analyst called the terminal emulation software vendor with the results of his experiment. The vendor discovered that the current version of software became confused when more than four routes were returned from the discovery process. This explained why deactivating one of the bridges (and reducing the number of responses from eight to four) enabled a successful host connection. A subsequent release of the terminal emulation software fixed this problem, and the deactivated bridge was then reinstated into the network.

6.3.3 Token Ring/SNA Multiple NetBIOS Broadcasts

In our final bridging example, an internetwork consisting of three 4 Mbps token rings is connected via bridges to an FDDI backbone (see Figure 6-7). The rings are on three separate floors and are designated by the floor number (002, 004, or 006). The problem was described to the analyst as multiple logins to the server. In other words, a PC on Ring 006 would initiate a login sequence to the server on Ring 006, and multiple login messages would appear on the PC's CRT. To track down the problem, we attached a network analyzer to Ring 006 and captured the login information.

As Trace 6.3.3a revealed, Gregg's workstation was initializing just as it should according to the IEEE 802.5 specification. First came the Duplicate Address Test (Frames 1 and 2), the Report SUA Change (Frame 3), and Request Initialization

(Frames 5 through 8). Note that a Ring Parameter Server was not active on the ring; therefore, Gregg's workstation used its default values after the fourth request in Frame 8. Various NetBIOS commands (Frames 12 through 40) verified names and groups. (Useful details on NetBIOS are found in References [6-41] through [6-44].) The server (Server 1) was requested and found in Frames 43 and 44. Gregg's workstation then initialized a session (Frame 49) and began to send data (Frame 53). At this point, the multiple login messages appeared at his workstation.

The reason for these multiple messages appeared in the next four transmissions (Frames 55 through 58), shown in Trace 6.3.3b. The first frame (55) was a legitimate NetBIOS Datagram from Gregg's workstation to the NetBIOS functional address (C00000000080H). The second frame (56) was a mirror image of Frame 55. The third and fourth frames (57 and 58) were slightly different, however, in the contents of their routing information fields:

Frame 55: Single route broadcast, all-routes broadcast return

Frame 56: Single route broadcast, all-routes broadcast return

Frame 57: Single route broadcast, all-routes broadcast return
006-6-FDD-2-002-2-FDD-6-006

Frame 58: Single route broadcast, all-routes broadcast return
006-6-FDD-4-004-4-FDD-6-006

As you review Figure 6-7, notice that Frame 57 took the path Ring 6 to Bridge 6, FDDI ring to Bridge 2, Ring 002 to Bridge 2, FDDI ring to Bridge 6, Ring 006 to Gregg. Frame 57 was similar, but crossed Bridge 4, took a trip around Ring 4, and returned. So there was an echo of the NetBIOS datagram at each bridge. Instead of passing through the bridge in only one direction, the datagram would pass through in one direction, go around that ring, and return to Gregg. Hence, his workstation was seeing multiple responses: the original (Frame 55) plus one echoed from each bridge: Bridge 6 echo (Frame 56), Bridge 2 echo (Frame 57), and Bridge 4 echo (Frame 58).

Furthermore, Frames 57 and 58 were returned with the frame copied indicators FCI = 00, which indicated that the frame had not gone past the bridge, when in reality it had gone past twice. All indications pointed towards the bridge as the source of the failure.

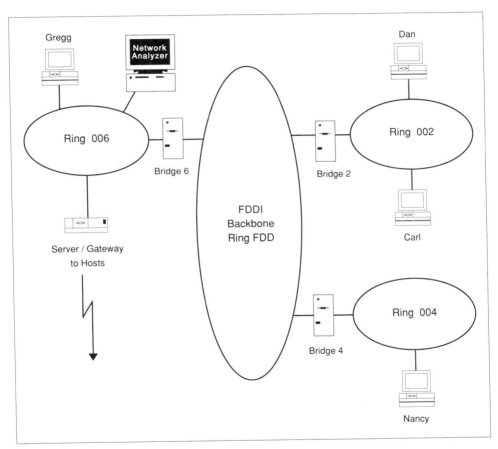

Figure 6-7. Token Ring/SNA with FDDI Backbone

Sniffer Network Analyzer data 16-May-91 at 12:28:08 file G0516A.TRC Pg 1

SUMMARY	Delta T	Destination	Source	Summary
M 1		Gregg	Gregg	MAC Duplicate Address Test
2	0.002	Gregg	Gregg	MAC Duplicate Address Test
3	0.458	Config Srv	Gregg	MAC Report SUA Change
4	0.016	Broadcast	Gregg	MAC Standby Monitor Present
5	0.001	Param Server	Gregg	MAC Request Initialization
6	0.000	Param Server	Gregg	MAC Request Initialization
7	0.001	Param Server	Gregg	MAC Request Initialization
8	0.001	Param Server	Gregg	MAC Request Initialization
9	0.011	NetBIOS	Gregg	NETB Check name <FB>
10	0.005	Gregg	Prteon0E25BF	MAC Request Station Address
11	0.001	Prteon0E25BF	Gregg	MAC Report Station Address
12	1.163	NetBIOS	Gregg	NETB Check name <FB>
13	0.005	NetBIOS	Gregg	NETB Check name <FB>
14	0.588	NetBIOS	Gregg	NETB Check name <FB>
15	0.593	NetBIOS	Gregg	NETB Check name <FB>
16	0.593	NetBIOS	Gregg	NETB Check name <FB>
17	0.593	NetBIOS	Gregg	NETB Check name <FB>
18	1.781	NetBIOS	Gregg	NETB Check name <F9>
19	1.187	NetBIOS	Gregg	NETB Check name <F9>
20	0.395	Broadcast	Gregg	MAC Standby Monitor Present
21	0.198	NetBIOS	Gregg	NETB Check name <F9>
22	0.593	NetBIOS	Gregg	NETB Check name <F9>
23	0.593	NetBIOS	Gregg	NETB Check name <F9>
24	0.593	NetBIOS	Gregg	NETB Check name <F9>
25	1.789	NetBIOS	Gregg	NETB Check name <FA>
26	1.179	NetBIOS	Gregg	NETB Check name <FA>
27	0.593	NetBIOS	Gregg	NETB Check name <FA>
28	0.593	NetBIOS	Gregg	NETB Check name <FA>
29	0.593	NetBIOS	Gregg	NETB Check name <FA>
30	0.197	Broadcast	Gregg	MAC Standby Monitor Present

31	0.395	NetBIOS	Gregg	NETB Check name <FA>
32	1.796	NetBIOS	Gregg	NETB Datagram
				THUNDERBOLT<-<FA>
33	0.097	NetBIOS	Gregg	NETB Check group BXA1RG1<00>
34	0.005	NetBIOS	Gregg	NETB Check group BXA1RG1<00>
35	1.084	NetBIOS	Gregg	NETB Check group BXA1RG1<00>
36	0.593	NetBIOS	Gregg	NETB Check group BXA1RG1<00>
37	0.593	NetBIOS	Gregg	NETB Check group BXA1RG1<00>
38	0.005	NetBIOS	Gregg	NETB Check group BXA1RG1<00>
39	0.588	NetBIOS	Gregg	NETB Check group BXA1RG1<00>
40	0.593	NetBIOS	Gregg	NETB Check group BXA1RG1<00>
41	1.187	Broadcast	Gregg	MAC Standby Monitor Present
42	6.927	Broadcast	Gregg	MAC Standby Monitor Present
43	3.265	NetBIOS	Gregg	NETB Find name BXA1
44	0.005	Gregg	Server 1	NETB Name BXA1 recognized
45	0.004	Server 1	Gregg	LLC C D=F0 S=F0 SABME P
46	0.005	Gregg	Server 1	LLC R D=F0 S=F0 UA F
47	0.000	Server 1	Gregg	LLC C D=F0 S=F0 RR NR=0 P
48	0.000	Gregg	Server 1	LLC R D=F0 S=F0 RR NR=0 F
49	0.001	Server 1	Gregg	NETB D=D9 S=01
				Session initialize
50	0.002	Gregg	Server 1	LLC R D=F0 S=F0 RR NR=1
51	0.002	Gregg	Server 1	NETB D=01 S=D9 Session confirm
52	0.001	Server 1	Gregg	LLC R D=F0 S=F0 RR NR=1
53	0.002	Server 1	Gregg	NETB D=D9 S=01 Data, 128 bytes
54	0.002	Gregg	Server 1	LLC R D=F0 S=F0 RR NR=2
55	0.013	NetBIOS	Gregg	NETB Datagram BXA1<-<FB>
56	0.005	NetBIOS	Gregg	NETB Datagram BXA1<-<FB>
57	0.000	NetBIOS	Gregg	NETB Datagram BXA1<-<FB>
58	0.005	NetBIOS	Gregg	NETB Datagram BXA1<-<FB>
59	1.471	Gregg	Server 1	NETB D=01 S=D9 Send more now
60	0.002	Server 1	Gregg	LLC R D=F0 S=F0 RR NR=2

Trace 6.3.3a. Token Ring/SNA Multiple NetBIOS Broadcast Summary

Sniffer Network Analyzer data 16-May-91 at 12:28:08, file G0516A.TRC Pg 1

- - - - - - - - - - - - - - - Frame 55 - - - - - - - - - - - - - - - -

DLC: —— DLC Header ——

DLC:

DLC: Frame 55 arrived at 12:29:15.724; frame size is 139 (008B hex) bytes.

DLC: AC: Frame priority 0, Reservation priority 0, Monitor count 1

DLC: FC: LLC frame, PCF attention code: None

DLC: FS: Addr recognized indicators: 11, Frame copied indicators: 11

DLC: Destination = Functional address C00000000080, NetBIOS

DLC: Source   = Station Prteon0E26B0, Gregg

DLC:

RI : —— Routing Indicators ——

RI :

RI : Routing control = C2

RI :   110. .... = Single-route broadcast, all-routes broadcast return

RI :   ...0 0010 = RI length is 2

RI : Routing control = 70

RI :   0... .... = Forward direction

RI :   .111 .... = Largest frame is unspecified maximum value

RI :   .... 0000 = Reserved

RI :

LLC: —— LLC Header ——

LLC:

LLC: DSAP = F0, SSAP = F0, Command, Unnumbered frame: UI

LLC:

NETB: —— NETBIOS Datagram ——

NETB:

NETB: Header length = 44, Data length = 76

NETB: Delimiter = EFFF (NETBIOS)

NETB: Command = 08

NETB: Data1 = 00

NETB: Data2 = 0000

NETB: Transmit correlator = 0000

NETB: Response correlator = 0000

NETB: Receiver's name = BXA1

NETB: Sender's name = <FB>

NETB: [76 bytes of datagram]

```
ADDR  HEX                                                          ASCII
0000  18 40 C0 00 00 00 00 80   C0 00 C9 0E 26 B0 C2 70   .@.........&..p
0010  F0 F0 03 2C 00 FF EF 08   00 00 00 00 00 00 00 42   ...,...........B
0020  58 41 31 20 20 20 20 20   20 20 20 20 20 20 FF FB   XA1           ..
0030  00 00 00 00 00 00 00 00   00 40 00 C9 0E 26 B0 FB   .........@...&..
0040  FB 00 00 00 00 00 00 00   00 00 40 00 C9 0E 26 B0   ..........@...&.
0050  42 58 41 31 20 20 20 20   20 20 20 20 20 20 20 FF   BXA1           .
0060  00 FF FF 00 00 00 00 00   00 00 00 61 64 6D 69 6E   ...........admin
0070  20 20 20 5D 6E 00 20 E7   87 50 56 42 58 41 31 52   ]n. ..PVBXA1R
0080  47 31 20 20 20 20 20 20   20 20 00                  G1          .
```

- - - - - - - - - - - - - - - Frame 56 - - - - - - - - - - - - - - - - -

DLC: ──── DLC Header ────

DLC:

DLC: Frame 56 arrived at 12:29:15.730; frame size is 139 (008B hex) bytes.

DLC: AC: Frame priority 0, Reservation priority 0, Monitor count 1

DLC: FC: LLC frame, PCF attention code: None

DLC: FS: Addr recognized indicators: 11, Frame copied indicators: 11

DLC: Destination = Functional address C00000000080, NetBIOS

DLC: Source   = Station Prteon0E26B0, Gregg

DLC:

RI : ──── Routing Indicators ────

RI :

RI : Routing control = C2

RI :   110. .... = Single-route broadcast, all-routes broadcast return

RI :   ...0 0010 = RI length is 2

RI : Routing control = 70

RI :   0... .... = Forward direction

RI :   .111 .... = Largest frame is unspecified maximum value

RI :   .... 0000 = Reserved

RI :

LLC: —— LLC Header ——

LLC:

LLC: DSAP = F0, SSAP = F0, Command, Unnumbered frame: UI

LLC:

NETB: —— NETBIOS Datagram ——

NETB:

NETB: Header length = 44, Data length = 76

NETB: Delimiter = EFFF (NETBIOS)

NETB: Command = 08

NETB: Data1 = 00

NETB: Data2 = 0000

NETB: Transmit correlator = 0000

NETB: Response correlator = 0000

NETB: Receiver's name = BXA1

NETB: Sender's name = <FB>

NETB: [76 bytes of datagram]

```
ADDR  HEX                                                              ASCII
0000  18 40 C0 00 00 00 00 80    C0 00 C9 0E 26 B0 C2 70    .@.........&..p
0010  F0 F0 03 2C 00 FF EF 08    00 00 00 00 00 00 00 42    ...,.........B
0020  58 41 31 20 20 20 20 20    20 20 20 20 20 20 FF FB    XA1          ..
0030  00 00 00 00 00 00 00 00    00 40 00 C9 0E 26 B0 FB    .........@...&..
0040  FB 00 00 00 00 00 00 00    00 00 40 00 C9 0E 26 B0    ..........@...&.
0050  42 58 41 31 20 20 20 20    20 20 20 20 20 20 20 FF    BXA1           .
0060  00 FF FF 00 00 00 00 00    00 00 00 61 64 6D 69 6E    ...........admin
0070  20 20 20 5D 6E 00 20 E7    87 50 56 42 58 41 31 52    ]n. ..PVBXA1R
0080  47 31 20 20 20 20 20 20    20 20 00                   G1        .
```

```
- - - - - - - - - - - - - - - Frame 57 - - - - - - - - - - - - - - - -

DLC: ---- DLC Header ----
DLC:
DLC: Frame 57 arrived at  12:29:15.731; frame size is 149 (0095 hex)
DLC: AC: Frame priority 0,  Reservation priority 0,  Monitor count 0
DLC: FC: LLC frame,  PCF attention code: None
DLC: FS: Addr recognized indicators: 00, Frame copied indicators: 00
DLC: Destination = Functional address C00000000080, NetBIOS
DLC: Source     = Station Prteon0E26B0, Gregg
DLC:
RI : ---- Routing Indicators ----
RI :
RI : Routing control = CC
RI :       110. .... = Single-route broadcast, all-routes broadcast return
RI :       ...0 1100 = RI length is 12
RI : Routing control = 20
RI :       0... .... = Forward direction
RI :       .010 .... = Largest frame is 2052
RI :       .... 0000 = Reserved
RI : Ring number 006 via bridge 6
RI : Ring number FDD via bridge 2
RI : Ring number 002 via bridge 2
RI : Ring number FDD via bridge 6
RI : Ring number 006
RI :
LLC: ---- LLC Header ----
LLC:
LLC: DSAP = F0, SSAP = F0, Command, Unnumbered frame: UI
LLC:
NETB: ---- NETBIOS Datagram ----
NETB:
NETB: Header length = 44, Data length = 76
```

NETB: Delimiter = EFFF (NETBIOS)

NETB: Command = 08

NETB: Data1 = 00

NETB: Data2 = 0000

NETB: Transmit correlator = 0000

NETB: Response correlator = 0000

NETB: Receiver's name = BXA1

NETB: Sender's name = <FB>

NETB: [76 bytes of datagram]

ADDR	HEX		ASCII
0000	10 40 C0 00 00 00 00 80	C0 00 C9 0E 26 B0 CC20	.@..........&..
0010	00 66 FD D2 00 22 FD D6	00 60 F0 F0 03 2C 00 FF	.f...".....,..
0020	EF 08 00 00 00 00 00 00	00 42 58 41 31 20 20 20	.........BXA1
0030	20 20 20 20 20 20 20 20	FF FB 00 00 00 00 00 00	....
0040	00 00 00 40 00 C9 0E 26	B0 FB FB 00 00 00 00 00	...@...&........
0050	00 00 00 00 40 00 C9 0E	26 B0 42 58 41 31 20 20	....@...&.BXA1
0060	20 20 20 20 20 20 20 20	20 FF 00 FF FF 00 00 00	....
0070	00 00 00 00 00 61 64 6D	69 6E 20 20 20 5D 6E 00	.....admin]n.
0080	20 E7 87 50 56 42 58 41	31 52 47 31 20 20 20 20	..PVBXA1RG1
0090	20 20 20 20 00		

- - - - - - - - - - - - - - - Frame 58 - - - - - - - - - - - - - - - - -

DLC: —— DLC Header ——

DLC:

DLC: Frame 58 arrived at 12:29:15.736; frame size is 149 (0095 hex)

DLC: AC: Frame priority 0, Reservation priority 0, Monitor count 0

DLC: FC: LLC frame, PCF attention code: None

DLC: FS: Addr recognized indicators: 00, Frame copied indicators: 00

DLC: Destination = Functional address C00000000080, NetBIOS

DLC: Source   = Station Prteon0E26B0, Gregg

DLC:

RI : —— Routing Indicators ——

RI :

RI : Routing control = CC

RI :   110. .... = Single-route broadcast, all-routes broadcast return

RI :   ...0 1100 = RI length is 12

RI : Routing control = 20

RI :   0... .... = Forward direction

RI :   .010 .... = Largest frame is 2052

RI :   .... 0000 = Reserved

RI : Ring number 006 via bridge 6

RI : Ring number FDD via bridge 4

RI : Ring number 004 via bridge 4

RI : Ring number FDD via bridge 6

RI : Ring number 006

RI :

LLC: —— LLC Header ——

LLC:

LLC: DSAP = F0, SSAP = F0, Command, Unnumbered frame: UI

LLC:

NETB: —— NETBIOS Datagram ——

NETB:

NETB: Header length = 44, Data length = 76

NETB: Delimiter = EFFF (NETBIOS)

NETB: Command = 08

NETB: Data1 = 00

NETB: Data2 = 0000

NETB: Transmit correlator = 0000

NETB: Response correlator = 0000

NETB: Receiver's name = BXA1

NETB: Sender's name = <FB>

NETB: [76 bytes of datagram]

ADDR	HEX		ASCII
0000	10 40 C0 00 00 00 00 80	C0 00 C9 0E 26 B0 CC20	.@.........&..
0010	00 66 FD D4 00 44 FD D6	00 60 F0 F0 03 2C 00 FF	.f...D...'...,..
0020	EF 08 00 00 00 00 00 00	00 42 58 41 31 20 20 20	.........BXA1
0030	20 20 20 20 20 20 20 20	FF FB 00 00 00 00 00 00	....
0040	00 00 00 40 00 C9 0E 26	B0 FB FB 00 00 00 00 00	...@...&........
0050	00 00 00 00 40 00 C9 0E	26 B0 42 58 41 31 20 20	....@...&.BXA1
0060	20 20 20 20 20 20 20 20	20 FF 00 FF FF 00 00 00	....
0070	00 00 00 00 00 61 64 6D	69 6E 20 20 20 5D 6E 00	.....admin]n.
0080	20 E7 87 50 56 42 58 41	31 52 47 31 20 20 20 20	..PVBXA1RG1
0090	20 20 20 20 00		

Trace 6.3.3.b. Token Ring/SNA Multiple NetBIOS Broadcast Details

We contacted the bridge manufacturer, who found a bug that was causing the token ring protocol software in the bridge to ignore the Frame Copied Indicator (FCI) bits. This problem allowed frames to go through a bridge in two directions instead of one. Thus, the frame would enter the ring via the bridge, go around the ring, and come off the ring via the bridge; instead, it should have gone into the ring via the bridge, circled the ring once, and then died. After the bridge software was patched, the proper routing sequences were:

Frame 57:   006-6-FDD-2-002
Frame 58:   006-6-FDD-4-004

Once the software patch was installed, the multiple NetBIOS broadcasts did not reoccur.

6.3.4 Token Ring/SNA RS/6000 Gateway to TCP/IP Environment

Because SNA environments are so popular, gateways into those environments are popular internetworking devices. In order for the gateway and host to communicate, however, a number of peer-to-peer protocols and parameters must be properly configured. Both gateway and host must agree on these parameters. If either end does not, connectivity problems can arise. In this case study, we'll focus on the gateway side of the connection. In the next section, we'll see what happens when the host is misconfigured.

The internetwork in this example used an IBM RS/6000 SNA gateway to connect a token ring and an Ethernet (see Figure 6-8). The token ring side included an ES/9000 host and a number of NetWare workstations. The Ethernet side was primarily running TCP/IP on Sun SPARCStations. One of the purposes of the gateway was to allow the host to access a plotter that resided on the Ethernet. The host could access the gateway and establish a session. When the gateway tried to respond, however, its SNA services would crash. Let's see why.

The engineer placed an analyzer on the token ring side to capture the data between the gateway and the host (Trace 6.3.4a). The trace began as expected, with the devices testing the communication path (Frames 1 through 4), then exchanging SNA information (Frames 5 through 11). The host established the link (Frame 12), activated the physical unit (Frame 16), and activated one logical unit (Frame 19). The gateway acknowledges the first LU in Frame 20, but then rejects a series of host commands (ACTLU) in Frames 22 through 82. The gateway continues with its business, however, and notifies the host of its session service capabilities (Frame 84). The host then issues a BIND command to the VTUBES session manager and begins to transfer data (Frames 96 through 132). The gateway abruptly issues an SNA NOTIFY command in Frame 134, stating that its LU-LU session capability is disabled. The host then UNBINDs (Frame 142) and disconnects (Frame 147). Two questions had to be answered: Why did the second ACTLU fail, and why was the session abruptly terminated?

Sniffer Network Analyzer data 14-Jun-91 at 13:19:54, file RS/6000.TRC Pg 1

SUMMARY		Delta T	Destination	Source	Summary
M	1		ES/9000 Host	SNA Gateway	LLC C D=00 S=04 TEST P
	2	0.004	SNA Gateway	ES/9000 Host	LLC R D=04 S=00 TEST F
	3	0.006	ES/9000 Host	SNA Gateway	LLC C D=04 S=04 XID P
	4	0.009	SNA Gateway	ES/9000 Host	LLC R D=04 S=04 XID F
	5	0.004	ES/9000 Host	SNA Gateway	SNA XID Fmt 3 T2
					AECLNET.PUT40

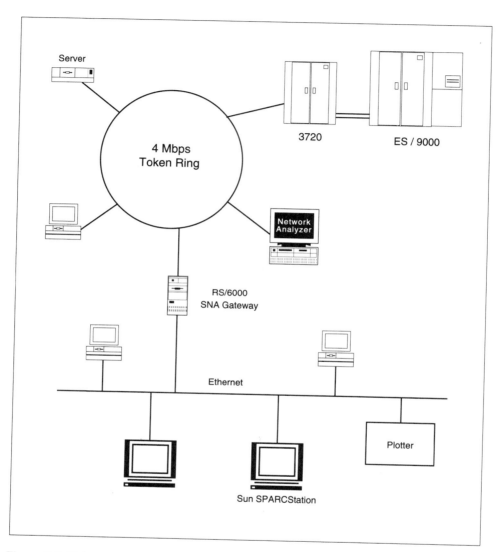

Figure 6-8. Token Ring/SNA RS/6000 Gateway

6	0.032	SNA Gateway	ES/9000 Host	SNA XID Fmt 3 T4
				AECLNET.CDRM4381
7	0.003	ES/9000 Host	SNA Gateway	SNA XID Fmt 3 T2
				AECLNET.PUT40
8	0.564	SNA Gateway	ES/9000 Host	SNA XID Fmt 3 T4
				AECLNET.CDRM4381
9	0.003	ES/9000 Host	SNA Gateway	SNA XID Fmt 3 T2
				AECLNET.PUT40
10	0.024	SNA Gateway	ES/9000 Host	SNA XID Fmt 3 T4
				AECLNET.CDRM4381
11	0.003	ES/9000 Host	SNA Gateway	SNA XID Fmt 3 T2
				AECLNET.PUT40
12	0.013	SNA Gateway	ES/9000 Host	LLC C D=04 S=04 SABME P
13	0.001	ES/9000 Host	SNA Gateway	LLC R D=04 S=04 UA F
14	0.019	SNA Gateway	ES/9000 Host	LLC C D=04 S=04 RR NR=0 P
15	0.001	ES/9000 Host	SNA Gateway	LLC R D=04 S=04 RR NR=0 F
16	0.233	SNA Gateway	ES/9000 Host	SNA C ACTPU PU5
17	0.004	ES/9000 Host	SNA Gateway	SNA R ACTPU
18	0.009	SNA Gateway	ES/9000 Host	LLC R D=04 S=04 RR NR=1
19	0.653	SNA Gateway	ES/9000 Host	SNA C ACTLU
20	0.547	ES/9000 Host	SNA Gateway	SNA R ACTLU
21	0.006	SNA Gateway	ES/9000 Host	SNA C ACTLU
22	0.033	ES/9000 Host	SNA Gateway	SNA R ACTLU, Reject code 4B
23	0.009	SNA Gateway	ES/9000 Host	SNA C ACTLU
24	0.033	ES/9000 Host	SNA Gateway	SNA R ACTLU, Reject code 4B
25	0.007	SNA Gateway	ES/9000 Host	SNA C ACTLU
26	0.033	ES/9000 Host	SNA Gateway	SNA R ACTLU, Reject code 4B
27	0.007	SNA Gateway	ES/9000 Host	SNA C ACTLU
28	0.033	ES/9000 Host	SNA Gateway	SNA R ACTLU, Reject code 4B
29	0.013	SNA Gateway	ES/9000 Host	SNA C ACTLU
30	0.034	ES/9000 Host	SNA Gateway	SNA R ACTLU, Reject code 4B
31	0.007	SNA Gateway	ES/9000 Host	SNA C ACTLU

32	0.033	ES/9000 Host	SNA Gateway	SNA R ACTLU, Reject code 4B
33	0.006	SNA Gateway	ES/9000 Host	SNA C ACTLU
34	0.033	ES/9000 Host	SNA Gateway	SNA R ACTLU, Reject code 4B
35	0.008	SNA Gateway	ES/9000 Host	SNA C ACTLU
36	0.033	ES/9000 Host	SNA Gateway	SNA R ACTLU, Reject code 4B
37	0.008	SNA Gateway	ES/9000 Host	SNA C ACTLU
38	0.033	ES/9000 Host	SNA Gateway	SNA R ACTLU, Reject code 4B
39	0.007	SNA Gateway	ES/9000 Host	SNA C ACTLU
40	0.033	ES/9000 Host	SNA Gateway	SNA R ACTLU, Reject code 4B
41	0.006	SNA Gateway	ES/9000 Host	SNA C ACTLU
42	0.033	ES/9000 Host	SNA Gateway	SNA R ACTLU, Reject code 4B
43	0.007	SNA Gateway	ES/9000 Host	SNA C ACTLU
44	0.033	ES/9000 Host	SNA Gateway	SNA R ACTLU, Reject code 4B
45	0.006	SNA Gateway	ES/9000 Host	SNA C ACTLU
46	0.033	ES/9000 Host	SNA Gateway	SNA R ACTLU, Reject code 4B
47	0.006	SNA Gateway	ES/9000 Host	SNA C ACTLU
48	0.033	ES/9000 Host	SNA Gateway	SNA R ACTLU, Reject code 4B
49	0.006	SNA Gateway	ES/9000 Host	SNA C ACTLU
50	0.033	ES/9000 Host	SNA Gateway	SNA R ACTLU, Reject code 4B
51	0.006	SNA Gateway	ES/9000 Host	SNA C ACTLU
52	0.033	ES/9000 Host	SNA Gateway	SNA R ACTLU, Reject code 4B
53	0.015	SNA Gateway	ES/9000 Host	SNA C ACTLU
54	0.034	ES/9000 Host	SNA Gateway	SNA R ACTLU, Reject code 4B
55	0.011	SNA Gateway	ES/9000 Host	SNA C ACTLU
56	0.033	ES/9000 Host	SNA Gateway	SNA R ACTLU, Reject code 4B
57	0.007	SNA Gateway	ES/9000 Host	SNA C ACTLU
58	0.033	ES/9000 Host	SNA Gateway	SNA R ACTLU, Reject code 4B
59	0.011	SNA Gateway	ES/9000 Host	SNA C ACTLU
60	0.033	ES/9000 Host	SNA Gateway	SNA R ACTLU, Reject code 4B
61	0.007	SNA Gateway	ES/9000 Host	SNA C ACTLU
62	0.033	ES/9000 Host	SNA Gateway	SNA R ACTLU, Reject code 4B
63	0.010	SNA Gateway	ES/9000 Host	SNA C ACTLU

64	0.033	ES/9000 Host	SNA Gateway	SNA R ACTLU, Reject code 4B
65	0.007	SNA Gateway	ES/9000 Host	SNA C ACTLU
66	0.033	ES/9000 Host	SNA Gateway	SNA R ACTLU, Reject code 4B
67	0.006	SNA Gateway	ES/9000 Host	SNA C ACTLU
68	0.033	ES/9000 Host	SNA Gateway	SNA R ACTLU, Reject code 4B
69	0.008	SNA Gateway	ES/9000 Host	SNA C ACTLU
70	0.033	ES/9000 Host	SNA Gateway	SNA R ACTLU, Reject code 4B
71	0.006	SNA Gateway	ES/9000 Host	SNA C ACTLU
72	0.033	ES/9000 Host	SNA Gateway	SNA R ACTLU, Reject code 4B
73	0.006	SNA Gateway	ES/9000 Host	SNA C ACTLU
74	0.034	ES/9000 Host	SNA Gateway	SNA R ACTLU, Reject code 4B
75	0.006	SNA Gateway	ES/9000 Host	SNA C ACTLU
76	0.033	ES/9000 Host	SNA Gateway	SNA R ACTLU, Reject code 4B
77	0.006	SNA Gateway	ES/9000 Host	SNA C ACTLU
78	0.034	ES/9000 Host	SNA Gateway	SNA R ACTLU, Reject code 4B
79	0.008	SNA Gateway	ES/9000 Host	SNA C ACTLU
80	0.033	ES/9000 Host	SNA Gateway	SNA R ACTLU, Reject code 4B
81	0.012	SNA Gateway	ES/9000 Host	SNA C ACTLU
82	0.033	ES/9000 Host	SNA Gateway	SNA R ACTLU, Reject code 4B
83	0.005	SNA Gateway	ES/9000 Host	LLC R D=04 S=04 RR NR=33
84	25.354	ES/9000 Host	SNA Gateway	SNA C NOTIFY
85	0.005	SNA Gateway	ES/9000 Host	LLC R D=04 S=04 RR NR=34
86	0.185	SNA Gateway	ES/9000 Host	SNA R NOTIFY
87	0.832	ES/9000 Host	SNA Gateway	LLC R D=04 S=04 RR NR=34
88	0.011	SNA Gateway	ES/9000 Host	SNA C FMD user data
89	0.246	ES/9000 Host	SNA Gateway	SNA R FMD
90	0.017	SNA Gateway	ES/9000 Host	LLC R D=04 S=04 RR NR=35
91	8.560	ES/9000 Host	SNA Gateway	SNA C FMD user data
92	0.013	SNA Gateway	ES/9000 Host	LLC R D=04 S=04 RR NR=36
93	0.199	SNA Gateway	ES/9000 Host	SNA C FMD user data
94	0.033	ES/9000 Host	SNA Gateway	SNA R FMD
95	0.007	SNA Gateway	ES/9000 Host	LLC R D=04 S=04 RR NR=37

289

96	0.213	SNA Gateway	ES/9000 Host	SNA C BIND LU2 VTUBES
97	0.057	ES/9000 Host	SNA Gateway	SNA R BIND
98	0.007	SNA Gateway	ES/9000 Host	LLC R D=04 S=04 RR NR=38
99	0.209	SNA Gateway	ES/9000 Host	SNA C SDT
100	0.003	ES/9000 Host	SNA Gateway	SNA R SDT
101	0.005	SNA Gateway	ES/9000 Host	LLC R D=04 S=04 RR NR=39
102	0.160	SNA Gateway	ES/9000 Host	SNA C FMD user data
103	0.049	ES/9000 Host	SNA Gateway	SNA R FMD
104	0.005	SNA Gateway	ES/9000 Host	LLC R D=04 S=04 RR NR=40
105	0.141	SNA Gateway	ES/9000 Host	SNA C FMD user data
106	0.010	ES/9000 Host	SNA Gateway	SNA R FMD
107	0.006	SNA Gateway	ES/9000 Host	LLC R D=04 S=04 RR NR=41
108	0.007	ES/9000 Host	SNA Gateway	SNA C FMD user data
109	0.005	SNA Gateway	ES/9000 Host	LLC R D=04 S=04 RR NR=42
110	0.206	SNA Gateway	ES/9000 Host	SNA C FMD user data
111	0.818	ES/9000 Host	SNA Gateway	LLC R D=04 S=04 RR NR=41
112	0.006	SNA Gateway	ES/9000 Host	SNA C FMD user data
113	0.049	ES/9000 Host	SNA Gateway	SNA R FMD
114	0.006	SNA Gateway	ES/9000 Host	LLC R D=04 S=04 RR NR=43
115	5.060	ES/9000 Host	SNA Gateway	SNA C FMD user data
116	0.005	SNA Gateway	ES/9000 Host	LLC R D=04 S=04 RR NR=44
117	0.381	SNA Gateway	ES/9000 Host	SNA C FMD user data
118	0.990	ES/9000 Host	SNA Gateway	LLC R D=04 S=04 RR NR=43
119	0.006	SNA Gateway	ES/9000 Host	SNA C FMD user data
120	0.031	ES/9000 Host	SNA Gateway	SNA R FMD
121	0.007	SNA Gateway	ES/9000 Host	LLC R D=04 S=04 RR NR=45
122	3.669	ES/9000 Host	SNA Gateway	SNA C FMD user data
123	0.010	SNA Gateway	ES/9000 Host	LLC R D=04 S=04 RR NR=46
124	0.303	SNA Gateway	ES/9000 Host	SNA C FMD user data
125	0.096	ES/9000 Host	SNA Gateway	SNA R FMD
126	0.007	SNA Gateway	ES/9000 Host	LLC R D=04 S=04 RR NR=47
127	3.690	ES/9000 Host	SNA Gateway	SNA C FMD user data

128	0.005	SNA Gateway	ES/9000 Host	LLC R D=04 S=04 RR NR=48
129	0.349	SNA Gateway	ES/9000 Host	SNA C FMD user data
130	0.821	ES/9000 Host	SNA Gateway	LLC R D=04 S=04 RR NR=46
131	0.006	SNA Gateway	ES/9000 Host	SNA C FMD user data
132	0.067	ES/9000 Host	SNA Gateway	SNA R FMD
133	0.005	SNA Gateway	ES/9000 Host	LLC R D=04 S=04 RR NR=49
134	4.635	ES/9000 Host	SNA Gateway	SNA C NOTIFY
135	0.009	SNA Gateway	ES/9000 Host	LLC R D=04 S=04 RR NR=50
136	0.010	ES/9000 Host	SNA Gateway	SNA C RSHUTD
137	0.005	SNA Gateway	ES/9000 Host	LLC R D=04 S=04 RR NR=51
138	0.125	SNA Gateway	ES/9000 Host	SNA R NOTIFY
139	0.634	ES/9000 Host	SNA Gateway	LLC R D=04 S=04 RR NR=48
140	0.005	SNA Gateway	ES/9000 Host	SNA R RSHUTD
141	1.008	ES/9000 Host	SNA Gateway	LLC R D=04 S=04 RR NR=49
142	0.005	SNA Gateway	ES/9000 Host	SNA C UNBIND (Normal)
143	0.009	ES/9000 Host	SNA Gateway	SNA R UNBIND
144	0.008	SNA Gateway	ES/9000 Host	LLC R D=04 S=04 RR NR=52
145	9.841	ES/9000 Host	SNA Gateway	SNA C TERM-SELF
146	0.006	SNA Gateway	ES/9000 Host	LLC R D=04 S=04 RR NR=53
147	0.002	ES/9000 Host	SNA Gateway	LLC C D=04 S=04 DISC P
148	0.007	SNA Gateway	ES/9000 Host	LLC R D=04 S=04 UA F

Trace 6.3.4a. Token Ring/SNA RS/6000 Gateway Initialization Summary

Since the host exhibited no other unusual behavior, we suspected the parameters of the RS/6000 gateway. The analyst returned to the SNA ACTPU command to trace the events (see Trace 6.3.4b). In Frame 16 the host activated the physical unit (ACTPU). The SNA Transmission Header (TH) of that packet assigned Destination Address = 00 and Origin Address = 00. The SNA Request Header activated PU Type = 5 (the host). In Frame 17 the gateway responded, followed by an LLC Receive Ready (RR) or acknowledgement in Frame 18. So far, so good.

Sniffer Network Analyzer data 22-Apr-91 at 13:03:32 file HOSTCONN.TRC Pg 1

SUMMARY	Delta T	Destination	Source	Summary
M 1		Ray	Ray	MAC Duplicate Address Test
2	0.001	Ray	Ray	MAC Duplicate Address Test
3	0.027	Config Srv	Ray	MAC Report SUA Change
4	0.012	Broadcast	Ray	MAC Standby Monitor Present
5	0.001	Param Server	Ray	MAC Request Initialization
6	0.006	Ray	40007FF134F1	MAC Initialize Ring Station
7	0.001	40007FF134F1	Ray	MAC Response
8	0.096	Host	Ray	LLC C D=00 S=04 XID P
9	0.001	Host	Ray	LLC C D=00 S=04 XID P
10	0.001	Host	Ray	LLC C D=00 S=04 XID P
11	0.001	Host	Ray	LLC C D=00 S=04 XID P
12	0.010	Ray	Host	LLC R D=04 S=00 XID F
13	0.001	Host	Ray	LLC C D=04 S=04 XID P
14	0.025	Ray	Host	LLC R D=04 S=04 XID F
15	0.001	Host	Ray	SNA XID Fmt 0 T2
16	0.436	Ray	Host	LLC C D=04 S=04 SABME P
17	0.001	Host	Ray	LLC R D=04 S=04 UA F
18	0.009	Ray	Host	LLC C D=04 S=04 RR NR=0 P
19	0.000	Host	Ray	LLC R D=04 S=04 RR NR=0 F
20	0.079	Ray	Host	SNA C ACTPU PU5
21	0.001	Host	Ray	LLC R D=04 S=04 RR NR=1
22	0.002	Host	Ray	SNA R ACTPU
23	0.010	Ray	Host	LLC R D=04 S=04 RR NR=1
24	0.178	Ray	Host	SNA C NMVT Request RTM
25	0.001	Host	Ray	LLC R D=04 S=04 RR NR=2
26	0.001	Host	Ray	SNA R NMVT, Request err:
				Fct not supported
27	0.013	Ray	Host	LLC R D=04 S=04 RR NR=2
28	0.074	Ray	Host	SNA C ACTLU
29	0.001	Host	Ray	LLC R D=04 S=04 RR NR=3

30	0.002	Host	Ray	SNA R ACTLU
31	0.007	Ray	Host	LLC R D=04 S=04 RR NR=3
32	0.001	Host	Ray	SNA C NOTIFY
33	0.009	Ray	Host	LLC R D=04 S=04 RR NR=4
34	0.013	Ray	Host	SNA C ACTLU
35	0.001	Host	Ray	LLC R D=04 S=04 RR NR=4
36	0.001	Host	Ray	SNA R ACTLU
37	0.011	Ray	Host	SNA C ACTLU
38	0.001	Host	Ray	LLC R D=04 S=04 RR NR=5
39	0.001	Host	Ray	SNA R ACTLU, Path err: Unrecognzd dest.
40	0.010	Ray	Host	LLC R D=04 S=04 RR NR=6
41	0.122	Ray	Host	SNA R NOTIFY
42	0.001	Host	Ray	LLC R D=04 S=04 RR NR=6
43	0.007	Ray	Host	SNA C FMD user data
44	0.001	Host	Ray	LLC R D=04 S=04 RR NR=7
45	0.001	Host	Ray	SNA R FMD, Request err: Category not spprtd
46	0.009	Ray	Host	SNA C FMD user data
47	0.001	Host	Ray	LLC R D=04 S=04 RR NR=8
48	0.085	Host	Ray	SNA R FMD
49	0.007	Ray	Host	LLC R D=04 S=04 RR NR=8
50	5.741	Broadcast	Ray	MAC Standby Monitor Present
51	7.009	Broadcast	Ray	MAC Standby Monitor Present
52	6.999	Broadcast	Ray	MAC Standby Monitor Present
53	1.961	Host	Ray	LLC C D=04 S=04 DISC P
54	0.012	Ray	Host	LLC R D=04 S=04 UA F
55	5.015	Broadcast	Ray	MAC Standby Monitor Present

Trace 6.3.1a. SNA/Token Ring Terminal Emulation Summary

Next, the host activated a Logical Unit (ACTLU), assigning Origin Address = 00 and Destination Address = 02 (Frame 19). The gateway again responded positively. The host next activated Destination Address = 03 and the gateway responded negatively, which indicated that the gateway was optioned to accommodate only one LU-LU session. This explained why the subsequent ACTLU commands (Frames 21 through 81) failed— the gateway could handle only one LU-LU session.

The solution was straightforward. The analyst reconfigured the gateway for a maximum of 32 LU-LU sessions. After that simple change, the host and gateway were able to communicate as required. In our next case study, we'll look at a misconfiguration on the host side. Readers interested in studying SNA gateways in further detail should consult References [6-45] through [6-48].

6.3.5 Token Ring/SNA Gateway Response Time Problems

In our final example, users on a Banyan VINES-based token ring network trying to access an IBM ES/9000 host over an SNA Gateway (see Figure 6-9) complained of very slow mainframe response. Upon closer examination, we determined that the response time was acceptable for small screens of data, but not for large screens.

We started our analysis by attaching a network analyzer to the backbone ring (review Figure 6-9) in order to capture the traffic from both the VINES server and the mainframe via the 3745 communication controllers.

The initial data (Trace 6.3.5) revealed stable operation of the MAC layer. Note that the Banyan server is the Active Monitor, and that the Active Monitor Present (Frames 1 through 3, 10, 13, 26, and so on) are transmitted every seven seconds as expected. The server would transmit its LU-LU Session Services capabilities (Frame 5), the host would request the application ID (the Function Management Data in Frame 7), and then BIND the session (Frame 19). Another session would BIND (Frames 29 and 30) and the host would start sending data (the Start Data Traffic—SDT in Frames 32 and 33.) The screen of data in Frame 32 was short (28 octets) and contained the request "ENTER USER ID," which was sent and acknowledged quickly. Beginning in Frame 44, a larger screen was then sent from the host. Because of its size, it was divided into four transmissions: Frame 44 (220 octets), Frame 48 (264 octets), Frame

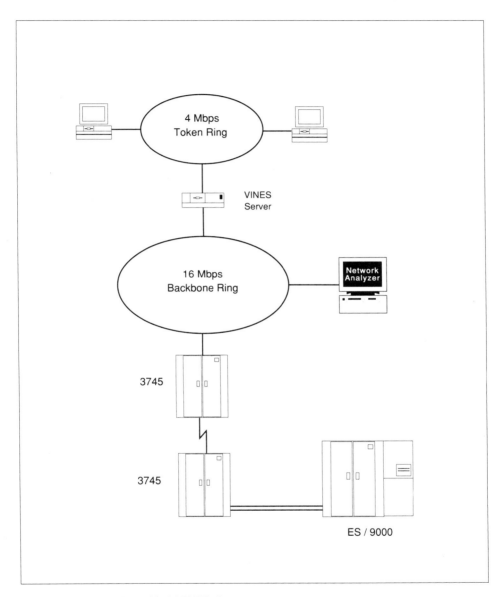

Figure 6-9. Token Ring/SNA VINES Gateway

51 (264 octets), and Frame 54 (269 octets). The server acknowledged this data in Frame 55. After each FMD frame, the host also transmitted an LLC Poll frame (Frames 46, 49, and 52). The time between the host data frame and the host polling frame was relatively long: 1.339 seconds (after Frame 44), 1.595 seconds (after Frame 48), and 1.595 seconds (after Frame 51). Thus, the host was inserting these polls after each data frame because the gateways was not responding. The lack of Acknowledgement (ACKs) was the source of the response time problem.

Sniffer Network Analyzer data 4-Apr-91 at 11:57:54, file 3745-TRN.TRC Pg 1

SUMMARY	Delta T	Size	Destination	Source	Summary
M 1		32	Broadcast	Banyan Svr	MAC Active Monitor Present
2	6.999	32	Broadcast	Banyan Svr	MAC Active Monitor Present
3	6.999	32	Broadcast	Banyan Svr	MAC Active Monitor Present
4	6.536	64	Broadcast	Banyan Svr	VIPC Datagram
					D=0013 S=02E8
5	0.019	38	3745 TIC	Banyan Svr	SNA C NOTIFY
6	0.002	18	Banyan Svr	3745 TIC	LLC R D=04 S=04 RR NR=35
7	0.068	101	Banyan Svr	3745 TIC	SNA C FMD user data
8	0.033	27	3745 TIC	Banyan Svr	SNA R FMD
9	0.002	30	Banyan Svr	3745 TIC	SNA R NOTIFY
10	0.351	32	Broadcast	Banyan Svr	MAC Active Monitor Present
11	1.222	18	Banyan Svr	3745 TIC	LLC C D=04 S=04 RR NR=36 P
12	0.000	18	3745 TIC	Banyan Svr	LLC R D=04 S=04 RR NR=36 F
13	5.776	28	Broadcast	Banyan Svr	MAC Active Monitor Present
14	5.112	31	3745 TIC	Banyan Svr	SNA C FMD user data
15	0.002	18	Banyan Svr	3745 TIC	LLC R D=04 S=04 RR NR=37
16	0.094	27	Banyan Svr	3745 TIC	SNA R FMD
17	1.510	18	Banyan Svr	3745 TIC	LLC C D=04 S=04 RR NR=37 P
18	0.000	18	3745 TIC	Banyan Svr	LLC R D=04 S=04 RR NR=37 F
19	0.002	62	Banyan Svr	3745 TIC	SNA C BIND LU2 A60TSO
20	0.009	28	3745 TIC	Banyan Svr	SNA R BIND
21	0.002	18	Banyan Svr	3745 TIC	LLC R D=04 S=04 RR NR=38

TROUBLESHOOTING IBM TOKEN RING/SNA INTERNETWORKS

22	0.100	28	Banyan Svr	3745 TIC	SNA C SDT
23	0.025	28	3745 TIC	Banyan Svr	SNA R SDT
24	0.002	18	Banyan Svr	3745 TIC	LLC R D=04 S=04 RR NR=39
25	0.128	29	Banyan Svr	3745 TIC	SNA C UNBIND
					(BIND forthcoming)
26	0.006	32	Broadcast	Banyan Svr	MAC Active Monitor Present
27	0.005	28	3745 TIC	Banyan Svr	SNA R UNBIND
28	0.002	18	Banyan Svr	3745 TIC	LLC R D=04 S=04 RR NR=40
29	0.132	64	Banyan Svr	3745 TIC	SNA C BIND LU2 A60TSO40
30	0.009	28	3745 TIC	Banyan Svr	SNA R BIND
31	0.002	18	Banyan Svr	3745 TIC	LLC R D=04 S=04 RR NR=41
32	0.065	28	Banyan Svr	3745 TIC	SNA C SDT
33	0.061	28	3745 TIC	Banyan Svr	SNA R SDT
34	0.002	18	Banyan Svr	3745 TIC	LLC R D=04 S=04 RR NR=42
35	0.036	69	Banyan Svr	3745 TIC	SNA C FMD user data
36	0.003	27	3745 TIC	Banyan Svr	SNA R FMD
37	0.003	18	Banyan Svr	3745 TIC	LLC R D=04 S=04 RR NR=43
38	0.012	27	3745 TIC	Banyan Svr	SNA R FMD
39	0.002	18	Banyan Svr	3745 TIC	LLC R D=04 S=04 RR NR=44
40	1.977	40	Broadcast	Banyan Svr	VRTP R Router Hello
41	4.680	32	Broadcast	Banyan Svr	MAC Active Monitor Present
42	4.885	40	3745 TIC	Banyan Svr	SNA C FMD user data
43	0.002	18	Banyan Svr	3745 TIC	LLC R D=04 S=04 RR NR=45
44	0.771	220	Banyan Svr	3745 TIC	SNA C FMD user data
45	1.339	32	Broadcast	Banyan Svr	MAC Active Monitor Present
46	0.218	18	Banyan Svr	3745 TIC	LLC C D=04 S=04 RR NR=45 P
47	0.000	18	3745 TIC	Banyan Svr	LLC R D=04 S=04 RR NR=44 F
48	0.004	264	Banyan Svr	3745 TIC	SNA FID Type 2
					continuation
49	1.595	18	Banyan Svr	3745 TIC	LLC C D=04 S=04 RR NR=45 P
50	0.000	18	3745 TIC	Banyan Svr	LLC R D=04 S=04 RR NR=45 F
51	0.003	264	Banyan Svr	3745 TIC	SNA FID Type 2
					continuation

52	1.595	18	Banyan Svr	3745 TIC	LLC C D=04 S=04 RR NR=45 P
53	0.000	18	3745 TIC	Banyan Svr	LLC R D=04 S=04 RR NR=46 F
54	0.003	269	Banyan Svr	3745 TIC	SNA FID Type 2
					continuation
55	0.005	27	3745 TIC	Banyan Svr	SNA R FMD
56	0.002	18	Banyan Svr	3745 TIC	LLC R D=04 S=04 RR NR=46
57	0.033	27	3745 TIC	Banyan Svr	SNA R FMD
58	0.002	18	Banyan Svr	3745 TIC	LLC R D=04 S=04 RR NR=47
59	3.534	32	Broadcast	Banyan Svr	MAC Active Monitor Present
60	6.999	32	Broadcast	Banyan Svr	MAC Active Monitor Present

Trace 6.3.5. Token Ring/SNA Response Time Problem

The analyst also noted, however, that the size of the frames transmitted from the host was unusually small (e.g. Frame 44 is only 220 octets in length). Since these captured frames were coming directly from the host (recall that the analyzer was placed on the backbone ring), we then questioned the host's configuration parameters. The host's VTAM switched majornode file revealed the following:

```
PAA882 PU    DISCNT=NO,
             ADDR=C5,
             IDBLK=017,
             IDNUM=A8802,
             MAXPATH=1,
             MAXOUT=1,
             MODETAB=MODTABLE,
             DLOGMOD=PC3270Y,
             PUTYPE=2,
             SSCPFM=USSSCS,
             USSTAB=USS24L1,
             VPACING=0,
             STATOPT='BACKBONE TOKEN'
```

After checking the VTAM documentation, we discovered that one line was missing:

MAXDATA = xxxx

MAXDATA is the host's maximum transmit buffer size. If this line is omitted from the switched majornode file, the PU definition defaults to MAXDATA = 265. This explained why the frame sizes were always less than a full screen's worth of data. Solving the problem was easy. The analyst added one line to that file:

MAXDATA = 2042

With this line in place, the host did not insert the polls, and the screen transfers occurred without delay. A second improvement in response time could be generated by setting MAXOUT = 7. This would allow the host to transmit seven frames of data (instead of only one) prior to expecting an acknowledgement. It's amazing what effect one line can have in a configuration file!

In this chapter, we have explored the complexities of both the token ring and SNA protocols. When combined into one internetwork, these two architectures make for a powerful combination for both LAN and WAN connections.

6.4 References

[6-1] Institute of Electrical and Electronics Engineers, *Token Ring Access Method and Physical Layer Specification*, IEEE Standard 802.5, 1989.

[6-2] Haugdahl, J. Scott. *Inside the Token-Ring*, 3rd Edition. Minneapolis, MN: Architecture Technology Corporation, 1990.

[6-3] Technology Research Corp., *The IBM Token-Ring Network*, 2nd Edition, 1991.

[6-4] Roetzheim, William H. *A C Programmer's Guide to the IBM Token Ring*. Englewood Cliffs, NJ: Prentice Hall, 1991.

[6-5] Miller, Mark A. *LAN Troubleshooting Handbook*. Redwood City, CA: M&T Books, Inc. 1989.

[6-6] Miller, Mark A. *LAN Protocol Handbook*. Redwood City, CA: M&T Books, Inc. 1990.

[6-7] Institute of Electrical and Electronic Engineers, Source Routing Supplement to IEEE 802.1d (MAC Bridges). IEEE Standard P802.5M/D5, August 15, 1991.

[6-8] *IBM Token-Ring Network Architecture Reference*, document SC30-3374-02.

[6-9] Miller, Mark A. *Internetworking: A Guide to Network Communications*. Redwood City, CA: M&T Books, Inc. 1991.

[6-10] Cypser, R.J. *Communications Architecture for Distributed Systems*. Reading, MA: Addison-Wesley Publishing Company, 1978.

[6-11] IBM. *Systems Network Architecture Concepts and Products*, document number GC30-3072-3.

[6-12] IBM. *Systems Network Architecture Technical Overview*, document number GC30-3073-2.

[6-13] Martin, James and Kathleen Kavanagh Chapman. *SNA: IBM's Networking Solution*. Englewood Cliffs, NJ: Prentice-Hall, Inc., 19 87.

[6-14] IBM. *IBM Synchronous Data Link Control General Information*, document number GA27-3093-2.

[6-15] Hoskins, Jim. *IBM AS/400: A Business Perspective*, 2nd Edition. New York: John Wiley & Sons, Inc., 1990.

[6-16] Carlo, Jim and John Hughes. "Token Ring Compatibility: It's Time to Plug and Play." *Data Communications* (November 21, 1989): 26-34.

[6-17] Guruge, Anura. "The New SNA: Router Backbones Unite Terminals and LANs," *Data Communications* (June 21, 1991): 24-36.

[6-18] Greenfield, David. "Multivendor Token Ring Networks Come of Age." *Data Communications* (November 21, 1989): 37-43.

[6-19] IBM. *SNA Sessions Between Logical Units*, document number GC20-1868.

[6-20] IBM. *Systems Network Architecture Format and Protocol Reference Manual: Architectural Logic*, document number SC30-3112.

[6-21] IBM. *Systems Network Architecture Reference Summary*, document number GA27-3136-4.

[6-22] Miller, Mark A. "Troubleshooting the Token Ring," *LAN Technology* (June 1989): 48-53.

[6-23] Schulman, Chris. "Complex Token-Ring Cabling Built on a Simple Foundation." *LAN Times* (November 19, 1990): 48-53.

[6-24] IBM. *Token-Ring Network Problem Determination Guide*, document number SX27-3710.

[6-25] Proteon, Inc., *Networking the SNA Environment: A Proteon Perspective*, May 1991.

[6-26] CrossComm Corporation. "How to Combine SNA and LAN Traffic Over a Common Wide Area Network," *Internetworking Solutions* Issue 1, February 1991.

[6-27] Texas Instruments, *TMS380 Second-Generation Token Ring User's Guide*, 1990.

[6-28] IBM. *Using the IBM Trace and Performance Program for Problem Determination on a Token-Ring Local Area Network*, document number GG22-9456-00, September 1989.

[6-29] IBM. *Managing Problems for NCP Gateways Token Ring Connections*, document number GG66-3205, June 1991.

[6-30] IBM. *Advanced Communications Function for VTAM (ACF/VTAM) SNA Problem Determination Reference Summary*, document number SX27-3030-0.

[6-31] Dixon, Roy C. and Daniel A. Pitt. "Source Routing Bridges: Addressing, Bridging, and Source Routing." *IEEE Network* (January 1988): 25-32.

[6-32] Hamner, M. Claire and Gerald R. Samsen. "Source Routing Bridge Implementation." *IEEE Network* (January 1988): 33-36.

[6-33] Thiele, Everett. "Source Routing for Token Ring LANs, Transparent Bridging Is Not The Only Way." *LAN Magazine* (February 1989): 80-87.

[6-34] Layland, Robin. "Gridlock Alert: Source Routing." *Network World* (November 12, 1990): 42-48.

[6-35] Layland, Robin. "Token Ring Bridges and Routers: Heirs to the SNA Throne." *Data Communications* (November 21, 1990): 30-44.

[6-36] Lothers, Robert. "Option Shock: Connecting Token-Ring LANs." *Business Communications Review* (February 1991): 31-37.

[6-37] Proteon, Inc., *NetPerspectives: Building Today's Token Ring Infrastructure*, Spring 1991.

[6-38] Cross Comm Corporation. *Token Ring Internetworking: A Guide for IBM Users*, Advertising Supplement to *Network World*, August 26, 1991.

[6-39] Tolly, Kevin. "Ring Bridges: Plug and Play or Plug and Pay?" *Data Communications* (August 1991): 60-76.

[6-40] Tolly, Kevin and Steven S. King. "Remote Token Ring Bridges, Part 2." *Data Communications* (September 21, 1991): 16-35.

[6-41] IBM. *Token-Ring Network NetBIOS Program, NetBIOS Formats, and Protocols*, Supplement to *IBM Token-Ring Network PC Adapter Technical Reference*, document number 6165876, November 1987.

[6-42] IBM. *Local Area Network Technical Reference*, document SC30-3383-2, Third Edition, 1988.

[6-43] Haugdahl, J. Scott. *Inside NetBIOS*, 3rd Edition. Minneapolis, MN: Architecture Technology Corporation, 1990.

[6-44] Schwaderer, W. David. "C Programmer's Guide to NetBIOS." Indianapolis, IN: Howard W. Sams & Company, 1988.

[6-45] Routt, Thomas J. "SNA to OSI: IBM Building Upper-Layer Gateways." *Data Communications* (May 1987): 120-142.

[6-46] Tolly, Kevin. "Playing to Win with IBM's LAN Gateways." *Data Communications* (February 1990): 74-95.

[6-47] Tolly, Kevin. "Opening the Gateways to SNA Connectivity." *Data Communications* (March 1990): 89-102.

[6-48] Tolly, Kevin. "Surprise! SNA Gateways Are More Than Mere Child's Play." *Data Communications* (October 1990): 79-96.

CHAPTER 7

Troubleshooting Novell NetWare Internetworks

Novell Inc.'s (Provo, UT) NetWare is the most popular of the available LAN operating systems. Market researchers report that NetWare accounts for the majority of the LAN market share and will continue to dominate the LAN market in the near future [7-1]. In addition to its strength in the LAN arena, Novell has been shifting NetWare in the direction of internetworking. To its traditional DOS base, NetWare has added support for new workstation types, such as the Macintosh and OS/2, new host environments, such as UNIX and VMS systems, and WANs. The latest version, 3.x, has added support for a number of non-Novell proprietary protocols. Before we examine Novell's internetworking protocols in depth, it's important to understand the architecture of NetWare 2.x and NetWare 3.x.

7.1 NetWare Architectures and Protocols

NetWare's success in the marketplace can be attributed to the rigor with which its architecture and protocols have been designed. Novell used proven Xerox Network Systems (XNS) protocols as the core of the operating system, then added internetwork communication options, such as specialized servers and gateways, as the need arose. Version 3.x further enhanced interoperability with support for additional protocols. Let's begin by looking at the architectural differences between NetWare version 2.x (286-based) and NetWare version 3.x (386-based).

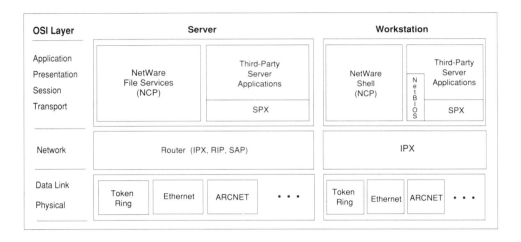

Figure 7-1a. NetWare 286 Architecture
(Courtesy Novell, Inc.)

7.1.1 NetWare 286 Architecture

NetWare 2.x, also referred to as NetWare 286, was introduced in 1983 and designed to run on virtually any type of LAN hardware. In the original version, Novell based its operating system on a proprietary file server that communicated with DOS-based workstations. Novell added support for OS/2 and Macintosh workstations in subsequent releases.

The NetWare architecture is comprised of four basic components: the NetWare File Services and the NetWare Core Protocol (NCP); Novell and third party server applications that use the Sequenced Packet Exchange (SPX) protocol; the Router function, which uses the Routing Information Protocol (RIP), the Internetwork Packet Exchange (IPX) protocol, and the Service Advertising Protocol (SAP); and the local network hardware (token ring, Ethernet, ARCNET, and so on.), as shown in Figure 7-1a.

The NetWare Shell, the SPX protocol, and the NetBIOS emulator allow workstation applications to communicate with the network. The NetWare Shell runs in the workstation or in a non-dedicated server and resides in a terminate-and-stay-resident (TSR) program called NETX.COM. Novell and third party server applica-

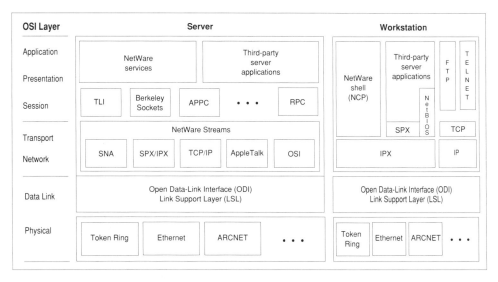

Figure 7-1b. NetWare 386 Architecture
(Courtesy Novell, Inc.)

tions (Value Added Processes (VAPs) in NetWare 2.x) use the SPX protocol to access the Router function for transmission over the network. Once the workstation has been hooked up to the network, IPX and NCP establish communications with the server. IPX is based upon the XNS protocol known as the *Internetwork Datagram Protocol* (IDP) [7-2]; NCP is a Novell-proprietary protocol. Basically, IPX establishes the route to the server. IPX.COM, another program that implements IPX protocols, provides hardware drivers for more than 100 different hardware architectures, including ARCNET, Ethernet, and so on. Thus, IPX.COM acts as a liaison between the NetWare Shell and the network hardware. NCP establishes the logical connection to the server.

To summarize, the Shell intercepts an application that requests network services, formulates a request packet and sends it to IPX.COM for transmission. The network hardware and cable complete the transmission path between workstation and server. Reference [7-3] provides further details on NetWare version 2.

7.1.2 NetWare 386 Architecture

As its name implies, NetWare 3.x, also called NetWare 386, supports the Intel 80386 processor family. NetWare 386 has enhanced NetWare version 2.x by allowing for greater numbers of workstations and offering more file storage, server applications, and communication options (see Figure 7-1b). The primary objective of the new version is to support a variety of LAN/WAN protocols from many vendors (see References [7-4] through [7-6]). The core of this architecture is a number of independent Transport and Network Layer protocol stacks such as IBM's SNA, Novell's SPX/IPX, TCP/IP, AppleTalk, and OSI. NetWare Streams manages the protocol stacks and provides interfaces both to these stacks and to server applications (called *NetWare Loadable Modules* (NLMs) in 3.x. An example of an NLM is Oracle NLM.SQL). The interfaces include AT&T's Transport Level Interface (TLI), Berkeley Sockets, IBM's Advanced Program-to-Program Communication (APPC), and Sun's Remote Procedure Calls (RPC) for NFS. The Link Support Layer (LSL) passes the Data Link Layer frame to the appropriate protocol stack. The Open Data-link Interface (ODI) is a common interface specification that allows LAN hardware vendors to develop a single device driver rather than individual drivers for each protocol stack in use (e.g. SPX/IPX, TCP/IP, etc.). By supporting ODI, a single NIC can access multiple protocol stacks and frame types. ODI also allows the administrator to reconfigure the protocol stacks dynamically without having to reboot the workstation. References [7-7] and [7-8] discuss the ODI in greater detail.

As a final note, Novell has also extended its operating system to encompass a variety of workstation and host environments [7-9]. The NetWare Requester for OS/2 [7-10], NetWare for Macintosh ([7-11] and [7-12]), and NetWare NFS for UNIX workstations, allow additional workstation platforms to run in the NetWare environment and share files. NetWare for VMS allows a host running DEC's VMS operating system to act as a NetWare server for both DOS and OS/2 workstations [7-13]. Portable NetWare permits non-NetWare hosts (such as UNIX hosts) to function as NetWare servers (see References [7-14] through [7-16]). Other products, such as Novell's Communications Server, NetWare Access Server, and Asynchronous Communications Server provide links into WAN environments (see Reference [7-17], Chapter 8).

In the next section, we'll study the protocols that are incorporated into the NetWare environment. The discussions relative to protocols apply to both NetWare 2.x and NetWare 3.x unless stated otherwise.

7.1.3 NetWare Physical and Data Link Layers

Novell has seen to it that NetWare can operate with virtually all LAN hardware (see Figure 7-2), including ARCNET, Ethernet, token ring, and StarLAN NICs from a number of vendors. NetWare also supports more specialized networks such as

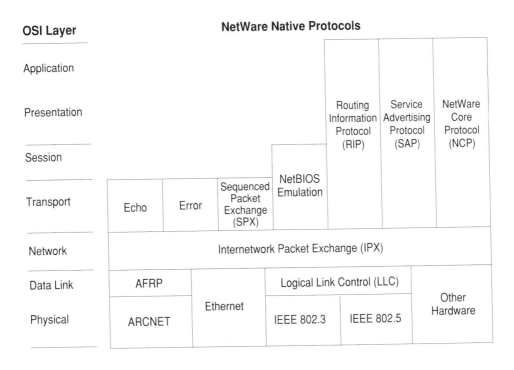

Figure 7-2. NetWare Native Protocols
(Courtesy Novell, Inc.)

Omninet (Corvus Systems, Inc., San Jose, CA), ProNET-10 (Proteon, Inc., Westborough, MA), Vista LAN (Allen-Bradley, Ann Arbor, MI), G/Net (Gateway Communications, Inc., Irvine, CA), and others.

As discussed above, Novell's architecture requires a LAN driver (IPX.COM) customized for the hardware in use. (In NetWare versions 2.2 and 3.x, the ODI and Link Support Layer (LSL) provide these functions.) With this driver, Higher Layer protocols and processes can be consistent across all hardware implementations. (Another protocol, known as the ARCNET Fragmentation Protocol (AFRP), is used for ARCNET, which has a maximum transmission frame size of 508 octets of data. AFRP breaks up and reassembles the NetWare packets into the smaller units required by the ARCNET hardware). NetWare's success in the marketplace can thus be attributed to its widespread support among hardware vendors. (Further details on specific hardware implementations can be found in Reference [7-18]. An example of diagnosing a hardware fault on an Ethernet running NetWare is given in Chapter 3 of Reference [7-19].)

7.1.4 NetWare Network Layer

The XNS protocols influence NetWare's Network and higher layers. The Internetwork Packet Exchange (IPX) protocol is a derivative of the XNS Internet Datagram Protocol (IDP). (References [7-20] and [7-21] are excellent references on the XNS protocols; References [7-22] and [7-23] describe IPX.) The IPX header is 30 octets long, and includes the internetwork addressing (see Section 7.1.6) required to move the NetWare packet from a source node to a destination node within the internetwork. IPX provides datagram (or connectionless) packet transport service. It transmits each data unit as an independent entity, without establishing a logical connection between the two endpoints. IPX, therefore, does not guarantee delivery of each packet. Instead, the Transport layer protocols, SPX or NCP, described below, offer the reliable delivery that IPX lacks.

7.1.5 NetWare Transport and Higher Layers

NetWare's Transport and Higher Layers use six protocols (as well as other Application Program Interfaces (APIs), such as NetBIOS). The Packet Type field within the IPX header specifies which of these protocols is in use.

The first protocol is known as the Sequenced Packet Exchange (SPX). SPX is a connection-oriented protocol used for reliable peer-to-peer communication. Based upon the XNS Sequenced Packet Protocol (SPP), SPX guarantees in-sequence and correct delivery of packets. SPX is often associated with IPX, as in SPX/IPX.

A second group of protocols, comprised of Echo and Error, is also derived from XNS. The Echo protocol tests a communication path between two workstations by returning a packet back to the sender. The Error protocol reports packet errors on the internetwork.

The third group of protocols consists of the Routing Information Protocol (RIP) and the Service Advertising Protocol (SAP) used for internetworking. RIP (also derived from XNS) allows various entities within the internetwork to exchange routing information. This allows routers to establish and maintain tables of the internetwork topology that workstations can use to determine the fastest route to a particular network. The RIP packet specifies the number of hops (how many routers must be traversed) and the number of "ticks" (1 second = 18.21 ticks) required to reach that network. Sending a packet via the route with the minimum number of ticks speeds the workstation's response time. RIP packets are broadcast every 60 seconds to inform all routers of the current internetwork topology. Each RIP packet can contain information on up to 50 networks. SAP allows service nodes, such as file servers, print servers, asynchronous communication servers, and gateways to advertise their service to the rest of the network. All of the routers on the internetwork collect and share this information so that workstations can inquire about, and find, the service that they need. Like RIP, this information is broadcast every 60 seconds. Each SAP packet can contain information regarding a maximum of seven servers.

Finally, the NetWare Core Protocol (NCP) is the heart of the NetWare operating system. The NCP facilitates interaction between clients (or workstations) and file servers. The NCP handles two aspects of the communication: It controls the connection between client and server, and it requests a particular type of service (e.g.

read from a file). The NetWare Shell or NetWare Requester for OS/2 handles the processing of NCP packets at the workstation. We will study the client/server interactions in Section 7.3.2.

7.1.6 NetWare Internetwork Addressing

The IPX header fields contain the address information necessary to route a NetWare packet from its source to its destination properly. A total of 12 octets specify a complete address. The 4-octet Destination and Source Network numbers contain the unique network number assigned to that segment on the NetWare internetwork. (This number is assigned during the NETGEN process when the network is configured in the NetWare 2.x environment (INSTALL for NetWare 2.2) or when the BIND IPX command is invoked in the NetWare 3.x environment.) The internetwork routers use the network number to transfer the packet to the correct network segment. A Destination Network Number = 0 implies that the destination node and source node reside on the same network so that no internetwork routing is necessary.

The 6-octet Destination and Source Node addresses specify the hardware address of the node in question. For IEEE 802.x compliant nodes, this number will be the 48-bit or 6-octet number resident in the address ROM on the NIC or assigned by the administrator through a Locally-Administered Address (LAA). For other hardware devices that require fewer than 6 octets of addressing (e.g. ARCNET requires only 1 octet), the address is placed in the least significant portion of the field and the remaining bits are set equal to zero. A Destination Node Address = FFFFFFFFFFFFH (48 ones in binary notation) is an all-stations broadcast message to all nodes on the destination network.

NetWare file servers may contain multiple NICs, each of which is connected to a specific network segment. The server performs routing internally between these network segments. NetWare 2.x can handle up to 4 NICs in the server, NetWare 3.x up to 16. In NetWare 2. x, these NICs are designated NICa, NICb, NICc, and NICd. In NetWare 3.x, the driver name identifies the specific card.

A NetWare 2.x server is identified with its NICa address. In NetWare 3.x, a number is assigned during system configuration to internally address the various file services. As a result, NetWare 3.x-based servers are identified to the internetwork (i.e. externally) by a Node Address = 1. The server's internal number further delineates the various attached networks.

Within a particular node, a 2-octet Socket address distinguishes the appropriate higher layer process for that packet. Novell has assigned sockets for specific purposes:

Device	Protocol	Socket (hex)	Socket (decimal)
File Servers	NCP	451	1105
Routers	SAP	452	1106
	RIP	453	1107
Workstations	NetBIOS	455	1109
	Diagnostics	456	1110
	* Ephemeral	4000-6000	16,384-24,576

*(used for file server and network communication)

Thus, a workstation with a ROM address of 02070108E2EEH on network EFFFFFFFH might use socket 4003H to communicate with a file server. The workstation's full address (Network:Node:Socket) would be EFFFFFFF:02070108E2EE:4003H. If the server was on network 0000100 0H, using the NCP protocol (socket 451H), the server's full address would be 00001000:000000000001:0451H.

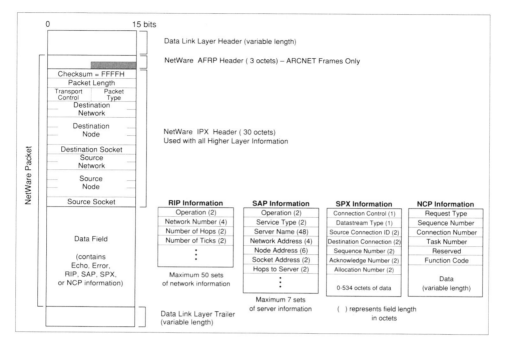

Figure 7-3. NetWare Packet Formats
(Courtesy Novell, Inc.)

7.1.7 NetWare Packet Formats

The NetWare packet can take on a number of formats, depending upon the function and the protocols being used (see Figure 7-3). The packet is encapsulated within the Data Link Layer frame header and trailer, defined by the hardware in use (Ethernet, token ring, etc.). If the Data Link Layer is ARCNET, then the 3-octet ARCNET Fragmentation Protocol (AFRP) will immediately follow the ARCNET header. In all cases, the IPX header is transmitted next. This 30-octet header is divided into a number of fields. The 2-octet checksum, 2-octet Packet length, 1-octet Transport Control, and 1-octet Packet type fields provide control information. A number of packet types are defined including RIP (Type = 1), Echo (Type = 2), Error (Type = 3), SPX (Type = 5), and NCP (Type = 17). The remainder of the IPX header is used for packet addressing: the 4-octet Destination Network, 6-octet Node, and 2-octet Socket, and similar fields for the Source addresses.

314

Information from one of the higher layer protocols is transmitted next. The most common are SPX, RIP, SAP, and NCP. The 12-octet SPX header contains the connection and sequence numbers necessary to assure reliable packet delivery. A RIP packet begins with a 2-octet operation field that specifies a Request (Operation = 1) or a Response (Operation = 2). Network information (total of 8 octets) comes next, with up to 50 sets per RIP packet. The SAP packet also begins with a 2-octet Operation field that specifies one of five different operations, including workstation and router requests, and periodic server and router responses. Server information (64 octets per server) follows, which includes the Service Type, Server Name and Address, and number of hops. An SAP packet can contain information on up to seven servers.

Finally, the NCP packet transfers the actual data between the client and the file server. This packet includes a Request Type (e.g. create connection, destroy connection), Sequence Number, Connection Number, Task Number, and Function Code. The data being sent would complete the packet. Several hundred NCP packet types exist. Figure 7-3 illustrates the general structure of the transmitted NCP information. Further details on SPX can be found in [7-24]; RIP, SAP, and NCP are described in [7-25]; and Error and Echo protocols are discussed in [7-26].

With this background in the native NetWare protocols, let's look at some techniques for analyzing Novell internetworks.

7.2 NetWare Protocol Analysis Techniques

Because NetWare is so popular, many reference books, including [7-27] through [7-29], are available to assist network managers with system administration. In this section, we'll offer suggestions for identifying some typical NetWare internetwork problems. Here are some guidelines:

1. Verify the integrity of the workstation, server, and cable plant hardware. Unlike networks such as SNA or DECnet that tend to be part of a large, well-controlled system, NetWare networks generally start small and grow as the need arises. As the network grows, certain liberties may be taken with the cable plant (e.g. extending the bus length beyond specification or using the

wrong type of coax cable or connector). It is, therefore, vital to verify that the cables, repeaters, terminators, hubs, and so on, are working. The diagnostic disk that comes with most vendors' NICs can also be a valuable diagnostic resource. Reference [7-30] discusses some techniques for hardware troubleshooting when a workstation displays the "File Server Not Found" message.

2. Become familiar with the NetWare management utilities, such as USERLIST (user list), SLIST (server list), FCONSOLE (file server console), and the Monitor (NetWare 3.11). These utilities offer the user many performance statistics, including current server utilization, routing buffers, and router (bridge) I/O. Reference [7-31] describes how the network administrator can more effectively use the built-in NetWare management tools.

3. Be aware of the NetWare utilities that affect internetwork transmission and routing. The DCONFIG utility [7-31] can change the node or network address, routing buffers, and so forth. The ECONFIG utility [7-13] configures the workstation driver to transmit Ethernet v.2.0 or IEEE 802.3 frames. (Differences in these two frame formats are shown in Appendix G.)

4. Check that the NetWare 3.x server is set up to load the proper Ethernet version 2.0 or IEEE 802.3 frame with the AUTOEXEC.NCF file. For example:

LOAD 3C507 PORT=30 MEM=D0000 INT=30 FRAME=ETHERNET_802.3 NAME=E8023

5. Verify that the workstation drivers (NETx.COM and IPX.COM) are the proper type for that hardware (ARCNET, Ethernet, etc.). For ARCNET, be alert to possible problems from having multiple versions of different vendors' IPX.COM files. The user should also watch for "turbo" versions of ARCNET IPX.COM that may not coexist with "non-turbo" versions.

6. Make sure that the NET.CFG or SHELL.CFG file is in the directory where NetWare modules are being executed.

7. Assure that all workstation node and network addresses are unique. The administrator defines the network address during network configuration, and the user may configure the node address (known locally as a *locally-administered address*).

8. Identify the servers and routers on the internetwork and verify the occurrence of periodic broadcasts. Every 60 seconds, servers broadcast SAP information and Routers broadcast RIP information. Consult Reference [7-25] for specifics on these broadcasts. Also verify that the server's watchdog process is operating. This process polls any workstation that has not been heard from for five minutes. The watchdog polls every minute until it has transmitted 11 polls (total time of 15 minutes). If no response is heard, the workstation connection is cleared. (The number and frequency of these broadcasts can be adjusted in NetWare 3.11.) We will discuss NetWare routing in Section 7.3.1.

9. If the problem relates to a custom application, such as a Value Added Process (VAP, on NetWare 2.x) or a NetWare Loadable Module (NLM, on NetWare 3.x), you may need to analyze the server. Reference [7-32], written by Novell's Developer Support Group, offers a step-by-step bit-level procedure for debugging the server. This reference includes forms that you can use to record and interpret information from the server's interval registers prior to contacting Novell for further assistance.

10. Become familiar with the NetWire database that is available on CompuServe (CompuServe Information Service, Columbus, OH). NetWire is an excellent source of NetWare documentation, technical bulletins, patches, and fixes. It's also a great way to trade information with other NetWare users and administrators. Reference [7-31] discusses the various NetWire options.

Let's now put these techniques to use by studying six case histories of NetWare internetwork problems.

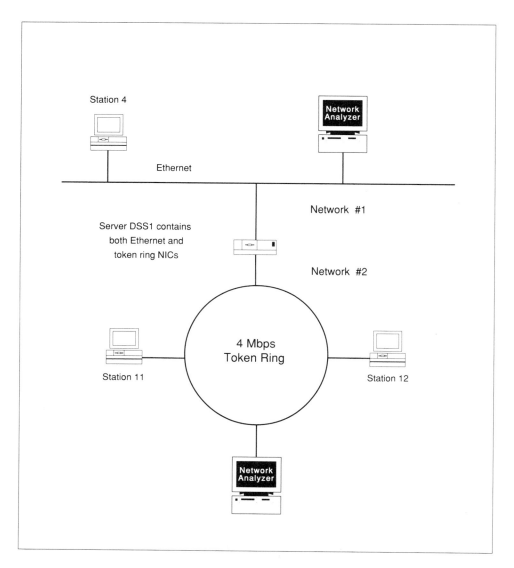

Station 4

Network Analyzer

Ethernet

Network #1

Server DSS1 contains
both Ethernet and
token ring NICs

Network #2

4 Mbps
Token Ring

Station 11

Station 12

Network Analyzer

Figure 7-4. NetWare Internal Router Operation

7.3 NetWare Internetwork Troubleshooting

Novell has included a number of internetworking protocols into its NetWare operating system, which may partially explain NetWare's success in the marketplace. Let's begin our study of NetWare internetwork analysis by looking at the operation of a NetWare server.

7.3.1 NetWare Internal Routing

In our discussion of the NetWare addressing schemes (Section 7.1.6), we said that a NetWare 2.x server can hold up to four NICs, each of which connects to a distinct LAN. In our first example, we will study a NetWare internetwork that contains both Ethernet and token ring segments (see Figure 7-4). The Ethernet segment is designated network Number 1, and the token ring segment is designated network Number 2. The NetWare server provides the internetworking between the Ethernet and token ring segments, using an option known as *internal routing*. (Note that this is a routing, not a bridging function, since the Network Layer protocol, IPX, is involved in the communication process.)

First, let's look at the token ring side of the internetwork and see what traffic the NetWare server (designated DSS1) is generating. Three stations are active on the token ring side: two PCs (Station 11 and Station 12) plus the token ring board in the server (Server-TR). In Trace 7.3.1a (filtered to show the MAC frames only), the server is acting as the active monitor, transmitting MAC Active Monitor Present frames every seven seconds. Stations 11 and 12 are also active on the network and respond with MAC Standby Monitor Present frames.

Sniffer Network Analyzer data 11-Sep-91 at 06:28:18 file ROUTNORM.TRC Pg 1

SUMMARY	Delta T	Destination	Source	Summary
M 1		Broadcast	Server-TR	MAC Active Monitor Present
2	0.013	Broadcast	Station 12	MAC Standby Monitor Present
3	0.019	Broadcast	Station 11	MAC Standby Monitor Present
4	6.965	Broadcast	Server-TR	MAC Active Monitor Present
5	0.013	Broadcast	Station 12	MAC Standby Monitor Present
6	0.019	Broadcast	Station 11	MAC Standby Monitor Present

319

7	6.965	Broadcast	Server-TR	MAC Active Monitor Present
8	0.013	Broadcast	Station 12	MAC Standby Monitor Present
9	0.019	Broadcast	Station 11	MAC Standby Monitor Present
11	6.965	Broadcast	Server-TR	MAC Active Monitor Present
12	0.013	Broadcast	Station 12	MAC Standby Monitor Present
13	0.019	Broadcast	Station 11	MAC Standby Monitor Present
14	6.965	Broadcast	Server-TR	MAC Active Monitor Present
16	0.013	Broadcast	Station 12	MAC Standby Monitor Present
17	0.019	Broadcast	Station 11	MAC Standby Monitor Present
18	6.980	Broadcast	Server-TR	MAC Active Monitor Present
19	0.013	Broadcast	Station 12	MAC Standby Monitor Present
20	0.018	Broadcast	Station 11	MAC Standby Monitor Present

Trace 7.3.1a. NetWare Internetwork token ring MAC frames

At the same time, the NetWare protocols are transmitting periodic information as well. The server transmits routing information (RIP) packets every 66 seconds to inform other routers about the other network (net = 00000001) that is one hop away (Frames 10, 40, and 72 in Trace 7.3.1b). The server advertises its presence by transmitting NetWare Service Advertising (SAP) packets every 66 seconds (Frames 24, 57, and 89). The server asks both stations if they are still active on the network by transmitting a NetWare Request Keep Alive (or watchdog) packet in Frames 70 and 99. Each station is queried every 297 seconds although this time period is not shown in Trace 7.3.1b.

Sniffer Network Analyzer data 11-Sep-91 at 06:28:18 file ROUTNORM.TRC Pg 1

SUMMARY	Delta T	Destination	Source	Summary
10		NetWare	Server-TR	XNS RIP response: 1 network, 00000001 at 1 hop
24	32.957	NetWare	Server-TR	XNS NetWare Service Adver
40	32.941	NetWare	Server-TR	XNS RIP response: 1 network, 00000001 at 1 hop

57	32.956	NetWare	Server-TR	XNS NetWare Service Adver
70	27.505	Station 12	Server-TR	XNS NetWare Request
				Keep alive C=7
71	0.002	Server-TR	Station 12	XNS NetWare Reply
				Keep alive C=7
72	5.433	NetWare	Server-TR	XNS RIP response: 1 network,
				00000001 at 1 hop
89	32.957	NetWare	Server-TR	XNS NetWare Service Adver
99	20.971	Station 11	Server-TR	XNS NetWare Request
				Keep alive C=9
100	0.002	Server-TR	Station 11	XNS NetWare Reply
				Keep alive C=9

Trace 7.3.1b. NetWare Internetwork Periodic Broadcasts (Token Ring Side)

The details of the broadcasts reveal the internetwork addresses in use (Trace 7.3.1c). Frame 10, a RIP packet, is broadcast from the Server-TR NIC (host = 10005A6FA28CH) on network 00000002 (the token ring). It identifies another network (net = 00000001, the Ethernet) one hop away. (The one hop is via the server's bus, as the packet would cross from the token ring to Ethernet side.) The SAP packet (Frame 24) informs the internetwork devices (routers) that a NetWare file server is on the network.

```
Sniffer Network Analyzer data 11-Sep-91 at 06:28:18 file ROUTNORM.TRC Pg 1
- - - - - - - - - - - - - - - Frame 10 - - - - - - - - - - - - - - - - -
XNS: —— XNS Header ——
XNS: \par XNS: Checksum = FFFF
XNS: Length = 40
XNS: Transport control = 00
XNS:     0000 .... = Reserved
XNS:     .... 0000 = Hop count
XNS: Packet type = 1 (RIP)
XNS:
```

XNS: Dest net = 00000002, host = FFFFFFFFFFFF, socket = 1107 (NetWare Routing)

XNS: Source net = 00000002, host = 10005A6FA28C, socket = 1107 (NetWare Routing)

XNS:

XNS: —— Novell Routing Information Protocol (RIP) ——

XNS:

XNS: Operation = 2 (response)

XNS:

XNS: Object network = 00000001, hop count = 1

XNS:

- - - - - - - - - - - - - - - Frame 24 - - - - - - - - - - - - - - - -

XNS: —— XNS Header ——

XNS:

XNS: Checksum = FFFF

XNS: Length = 96

XNS: Transport control = 00

XNS: 0000 .... = Reserved

XNS: .... 0000 = Hop count

XNS: Packet type = 4 (PEP)

XNS:

XNS: Dest net = 00000002, host = FFFFFFFFFFFF, socket = 1106 (NetWare Service Advertising)

XNS: Source net = 00000002, host = 10005A6FA28C, socket = 1106 (NetWare Service Advertising)

XNS:

Trace 7.3.1c. NetWare Internetwork Periodic Broadcast Details

When the network analyzer is moved to the Ethernet side of the internetwork, we find that NetWare broadcasts are similar to those from the token ring network. In Trace 7.3.1d, the server periodically transmits NCP packets that identify the server name (DSS1) and the network that the server is connected to, network 00000001 (see Frames 1, 3, 5, and 7). The RIP packet broadcasts (Frames 2, 4, 6, and 8) now indicate the presence of the token ring network (net = 00000002) at a distance of one hop.

Sniffer Network Analyzer data 11-Sep-91 at 05:56:16, file SRVNORM.ENC Pg 1

SUMMARY	Delta T	Destination	Source	Summary
M 1		Broadcast	DSS Server	NCP R DSS1
2	32.9546	Broadcast	DSS Server	XNS RIP response: 1 network, 00000002 at 1 hop
3	32.9547	Broadcast	DSS Server	NCP R DSS1
4	32.9546	Broadcast	DSS Server	XNS RIP response: 1 network, 00000002 at 1 hop
5	32.9547	Broadcast	DSS Server	NCP R DSS1
6	32.9546	Broadcast	DSS Server	XNS RIP response: 1 network, 00000002 at 1 hop
7	32.9548	Broadcast	DSS Server	NCP R DSS1
8	32.9546	Broadcast	DSS Server	XNS RIP response: 1 network, 00000002 at 1 hop
9	1.1533	Station 4	DSS Server	XNS NetWare Request Keep alive C=8
10	0.0006	DSS Server	Station 4	XNS NetWare Reply Keep alive C=8

Trace 7.3.1d. NetWare Internetwork Periodic Broadcasts (Ethernet side)

Now let's trace an electronic mail message from the Ethernet to the token ring side of the internet to verify connectivity. (Electronic mail is included with most network operating systems and is an extremely useful "built-in" troubleshooting tool.) The network analyst goes to an Ethernet station (Station 4 in Figure 7-4) and enters SEND "hello carl" TO STATION 11 (see Trace 7.3.1e). The NetWare server must first find the E-mail file (SEND.EXE discovered in Frame 15). The server then opens the file (Frames 22 and 23), and reads/transfers the file to Station 4 (Frames 24 through 59). Next, Station 4 must look for the intended message recipient (Frame 68) and enter the message (Frame 72). The task is completed in Frame 77.

TROUBLESHOOTING INTERNETWORKS

Sniffer Network Analyzer data 11-Sep-91 at 05:54:08, file MAIL411.ENC Pg 1

SUMMARY	Delta T	Destination	Source	Summary
M 1	3Com	3C616B	DSS Server	XNS NetWare Request
				Keep alive C=11
2	14.6387	DSS Server	Station 4	NCP C Get dir path of handle 05
3	0.0009	Station 4	DSS Server	NCP R OK Path=SYS:HOME/
				DSS4
4	0.0015	DSS Server	Station 4	NCP C Dir search parms
				for [null]
5	0.0005	Station 4	DSS Server	NCP R OK Next=-1
6	0.0009	DSS Server	Station 4	NCP C Dir search SEND.???
7	0.0007	Station 4	DSS Server	NCP R File not found
8	0.0009	DSS Server	Station 4	NCP C Dir search SEND.???
9	0.0007	Station 4	DSS Server	NCP R File not found
10	0.0012	DSS Server	Station 4	NCP C Get dir path of handle 02
11	0.0008	Station 4	DSS Server	NCP R OK Path=SYS:PUBLIC
12	0.0015	DSS Server	Station 4	NCP C Dir search parms for ./
13	0.0021	Station 4	DSS Server	NCP R OK Next=-1
14	0.0009	DSS Server	Station 4	NCP C Dir search SEND.???
15	0.0066	Station 4	DSS Server	NCP R OK File=SEND.EXE
16	0.0011	DSS Server	Station 4	NCP C Dir search SEND.???
17	0.0076	Station 4 D	SS Server	NCP R File not found
18	0.0009	DSS Server	Station 4	NCP C Dir search SEND.???
19	0.0109	Station 4	DSS Server	NCP R File not found
20	0.0011	DSS Server	Station 4	NCP C Get dir path of handle 02
21	0.0008	Station 4	DSS Server	NCP R OK Path=SYS:PUBLIC
22	0.0021	DSS Server	Station 4	NCP C Open file
				/PUBLIC/SEND.EXE
23	0.0089	Station 4	DSS Server	NCP R F=B316 OK Opened
24	0.0019	DSS Server	Station 4	NCP C F=B316 Read 30 at 0
25	0.0006	Station 4	DSS Server	NCP R OK 30 bytes read
26	0.0021	DSS Server	Station 4	NCP C F=B316 Read 512 at 512

27	0.0011	Station 4	DSS Server	NCP R OK 512 bytes read
28	0.0016	DSS Server	Station 4	NCP C F=B316 Read 1024 at 1024
29	0.0016	Station 4	DSS Server	NCP R OK 1024 bytes read
30	0.0023	DSS Server	Station 4	NCP C F=B316 Read 1024 at 2048
31	0.0017	Station 4	DSS Server	NCP R OK 1024 bytes read
32	0.0023	DSS Server	Station 4	NCP C F=B316 Read 1024 at 3072
33	0.0017	Station 4	DSS Server	NCP R OK 1024 bytes read
34	0.0022	DSS Server	Station 4	NCP C F=B316 Read 1024 at 4096
35	0.0017	Station 4	DSS Server	NCP R OK 1024 bytes read
36	0.0023	DSS Server	Station 4	NCP C F=B316 Read 1024 at 5120
37	0.0016	Station 4	DSS Serer	NCP R OK 1024 bytes read
38	0.0023	DSS Server	Station 4	NCP C F=B316 Read 1024 at 6144
39	0.0017	Station 4	DSS Server	NCP R OK 1024 bytes read
40	0.0023	DSS Server	Station 4	NCP C F=B316 Read 1024 at 7168
41	0.0017	Station 4	DSS Server	NCP R OK 1024 bytes read
42	0.0023	DSS Server	Station 4	NCP C F=B316 Read 1024 at 8192
43	0.0017	Station 4	DSS Server	NCP R OK 1024 bytes read
44	0.0023	DSS Server	Station 4	NCP C F=B316 Read 1024 at 9216
45	0.0016	Station 4	DSS Server	NCP R OK 1024 bytes read
46	0.0023	DSS Server	Station 4	NCP C F=B316 Read 1024 at 10240
47	0.0017	Station 4	DSS Server	NCP R OK 1024 bytes read

48	0.0023	DSS Server	Station 4	NCP C F=B316 Read 1024 at11264
49	0.0017	Station 4	DSS Server	NCP R OK 1024 bytes read
50	0.0023	DSS Server	Station 4	NCP C F=B316 Read 1024 at12288
51	0.0016	Station 4	DSS Server	NCP R OK 1024 bytes read
52	0.0023	DSS Server	Station 4	NCP C F=B316 Read 1024 at13312
53	0.0017	Station 4	DSS Server	NCP R OK 1024 bytes read
54	0.0023	DSS Server	Station 4	NCP C F=B316 Read 1024 at14336
55	0.0016	Station 4	DSS Server	NCP R OK 1024 bytes read
56	0.0023	DSS Server	Station 4	NCP C F=B316 Read 1024 at15360
57	0.0017	Station 4	DSS Server	NCP R OK 1024 bytes read
58	0.0026	DSS Server	Station 4	NCP C F=B316 Close file
59	0.0008	Station 4	DSS Server	NCP R OK
60	0.0329	DSS Server	Station 4	NCP C Check server version
61	0.0007	Station 4	DSS Server	NCP R OK
62	0.0013	DSS Server	Station 4	NCP C Get station number
63	0.0005	Station 4	DSS Server	NCP R OK Station is 08
64	0.0529	DSS Server	Station 4	NCP C Get station number
65	0.0005	Station 4	DSS Server	NCP R OK Station is 08
66	0.0009	DSS Server	Station 4	NCP C Get connection info
67	0.0028	Station 4	DSS Server	NCP R OK
68	0.0013	DSS Server	Station 4	NCP C Search bindery for DSS11
69	0.0030	Station 4	DSS Server	NCP R OK Found DSS11
70	0.0011	DSS Server	Station 4	NCP C Map DSS11 to station
71	0.0044	Station 4	DSS Server	NCP R OK
72	0.0013	DSS Server	Station 4	NCP C Log msg to <09>
73	0.0006	Station 4	DSS Server	NCP R OK Msg status: [null]

74	0.0663	DSS Server	Station 4	NCP C End of task
75	0.0006	Station 4	DSS Server	NCP R OK
76	0.0477	DSS Server	Station 4	NCP C End of task
77	0.0006	Station 4	DSS Server	NCP R OK
78	0.0016	DSS Server	Station 4	NCP C Get dir path of handle 05
79	0.0009	Station 4	DSS Server	NCP R OK Path=SYS:HOME/DSS4
80	10.2255	Broadcast	DSS Server	XNS RIP response: 1 network, 00000002 at 1 hop

Trace 7.3.1e. NetWare Internetwork E-Mail Transmission (Ethernet side)

With the analyzer on the token ring side, a message is received for Station 11 (Trace 7.3.1f). The station sends the server a "Check For A General Message Request" packet in Frame 16. This packet is transmitted from Station 11 (host = 10005A3AA020H) on the token ring (net = 00000002) to the server (host = 02608C4B4680H) on the Ethernet (net = 00000001). The server responds with the actual message in Frame 17: "Message = From DSS4 [8]: hello carl."

This simple exercise has verified a number of internetwork operations: Both the Ethernet and the token ring LAN sides are healthy, the server and its addressing are properly configured, and the NetWare internal routing is functioning.

7.3.2 NetWare Preferred Server Operation

Most internetworks are designed with multiple file servers for a number of good reasons. Multiple servers increase the fault tolerance of the network, spread the disk storage load among several machines, and minimize the traffic across bridges. In order for multiple servers to function effectively, users need one server to be their primary server, with other servers used less frequently. If the internetwork includes bridges or routers, the user's workstation and most frequently-accessed server should be on the same side to minimize the internetwork traffic.

Sniffer Network Analyzer data 11-Sep-91 at 06:25:54, file RMAIL422.TRC Pg 1

- - - - - - - - - - - - - - - - Frame 16 - - - - - - - - - - - - - - - - -

DLC: —— DLC Header ——

DLC:

DLC: Frame 16 arrived at 06:26:23.748; frame size is 57 (0039 hex) bytes.

DLC: AC: Frame priority 0, Reservation priority 0, Monitor count 0

DLC: FC: LLC frame, PCF attention code: None

DLC: FS: Addr recognized indicators: 00, Frame copied indicators: 01

DLC: Destination = Station IBM   6FA28C, Server-TR

DLC: Source   = Station IBM   3AA020, Station 11

DLC:

LLC: —— LLC Header ——

LLC:

LLC: DSAP = E0, SSAP = E0, Command, Unnumbered frame: UI

LLC:

XNS: —— XNS Header ——

XNS:

 XNS: Checksum = FFFF

XNS: Length = 40

XNS: Transport control = 00

XNS: 0000 .... = Reserved

XNS: .... 0000 = Hop count

XNS: Packet type = 17 (Novell NetWare)

XNS:

XNS: Dest   net = 00000001, host = 02608C4B4680, socket = 1105 (NetWare Server)

XNS: Source net = 00000002, host = 10005A3AA020, socket = 16387 (4003)

XNS:

XNS: —— Novell Advanced NetWare ——

XNS:

XNS: Request type = 2222 (Request)

XNS: Seq no=209 Connection no=9   Task no=1

XNS:

NCP: —— Check For A General Message Request ——

NCP:

NCP: Request/sub-function code = 21,1

NCP:

NCP: (No parameters)

NCP:

NCP: [Normal end of NetWare "Check For A General Message Request" packet.]

NCP:

- - - - - - - - - - - - - - - - Frame 17 - - - - - - - - - - - - - - - - -

DLC: —— DLC Header ——

DLC:

DLC: Frame 17 arrived at 06:26:23.750; frame size is 80 (0050 hex) bytes.

DLC: AC: Frame priority 0, Reservation priority 0, Monitor count 0

DLC: FC: LLC frame, PCF attention code: None

DLC: FS: Addr recognized indicators: 00, Frame copied indicators: 01

DLC: Destination = Station IBM   3AA020, Station 11

DLC: Source   = Station IBM   6FA28C, Server-TR

DLC:

LLC: —— LLC Header ——

LLC:

LLC: DSAP = E0, SSAP = E0, Command, Unnumbered frame: UI

LLC:

XNS: —— XNS Header ——

XNS:

XNS: Checksum = FFFF

XNS: Length = 63

XNS: Transport control = 00

XNS: 0000 .... = Reserved

XNS: .... 0000 = Hop count

XNS: Packet type = 17 (Novell NetWare)

XNS:

XNS: Dest   net = 00000002, host = 10005A3AA020, socket = 16387 (4003)

XNS: Source net = 00000001, host = 02608C4B4680, socket = 1105 (NetWare Server)

XNS:

XNS: —— Novell Advanced NetWare ——

XNS:

XNS: Request type = 3333 (Reply)

XNS: Seq no=209 Connection no=9   Task no=0

XNS:

NCP: —— Check For A General Message Reply ——

NCP:

NCP: Request/sub-function code = 21,1 (reply to frame 16)

NCP:

NCP: Completion code = 00 (OK)

NCP: Connection status flags = 00 (OK)

NCP: Message = "From DSS4[8]: hello carl"

NCP:

NCP: [Normal end of NetWare "Check For A General Message Reply" packet.]

NCP:

Trace 7.3.1f. NetWare Internetwork E-Mail Transmission (Token Ring side)

To facilitate server selection, NetWare's Shell driver includes a parameter that selects the server to attach to. This server is designated as the Preferred Server (PS) and is specified on the NETX command line, the SHELL.CFG, or NET.CFG file:

NETx [I]|[U]|[PS = server name]

Where   I: to view the NetWare Shell version

U: unload NETx PS: specifies the server to attach to

|: either, or (i.e. only one of the I, U, or PS options)

In this example, four servers (designated Server 013, 014, 015, and 021) reside on a network. A workstation (designated NW Client) wishes to connect to its preferred server, which is Server 013. Trace 7.3.2 illustrates the steps that are

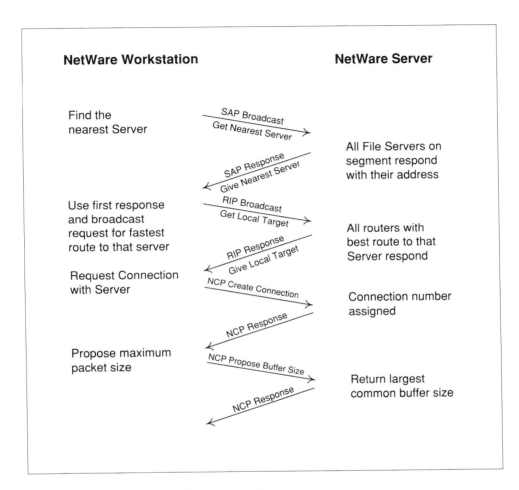

NetWare Workstation   **NetWare Server**

Find the
nearest Server

SAP Broadcast
Get Nearest Server

All File Servers on
segment respond
with their address

SAP Response
Give Nearest Server

Use first response
and broadcast
request for fastest
route to that server

RIP Broadcast
Get Local Target

All routers with
best route to that
Server respond

RIP Response
Give Local Target

Request Connection
with Server

NCP Create Connection

Connection number
assigned

NCP Response

Propose maximum
packet size

NCP Propose Buffer Size

Return largest
common buffer size

NCP Response

Figure 7-5a. Netware Server Connection Sequence

involved in this process. The process is illustrated graphically in Figure 7-5a. In
Frame 1 the NW Client broadcasts an SAP packet looking for the nearest server. Four
servers on that segment respond: Server 021 (Frame 2), Server 014 (Frame 3), Server
013 (Frame 4), and Server 015 (Frame 5). A late response is also shown in Frame 11.

Sniffer Network Analyzer data 27-Nov-90 at 09:53:50, P_SRVR_1.TRC Pg 1

SUMMARY	Delta T	Destination	Source	Summary
M 1		NetWare	NW Client	XNS NetWare Service Adv
2	0.003	NW Client	Server 021	NCP R SVR021
3	0.000	NW Client	Server 014	NCP R SVR014
4	0.000	NW Client	Server 013	NCP R SVR013
5	0.001	NW Client	Server 015	NCP R SVR015
6	0.001	NetWare	NW Client	XNS RIP request:
				find 1 network, 00107001
7	0.000	NW Client	Server 021	XNS RIP response: 1 network
				00107001 at 1 hop
8	0.000	NW Client	Server 014	XNS RIP response: 1 network
				00107001 at 1 hop
9	0.000	NW Client	Server 013	XNS RIP response: 1 network
				00107001 at 1 hop
10	0.000	NW Client	Server 015	XNS RIP response: 1 network
				00107001 at 1 hop
11	0.000	NW Client	Prteon04A084	NCP R SVR021
12	0.000	Server 021	NW Client	NCP C Create Connection
13	0.000	NW Client	Server 021	NCP R OK
14	0.001	Server 021	NW Client	NCP C Propose buffer size of 1024
15	0.001	NW Client	Server 021	NCP R OK Accept buffer size of 1024
16	0.002	Server 021	NW Client	NCP C Read SVR013's properties
17	0.002	NW Client	Server 021	NCP R OK
18	0.002	Server 013	NW Client	NCP C Create Connection
19	0.056	NW Client	Server 013	NCP R OK
20	0.001	Server 013	NW Client	NCP C Propose buffer size of 1024
21	0.002	NW Client	Server 013	NCP R OK Accept buffer size of 1024
22	0.037	Server 021	NW Client	NCP C Destroy Connection
23	0.004	NW Client	Server 021	NCP R OK
24	0.002	Server 021	NW Client	NCP C Logout
25	0.027	NW Client	Server 021	NCP R OK

Trace 7.3.2. NetWare Preferred Server Shell Connection Sequence

The NW Client then broadcasts a RIP request, looking for the fastest route to the server that responded first (Server 021). All routers, which are internal functions of the server, that have a route to Server 021 respond (Frames 7 through 10). The NW Client then requests a connection with Server 021 (Frame 12), and Server 021 responds by assigning a connection number (Frame 13). In Frame 14 the NW Client proposes a maximum packet size of 1,024 octets, and the Server 021 agrees (Frame 15). If the standard (i.e. non-preferred) NetWare Shell was involved, the workstation would then log in to Server 021.

Additional steps are required when logging in to the preferred server (see Figure 7-5b). In Frame 16 the NW client asks for the address of the preferred server (Server 013), and the first server (Server 021) responds (Frame 17). The NW Client once again goes through the connection process with the preferred server, Server 013: Create Connection (Frames 18 and 19) and Propose Packet Size (Frames 20 and 21). (Note that the preferred server's NIC is attached to the same segment as the NW Client; therefore, no RIP Get Local Target broadcasts were necessary.) With the connection established with the preferred server, the previous connection to the first responding server (Server 021) is no longer necessary. That connection is destroyed in Frames 22 through 25. The NW Client would then execute the LOGIN.EXE command and begin the login sequence.

From an internetwork analysis point of view, the correct assignment and identification of the preferred server is a key to troubleshooting a multiserver NetWare internetwork. Look for the significant events that are summarized in Figures 7-5a and 7-5b as you proceed with your analysis.

7.3.3 NetWare Addressing Confusion

As we discussed in Section 7.1.6, a complete NetWare internetwork address consists of three parts: node (or host), network, and socket. These addresses are contained within the IPX header (review Figure 7-3). If these addresses are incorrect or inconsistent, the internetwork will become confused.

In this case study, an Ethernet contained a number of segments, connected by bridges to a backbone (see Figure 7-6). Each segment contained at least one server. In addition, different versions of NetWare, including NetWare version 2.15, 3.0, 3.1,

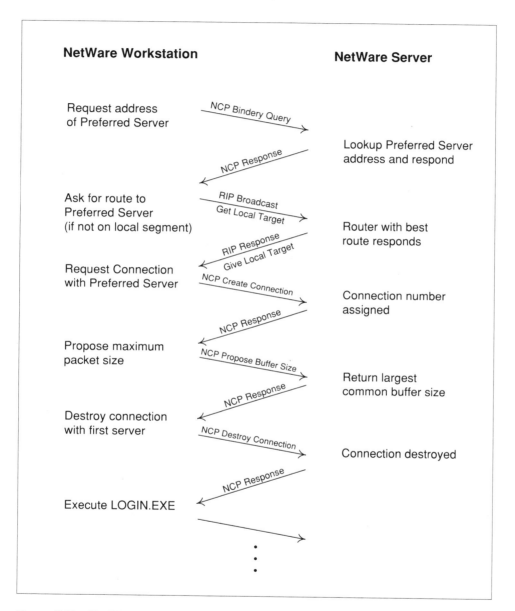

Figure 7-5b. NetWare Preferred Server Connection Sequence

and Portable NetWare were being used. The problem was that the servers could only communicate to other servers on their own segment, not on other segments. Thus, RGOSP could communicate with EVE but not with RESTONOCG or AVIION. Likewise, EVE could only communicate with RGOSP. Servers RESTONOCG and AVIION could see RGOSP and EVE (using the SLIST command), but could not log in. The error message displayed was "Router configuration error detected." Addressing confusion was suspected.

We attached a network analyzer to the segment where RGOSP and EVE resided. A workstation (shown as JANE) attempted to log in to the remote server RESTONOCG (see Trace 7.3.3a). That process failed (Frame 11). A login to a server on the same segment (RGOSP) as Jane was successful, however (Frames 25 through 36). Thus, the workstation could access a server on its own network, but not one on the internetwork. A further analysis of the internetwork addresses provided the answer.

When the network was planned, it was designed to be one logical network (net = 00000001). Unfortunately, five vendors had participated in various stages of the installation, and were not consistent with this assumption. In Trace 7.3.3b, when the RGOSP server communicated with Jane's workstation, the Destination and Source Networks within the IPX header were both equal to 00000001. Communication was successful. When the workstation requested a connection in Frame 2, it requested a connection with a destination network (00000003) that was unknown to the RGOSP server. As a result, the connection via the internetwork failed, while a network connection could succeed. The bridges were not the problem—the internal addressing of the servers was. When the servers were reconfigured so that they all resided on network 00000001, no further problems arose. If nothing else, this makes a strong argument against multivendor participation in internetwork installations!

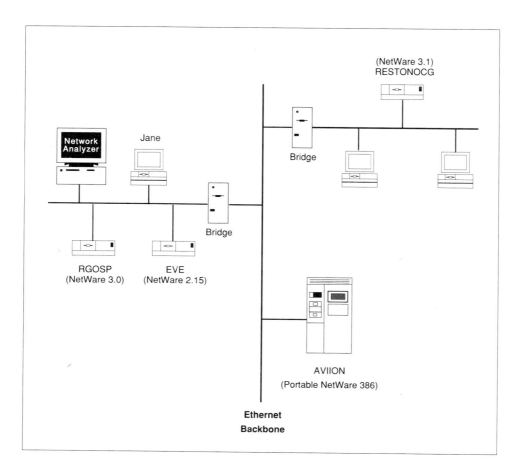

Figure 7-6. NetWare Misconfigured Addresses

Sniffer Network Analyzer data 8-Jan-91 at 14:33:42, file USGS1BAD.ENC, Pg 1

SUMMARY	Delta T	Destination	Source	Summary
M 1		Jane	SVR RGOSP	XNS RIP response: 1 network
				00000003 at 1 hop
2	0.0007	SVR RGOSP	Jane	NCP C Create Connection
3	0.0009	Jane	SVR RGOSP	NCP R OK
4	0.0006	SVR RGOSP	Jane	NCP C Propose buffer size of 1024
5	0.0007	Jane	SVR RGOSP	NCP R OK Accept buffer size of 1024
6	0.0007	SVR RGOSP	Jane	NCP C Request=23
7	0.0006	Jane	SVR RGOSP	NCP R OK
8	0.0009	SVR RGOSP	Jane	NCP C Map RESTONOCG to trustee
9	0.0008	Jane	SVR RGOSP	NCP R OK Mapped: RESTONOCG
10	0.0036	SVR RGOSP	Jane	NCP C Request=23
11	0.0042	Jane	SVR RGOSP	NCP R Verification failed
12	1.0697	Broadcast	SVR RGOSP	NCP R RGOSP
13	0.1310	SVR RGOSP	Jane	NCP C Request=23
14	0.0007	Jane	SVR RGOSP	NCP R OK
15	0.0009	SVR RGOSP	Jane	NCP C Map RESTONOCG to trustee
16	0.0008	Jane	SVR RGOSP	NCP R OK Mapped: RESTONOCG
17	0.0038	SVR RGOSP	Jane	NCP C Request=23
18	0.0046	Jane	SVR RGOSP	NCP R OK
19	0.0233	SVR RGOSP	Jane	NCP C End of task
20	0.0006	Jane	SVR RGOSP	NCP R OK
21	27.3933	SVR RGOSP	Jane	NCP C Get client's bindery access level
22	0.0006	Jane	SVR RGOSP	NCP R OK
23	0.0007	SVR RGOSP	Jane	NCP C Map Trustee to user
24	0.0011	Jane	SVR RGOSP	NCP R OK Mapped: RESTONOCG
25	0.0009	SVR RGOSP	Jane	NCP C Search bindery for RGOSP
26	0.0009	Jane	SVR RGOSP	NCP R OK Found RGOSP
27	0.0010	SVR RGOSP	Jane	NCP C Get server's clock
28	0.0006	Jane	SVR RGOSP	NCP R OK
29	0.0009	SVR RGOSP	Jane	NCP C Get connection info

30	0.0007	Jane	SVR RGOSP	NCP R OK
31	0.0009	SVR RGOSP	Jane	NCP C Logout
32	0.0011	Jane	SVR RGOSP	NCP R OK
33	0.0008	SVR RGOSP	Jane	NCP C Logout
34	0.0010	Jane	SVR RGOSP	NCP R OK
35	0.0006	SVR RGOSP	Jane	NCP C Destroy Connection
36	0.0009	Jane	SVR RGOSP	NCP R OK

Trace 7.3.3a. NetWare Addressing Confusion Summary

Sniffer Network Analyzer data 8-Jan-91 at 14:33:42, file USGS1BAD.ENC Pg 1

- - - - - - - - - - - - - - - - Frame 1 - - - - - - - - - - - - - - - -

DLC: —— DLC Header ——

DLC:

DLC: Frame 1 arrived at 14:33:52.7236; frame size is 60 (003C hex) bytes.

DLC: Destination = Station 3Com 4BD156, Jane

DLC: Source   = Station Novell140BCD, SVR RGOSP

DLC: 802.3 length = 40

DLC:

XNS: —— XNS Header ——

XNS:

XNS: Checksum = FFFF

XNS: Length = 40

XNS: Transport control = 00

XNS: 0000 .... = Reserved

XNS: .... 0000 = Hop count

XNS: Packet type = 0 (Novell)

XNS:

XNS: Dest net = 00000001, host = 02608C4BD156, socket = 1107 (NW Rout)

XNS: Source net = 00000001, host = 00001B140BCD, socket = 1107 (NW Rout)

XNS:

XNS: —— Novell Routing Information Protocol (RIP) ——

XNS:

XNS: Operation = 2 (response)

XNS:

XNS: Object network = 00000003, hop count = 1

XNS:

- - - - - - - - - - - - - - - - Frame 2 - - - - - - - - - - - - - - - - -

DLC: —— DLC Header ——

DLC:

DLC: Frame 2 arrived at 14:33:52.7244; frame size is 60 (003C hex) bytes.

DLC: Destination = Station Novell140BCD, SVR RGOSP

DLC: Source   = Station 3Com 4BD156, Jane \par DLC: 802.3 length = 38

DLC:

XNS: —— XNS Header ——

XNS:

XNS: Checksum = FFFF

XNS: Length = 37

XNS: Transport control = 00

XNS: 0000 .... = Reserved

XNS: .... 0000 = Hop count

XNS: Packet type = 17 (Novell NetWare)

XNS:

XNS: Dest   net = 00000003, host = 000000000001, socket = 1105 (NW Svr)

XNS: Source net = 00000001, host = 02608C4BD156, socket = 16387 (4003)

XNS:

XNS: —— Novell Advanced NetWare ——

XNS:

XNS: Request type = 1111 (Create Connection)

XNS: Seq no=0   Connection no=255 Task no=2

XNS:

NCP: —— Create Service Connection ——

NCP:

NCP: [Normal end of NetWare "Create Service Connection" packet.]

NCP:

```
- - - - - - - - - - - - - - - Frame 3 - - - - - - - - - - - - - - - - -
DLC:  —— DLC Header ——
DLC:
DLC:  Frame 3 arrived at  14:33:52.7253; frame size is 60 (003C hex) bytes.
DLC:  Destination = Station 3Com  4BD156, Jane
DLC:  Source     = Station Novell140BCD, SVR RGOSP
DLC:  802.3 length = 38
DLC:
XNS:  —— XNS Header ——
XNS:
XNS:  Checksum = FFFF
XNS:  Length = 38
XNS:  Transport control = 00
XNS:        0000 .... = Reserved
XNS:        .... 0000 = Hop count
XNS:  Packet type = 17 (Novell NetWare)
XNS:
XNS:  Dest   net = 00000001, host = 02608C4BD156, socket = 16387 (4003)
XNS:  Source net = 00000003, host = 000000000001, socket = 1105 (NW Svr)  XNS: \par XNS: —
— Novell Advanced NetWare ——
XNS:
XNS:  Request type = 3333 (Reply)
XNS:  Seq no=0    Connection no=2    Task no=1
XNS:
NCP:  —— Create Service Connection Reply ——
NCP:
NCP:  Completion code = 00 (OK)
NCP:  Connection status flags = 00 (OK)
NCP:  [Normal end of NetWare "Create Service Connection Reply" packet.] \par NCP:
```

Trace 7.3.3b. NetWare Addressing Confusion Details

7.3.4 NetWare Source Routing Bridges

One of the emerging standards for token ring (IEEE 802.5) networks is the Source Routing (SR) bridging standard [7-33]. (Reference [7-34] discusses Novell's Source Routing implementation.) As its name implies, the source of the information (i.e. the message originator) supplies the route to the message recipient. This message may traverse multiple bridges between the source and destination (review Section 6.2). As the frame passes from one ring to the next via a bridge, a special field known as the Routing Information (RI) field directs its path. The RI field contains a number of parameters (review Figures 6-1a, b), one of which is the Largest Frame (LF) specification. This parameter defines the largest MAC frame that can be carried on the route, and all communicating devices along the route, such as workstations and bridges, must agree with that value. The SR Standard defines a small number of valid LF values:

LF in octets	Application
516	ISO 8473 and IEEE 802.2
1500	ISO 08802-3, CSMA/CD LAN
2052	80 x 20 character screen
4472	ISO 8802-5 (token ring LAN and ISO 9314-2 (FDDI LAN)
8144	ISO 8802-4, token bus LAN
11407	ISO 8802-5, token ring LAN
17800	ISO 8802-5, token ring LAN
65535	ISO 8348

Depending upon the manufacturer, a bridge may default to either a smaller or larger LF size upon initialization. So the LF size may need adjustment. Further parameter customization may be required based upon the network's unique applications, network operating system, and so on.

In this case study, two token ring locations were connected via remote source routing bridges (Figure 7-7). A total of three bridges (one local and two remote) plus one leased line operating at 9.6 Kbps comprised the internetwork topology. In most

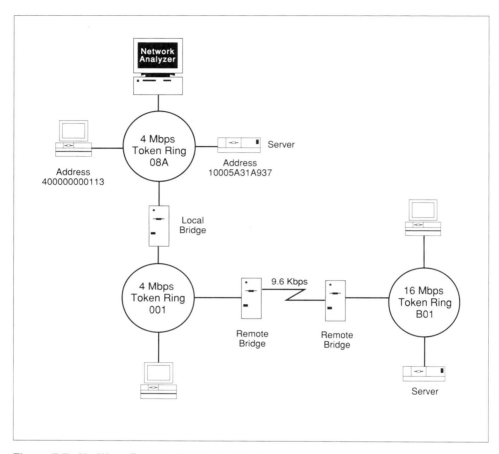

Figure 7-7. NetWare Remote Bridge Connection

situations, the workstations accessed a server on their own ring; however, communication to a distant server via the remote bridge was occasionally necessary. When this remote access was required, the user was able to attach to the remote server, but login would fail. In other words, the workstation's NetWare Shell would load properly, and access to a local server on the same ring would proceed smoothly. If that local server was unavailable, the workstation would attempt to access a remote server via the remote bridges and 9.6 Kbps line, but the login would fail.

To diagnose the problem, we placed a network analyzer on the server's ring (designated ring 08AH) and instructed a local workstation (designated Station 113) to log in to the server (see Trace 7.3.4a). We configured this workstation identically to the remote workstation experiencing the difficulty. The purpose of this initial step was to determine the type and size of the frames transmitted between any workstation and the server in question. In Frame 6 the workstation login sequence begins, and in Frame 19 the file LOGIN.EXE is opened on the server. Subsequent commands read data from the server in 30-octet (Frame 21), 512-octet (Frame 23), and 1,024-octet (Frames 25 and following) blocks.

Sniffer Network Analyzer data 4-Oct-90 at 09:07:44, file SVRTEST.TRC Pg 1

SUMMARY	Delta T	Size	Destination	Source	Summary
6	1.092	60	NetWare Svr	Station 113	NCP C Get dir path
					of handle 01
7	0.002	67	Station 113	NetWare Svr	NCP R OK Path=SYS:LOGIN
8	0.003	58	NetWare Svr	Station 113	NCP C Dir search parms for [null]
9	0.001	63	Station 113	NetWare Svr	NCP R OK Next=-1
10	0.002	74	NetWare Svr	Station 113	NCP C Dir search
					LOGIN.???
11	0.002	89	Station 113	NetWare Svr	NCP R OK File=LOGIN.EXE
12	0.002	74	NetWare Svr	Station 113	NCP C Dir search
					LOGIN.???
13	0.002	89	Station 113	NetWare Svr	NCP R File not found
14	0.002	74	NetWare Svr	Station 113	NCP C Dir search
					LOGIN.???
15	0.002	89	Station 113	NetWare Svr	NCP R File not found
16	0.002	60	NetWare Svr	Station 113	NCP C Get dir path
					of handle 01
17	0.002	67	Station 113	NetWare Svr	NCP R OK Path=SYS:LOGIN
18	0.003	76	NetWare Svr	Station 113	NCP C Open file
					/LOGIN/LOGIN.EXE
19	0.004	93	Station 113	NetWare Svr	NCP R F=7A79 OK Opened
20	0.003	69	NetWare Svr	Station 113	NCP C F=7A79 Read 30 at 0

343

21	0.002	89	Station 113	NetWare Svr	NCP R OK 30 bytes read
22	0.004	69	NetWare Svr	Station 113	NCP C F=7A79 Read 512 at 512
23	0.003	571	Station 113	NetWare Svr	NCP R OK 512 bytes read
24	0.002	69	NetWare Svr	Station 113	NCP C F=7A79 Read 1024 at 1024
25	0.005	1083	Station 113	NetWare Svr	NCP R OK 1024 bytes read
26	0.003	69	NetWare Svr	Station 113	NCP C F=7A79 Read 1024 at 2048
27	0.005	1083	Station 113	NetWare Svr	NCP R OK 1024 bytes read
28	0.003	69	NetWare Svr	Station 113	NCP C F=7A79 Read 1024 at 3072
29	0.005	1083	Station 113	NetWare Svr	NCP R OK 1024 bytes read
30	0.003	69	NetWare Svr	Station 113	NCP C F=7A79 Read 1024 at 4096
31	0.005	1083	Station 113	NetWare Svr	NCP R OK 1024 bytes read
32	0.003	69	NetWare Svr	Station 113	NCP C F=7A79 Read 1024 at 5120
33	0.005	1083	Station 113	NetWare Svr	NCP R OK 1024 bytes read
34	0.003	69	NetWare Svr	Station 113	NCP C F=7A79 Read 1024 at 6144
35	0.005	1083	Station 113	NetWare Svr	NCP R OK 1024 bytes read

Trace 7.3.4a. NetWare Source Routing Bridge Summary

We identified the problem by examining the size of the frames sent from the workstation and the server. Each data request from the workstation required a frame length of only 69 octets (Frames 20, 22, 24, 26, and so on). This small frame size is a result of the relatively small size of the NetWare Read File Data Request packet. Because of the amount of data that the workstation requested, the server responded with a much larger frame. In Frames 20 through 23, the server's response is 512 octets or less; but beginning with Frame 24, the response increased to 1,024 octets.

The details of two request/response frames identify the problem (see Trace 7.3.4b). The workstation's request (Frame 24) requires a 69-octet frame. The routing indicators within that frame are set to pass a maximum frame size of 516 octets, so the Read File Data Request packet goes through. The server's response (Frame 25) is a different story. The response requires a frame of 1,083 octets (1,024 octets of data plus the frame and packet header overhead). Yet the routing indicators in Frame 25 are still set at 516 octets. In other words, the server is trying to pass 1,083 octets of data across a bridge that will only accommodate 516 octets; thus its response is blocked.

Sniffer Network Analyzer data 4-Oct-90 at 09:07:44, file SVRTEST.TRC Pg 1

- - - - - - - - - - - - - - - Frame 24 - - - - - - - - - - - - - - - - -

DLC: —— DLC Header ——

DLC:

DLC: Frame 24 arrived at 09:07:52.079; frame size is 69 (0045 hex) bytes.

DLC: AC: Frame priority 0, Reservation priority 0, Monitor count 0

DLC: FC: LLC frame, PCF attention code: None

DLC: FS: Addr recognized indicators: 11, Frame copied indicators: 11

DLC: Destination = Station IBM 31A937, NetWare Svr

DLC: Source   = Station 400000000113, Station 113

DLC:

RI : —— Routing Indicators ——

RI :

RI : Routing control = 02

RI :   000. .... = Non-broadcast

RI :   ...0 0010 = RI length is 2

RI : Routing control = 00

RI :   0... .... = Forward direction

RI :   .000 .... = Largest frame is 516

RI :   .... 0000 = Reserved

RI :

LLC: —— LLC Header ——

LLC:

LLC: DSAP = E0, SSAP = E0, Command, Unnumbered frame: UI

LLC:

XNS: —— XNS Header ——

XNS:

XNS: Checksum = FFFF

XNS: Length = 50

XNS: Transport control = 00

XNS: 0000 .... = Reserved

XNS: .... 0000 = Hop count

XNS: Packet type = 17 (Novell NetWare)

XNS:

XNS: Dest net = 0000008A, host = 10005A31A937, socket = 1105 (NetWare Server)

XNS: Source net = 0000008A, host = 400000000113, socket = 16387 (4003)

XNS:

XNS: —— Novell Advanced NetWare ——

XNS:

XNS: Request type = 2222 (Request)

 XNS: Seq no=141 Connection no=33 Task no=1

XNS:

NCP: —— Read File Data Request ——

NCP:

NCP: Request code = 72

NCP:

NCP: File handle = 0000 2E19 5460

NCP: Starting byte offset = 1024

NCP: Number of bytes to read = 1024 \par NCP:

NCP: [Normal end of NetWare "Read File Data Request" packet.]

NCP:

- - - - - - - - - - - - - - - - Frame 25 - - - - - - - - - - - - - - - - -

DLC: —— DLC Header ——

DLC:

DLC: Frame 25 arrived at 09:07:52.085; frame size is 1083 (043B hex) bytes.

DLC: AC: Frame priority 0, Reservation priority 0, Monitor count 0

DLC: FC: LLC frame, PCF attention code: None

DLC: FS: Addr recognized indicators: 00, Frame copied indicators: 00

DLC: Destination = Station 400000000113, Station 113

DLC: Source   = Station IBM   31A937, NetWare Svr

DLC:

RI : —— Routing Indicators ——

RI :

346

RI : Routing control = 02

RI :   000. .... = Non-broadcast

RI :   ...0 0010 = RI length is 2

RI : Routing control = 80

RI :   1... .... = Backward direction

RI :   .000 .... = Largest frame is 516

RI :   .... 0000 = Reserved

RI :

LLC: —— LLC Header ——

LLC:

LLC: DSAP = E0, SSAP = E0, Command, Unnumbered frame: UI

LLC:

XNS: —— XNS Header ——

XNS:

XNS: Checksum = FFFF

XNS: Length = 1064

XNS: Transport control = 00

XNS: 0000 .... = Reserved

XNS: .... 0000 = Hop count

XNS: Packet type = 17 (Novell NetWare)

XNS:

XNS: Dest   net = 0000008A, host = 400000000113, socket = 16387 (4003)

XNS: Source net = 0000008A, host = 10005A31A937, socket = 1105 (NetWare Server)

XNS:

XNS: —— Novell Advanced NetWare ——

XNS:

XNS: Request type = 3333 (Reply)

XNS: Seq no=141 Connection no=33   Task no=0

XNS:

NCP: —— Read File Data Reply ——

NCP:

NCP: Request code = 72 (reply to frame 24)

NCP:

NCP: Completion code = 00 (OK)

NCP: Connection status flags = 00 (OK)

NCP: Number of bytes read = 1024

NCP: [1024 byte(s) of read data]

NCP:

NCP: [Normal end of NetWare "Read File Data Reply" packet.]

NCP:

Trace 7.3.4b. NetWare Source Routing Bridge Details

The solution was easy—the remote bridge had been configured for a Maximum Frame Size (LF) of 516 octets (the default). When we increased this parameter to 1,500 octets, we encountered no further problems with remote server access. A straightforward answer to a frustrating problem!

7.3.5 NetWare Extraneous Frame Copied Errors

The token ring (IEEE 802.5) standard contains a number of network management functions that control errors, govern the initialization of workstations, and manage network parameters, such as ring numbers, identifying the active monitor, and so on. In the 802.5 standard [7-35], 25 specific frame formats, known as *Medium Access Control* (MAC) frames, perform these functions. One of these is the MAC Report Soft Error frame. A workstation transmits this frame to a functional address, known as the *Error Monitor*, that logs the errors. (The Error Monitor may actually be part of a network management software package that may provide a report to the network administrator.) There are two types of errors: hard errors, such as a cable break, and soft errors, such as noise on the cable. A soft error degrades network performance by causing the retransmission of data frames. The workstation NIC detects these soft errors, records them in registers, and transmits the data on these errors in a Report Soft Error MAC frame to the Error Monitor. The NICs report two types of soft errors: Isolating Errors can be isolated to two workstations or the transmission media between them; non-isolating Errors are errors that could have been caused by any other workstation or device on the ring.

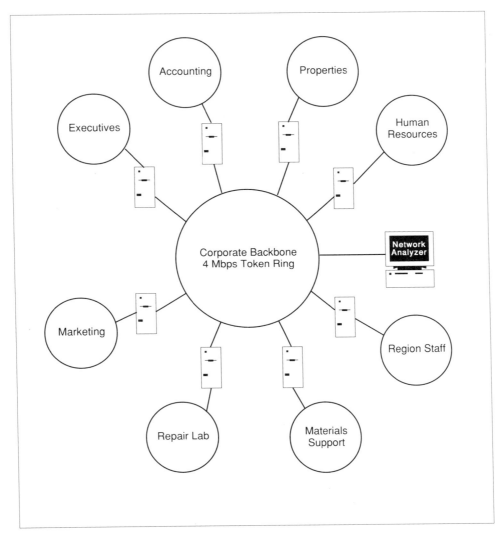

Figure 7-8. NetWare Local Bridges

In this case study, a 4 Mbps backbone token ring was connected to a number of departmental rings (also 4 Mbps) via bridges (see Figure 7-8). The entire internetwork was running NetWare. Under normal operation, the Report Error MAC frames would account for about 1% of the entire network traffic. (Some Report Error frames are always expected. For example, every time that a workstation enters the ring, the relay in the Multi-Station Access Unit (MSAU) changes state, corrupting a frame. This error degrades the network performance because it requires a retransmission of that frame. As a result, an analyzer will see a Report Soft Error frame two seconds after a workstation enters the ring. However, the number of error frames on this internetwork was excessive.

An analyzer placed on the backbone revealed these Report Soft Error frames (Trace 7.3.5a). When we studied the details of these frames, we found that the type of soft error being reported was a non-isolating frame copied error (see Trace 7.3.5b). This error occurs when the IEEE 802.5 Frame Status field A bit (Address Recognized) is improperly set to 1. The workstation sets the A bit when it recognizes its own address in a transmitted frame traversing the ring. Every workstation should have a unique address; therefore, all frames entering a particular workstation should have A = 0. All outgoing frames would have A = 1. If an incoming frame has A = 1, either a line hit (noise) has corrupted the bit or a workstation with a duplicate address exists. In either case, the Frame Copied (FC) error counter would be incremented. Since the FC error is non-isolating, detecting the source of the problem is more difficult.

Sniffer Network Analyzer data 25-Jun-91 at 15:09:10, file BEFORE.TRC, Pg 1

SUMMARY	Delta T	Destination	Source	Summary
65	708.620	Error Mon.	5000E0000315	MAC Report Soft Error
66	0.227	Error Mon.	5000E0002919	MAC Report Soft Error
67	0.366	Error Mon.	5000E0002263	MAC Report Soft Error
68	0.142	Error Mon.	5000E0001E3B	MAC Report Soft Error
69	0.058	Error Mon.	IBM 128B56	MAC Report Soft Error
70	0.180	Error Mon.	5000E0003275	MAC Report Soft Error
71	0.005	Error Mon.	GH333004452	MAC Report Soft Error
72	0.019	Error Mon.	5000E00006D0	MAC Report Soft Error

73	0.011	Error Mon.	10002410F32E	MAC Report Soft Error
74	0.075	Error Mon.	5000E000234B	MAC Report Soft Error
75	0.638	Error Mon.	5000E0001E47	MAC Report Soft Error
76	0.046	Error Mon.	Olin	MAC Report Soft Error

Trace 7.3.5a. NetWare Report Soft Error (IEEE 802.5) MAC Frame Summary

Sniffer Network Analyzer data from 25-Jun-91 at 15:09:10, BEFORE.TRC, Pg 1

- - - - - - - - - - - - - - - - Frame 71 - - - - - - - - - - - - - - - - -

DLC: —— DLC Header ——

DLC:

DLC: Frame 71 arrived at 15:46:11.322; frame size is 48 (0030 hex) bytes.

DLC: AC: Frame priority 0, Reservation priority 0, Monitor count 0

DLC: FC: MAC frame, PCF attention code: None

DLC: FS: Addr recognized indicators: 00, Frame copied indicators: 00

DLC: Destination = Functional address C00000000008, Error Mon.

DLC: Source   = Station IBM   8AD9C3, GH333004452

DLC:

MAC: —— MAC data ——

MAC:

MAC: MAC Command: Report Soft Error

MAC: Source: Ring station, Destination: Ring Error Monitor

MAC: Subvector type: Isolating Error Counts

MAC: 0 line errors,   0 internal errors,   0 burst errors

MAC: 0 AC errors,   0 abort delimiters transmitted

MAC: Subvector type: Non-Isolating Error Counts

MAC: 0 lost frame errors, 0 receiver congestion, 5 FC errors

MAC: 0 frequency errors,   0 token errors

MAC: Subvector type: Physical Drop Number 00000000

MAC: Subvector type: Upstream Neighbor Address IBM   3039F7

MAC:

Trace 7.3.5b. NetWare Report Soft Error (IEEE 802.5) MAC Frame Detail

We needed the bridge manufacturer's assistance to isolate the problem to one of the 14 bridges on the backbone. Through their remote diagnostic procedures, the manufacturer dialed into the bridge's diagnostic port and looked at the address cache (i.e. forwarding /filtering table) of each bridge. We found that one bridge, designated GPCO_CASSBACK, had an abnormal address cache, and this bridge was transmitting internetwork topology changes to the other bridges on the internetwork. When it copied those frames, it set the A bit = 1. When the next bridge or server downstream would get the frame, it would see A = 1 and set the FC register = 1 also. After two minutes, the contents of the FC register were reported to the Error Monitor. (No report is issued if all error registers = 0.) As a result, the network was congested with excessive Report Soft Error frames.

After we replaced the bridge, we performed a second analysis (Trace 7.3.5c). This trace showed almost no Report Soft Error frames. The MAC frames indicated stable token ring operation. The bridge (Frame 102) now transmitted the expected MAC Standby Monitor Present frame, and all other NetWare file and print services were normal.

Sniffer Network Analyzer data from 9-May-91 at 14:20:36, AFTER.TRC, Pg 1

SUMMARY	Delta T	Destination	Source	Summary
91	0.001	GSMAC990	EXTERNALGW	NCP C Open file KEY
92	0.000	5000E00002C4	GH333019	NBP C Request ID=144
93	0.026	EXTERNALGW	GSMAC990	NCP R F=7E9C OK Opened
94	0.002	GSMAC990	EXTERNALGW	NCP C F=7E9C Read 560 at 0
95	0.048	EXTERNALGW	GSMAC990	NCP R OK 560 bytes read
96	0.002	GSMAC990	EXTERNALGW	NCP C F=7E9C Close file
97	0.015	Broadcast	ITLANBACK	MAC Active Monitor Present
98	0.005	EXTERNALGW	GSMAC990	NCP R OK
99	0.004	GSMAC990	EXTERNALGW	NCP C Open file KEY
100	0.006	GH333993	GH333019	NCP C Check for a msg
101	0.001	GH333019	GH333993	NCP R
102	0.000	Broadcast	GPCO_CASSB..	MAC Standby Monitor Present
103	0.017	EXTERNALGW	GSMAC990	NCP R F=7F9C OK Opened

104	0.001	Broadcast	GPCO_POWGE..MAC Standby Monitor Present
105	0.001	GSMAC990	EXTERNALGW NCP C F=7F9C Read 560 at 0
106	0.016	802.2B	IBM 21C8CE XNS SPP D=833A S=88F8 NR=135
107	0.002	IBM	21C8CE 802.2B XNS SPP A D=88F8 S=833A NR=60
108	0.000	Broadcast	GPCO_MKTGB.. MAC Standby Monitor Present
109	0.004	3174B	802.2B SNA C FMD user data

Trace 7.3.5c. NetWare Stable Backbone Operation

7.3.6 NetWare SNA Gateway

Novell has addressed the internetworking requirements of its customers with a number of gateway products that can connect to other types of computer networks. One of these gateways is the NetWare SNA Gateway, which allows workstations on the LAN to attach to an IBM SNA mainframe, thus enabling two incompatible computing systems to communicate.

The NetWare SNA Gateway consists of hardware and software components. The gateway resides in a workstation and includes two hardware interfaces. One interface connects to the LAN, and maybe an ARCNET, Ethernet, or token ring NIC. The other interface connects to the IBM host via coaxial cable, a remote Synchronous Data Link Control (SDLC) connection, or a token ring NIC. (Note the recurring theme of NetWare hardware flexibility: This gateway allows an ARCNET LAN to communicate with an IBM host—an unusual combination.)

The gateway software resides in two modules: Gateway Server and Workstation (see Figure 7-9). The server contains two parallel protocol stacks. One of these stacks communicates with the SNA environment, receiving its Data Link information from the host connection. The SNA information is translated into Novell's SPX/IPX protocols, which are then transmitted through the LAN Driver onto the LAN (ARCNET, Ethernet, etc.). The Gateway Server performs within the OSI Physical through Session layers. The workstation component contains two parallel protocol stacks. The first stack receives the information from the LAN Driver and decodes the SPX/IPX protocols. The second stack contains a Presentation Services Process (PSP) that performs an EBCDIC to ASCII translation and an Application Programming Interface (API) that delivers the information to the user application. Thus, these

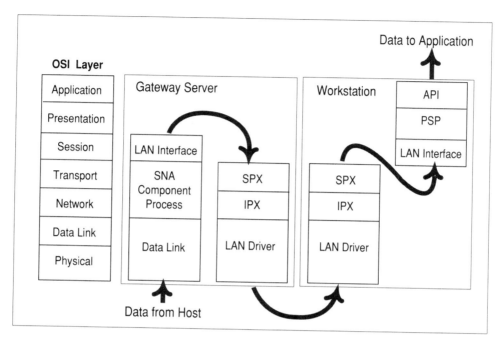

Figure 7-9. NetWare SNA Gateway Architecture

(Courtesy Novell, Inc.)

multiple protocol stacks translate the SNA information into a format that can be transmitted on the LAN and understood by the workstation user. References [7-36] through [7-38] provide further details on NetWare-to-SNA gateway services.

Given these complexities, it's not surprising that interoperability problems between host and gateway sometimes arise. In this example, the NetWare SNA Gateways were attached between two backbone token rings (see Figure 7-10). One backbone connects to a 3745 Communications Controller and the IBM host. The intermediate backbone ring connects to other rings on each floor via NetWare servers. The NetWare workstations are connected to the networks on each floor.

The IBM 3090 mainframe was taken down every Saturday evening for its weekly maintenance and system update procedures. When it was restarted on Sunday morning, NetView, IBM's network management system, was not the first

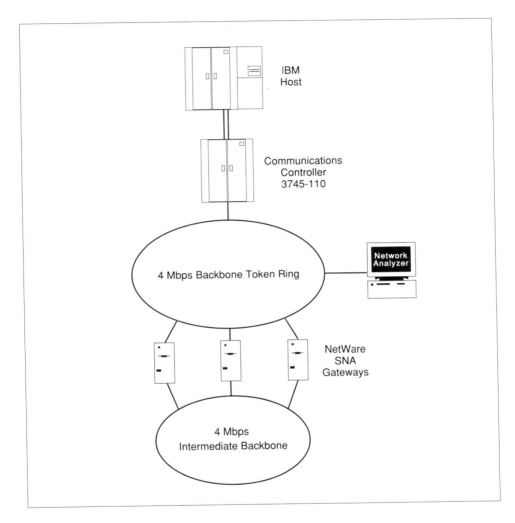

Figure 7-10. NetWare SNA Gateway Connections

application to be loaded: Other applications came up first. During this period of host downtime, the gateway remained operational, but because the maintenance procedure was performed on Saturday evening, users were unaffected. The host's maintenance log was affected, however.

Part of the SNA Component Process within the Gateway Server software (review Figure 7-9) includes an algorithm that attempts to re-establish the Physical Unit (PU) connection to the host if that connection is lost. This algorithm issues a Logical Link Control (LLC) TEST frame to the host (shown as 3745-110) every three seconds. If the host responds, the session is re-established. If not, six more TEST frames, followed by one Disconnected Mode (DM) frame, are sent. This process continues indefinitely (see Trace 7.3.6).

Sniffer Network Analyzer data 24-May-91 at 16:44:48 file NOVGTWY.TRC, Pg 1

SUMMARY		Delta T	Destination	Source	Summary
M	1		3745-110	NW Gateway	LLC C D=04 S=04 RR NR=104 P
	2	0.003	NW Gateway	3745-110	LLC R D=04 S=04 RR NR=102 F
	3	0.404	NW Gateway	3745-110	LLC C D=04 S=04 DISC P
	4	0.000	3745-110	NW Gateway	LLC R D=04 S=04 UA F
	5	0.026	3745-110	NW Gateway	LLC R D=04 S=04 DM
	6	0.063	3745-110	NW Gateway	LLC C D=00 S=04 TEST P
	7	3.569	3745-110	NW Gateway	LLC C D=00 S=04 TEST P
	8	3.020	3745-110	NW Gateway	LLC C D=00 S=04 TEST P
	9	2.965	3745-110	NW Gateway	LLC C D=00 S=04 TEST P
	10	3.020	3745-110	NW Gateway	LLC C D=00 S=04 TEST P
	11	3.020	3745-110	NW Gateway	LLC C D=00 S=04 TEST P
	12	2.965	3745-110	NW Gateway	LLC C D=00 S=04 TEST P
	13	3.019	3745-110	NW Gateway	LLC R D=04 S=04 DM
	14	0.048	3745-110	NW Gateway	LLC C D=00 S=04 TEST P
	15	3.960	3745-110	NW Gateway	LLC C D=00 S=04 TEST P
	16	2.965	3745-110	NW Gateway	LLC C D=00 S=04 TEST P
	17	3.020	3745-110	NW Gateway	LLC C D=00 S=04 TEST P
	18	3.020	3745-110	NW Gateway	LLC C D=00 S=04 TEST P

19	2.965	3745-110	NW Gateway	LLC C D=00 S=04 TEST P
20	3.034	3745-110	NW Gateway	LLC C D=00 S=04 TEST P
21	3.019	3745-110	NW Gateway	LLC R D=04 S=04 DM
22	0.048	3745-110	NW Gateway	LLC C D=00 S=04 TEST P
23	3.905	3745-110	NW Gateway	LLC C D=00 S=04 TEST P
24	3.020	3745-110	NW Gateway	LLC C D=00 S=04 TEST P

Trace 7.3.6. NetWare Gateway Reconnection Frames

Under most circumstances, this reconnection algorithm would not cause any host interaction difficulties. When the host re-initialized, the PUs would be re-established, and the user sessions could proceed. In this case, however, the gateway's TEST frames caused an error log on the host (LOGREC) to overflow. Since NetView was not active, it was impossible to determine whether the source of the errors was the recently-added maintenance changes and updates or some other network device. As a result, the mainframe operators would remove the updates, thinking they were the source of the problem.

The solution was to initiate NetView as the first operation when the host was re-activated. NetView understood the source of the multiple LLC TEST frames and realized that they were a normal operation. A second solution was to install an upgrade to the NetWare SNA Gateway software that extended the transmission period between LLC TEST frames from three seconds to 15 seconds. This prevented the host error log from filling so rapidly. With these two modifications, the host and Gateway were able to coexist peacefully.

7.4 References

[7-1] Forrester Research. "LAN Manager's Now on the Rebound." *LAN Times* (March 4, 1991): 65.

[7-2] Neibaur, Dale. "Understanding XNS: The Prototypical Internetwork Protocol." *Data Communications* (September 21, 1989): 43-51.

[7-3] Novell, Inc. *Advanced NetWare Theory of Operations*, version 2.1, document number 420-020462-001, June 1987.

[7-4] Novell, Inc. *NetWare 386 Technical Overview*, document number 471-000011-002, July 1989.

[7-5] Major, Drew. "The Architecture of NetWare 386." *NetWare Technical Journal* (July 1989): 35-44.

[7-6] Novell, Inc. *NetWare 386 Theory of Operations*, versions 3.0 and 3.1, document 479-000042-001, August 1989.

[7-7] Lemon, Scott and Deni Connor. "A New Driver Choice, The Open Data-Link Interface." *LAN Times* (July 1989): 123-125.

[7-8] Dixon, Drew C. "NetWare 386 in the LAN Driver's Seat." *NetWare Technical Journal* (July 1989): 73-87.

[7-9] Novell, Inc. "The Big Picture." *Bullets* (July 1990): 2-13.

[7-10] Knutson, Charles D. "Connecting OS/2 To NetWare." *LAN Times* (May 1990): 62-64.

[7-11] Aston, Timothy W. "Bridging Macs and PCs." *LAN Technology* (July 1991): 59-69.

[7-12] Day, Michael. "A Look Inside NetWare for Macintosh 3.0." *LAN Times* (August 5, 1991): 21.

[7-13] Powell, Todd. "Changing Horses Midstream: The ECONFIG Program with NetWare for VMS." *LAN Times* (February 1989): 98.

[7-14] Sparks, Brian. "Connectivity and Freedom of Choice: An Introduction to Portable NetWare." *NetWare Technical Journal* (July 1989): 101-106.

[7-15] Day, Michael. "Puzzle Piece: Solving Mysteries of Portable NetWare." *LAN Times* (September 1989): 112-113.

[7-16] Millikin, Michael D. "Portable NetWare: Extending the Red Reach." *Patricia Seybold's Network Monitor* (January 1991): 1-11.

[7-17] Miller, Mark A. *Internetworking: A Guide to Network Communications*. Redwood City, CA: M&T Books, 1991.

[7-18] Foster, Jennifer. *The Hardware Guide for Novell NetWare*. New York: John Wiley & Sons, 1991.

[7-19] Miller, Mark A. *LAN Protocol Handbook*. Redwood City, CA: M&T Books, 1990.

[7-20] X*erox Network System Architecture General Information Manual*, Document XNSG068504, Xerox Corporation, April 1985.

[7-21] Xerox Corporation, *Internet Transport Protocols*, document XNSS 028112, 1981.

[7-22] Novell, Inc. *NetWare V2.1, Internetwork Packet Exchange Protocol (IPX) with Asynchronous Event Scheduler (AES)*, document number 100-000405-001, February 1988.

[7-23] *NetWare System Interface Technical Overview*, document 100-00569-001, Novell, Inc. 1989.

[7-24] Novell, Inc. *NetWare V2.1, Sequenced Packet Exchange Protocol (SPX)*, February 1988.

[7-25] Turner, Paul. "NetWare Communication Processes." *NetWare Application Notes*, Novell, Inc., (September 1990): 25-81.

[7-26] Malamud, Carl. *Analyzing Novell Networks*. New York: Van Nostrand Reinhold, 1990.

[7-27] Liebing, Edward. *NetWare User's Guide*. Redwood City, CA: M&T Books, 1989.

[7-28] McCann, John T., with Adam T. Ruef and Steven L. Guengerich. *NetWare Supervisor's Guide*. Redwood City, CA: M&T Books, 1989.

[7-29] Ivie, Scott and Cheryl D. Snapp. *Troubleshooting NetWare for the 286*. Redwood City, CA: M&T Books, 1991.

[7-30] Adicoff, Sam. "The Case of FSNF." *LAN Magazine* (July 1991): 57-64.

[7-31] Christian, Robert. "Troubleshooting NetWare, Part 1." *LAN Technology* (June 1991): 43-56, and "Troubleshooting NetWare, Part 2." *LAN Technology* (July 1991): 59-64.

[7-32] Novell, Inc. "A Guide to Debugging Your Server." *Bullets*, June/July 1991.

[7-33] Institute of Electrical and Electronics Engineers. *Source Routing Supplement to IEEE 802.1d (MAC Bridges)*. IEEE Standard P8 02.5M/D5, August 15, 1991.

[7-34] Rosenfeld, David, "Installing and Configuring Novell's Token-Ring Source Routing Drivers." *NetWare Application Notes*, Novell, Inc., (October 1991): 1-18.

[7-35] Institute of Electrical and Electronics Engineers. "Token Ring Access Method." IEEE Standard 802.5. 1989.

[7-36] Novell, Inc. *Accessing IBM Mainframe Computers: An In-Depth Look*, document number 481-000019-001, January 1990.

[7-37] Novell, Inc. *NetWare SNA Gateway, Technology & Techniques*, document number 100-000740-001 Rev. A.

[7-38] Au, Adam, Charles York, and Suzanne Ahmed. "The NetWare SNA Gateway." *LAN Times* (April 1990): 101-104.

CHAPTER 8

Troubleshooting TCP/IP-Based Internetworks

In the previous chapters, we studied proprietary protocol suites, such as DEC's DECnet, IBM's SNA and Novell's NetWare. All proprietary networks are designed with one major objective—keeping control of the customer's account. Vendors do this by holding details about their protocols' architecture and operating system close to the vest. They might publish the specifications for their Network and Transport Layer protocols, for instance, but withhold the Upper layer protocol details. This would enable other vendors to internetwork, but not interoperate (review Figure 1-6). It's not surprising that vendors are reluctant to share their secrets with their competition, since interoperability is tied closely to sales.

This chapter examines a suite of protocols that are the antithesis of a proprietary architecture. These protocols are known by several names: the Department of Defense (DOD) protocols; the Internet Protocols; and the Transmission Control Protocol/Internet Protocol suite, or simply TCP/IP.

Because the U.S. Government Department of Defense Advanced Research Projects Agency (DARPA) funded the development of the TCP/IP protocols, they're considered to be in the public domain. Documents describing the protocols are known as Request for Comments (RFC) papers, and are readily available [8-1]. DARPA developed these protocols expressly to facilitate multivendor communication. This idea has only recently become popular among private vendors with the advent of the OSI's ISO Standards.

Thus, three factors have contributed to TCP/IP's popularity: It was designed expressly for internetworking, documentation is readily obtainable, and most importantly, the protocols themselves are readily available (unlike some of the OSI protocols which are still in the various stages of development).

For more information on these protocols, consult the following references. Information on related networks that make up the Internet is given in [8-2] and [8-3]. Readers desiring to connect to the Internet should obtain the DDN Subscriber Interface Guide [8-4] and and the DDN New User Guide [8-5]. Chapter 6 of Reference [8-6] provides further details on the history of the protocols' development; References [8-7] through [8-16] are current journal articles attesting to their continuing popularity.

We'll commence our study of these protocols by comparing the architecture of the DOD Internet with OSI.

8.1 TCP/IP and Related Protocols

Developed in the early 1970s, the DOD Internet protocols preceded the familiar OSI Reference Model by several years. Not surprisingly then, the DOD architecture varies considerably from the OSI Model. We'll begin by exploring how.

8.1.1 DOD Internet Architecture

As you can see in Figure 8-1, in contrast to the seven-layer OSI Reference Model, the DOD architecture uses a four-layer model. These four layers, starting with the hardware, are designated Network Access or Local Network; Internet; Host-to-Host; and Process/Application.

The lowest layer deals with the physical hardware. Since the DOD protocols can be used on either LANs or WANs, the two names *Network Access* (i.e. WAN) and *Local Network* (i.e. LAN) apply equally. The Internet Layer determines the datagram's route from one network to another, a function that is clearly within the OSI Network Layer definition. The DOD Host-to-Host Layer, like its OSI counterpart, the Transport Layer, assures reliable end-to-end communication.

The functions defined by the three highest OSI layers, the Session, Presentation and Application layers, reside within a single layer in the DOD model, the Process/Application layer. In the DOD Model, each application (e.g. terminal emulation, file transfer, electronic mail, and so on) requires unique support functions. In contrast, OSI Application Layer protocols are more granular. Thus OSI applications, such as X.400 electronic messaging and File Transfer and Management (FTAM), can share

OSI Layer	Protocol Implementation				DOD Layer
Application	File Transfer	Electronic Mail	Terminal Emulation	Network Management	Process / Application
Presentation	File Transfer Protocol (FTP)	Simple Mail Transfer Protocol (SMTP)	TELNET Protocol	Simple Network Management Protocol (SNMP)	
Session	MIL-STD-1780 RFC 959	MIL-STD-1781 RFC 821	MIL-STD-1782 RFC 854	RFC 1098	
Transport	Transmission Control Protocol (TCP) MIL-STD-1778 RFC 793		User Datagram Protocol (UDP) RFC 768		Host-to-Host
Network	Address Resolution ARP RFC 826 RARP RFC 903	Internet Protocol (IP) MIL-STD-1777 RFC 791		Internet Control Message Protocol (ICMP) RFC 792	Internet
Data Link	Network Interface Cards: Ethernet, StarLAN, Token Ring, ARCNET RFC 894, RFC 1042, RFC 1051				Network Access or Local Network
Physical	Transmission Media: Twisted Pair, Coax, Fiber Optics, Wireless Media, etc.				

Figure 8-1. Comparing DOD Protocols with OSI and DOD Architectures

common Presentation Layer functions, such as data encryption or data compression protocol. Because the functions that the OSI Model delineates in its Session and Presentation Layers are application-specific in the DOD model, the DOD combines them into one group. Reference [8-17] provides further insight into the DOD architecture.

8.1.2 DOD Local Network Layer Protocols

One of the great advantages of the TCP/IP protocols is that they were designed under the assumption that the underlying hardware could be a heterogeneous mixture of LANs and WANs. As a result, they support all popular network hardware.

RFCs are available to describe much of the hardware that TCP/IP supports. Ethernet hardware support (the DIX version) is described in RFC 894 [8-18]. IEEE 802 networks (e.g. 802.3, 802.5, and so on) have their own document, RFC 1042 [8-19]. One significant difference between these two Ethernet standards is that the Sub-Network Access Protocol (SNAP) header is added to a transmitted 802.x frame, shown in Appendix G, Figure G-6. (Recall that SNAP provides a mechanism for including the Ethernet type (or Ethertype) field within an 802.x frame.) Also addressed by RFC 1042 is the IEEE 802.5 Source Routing Method that we studied in Section 6.1.1.

ARCNET networks are delineated in RFC 1051 [8-20]. One consideration unique to ARCNET networks is their small frame size, which can accommodate only 508 octets of data. As a result, engineering judgment would dictate that an ARCNET not be used to connect two higher speed networks, such as token rings. The fragmentation required to fit the larger token ring frame into a size that ARCNET frames could handle might cause performance problems.

The distributed nature of TCP/IP-based internetworks demands that wide-area links connect the local networks. Specifications for the popular X.25 protocols are given in RFC 877 [8-21] and low-speed serial links in RFC 1144 [8-22].

8.1.3 DOD Internet Layer Protocols

Two protocols translate between Local Network (i.e. Data Link Layer) addresses and the Internet (i.e. Network Layer) addresses: The Address Resolution Protocol (ARP) described by RFC 826 [8-23] converts the 32-bit IP addresses into 48-bit Ethernet or IEEE 802.x addresses; the Reverse Address Resolution Protocol (RARP), RFC 903 [8-24], provides Ethernet/IEEE 802.x-to-IP address Conversion. We will see examples of the ARP translation mechanism in the case studies presented in Section 8.3.2.

The Internet Protocol (IP) transports a datagram from its source to its destination network [8-25] using a 32-bit network address. The local network then delivers the datagram to the appropriate station using a local address (e.g. the 48-bit Ethernet address.) Thus, both the local and network addresses are necessary to deliver the datagram from its source to its ultimate destination properly. The network address is carried inside the IP header, which will be discussed in detail in Section 8.1.6.

Should there be a problem with the datagram's delivery, you can use the Internet Control Message Protocol (ICMP), described in RFC 792, for diagnostic purposes [8-26]. ICMP allows the IP process on one host or router to communicate with its peer on another host. Examples of these messages include Destination Unreachable (used when the datagram can't be delivered as requested), Redirect (to change a particular route), and Echo Request (to test the communication path between two stations). The Echo Request message, commonly known as a "Ping," is particularly interesting to internetwork analysts. If the status of the link to a remote station is questionable, the user can send an Echo Request message to test that path. If the path is good and the remote host is ready to respond, an Echo Reply message will return. The ICMP message is transmitted within the IP datagram's data field, i.e. both IP and ICMP are involved in this process. We will show an example of using the Echo Request/Reply in Section 8.3.2.

8.1.4 DOD Host-to-Host Layer Protocols

The Host-to-Host Layer is analogous to the OSI Transport Layer. It works on top of IP to provide reliable end-to-end data delivery. Depending upon the application process requirements, it may use one of two protocols: the User Datagram Protocol (UDP) or the Transmission Control Protocol (TCP).

UDP is a relatively simple protocol that delivers data to its destination but does not rigorously check the reliability of that data [8-27]. UDP transmits the data to and from the upper layer Source or Destination ports. These ports are identified with 16-bit addresses, sometimes known as *socket addresses*. The UDP header carries the Source and Destination Port addresses, the length of the datagram, and a checksum on the UDP header.

The purpose of UDP is to transfer data with a minimum of protocol overhead. The UDP header includes no mechanisms for data sequencing, acknowledgements, or flow control. Therefore, the UDP data transfer entity is referred to as a *datagram*, with UDP providing connectionless service. Applications that use UDP require less overhead but receive less reliable transport; thus, the designer must decide on the optimum tradeoff. When the physical transmission channel is reliable, such as a LAN, or the application is not absolutely critical, such as electronic mail, UDP can be an efficient choice. For applications requiring greater reliability, such as under battlefield conditions, TCP becomes the protocol of choice [8-28].

TCP provides excellent data reliability at the cost of greater protocol overhead. The minimum TCP header length is 20 octets, compared with UDP's maximum of 8 octets. The data itself is treated as a continuous stream, divided into units called *segments*, which can each be up to 65,535 octets long. To provide reliable data transfer, TCP assigns each octet of the segment a sequence number for use by the error control and flow control mechanisms.

While UDP is connectionless, TCP is considered a connection-oriented protocol. The TCP header uses six control flags to control the establishment or disconnect of the end-to-end connection, synchronize the sequence numbers on either end, acknowledge the receipt of data, and so on. We will discuss these six control flags in Section 8.1.7—they are very important to the analysis of the host-to-host connection.

8.1.5 DOD Process/Application Layer Protocols

Reviewing Figure 8-1, note that within the DOD architecture the Upper Layer Protocols (ULPs) are grouped into a single layer called the *Process/Application Layer*. The architecture offers several user applications, each of which could be the subject of a discussion in itself. Since we're primarily concerned with internetwork analysis (i.e. TCP/IP), we'll summarize the ULPs and refer interested readers to the source documents. The File Transfer Protocol (FTP) is defined by both RFC 959 and MIL-STD-1780 [8-29]. The Simple Mail Transfer Protocol (SMTP), probably the most popular application, is described in RFC 821 [8-30] and MIL-STD-1781. The Telecommunications Network (TELNET) program provides terminal emulation, RFC 854 [8-31], and MIL-STD-1782. And the Simple Network Management Protocol (SNMP) offers internetwork management. SNMP has recently received a great deal of press and many industry analysts expect it to be included with most internetworking devices, such as bridges and routers, within the next few years. SNMP is described in RFC 1098 [8-32].

Readers interested in learning the extent to which various hardware and software vendors support the TCP/IP protocols should consult the *DDN Protocol Implementations and Vendors Guide*, Reference [8-33]. In addition, the *DDN Protocol Handbook* [8-34] offers an excellent compilation of RFCs. An in-depth study of the protocols themselves can be found in References [8-35] and [8-36].

8.1.6 DOD Internet Addressing

The DOD Internet protocols define addresses at the Local Network Layer, the Internet Layer, and the Host-to-Host Layer. These were discussed briefly in previous sections of this book.

The Application/Process Layer uses the 16-bit port address (which was defined in the Host-to-Host Layer and is included in the UDP or TCP header) to identify a particular process or name a logical connection. For example, FTP, Telnet, and SMTP all have unique port addresses. The various assignments are listed in a very useful document, RFC 1060, entitled "Assigned Numbers" [8-37].

The internet address is a 32-bit number included within the IP header. The agency administering the network, such as the DDN Network Information Center [8-1], assigns the internet address. Depending on the intended use for the network, you may assign various classes (designated Classes A, B, C, D, and E) of IP addresses. The classes divide the 32-bit field into a network number plus a host number. (Chapter 6 of Reference [8-6] discusses the various classes in depth.)

The last address used is a hardware address unique to the local network. An example of this address would be the 48-bit address contained within a ROM on an Ethernet or token ring network interface card.

For those keeping track, a total of 96 bits (16 for the Port Address, 32 for the Internet Address, and up to 48 for the Local Network) identify the proper source and destination of the data. Reference [8-38] is an excellent tutorial on TCP/IP addressing. In the next section, we'll see how all of these addresses fit into the IP datagram.

8.1.7 DOD IP Datagram Format

As discussed in Section 8.1.3, the Internet Protocol (IP) provides connectionless delivery of datagrams from a source node to a destination node within the internetwork. The IP datagram is situated within a Data Link Layer frame, as shown in Figure 8-2. Immediately following the IP header is either a UDP header for host-to-host connectionless service or a TCP header for host-to-host connection-oriented service. As we saw in Section 8.1.4, the choice of UDP or TCP depends upon the application. For example, electronic mail might do fine with UDP, while a file transfer, which is more likely to require a reliable connection, might require TCP. Immediately following the UDP or TCP header is the ULP information, which completes the IP datagram. The Data Link Layer Trailer completes the frame. Note that in Figure 8-2 the TCP/IP header fields are described in 32-bit words (4 octets).

The IP header requires a minimum of 20 octets, and contains a number of fields. Note that the sizes of the fields in the IP header are specified primarily in bits rather than octets. The 4-bit vers or version specifies the version of IP in use. The current version is 4. The Internet Header Length (IHL) measures the IP header length in 32-bit words. The minimum value for headers without options or padding is five words or 20 octets. Total Length, 16 bits, measures the total length of the IP datagram in octets. (Note that some measurements are in 32-bit units.) The maximum value in this field is 65,535 octets. Type of Service (8 bits) are flags that specify the precedence, delay, throughput, and reliability parameters for that datagram. Identifier (16 bits) is a unique number that identifies the datagram.

Flags (3 bits) indicate whether fragmentation is permitted and/or used. Fragment Offset (13 bits) indicates where a fragment belongs in the datagram and is measured in 64-bit, or 8-octet, units.

The 8-bit Time to Live (TTL) measures how long this particular datagram can exist, and is measured in either router hops or seconds. (The maximum time the datagram can live is 255 seconds or 4.25 minutes.) Protocol (8 bits) identifies the protocol of the next header, such as UDP or TCP. Header Checksum (16 bits) is a checksum on the IP header, not the data following the header. Source Address (32 bits) and Destination Address (32 bits) identify the internetwork address of the sending and receiving stations. Options, which can vary in length, are options from the sender that could control the datagram route, include a timestamp, or can be used for internetwork testing. Padding (variable length) assures that the IP header ends on a 32-bit boundary.

Either a UDP or TCP header (the TCP header is shown in Figure 8-2) would follow the IP header. The UDP header includes 16-bit Source Port and Destination Port addresses; a 16-bit Length indicating the length of the UDP datagram; and a 16-bit checksum on the UDP header and data. The TCP header is more complex because TCP must provide reliable data delivery. The minimum length of the TCP header is 20 octets, divided into several fields. Source Port and Destination Port (16 bits each)

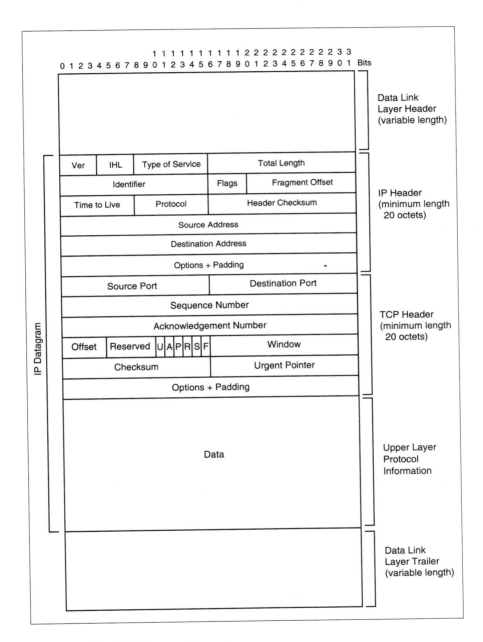

Figure 8-2. The IP Datagram Format

identify the application processes (e.g. Telnet) in use at either end of the connection. Sequence Number (32 bits) indicates where this segment belongs in the sender's data stream (measured in octets). Acknowledgement Number (32 bits) is an acknowledgement of the last data packet that piggybacks onto the next data transmission. Offset (4 bits) indicates the number of 32-bit words in the header, i.e. the offset of where the TCP data field starts. Reserved (6 bits), which are undefined, are set to zero.

Flag bits (six one-bit fields) provide control functions:

URG: Urgent pointer field significant, i.e. do urgent processing on the data.

ACK: Acknowledgement field significant, i.e. contains the next expected sequence number.

PSH: Push function, i.e. this segment contains data that must be pushed through.

RST: Reset connection, i.e. the receiver should reset that connection.

SYN: Synchronize sequence number, i.e. initiate the connection with this sequence number.

FIN: Finish, i.e. no more data from the sender.

Window (16 bits) is the size of the receive window and indicates the number of additional octets of data that the sender of the window is ready to receive. Checksum provides error control on the IP addresses, the TCP header, plus data. Urgent Pointer (16 bits) identifies the sequence number where the urgent data ends. Options (variable length) negotiate various parameters, such as the maximum segment size, with the TCP process at the other end of the connection.

8.2 TCP/IP Protocol Analysis Techniques

Although there are many advantages to a defacto standard such as TCP/IP, the need to support a multivendor (rather than a single vendor) internetwork can be a disadvantage. As we've all seen, multivendor networks provide fertile ground for finger-pointing, with all vendors assigning blame for a particular failure and none accepting responsibility.

With these caveats in mind, the following are hints for analyzing multivendor TCP/IP internetworks:

1. Verify the stability of the hardware layers. With TCP/IP-based internetworks, the hardware is invariably an interesting mixture of LAN, WAN, and PSPDN (via the X.25 protocol) connections. For LANs, review the Ethernet hints (Section 5.2) and token ring hints (Section 6.2) as necessary.

2. Older TCP/IP-based internetworks typically use the DEC, Intel, and Xerox (DIX) Ethernet frame format, while newer implementations use the IEEE 802.3 format. Verify that both sender and receiver are using the same format consistently. This technique is illustrated in Section 8.3.2.

3. Workstations should save (cache) responses from the ARP server. If they do not, internetwork bandwidth will be needlessly consumed in retransmitting ARP requests. Use the analyzer to capture only the ARP packets to determine whether one workstation or host is causing the problem.

4. The ARP protocol broadcasts requests from a workstation needing to convert an IP address to a Local Network (i.e. Ethernet) address on the network. Make sure that all stations define the same address for the broadcast. For example BSD 4.2 UNIX defines the broadcast as a destination address of all zeros. BSD 4.3 UNIX and AT&T System V UNIX define the same address as all ones. When hosts using both of these operating systems reside on the same network, excessive traffic, known as a *broadcast storm*, can result. Identify the broadcasting host using the source address field and make the broadcast address consistent with all other hosts on the network.

5. Verify that all bridges and routers are operational. Capture routing (e.g. RIP) packets and look for any broadcasts that are abnormal for that internetwork, such as multiple or incorrect routes.

6. Check for unknown hosts on the local network. A change or recent addition is often the source of problems, such as duplicate IP addresses.

7. ICMP messages (e.g. network unreachable or host unreachable) are clear hints that an internetwork problem exists. Decode the ICMP messages and see what they say. Also use ICMP's debugging capabilities, such as the ICMP Echo request (Ping) command.

8. Verify that packet fragmentation at the IP Layer is functioning properly for all networks along the internetwork transmission path. One of IP's strengths is its ability to fragment, reassemble, then refragment data as it traverses LANs and WANs to accommodate varying maximum frame sizes. Some application software supports a limited number of fragments (e.g. two fragments maximum). Problems can result when an intermediate network (such as an Ethernet with its maximum frame size of 1,500 octets) requires more than the maximum number of fragments.

9. Identify the significant events associated with TCP connections. These include the three-way handshakes that establish or disconnect the host-to-host connections. Use these events to define logical boundaries before and after the application data is sent. Identify the cause of any abnormal events, such as a connection reset. Section 8.3.1 is an example of this tip in action.

10. Unacceptably slow file transfers are often the result of a TCP window size that is too small or data traffic congestion on the slowest path.

11. Look for application-specific problems. One example would be a Telnet option (such as the terminal type) that is incompatible with the desired host.

Another would be a host that allocates insufficient buffer space for a particular application. This lack of buffer space can cause reassembly of the incoming packets to lock up, thereby slowing the response time.

References [8-39] and [8-40] provide further information on TCP/IP analysis.

8.3 TCP/IP Internetwork Troubleshooting

With our newly acquired understanding of TCP/IP protocols, let's examine four problems that internetwork managers typically face. The first may be a familiar user complaint: "I can't log in to the server."

8.3.1 TCP/IP Server Login Failure

In our first example, a PC user attempted to log in to a Sun server running the Sun OS operating system and perform a file transfer. Both devices were resident on the same Ethernet network. After several unsuccessful attempts, the user called for assistance. The network analyst captured the data from the PC and quickly determined the failure. Let's follow his steps (see Trace 8.3.1) and record the significant events. Figure 8-3 shows the TCP Connect/Disconnect events described below.

Sniffer Network Analyzer data 27-Mar-91 at 09:04:54, file TCPMEDLY.ENC Pg 1

SUMMARY	Delta T	Destination	Source	Summary
559	23.1535	Sun Server	PC	TCP D=21 S=1218 SYN
				SEQ=160830004
				LEN=0 WIN=1024
560	0.0009	PC	Sun Server	TCP D=1218 S=21 SYN
				ACK=160830005 SEQ=1961856000
				LEN=0 WIN=4096
561	0.0131	Sun Server	PC	TCP D=21 S=1218
				ACK=1961856001 WIN=1024
562	0.0530	PC	Sun Server	FTP R PORT=1218 220 h0008
				FTP server (SunOS 4.1)
				ready .<0D><0A>

563	0.1402	Sun Server	PC	TCP D=21 S=1218
				ACK=1961856042 WIN=983
564	1.1425	Sun Server	PC	FTP C PORT=1218
				USER kpa<0D><0A>
565	0.0130	PC	Sun Server	FTP R PORT=1218 331
				Password required for
				kpa.<0D><0A>
566	0.1621	Sun Server	PC	TCP D=21 S=1218
				ACK=1961856074 WIN=992
567	1.3071	Sun Server	PC	FTP C PORT=1218 PASS <0D><0A>
568	0.0321	PC	Sun Server	FTP R PORT=1218 530
				Login incorrect.<0D><0A>
569	0.1434	Sun Server	PC	TCP D=21 S=1218
				ACK=1961856096 WIN=1002
570	53.9247	Sun Server	PC	FTP C PORT=1218 QUIT<0D><0A>
571	0.0064	PC	Sun Server	FTP R PORT=1218
				221 Goodbye.<0D><0A>
572	0.0072	PC	Sun Server	TCP D=1218 S=21 FIN
				ACK=160830028 SEQ=1961856110
				LEN=0 WIN=4096
573	0.0142	Sun Server	PC	TCP D=21 S=1218
				ACK=1961856111 WIN=1010
574	0.0601	Sun Server	PC	TCP D=21 S=1218 FIN
				ACK=1961856111 SEQ=160830028
				LEN=0 WIN=1010
575	0.0006	PC	Sun Server	TCP D=1218 S=21
				ACK=160830029 WIN=4096
576	27.3807	Sun Server	PC	TCP D=21 S=1219 SYN
				SEQ=53219892 LEN=0 WIN=1024
577	0.0009	PC	Sun Server	TCP D=1219 S=21 SYN
				ACK=53219893 SEQ=1972864000
				LEN=0 WIN=4096
578	0.0130	Sun Server	PC	TCP D=21 S=1219

				ACK=1972864001 WIN=1024
579	0.0660	PC	Sun Server	FTP R PORT=1219 220 h0008
				FTP server (SunOS 4.1)
				ready.<0D><0A>
580	0.1440	Sun Server	PC	TCP D=21 S=1219
				ACK=1972864042 WIN=983
581	0.8431	Sun Server	PC	FTP C PORT=1219
				USER kpa<0D><0A>
582	0.0132	PC	Sun Server	FTP R PORT=1219 331
				Password required for
				kpa.<0D><0A>
583	0.1305	Sun Server	PC	TCP D=21 S=1219
				ACK=1972864074 WIN=992
584	4.2954	Sun Server	PC	FTP C PORT=1219
				PASS kpa-kpa<0D><0A>
585	0.0786	PC	Sun Server	TCP D=1219 S=21
				ACK=53219917 WIN=4096
586	0.0089	PC	Sun Server	FTP R PORT=1219 230
				User kpa logged in.<0D><0A>
587	0.1757	Sun Server	PC	TCP D=21 S=1219
				ACK=1972864099 WIN=999

Trace 8.3.1. TCP/IP Login Attempt Summary

In Frame 559, the PC initiates a TCP connection with a three-way handshake. The first transmission sends a Synchronize Sequence Numbers (SYN) command along with the PC's sequence number (SEQ = 160830004). The second is a response from the Sun (Frame 560), which includes a SYN, an acknowledgement for the PC's sequence number (ACK = 160830005), and the sequence number selected by the Sun (SEQ = 1961856000). The Sun permits a window size of 4,096 octets (WIN = 4096). The final step (Frame 561) is the PC's acknowledgement of the Sun's sequence number (ACK = 1961856001) and a statement regarding the PC's available window size (WIN = 1024). The connection is now established, and the server indicates its readiness (Frame 562).

375

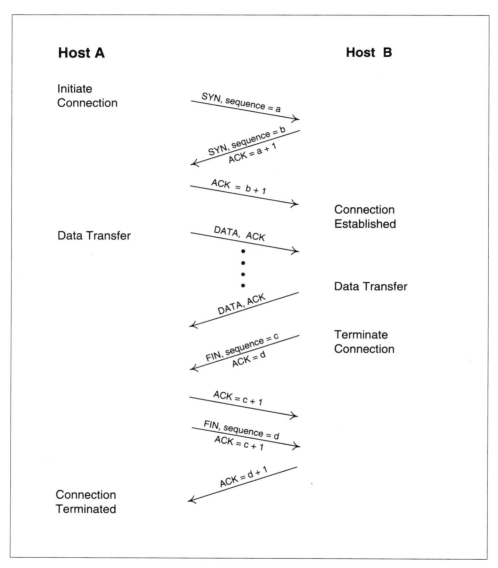

Figure 8-3. TCP/IP Connection Establishment/Disconnect Events

Next, the PC states its intentions to log in to the server and identifies itself as station user kpa (Frame 564). The server responds that a password is required for kpa (Frame 565). This confused the PC user because he expected the password to be acquired automatically from the server's login tables. Perplexed, the user presses the carriage return (Frame 567), but the server doesn't like what it sees and notes an incorrect login (Frame 568). The higher layer FTP process of both devices acknowledges the problem and terminates the application/process connection (Frames 570-571).

The server's final step is to disconnect the TCP connection (i.e. tear down the host-to-host communication path). The server initiates this process (although TCP would allow either end to terminate the connection) in Frame 572 by sending a TCP segment with the FIN (finish) flag set. The PC responds with two segments: The first (Frame 573) acknowledges the Server's FIN; the second (Frame 574) is a FIN terminating its data connection. (Two FINs are necessary because there are two independent data streams—one from the PC to the Server, and another from the Server to the PC.) The final step in the process is another acknowledgement (ACK = 160830029) from the Server confirming the PC's FIN segment. Thus, the TCP connection was established, but the user could not login.

The network analyst theorizes that the server may be misconfigured, so he attempts to make the connection a second time. Frames 576 through 578 are the initial three-way handshake, and Frames 579 and 580 indicate the Server's readiness. The user identifies himself in Frame 581 (USER kpa), and this time enters a different password (PASS kpa-kpa in Frame 584). This time the process succeeds. The server responds with the login message (Frame 586) which the user happily responds to (Frame 587). The file transfer may now begin.

The problem was traced to a configuration file on the server. The FTP process was not automatically acquiring the password when the user transmitted its login (e.g. kpa). Instead, the FTP process wanted to see the transmission of "user-user" (e.g. kpa-kpa). The misconfigured parameter caused the user login to fail. Through experimentation, the analyst discovered that the kpa-kpa sequence solved the problem. The moral of the story is not to assume that the user has done something wrong, but to question the server as well. Both ends of the communication link must agree on all of these details. After all, that's where the name "peer" comes from in the term "peer-to-peer" protocols!

8.3.2 TCP/IP Incompatible Frame Formats

In this example, a newly installed IBM RS/6000 workstation on a bridged Ethernet network demonstrated that TCP/IP internetwork problems aren't always what they seem.

The internetwork in question included bridged Ethernet segments with a Sun-3 server on one side and the new RS/6000 workstation on the other (see Figure 8-4). After the initial configuration, we discovered that the new workstation could not communicate with the server. Several hypotheses came to mind immediately, including a possible problem with the bridge.

The first step was to connect a network analyzer to the same segment as the RS/6000 and observe its data transmission (see Trace 8.3.2a). Frames 1 through 13 are an ARP broadcast from the RS/6000 looking for its server. The RS/6000 knows the target protocol address (PA = 132.163.250.255), but the hardware address (HA) of the server is unknown. An ARP request for a second server (PA = 132.163.150.255 in Frame 2) also goes unanswered. The ARP message (Trace 8.3.2b) identifies the address elements that are known (the sender's hardware and protocol addresses and the target protocol address) and fills the unknown field (the Target Hardware Address) with zeros. Note that the ARP requests are sent at 30 second intervals. Having no success finding the hardware address of the server, the analyst sends an ICMP Echo Request (Ping) message from the RS/6000 to the Sun-3 server (Trace 8.3.2c). This transmission correctly specifies the RS/6000 as the source address (132.163.200.19) and the Sun-3 (132.163.200.1) as the destination. These messages are transmitted at one-second intervals (Frames 14 through 20 in Trace 8.3.2a). Unfortunately, the Sun-3 never responds.

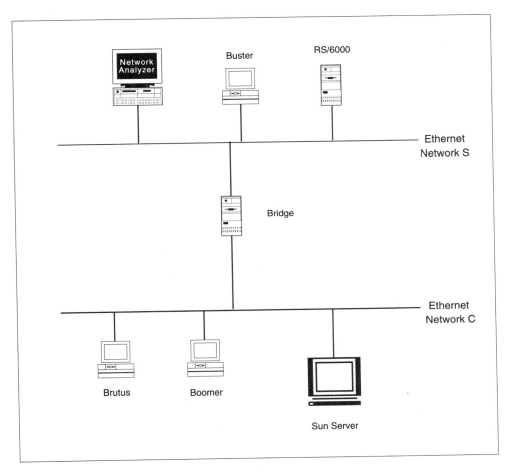

Figure 8-4. TCP/IP Incompatible Frame Formats

Sniffer Network Analyzer data 3-Jan-91 at 13:03:50, file M01.ENC Pg 1

SUMMARY	Delta T	Destination	Source	Summary
M 1		Broadcast	RS/6000	ARP C PA=[132.163.250.255] PRO=IP
2	3.7148	Broadcast	RS/6000	ARP C PA=[132.163.150.255] PRO=IP
3	29.9955	Broadcast	RS/6000	ARP C PA=[132.163.150.255] PRO=IP
4	29.9956	Broadcast	RS/6000	ARP C PA=[132.163.150.255] PRO=IP
5	29.9955	Broadcast	RS/6000	ARP C PA=[132.163.150.255] PRO=IP
6	29.9955	Broadcast	RS/6000	ARP C PA=[132.163.150.255] PRO=IP
7	13.1317	Broadcast	RS/6000	ARP C PA=[132.163.250.255] PRO=IP
8	16.8638	Broadcast	RS/6000	ARP C PA=[132.163.150.255] PRO=IP
9	26.3839	Broadcast	RS/6000	ARP C PA=[132.163.250.255] PRO=IP
10	3.6115	Broadcast	RS/6000	ARP C PA=[132.163.150.255] PRO=IP
11	29.9955	Broadcast	RS/6000	ARP C PA=[132.163.150.255] PRO=IP
12	29.9955	Broadcast	RS/6000	ARP C PA=[132.163.150.255] PRO=IP
13	29.9955	Broadcast	RS/6000	ARP C PA=[132.163.150.255] PRO=IP
14	10.2418	Sun-3	RS/6000	ICMP Echo
15	1.0015	Sun-3	RS/6000	ICMP Echo
16	1.0016	Sun-3	RS/6000	ICMP Echo
17	1.0016	Sun-3	RS/6000	ICMP Echo
18	1.0016	Sun-3	RS/6000	ICMP Echo
19	1.0017	Sun-3	RS/6000	ICMP Echo
20	1.0016	Sun-3	RS/6000	ICMP Echo

Trace 8.3.2a. TCP/IP Incompatible Frames Summary

Sniffer Network Analyzer data 3-Jan-91 at 13:03:50, file M01.ENC Pg 1

- - - - - - - - - - - - - - - - Frame 1 - - - - - - - - - - - - - - - - -

DLC: —— DLC Header ——

DLC:

DLC: Frame 1 arrived at 13:04:02.3236; frame size is 82 (0052 hex) bytes.

DLC: Destination = BROADCAST FFFFFFFFFFFF, Broadcast

DLC: Source   = Station 3Com 2E9E53, RS/6000

DLC: 802.3 length = 68

DLC:

LLC: —— LLC Header ——

LLC:

LLC: DSAP = AA, SSAP = AA, Command, Unnumbered frame: UI

LLC:

SNAP: —— SNAP Header ——

SNAP:

SNAP: Type = 0806 (ARP)

SNAP:

ARP: —— ARP/RARP frame ——

ARP:

ARP: Hardware type = 6 (4Mb 802.5 token ring)

ARP: Protocol type = 0800 (IP)

ARP: Length of hardware address = 6 bytes

ARP: Length of protocol address = 4 bytes

ARP: Opcode 1 (ARP request)

ARP: Sender's hardware address = 02608C2E9E53

ARP: Sender's protocol address = [132.163.200.19]

ARP: Target hardware address = 000000000000

ARP: Target protocol address = [132.163.250.255]

ARP:

Trace 8.3.2b. TCP/IP Repeated ARP Broadcasts

Sniffer Network Analyzer data 3-Jan-91 at 13:03:50, file M01.ENC Pg 1

- - - - - - - - - - - - - - - - Frame 14 - - - - - - - - - - - - - - - -

DLC: ——— DLC Header ———

DLC:

DLC: Frame 14 arrived at 13:08:46.2402; frame size is 106 (006A hex) bytes.

DLC: Destination = Station Sun   0165B2, Sun-3

DLC: Source   = Station 3Com 2E9E53, RS/6000

DLC: 802.3 length = 92

DLC:

LLC: ——— LLC Header ———

LLC:

LLC: DSAP = AA, SSAP = AA, Command, Unnumbered frame: UI

LLC:

SNAP: ——— SNAP Header ———

SNAP:

SNAP: Type = 0800 (IP)

SNAP:

IP: ——— IP Header ———

IP:

IP: Version = 4, header length = 20 bytes

IP: Type of service = 00

IP: 000. .... = routine

IP: ...0 .... = normal delay

IP: .... 0... = normal throughput

IP: .... .0.. = normal reliability

IP: Total length = 84 bytes

IP: Identification = 3769

IP: Flags = 0X

IP: .0.. .... = may fragment

IP: ..0. .... = last fragment

IP: Fragment offset = 0 bytes

IP: Time to live = 255 seconds/hops

```
IP:  Protocol = 1 (ICMP)

IP:  Header checksum = A194 (correct)

IP:  Source address = [132.163.200.19]

IP:  Destination address = [132.163.200.1]

IP:  No options

IP:

ICMP: ──── ICMP header ────

ICMP:

ICMP:  Type = 8 (Echo)

ICMP:  Code = 0

ICMP:  Checksum = F4EE (correct)

ICMP:  Identifier = 4063

ICMP:  Sequence number = 0

ICMP:  [56 bytes of data]

ICMP:

ICMP:  [Normal end of "ICMP header".]
```

Trace 8.3.2c. TCP/IP Repeated ICMP Echo (Ping) Messages

The analyst then examined the Data Link Layer frame format transmitted from the RS/6000. He noted that the network card in the RS/6000 workstation had been configured to transmit IEEE 802.3 frames (see Figure G-3 in Appendix G) instead of Ethernet v2.0 (see Figure G-4). These frames are identical in length, but differ in two significant respects. First, Ethernet v2.0 frames always use 6-octet addressing. IEEE 802.3 may use either 2-octet or 6-octet addressing, although most manufacturers have chosen the 6-octet alternative. Second, the 2-octet field preceding the data identifies the protocol TYPE for Ethernet v2.0, while it specifies the data LENGTH for 802.3. (Appendix E lists commonly-used Ethernet Types, sometimes called Ethertypes.)

In this example, the server, running Ethernet v2.0, could not interpret the LENGTH field transmitted within the IEEE 802.3 frame since it was expecting a TYPE in the same position. Because the transmitted LENGTH did not match the expected TYPE, the server failed to recognize the frame.

Reconfiguring the RS/6000 workstation driver to transmit Ethernet v2.0 frames solved the problem. Several ICMP Echo Request commands (Trace 8.3.2d) verified proper bridge operation. This time, the Sun-3 server provided the expected Echo Reply. Details of the ICMP messages (Trace 8.3.2e) verify that the source and destination addresses change place between the Echo Request (Frame 5) and the Echo Reply (Frame 6). In addition, the 56 bytes of transmitted test data is also returned. Thus, the connectivity path is verified, and the bridge is eliminated as a source of trouble. All that was necessary was to reconfigure the RS/6000 to provide frame compatibility between itself and the server. For this internetwork, the problem was not as complex as it originally seemed.

Sniffer Network Analyzer data 3-Jan-91 at 14:56:22, file M_OK.ENC Pg 1

SUMMARY	Delta T	Destination	Source	Summary
M 1		Broadcast	RS/6000	ARP C PA=[132.163.250.255]
				PRO=IP
2	0.0008	WstDig760A07	RS/6000	ICMP Redirect (Redirect
				datagrams for the host)
3	6.2017	Sun-3	RS/6000	DNS C ID=1 OP=QUERY NAME=
4	0.0159	RS/6000	Sun-3	DNS R ID=1 STAT=OK NAME=
5	0.0099	Sun-3	RS/6000	ICMP Echo
6	0.0041	RS/6000	Sun-3	ICMP Echo reply
7	0.9974	Sun-3	RS/6000	ICMP Echo
8	0.0033	RS/6000	Sun-3	ICMP Echo reply
9	0.9983	Sun-3	RS/6000	ICMP Echo
10	0.0051	RS/6000	Sun-3	ICMP Echo reply
11	0.9964	Sun-3	RS/6000	ICMP Echo
12	0.0046	RS/6000	Sun-3	ICMP Echo reply
13	0.9969	Sun-3	RS/6000	ICMP Echo
14	0.0044	RS/6000	Sun-3	ICMP Echo reply
15	0.9973	Sun-3	RS/6000	ICMP Echo
16	0.0033	RS/6000	Sun-3	ICMP Echo reply

17	0.9982	Sun-3	RS/6000	ICMP Echo
18	0.0033	RS/6000	Sun-3	ICMP Echo reply
19	0.9982	Sun-3	RS/6000	ICMP Echo
20	0.0033	RS/6000	Sun-3	ICMP Echo reply

Trace 8.3.2d. TCP/IP Successful ICMP Echo (Ping) Message Summary

Sniffer Network Analyzer data 3-Jan-91 at 14:56:22, file M_OK.ENC Pg 1

- - - - - - - - - - - - - - - Frame 5 - - - - - - - - - - - - - - - - -

DLC: —— DLC Header ——

DLC:

DLC: Frame 5 arrived at 14:56:40.5168; frame size is 98 (0062 hex) bytes.

DLC: Destination = Station Sun   0165B2, Sun-3

DLC: Source   = Station 3Com 2E9E53, RS/6000

DLC: Ethertype = 0800 (IP)

DLC:

IP: —— IP Header ——

IP:

IP: Version = 4, header length = 20 bytes

IP: Type of service = 00

IP: 000. .... = routine

IP: ...0 .... = normal delay

IP: .... 0... = normal throughput

IP: .... .0.. = normal reliability

IP: Total length = 84 bytes

IP: Identification = 21024

IP: Flags = 0X

IP: .0.. .... = may fragment

IP: ..0. .... = last fragment

IP: Fragment offset = 0 bytes

IP: Time to live = 255 seconds/hops

IP: Protocol = 1 (ICMP)

IP: Header checksum = 5E2D (correct)

IP: Source address = [132.163.200.19]

IP: Destination address = [132.163.200.1]

IP: No options

IP:

ICMP: —— ICMP header ——

ICMP:

ICMP: Type = 8 (Echo)

ICMP: Code = 0

ICMP: Checksum = 0761 (correct)

ICMP: Identifier = 4740

ICMP: Sequence number = 0

ICMP: [56 bytes of data]

ICMP:

ICMP: [Normal end of "ICMP header".]

ICMP:

- - - - - - - - - - - - - - - Frame 6 - - - - - - - - - - - - - - - - -

DLC: —— DLC Header ——

DLC:

DLC: Frame 6 arrived at 14:56:40.5210; frame size is 98 (0062 hex) bytes.

DLC: Destination = Station 3Com 2E9E53, RS/6000

DLC: Source = Station Sun 0165B2, Sun-3

DLC: Ethertype = 0800 (IP)

DLC:

IP: —— IP Header ——

IP:

IP: Version = 4, header length = 20 bytes

IP: Type of service = 00

IP: 000. .... = routine

IP: ...0 .... = normal delay

IP: .... 0... = normal throughput

IP: .... .0.. = normal reliability

IP: Total length = 84 bytes

IP: Identification = 49697

IP: Flags = 0X

IP: .0.. .... = may fragment

IP: ..0. .... = last fragment

IP: Fragment offset = 0 bytes

IP: Time to live = 255 seconds/hops

IP: Protocol = 1 (ICMP)

IP: Header checksum = EE2B (correct)

IP: Source address = [132.163.200.1]

IP: Destination address = [132.163.200.19]

IP: No options

IP:

ICMP: —— ICMP header ——

ICMP:

ICMP: Type = 0 (Echo reply)

ICMP: Code = 0

ICMP: Checksum = 0F61 (correct)

ICMP: Identifier = 4740

ICMP: Sequence number = 0

ICMP: [56 bytes of data]

ICMP:

ICMP: [Normal end of "ICMP header".]

ICMP:

Trace 8.3.2e. TCP/IP Successful ICMP Echo (Ping) Message Details

8.3.3 TCP/IP Incompatible Terminal Type

As we studied in Section 8.1, the DOD architecture groups all the upper-layer functions into the Process/Application Layer. This single (DOD) layer includes the OSI Session, Presentation, and Application Layer services. The Presentation layer performs any code conversion required to assure that the sending station and receiving station are speaking the same "language." For example, if my IBM host terminal spoke ASCII and the host machine spoke EBCDIC, some process would be necessary to perform a code conversion—otherwise the two of us could never communicate. In most cases, the PC does the conversion so as not to burden the host with this seemingly trivial issue.

In this case study, a PC on an Ethernet needed to establish communication with a remote IBM host (see Figure 8-5). The PC would establish a connection, but then the connection would abruptly fail. We placed a network analyzer on the Ethernet segment to determine the source of the failure. The initial analysis (see Trace 8.3.3a) indicated normal operation. The Emulator issued a query to the Domain Name Server to find the host's internet address (Frame 1), and the server responded with the address in Frame 2. Since the host was located on another network (network 129.6.x.x), a connection via the router was required. The TCP three-way handshake starts in Frame 3 and completes in Frames 4 and 6. (Note that any subsequent information to or from the remote host will go via the router. If our analyzer was placed on the same segment as the host, we could observe the host responding directly.)

Sniffer Network Analyzer data 21-Jun-90 at 09:06:50 file TERMTYPE.ENC Pg 1

SUMMARY	Delta T	Destination	Source	Summary
M 1		Name Server	Emulator	DNS C ID=17 OP=QUERY
2	0.0028	Emulator	Name Server	DNS R ID=17 STAT=OK
3	0.1023	Router	Emulator	TCP D=23 S=3158 SYN
				SEQ=4660 LEN=0 WIN=1024
4	4.0014	Router	Emulator	TCP D=23 S=3158 SYN
				SEQ=4660 LEN=0 WIN=1024
5	0.1316	Router	Emulator	ARP R PA=[132.163.200.15]
				HA=02608C1AB9BE PRO=IP

6	3.0033	Emulator	Router	TCP D=3158 S=23 SYN ACK=4661 SEQ=1051902676 LEN=0 WIN=8192
7	0.0033	Router	Emulator	TCP D=23 S=3158 ACK=1051902677 WIN=1024
8	0.2502	Emulator	Router	Telnet R PORT=3158 IAC Do Terminal type
9	0.1262	Router	Emulator	TCP D=23 S=3158 ACK=1051902680 WIN=1021
10	2.7604	Router	Emulator	Telnet C PORT=3158 IAC Will Terminal type
11	0.1311	Emulator	Router	TCP D=3158 S=23 ACK=4664 WIN=8189
12	0.0122	Emulator	Router	Telnet R PORT=3158 IAC SB ...
13	0.0048	Router	Emulator	Telnet C PORT=3158 IAC SB ...
14	0.1418	Emulator	Router	TCP D=3158 S=23 ACK=4675 WIN=8178
15	0.0142	Emulator	Router	Telnet R PORT=3158 IAC SB ...
16	0.0049	Router	Emulator	Telnet C PORT=3158 IAC SB ...
17	0.1404	Emulator	Router	TCP D=3158 S=23 ACK=4686 WIN=8167
18	0.0142	Emulator	Router	TCP D=3158 S=23 FIN ACK=4686 SEQ=1051902692 LEN=0 WIN=8167
19	0.0029	Router	Emulator	TCP D=23 S=3158 ACK=1051902693 WIN=1009
20	0.0021	Router	Emulator	TCP D=23 S=3158 FIN ACK=1051902693 SEQ=4686 LEN=0 WIN=1009
21	0.1492	Emulator	Router	TCP D=3158 S=23 ACK=4687 WIN=8166

Trace 8.3.3a. TCP/IP Terminal Emulation Incompatibility Summary

389

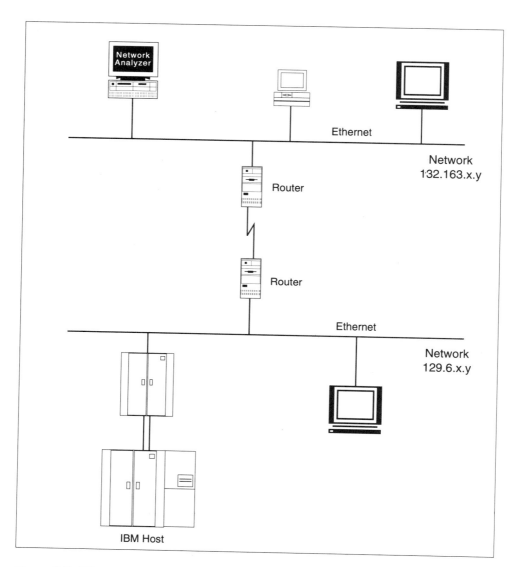

Figure 8-5. TCP/IP Incompatible Terminal Type

Next, the emulator initiates the Telnet session (see Reference [8-31]) with the remote host. All appears to be going well until the remote host terminates the connection in Frame 18. Frames 19 and 20 complete the TCP disconnect. The question is: Why did the session terminate abruptly before data could be transferred?

The answer is found in the details of the Telnet parameters that were passed from the emulator to the host (Trace 8.3.3b). Note that the source and destination stations are on different networks (see the IP address fields) and that the Telnet part of the host is being used (see the TCP header of Frame 12). The answer to the interoperability problem is found within the ASCII decode of the data in the details of Frame 13. The emulator has selected a Terminal Type = DUMB, indicating that it will emulate a dumb terminal. This selection might work well for ASCII-based hosts, such as a DEC or Hewlett-Packard minicomputer, but it is unacceptable to the IBM host. The remote host wants to speak to a terminal of its own type (e.g. 3278 or 3279 display station) and rebels when asked to speak to a dumb terminal. The host's dissatisfaction is demonstrated by the TCP disconnect in Frames 18 through 20. In Frame 12 the host (via the router) negotiates a parameter option with the terminal. The designation "IAC SB..." means "interpret as command, start of option subnegotiation." In other words, the host has a particular parameter option that must be negotiated. The emulator's response is given in Frame 13.

```
Sniffer Network Analyzer data 21-Jun-90 at 09:06:50 file TERMTYPE.ENC Pg 1

- - - - - - - - - - - - - - - - Frame 12 - - - - - - - - - - - - - - - - -

IP:  ——— IP Header ———
IP:
IP:  Version = 4, header length = 20 bytes
IP:  Type of service = 00
IP:      000. .... = routine
IP:      ...0 .... = normal delay
IP:      .... 0... = normal throughput
IP:      .... .0.. = normal reliability
IP:  Total length = 46 bytes
IP:  Identification = 47266
```

```
IP:   Flags = 0X
IP:   .0.. .... = may fragment
IP:   ..0. .... = last fragment
IP:   Fragment offset = 0 bytes
IP:   Time to live = 58 seconds/hops
IP:   Protocol = 6 (TCP)
IP:   Header checksum = 316B (correct)
IP:   Source address = [129.6.16.4]
IP:   Destination address = [132.163.200.15]
IP:   No options
IP:
TCP:  —— TCP header ——
TCP:
TCP:  Source port = 23 (Telnet)
TCP:  Destination port = 3158
TCP:  Sequence number = 1051902680
TCP:  Acknowledgment number = 4664
TCP:  Data offset = 20 bytes
TCP:  Flags = 18
TCP:  ..0. .... = (No urgent pointer)
TCP:  ...1 .... = Acknowledgment
TCP:  .... 1... = Push
TCP:  .... .0.. = (No reset)
TCP:  .... ..0. = (No SYN)
TCP:  .... ...0 = (No FIN)
TCP:  Window = 8189
TCP:  Checksum = 929F (correct)
TCP:  No TCP options
TCP:  [6 byte(s) of data]
TCP:
```

Telnet:———— Telnet data ————

Telnet:

Telnet:IAC SB ...

ADDR	HEX		ASCII
0000	02 60 8C 1A B9 BE 00 00	93 E0 80 7B 08 00 45 00	.'.........{..E.
0010	00 2E B8 A2 00 00 3A 06	31 6B 81 06 10 04 84 A3	.......:.1k......
0020	81 0F 00 17 0C 56 3E B2	C2 D8 00 00 12 38 50 18	.....V>......8P.
0030	1F FD 92 9F 2E 50 FF FA	18 01 FF F0	.....P......

- - - - - - - - - - - - - - - Frame 13 - - - - - - - - - - - - - - - -

IP: ———— IP Header ————

IP:

IP: Version = 4, header length = 20 bytes

IP: Type of service = 00

IP: 000. .... = routine

IP: ...0 .... = normal delay

IP: .... 0... = normal throughput

IP: .... .0.. = normal reliability

IP: Total length = 51 bytes

IP: Identification = 7052

IP: Flags = 0X

IP: .0.. .... = may fragment

IP: ..0. .... = last fragment

IP: Fragment offset = 0 bytes

IP: Time to live = 64 seconds/hops

IP: Protocol = 6 (TCP)

IP: Header checksum = C87C (correct)

IP: Source address = [132.163.200.15]

IP: Destination address = [129.6.16.4]

IP: No options

IP:

TCP: —— TCP header ——

TCP:

TCP: Source port = 3158

TCP: Destination port = 23 (Telnet)

TCP: Sequence number = 4664

TCP: Acknowledgment number = 1051902686

TCP: Data offset = 20 bytes

TCP: Flags = 18

TCP: ..0. .... = (No urgent pointer)

TCP: ...1 .... = Acknowledgment

TCP: .... 1... = Push

TCP: .... .0.. = (No reset)

TCP: .... ..0. = (No SYN)

TCP: ....0 = (No FIN)

TCP: Window = 1015

TCP: Checksum = 5A45 (correct)

TCP: No TCP options

TCP: [11 byte(s) of data]

TCP:

Telnet:—— Telnet data ——

Telnet:

Telnet:IAC SB ...

ADDR	HEX		ASCII
0000	00 00 93 E0 80 7B 02 60	8C 1A B9 BE08 00 45 00	.....{.'......E.
0010	00 33 1B 8C 00 00 40 06	C8 7C 84 A3 81 0F 81 06	.3....@..I......
0020	10 04 0C 56 00 17 00 00	12 38 3E B2 C2 DE 50 18	...V.....8>...P.
0030	03 F7 5A 45 00 00 FF FA	18 00 44 55 4D 42 00 FF	..ZE......DUMB..
0040	F0		

Trace 8.3.3b. TCP/IP Terminal Emulation Incompatibility Details

Once the problem was analyzed, the solution was straightforward. The analyst returned to the terminal emulation menu at the workstation and entered an IBM terminal type. This change assured compatibility between the two Presentation Layer processes (terminal and host) and solved the interoperability problem.

8.3.4 TCP/IP Router Problems

For our last example, we'll consider the effects that a misconfigured router can have on the internetwork. In this case (Figure 8-6), a new router (designated NewRouter) was being configured as an addition to an existing internetwork. When the new router was initialized, it began interfering with the router that should have been handling the traffic (OldRouter). Here's what happened.

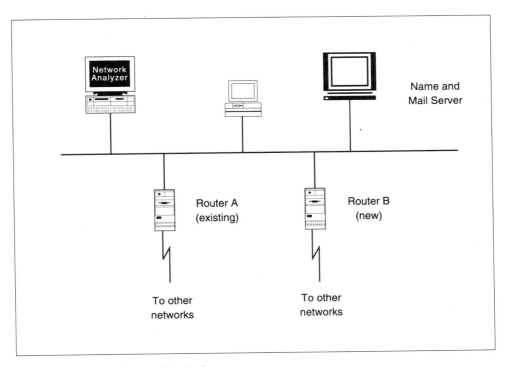

Figure 8-6. TCP/IP Router Confusion

We began our analysis by placing a network analyzer on the same segment as the two routers and captured the data from all devices (Trace 8.3.4a.) Three significant events can be observed. First, multiple ARP responses are coming from the new router (Frames 16, 17, 20, and 21.) Second, the old and new routers are attempting to exchange their routing tables using the Routing Information Protocol (RIP) in Frames 13, 15, 38, and 58. Finally, other devices on the internetwork are transmitting ICMP messages, indicating that an addressing problem exists (Frames 18, 19, 22, 39, 40, and so on) We'll examine these three issues separately.

Sniffer Network Analyzer data 10-Apr-90 at 17:13:12, file NEWROUTE.ENC Pg 1

SUMMARY	Delta T	Destination	Source	Summary
M 1		NewRouter	Name Svr	UDP D=1001 S=1171 LEN=524
2	0.0080	Name Svr	NewRouter	UDP D=1171 S=1001 LEN=12
3	0.0017	NewRouter	Name Svr	UDP D=1001 S=1171 LEN=524
4	0.0080	Name Svr	NewRouter	UDP D=1171 S=1001 LEN=12
5	0.0017	NewRouter	Name Svr	UDP D=1001 S=1171 LEN=524
6	0.0080	Name Svr	NewRouter	UDP D=1171 S=1001 LEN=12
7	0.0018	NewRouter	Name Svr	UDP D=1001 S=1171 LEN=467
8	0.0078	Name Svr	NewRouter	UDP D=1171 S=1001 LEN=12
9	2.0560	OldRouter	OldRouter	Ethertype=7030 (Interlan test)
10	0.0387	NewRouter	NewRouter	Ethertype=AAAA (Unknown)
11	0.0011	NewRouter	NewRouter	Ethertype=7030 (Interlan test)
12	0.4944	Broadcast	NewRouter	ARP R PA=[132.163.100.3]
				HA=000093E050F0 PRO=IP
13	0.0038	Broadcast	NewRouter	RIP C Requests=1
14	0.0071	Broadcast	OldRouter	ARP C PA=[132.163.100.3]
				PRO=IP
15	0.0002	Broadcast	NewRouter	RIP R Routing entries=3
16	0.0016	OldRouter	NewRouter	ARP R PA=[132.163.100.3]
				HA=000093E050F0 PRO=IP
17	0.0075	DG 01029E	NewRouter	ARP R PA=[132.163.100.3]
				HA=000093E050F0 PRO=IP

18	0.0098	NewRouter	DG 01029E	ICMP Destination unreachable
				(Port unreachable)
19	0.0027	NewRouter	DG 01029E	ICMP Destination unreachable
				(Port unreachable)
20	0.0192	Intrln01CE28	NewRouter	ARP R PA=[132.163.100.3]
				HA=000093E050F0 PRO=IP
21	0.0322	Intrln01CE28	NewRouter	ARP R PA=[132.163.100.3]
				HA=000093E050F0 PRO=IP
22	0.0380	NewRouter	Intrln01CE28	ICMP Destination unreachable
				(Net unreachable)
23	1.7174	Apollo00FDF6	OldRouter	Telnet C PORT=1939 r
24	0.0250	OldRouter	Apollo00FDF6	Telnet R PORT=1939 r
25	0.1329	Apollo00FDF6	OldRouter	TCP D=23 S=1939
				ACK=665728256 WIN=4096
26	1.2361	NewRouter	NewRouter	Ethertype=7030 (Interlan test)
27	0.2358	OldRouter	OldRouter	Ethertype=7030 (Interlan test)
28	2.3947	Apollo00FDF6	OldRouter	Telnet C PORT=1939 <0D>
29	0.0246	OldRouter	Apollo00FDF6	Telnet R PORT=1939 <0D><0A>
30	0.0373	OldRouter	Apollo00FDF6	Telnet R PORT=1939 <0D><0A>
				You are flying over
31	0.0068	Apollo00FDF6	OldRouter	Telnet C PORT=1939 <0A>
32	0.0555	OldRouter	Apollo00FDF6	TCP D=1939 S=23
				ACK=722497816 WIN=9116
33	0.2082	Apollo00FDF6	OldRouter	TCP D=23 S=1939
				ACK=665728488 WIN=4096
34	1.2768	OldRouter	OldRouter	Ethertype=7030 (Interlan test)
35	4.0041	OldRouter	OldRouter	Ethertype=7030 (Interlan test)
36	4.0042	OldRouter	OldRouter	Ethertype=7030 (Interlan test)
37	4.0040	OldRouter	OldRouter	Ethertype=7030 (Interlan test)
38	2.0242	Broadcast	OldRouter	RIP R Routing entries=1
39	0.0102	OldRouter	DG 01029E	ICMP Destination unreachable
				(Port unreachable)

40	0.0108	OldRouter	Intrln01CE28	ICMP Destination unreachable
				(Net unreachable)
41	1.9588	OldRouter	OldRouter	Ethertype=7030 (Interlan test)
42	4.0041	OldRouter	OldRouter	Ethertype=7030 (Interlan test)
43	2.5355	Apollo00FDF6	OldRouter	Telnet C PORT=1939 a
44	0.0274	OldRouter	Apollo00FDF6	Telnet R PORT=1939 a
45	0.1404	Apollo00FDF6	OldRouter	TCP D=23 S=1939
				ACK=665728489 WIN=4096
46	0.0953	Apollo00FDF6	OldRouter	Telnet C PORT=1939 <0D>
47	0.0246	OldRouter	Apollo00FDF6	Telnet R PORT=1939 <0D><0A>
48	0.0214	OldRouter	Apollo00FDF6	Telnet R PORT=1939 <0D><0A
				You are flying over <0D>...
49	0.0237	Apollo00FDF6	OldRouter	Telnet C PORT=1939 <0A>
50	0.0144	OldRouter	Apollo00FDF6	TCP D=1939 S=23
				ACK=722497819 WIN=9115
51	0.0220	Apollo00FDF6	OldRouter	TCP D=23 S=1939
				ACK=665728542 WIN=4096
52	1.0989	OldRouter	OldRouter	Ethertype=7030 (Interlan test)
53	4.0041	OldRouter	OldRouter	Ethertype=7030 (Interlan test)
54	4.0041	OldRouter	OldRouter	Ethertype=7030 (Interlan test)
55	4.0041	OldRouter	OldRouter	Ethertype=7030 (Interlan test)
56	4.0041	OldRouter	OldRouter	Ethertype=7030 (Interlan test)
57	4.0041	OldRouter	OldRouter	Ethertype=7030 (Interlan test)
58	0.0221	Broadcast	OldRouter	RIP R Routing entries=1
59	0.0102	OldRouter	DG 01029E	ICMP Destination unreachable
				(Port unreachable)
60	0.0106	OldRouter	Intrln01CE28	ICMP Destination unreachable
				(Net unreachable)
61	3.9610	OldRouter	OldRouter	Ethertype=7030 (Interlan test)

Trace 8.3.4a. TCP/IP Router Confusion Summary

In Frame 14 (see Trace 8.3.4b), OldRouter (IP address 132.163.100.1) wants to identify the hardware address of the new kid on the block (NewRouter). NewRouter's IP address (132.163.100.3) is transmitted in the ARP request packet with the hardware address to be filled in by the responding device. When the NewRouter recognizes its address, it should transmit an ARP Response packet to the requester (OldRouter). It does this in Frame 16, identifying its hardware address. Unfortunately, NewRouter does not stop with that response. It sends packets to other devices on the network as well (Frames 17, 20, 21.) These extra transmissions provide another clue that NewRouter is confused.

```
Sniffer Network Analyzer data 10-Apr-90 at 17:13:12 NEWROUTE.ENC Pg 1

- - - - - - - - - - - - - - - Frame 14 - - - - - - - - - - - - - - - - -

SUMMARY  Delta T   Destination  Source      Summary
   14    0.0109  Broadcast   OldRouter    ARP C PA=[132.163.100.3] PRO=IP



ARP: ——— ARP/RARP frame ———

ARP:

ARP: Hardware type = 1 (10Mb Ethernet)

ARP: Protocol type = 0800 (IP)

ARP: Length of hardware address = 6 bytes

ARP: Length of protocol address = 4 bytes

ARP: Opcode 1 (ARP request)

ARP: Sender's hardware address = XXXXXXE0807B, OldRouter

ARP: Sender's protocol address = [132.163.100.1]

ARP: Target hardware address = XXXXXX080208

ARP: Target protocol address = [132.163.100.3]

ARP:
```

- - - - - - - - - - - - - - - Frame 16 - - - - - - - - - - - - - - - - -

SUMMARY Delta T   Destination Source   Summary

  16   0.0018 OldRouter   NewRouter   ARP R PA=[132.163.100.3]

                                                  HA=XXXXXXE050F0 PRO=IP

ARP: —— ARP/RARP frame ——

ARP:

ARP: Hardware type = 1 (10Mb Ethernet)

ARP: Protocol type = 0800 (IP)

ARP: Length of hardware address = 6 bytes

ARP: Length of protocol address = 4 bytes

ARP: Opcode 2 (ARP reply)

ARP: Sender's hardware address = XXXXXXE050F0, NewRouter

ARP: Sender's protocol address = [132.163.100.3]

ARP: Target hardware address = XXXXXXE0807B, OldRouter

ARP: Target protocol address = [132.163.100.1]

ARP:

- - - - - - - - - - - - - - - Frame 17 - - - - - - - - - - - - - - - - -

SUMMARY Delta T   Destination Source   Summary

  17   0.0075 DG   01029E NewRouter   ARP R PA=[132.163.100.3]

                                                  HA=XXXXXXE050F0 PRO=IP

ARP: —— ARP/RARP frame ——

ARP:

ARP: Hardware type = 1 (10Mb Ethernet)

ARP: Protocol type = 0800 (IP)

ARP: Length of hardware address = 6 bytes

ARP: Length of protocol address = 4 bytes

ARP: Opcode 2 (ARP reply)

ARP: Sender's hardware address = XXXXXXE050F0, NewRouter

ARP: Sender's protocol address = [132.163.100.3]

400

ARP: Target hardware address = XXXXXX01029E

ARP: Target protocol address = [132.163.224.12]

ARP:

- - - - - - - - - - - - - - - Frame 20 - - - - - - - - - - - - - - - - -

SUMMARY Delta T   Destination Source   Summary

  20   0.0317 Intrln01CE28 NewRouter   ARP R PA=[132.163.100.3]

                                                HA=XXXXXXE050F0 PRO=IP

ARP: —— ARP/RARP frame ——

ARP:

ARP: Hardware type = 1 (10Mb Ethernet)

ARP: Protocol type = 0800 (IP)

ARP: Length of hardware address = 6 bytes

ARP: Length of protocol address = 4 bytes

ARP: Opcode 2 (ARP reply)

ARP: Sender's hardware address = XXXXXXE050F0, NewRouter

ARP: Sender's protocol address = [132.163.100.3]

ARP: Target hardware address = XXXXXX01CE28

ARP: Target protocol address = [132.163.250.201]

ARP:

- - - - - - - - - - - - - - - Frame 21 - - - - - - - - - - - - - - - - -

SUMMARY Delta T   Destination Source   Summary

  21   0.0322 Intrln01CE28 NewRouter   ARP R PA=[132.163.100.3]

                                                 HA=XXXXXXE050F0 PRO=IP

ARP: —— ARP/RARP frame ——

ARP:

ARP: Hardware type = 1 (10Mb Ethernet)

ARP: Protocol type = 0800 (IP)

ARP: Length of hardware address = 6 bytes

ARP: Length of protocol address = 4 bytes

ARP: Opcode 2 (ARP reply)

ARP: Sender's hardware address = XXXXXXE050F0, NewRouter

ARP: Sender's protocol address = [132.163.100.3]

ARP: Target hardware address = XXXXXX01CE28

ARP: Target protocol address = [132.163.64.201]

ARP:

Trace 8.3.4b. TCP/IP Router Confusion ARP Details

Next, the analyst examines the routing processes within the internetwork to determine if they are stable. The routing protocol used is the Routing Information Protocol (RFC 1058). The RIP process broadcasts routing table information from routers every 30 seconds. When the data is filtered to show only the RIP packets (Trace 8.3.4c), two points are identified. First, NewRouter requests the entire contents of the table from its neighboring routers (Frame 13), but responds to its own request in the next frame. Notice that NewRouter's tables do not contain much useful information: Two of the routers identified in Frame 15 are unreachable (their hop count exceeds the maximum of 16 hops). OldRouter's responses occur every 30 seconds (Frames 38 and 58) and appear to be stable. Thus, the RIP analysis points to NewRouter with some suspicion.

Sniffer Network Analyzer data 10-Apr-90 at 17:13:12 file NEWROUTE.ENC Pg 1

- - - - - - - - - - - - - - - Frame 13 - - - - - - - - - - - - - - - -

SUMMARY Delta T   Destination Source   Summary

  13   Broadcast   NewRouter   RIP C Requests=1

RIP: —— RIP Header ——

RIP:

RIP: Command = 1 (Request)

RIP: Version = 1

RIP: Unused = 0

RIP:

RIP: Routing data frame 1: Request for entire table

RIP: Address family identifier = 0

RIP: Metric   = 16

RIP:

- - - - - - - - - - - - - - - Frame 15 - - - - - - - - - - - - - - - - -

SUMMARY Delta T   Destination Source   Summary

   15   0.0073 Broadcast   NewRouter   RIP R Routing entries=3

RIP: —— RIP Header ——

RIP:

RIP: Command = 2 (Response)

RIP: Version = 1

RIP: Unused = 0

RIP:

RIP: Routing data frame 1

RIP: Address family identifier = 2 (IP)

RIP: IP Address = [X.X.X.X]

RIP: Metric   = 16 (Unreachable)

RIP:

RIP: Routing data frame 2

RIP: Address family identifier = 2 (IP)

RIP: IP Address = [X.X.X.X]

RIP: Metric   = 16 (Unreachable)

RIP:

RIP: Routing data frame 3

RIP: Address family identifier = 2 (IP)

RIP: IP Address = [X.X.X.X]

RIP: Metric   = 1

RIP:

- - - - - - - - - - - - - - - Frame 38 - - - - - - - - - - - - - - - - -

SUMMARY Delta T   Destination Source   Summary

   38   21.4995 Broadcast   OldRouter   RIP R Routing entries=1

```
RIP: ——— RIP Header ———
RIP:
RIP: Command = 2 (Response)
RIP: Version = 1
RIP: Unused  = 0
RIP:
RIP: Routing data frame 1
RIP:    Address family identifier = 2 (IP)
RIP:    IP Address = [0.0.0.0] (Default route)
RIP:    Metric    = 2
RIP:
```

```
- - - - - - - - - - - - - - - Frame 58 - - - - - - - - - - - - - - - - -
SUMMARY  Delta T    Destination  Source     Summary
   58   30.0313  Broadcast   OldRouter    RIP R Routing entries=1
```

```
RIP: ——— RIP Header ———
RIP:
RIP: Command = 2 (Response)
RIP: Version = 1
RIP: Unused  = 0
RIP:
RIP: Routing data frame 1
RIP:    Address family identifier = 2 (IP)
RIP:    IP Address = [0.0.0.0] (Default route)
RIP:    Metric    = 2
RIP:
```

Trace 8.3.4c. TCP/IP Router Confusion RIP Details

For a final analysis, we identified the ICMP packets (Trace 8.3.4d). The first observation is that the destination for all the ICMP messages are routers: NewRouter in Frames 18, 19, and 22, and OldRouter in Frames 39, 40, 59, and 60. ICMP reports errors back to the original source of the data, not an intermediate router. From the IP Source Address, notice that the source of error in all these ICMP packets is one of the two routers in question (addresses 132.163.100.1 or 132.163.100.3). Second, the type of ICMP message is Destination Unreachable; specifically Port Unreachable (Frames 18, 19, 39, and 59) or Net Unreachable (Frames 22, 40, and 60). There appears to be no correlation between the source of the errors (NewRouter or OldRouter) and the message type (Port or Net Unreachable). The only conclusion that can be drawn is that some type of routing errors (from the Net Unreachable messages) have occurred.

```
Sniffer Network Analyzer data 10-Apr-90 at 17:13:12, NEWROUTE.ENC Pg 1

- - - - - - - - - - - - - - - - Frame 18 - - - - - - - - - - - - - - - - - -

SUMMARY  Delta T   Destination  Source     Summary
   18        NewRouter   DG   01029E  ICMP Destination unreachable (Port unreachable)
ICMP: ------ ICMP header ------
ICMP:
ICMP: Type = 3 (Destination unreachable)
ICMP: Code = 3 (Port unreachable)
ICMP: Checksum = 9AF8 (correct)
ICMP: IP header of originating message (description follows)
ICMP:
IP: ------ IP Header ------
IP:
IP: Version = 4, header length = 20 bytes
IP: Type of service = 00
IP:    000. .... = routine
IP:    ...0 .... = normal delay
IP:    .... 0... = normal throughput
IP:    .... .0.. = normal reliability
```

IP: Total length = 52 bytes

IP: Identification = 1

IP: Flags = 0X

IP: .0.. .... = may fragment

IP: ..0. .... = last fragment

IP: Fragment offset = 0 bytes

IP: Time to live = 30 seconds/hops

IP: Protocol = 17 (UDP)

IP: Header checksum = 0000, should be 926F

IP: Source address = [132.163.100.3]

IP: Destination address = [132.163.255.255]

IP: No options

ICMP:

ICMP: [First 8 byte(s) of data of originating message]

ICMP:

ICMP: [Normal end of "ICMP header".]

ICMP:

- - - - - - - - - - - - - - - Frame 19 - - - - - - - - - - - - - - - -

SUMMARY Delta T   Destination Source   Summary

   19   0.0027 NewRouter   DG   01029E ICMP Destination unreachable (Port unreachable)

ICMP: —— ICMP header ——

ICMP:

ICMP: Type = 3 (Destination unreachable)

ICMP: Code = 3 (Port unreachable)

ICMP: Checksum = 3AE4 (correct)

ICMP: IP header of originating message (description follows)

ICMP:

IP: —— IP Header ——

IP:

IP: Version = 4, header length = 20 bytes

IP: Type of service = 00

IP: 000. .... = routine

IP: ...0 .... = normal delay

IP: .... 0... = normal throughput

IP: .... .0.. = normal reliability

IP: Total length = 92 bytes

IP: Identification = 3

IP: Flags = 0X

IP: .0.. .... = may fragment

IP: ..0. .... = last fragment

IP: Fragment offset = 0 bytes

IP: Time to live = 30 seconds/hops

IP: Protocol = 17 (UDP)

IP: Header checksum = 0000, should be 9245

IP: Source address = [132.163.100.3]

IP: Destination address = [132.163.255.255]

IP: No options

ICMP:

ICMP: [First 8 byte(s) of data of originating message]

ICMP:

ICMP: [Normal end of "ICMP header".]

ICMP:

- - - - - - - - - - - - - - - - Frame 22 - - - - - - - - - - - - - - - - -

SUMMARY Delta T   Destination Source   Summary

22   0.0894 NewRouter   Intrln01CE28 ICMP Destination unreachable (Net unreachable)

ICMP: —— ICMP header ——

ICMP:

ICMP: Type = 3 (Destination unreachable)

ICMP: Code = 0 (Net unreachable)

ICMP: Checksum = 3AD3 (correct)

ICMP: IP header of originating message (description follows)

ICMP:

IP: ——— IP Header ———

IP:

IP: Version = 4, header length = 20 bytes

IP: Type of service = 00

IP: 000. .... = routine

IP: ...0 .... = normal delay

IP: .... 0... = normal throughput

IP: .... .0.. = normal reliability

IP: Total length = 112 bytes

IP: Identification = 3

IP: Flags = 0X

IP: .0.. .... = may fragment

IP: ..0. .... = last fragment

IP: Fragment offset = 0 bytes

IP: Time to live = 30 seconds/hops

IP: Protocol = 17 (UDP)

IP: Header checksum = 0000, should be 9231

IP: Source address = [132.163.100.3]

IP: Destination address = [132.163.255.255]

IP: No options

ICMP:

ICMP: [First 8 byte(s) of data of originating message]

ICMP:

ICMP: [Normal end of "ICMP header".]

ICMP:

- - - - - - - - - - - - - - - - Frame 39 - - - - - - - - - - - - - - - - -

SUMMARY Delta T   Destination Source   Summary

  39 21.3986 OldRouter   DG   01029E ICMP Destination unreachable (Port unreachable)

ICMP: ——— ICMP header ———

ICMP:

ICMP: Type = 3 (Destination unreachable)

ICMP: Code = 3 (Port unreachable)

ICMP: Checksum = 1B23 (correct)

ICMP: IP header of originating message (description follows)

ICMP:

IP: —— IP Header ——

IP:

IP: Version = 4, header length = 20 bytes

IP: Type of service = 00

IP: 000. .... = routine

IP: ...0 .... = normal delay

IP: .... 0... = normal throughput

IP: .... .0.. = normal reliability

IP: Total length = 52 bytes

IP: Identification = 32970

IP: Flags = 0X

IP: .0.. .... = may fragment

IP: ..0. .... = last fragment

IP: Fragment offset = 0 bytes

IP: Time to live = 30 seconds/hops

IP: Protocol = 17 (UDP)

IP: Header checksum = 0000, should be 11A8

IP: Source address = [132.163.100.1]

IP: Destination address = [132.163.255.255]

IP: No options

ICMP:

ICMP: [First 8 byte(s) of data of originating message]

ICMP:

ICMP: [Normal end of "ICMP header".]

ICMP:

- - - - - - - - - - - - - - - Frame 40 - - - - - - - - - - - - - - - -

SUMMARY Delta T   Destination Source   Summary

  40   0.0108 OldRouter   Intrln01CE28 ICMP Destination unreachable (Net unreachable)

ICMP: —— ICMP header ——

ICMP:

ICMP: Type = 3 (Destination unreachable)

ICMP: Code = 0 (Net unreachable)

ICMP: Checksum = 1B12 (correct)

ICMP: IP header of originating message (description follows)

ICMP:

IP: —— IP Header ——

IP:

IP: Version = 4, header length = 20 bytes

IP: Type of service = 00

IP: 000. .... = routine

IP: ...0 .... = normal delay

IP: .... 0... = normal throughput

IP: .... .0.. = normal reliability

IP: Total length = 72 bytes

IP: Identification = 32970

IP: Flags = 0X

IP: .0.. .... = may fragment

IP: ..0. .... = last fragment

IP: Fragment offset = 0 bytes

IP: Time to live = 30 seconds/hops

IP: Protocol = 17 (UDP)

IP: Header checksum = 0000, should be 1194

IP: Source address = [132.163.100.1]

IP: Destination address = [132.163.255.255]

IP: No options

ICMP:

ICMP: [First 8 byte(s) of data of originating message]

ICMP:

ICMP: [Normal end of "ICMP header".]

ICMP:

- - - - - - - - - - - - - - - Frame 59 - - - - - - - - - - - - - - - - -

SUMMARY Delta T   Destination Source   Summary

  59 30.0205 OldRouter   DG   01029E ICMP Destination unreachable (Port unreachable)

ICMP: —— ICMP header ——

ICMP:

ICMP: Type = 3 (Destination unreachable)

ICMP: Code = 3 (Port unreachable)

ICMP: Checksum = 1B20 (correct)

ICMP: IP header of originating message (description follows)

ICMP:

IP: —— IP Header ——

IP:

IP: Version = 4, header length = 20 bytes

IP: Type of service = 00

IP: 000. .... = routine

IP: ...0 .... = normal delay

IP: .... 0... = normal throughput

IP: .... .0.. = normal reliability

IP: Total length = 52 bytes

IP: Identification = 32973

IP: Flags = 0X

IP: .0.. .... = may fragment

IP: ..0. .... = last fragment

IP: Fragment offset = 0 bytes

IP: Time to live = 30 seconds/hops

IP: Protocol = 17 (UDP)

IP: Header checksum = 0000, should be 11A5

IP: Source address = [132.163.100.1]

IP: Destination address = [132.163.255.255]

IP: No options

ICMP:

ICMP: [First 8 byte(s) of data of originating message]

ICMP:

ICMP: [Normal end of "ICMP header".]

ICMP:

- - - - - - - - - - - - - - - - Frame 60 - - - - - - - - - - - - - - - - -

SUMMARY Delta T   Destination   Source   Summary

  60   0.0106   OldRouter   Intrln01CE28 ICMP Destination unreachable (Net unreachable)

ICMP: —— ICMP header ——

ICMP:

ICMP: Type = 3 (Destination unreachable)

ICMP: Code = 0 (Net unreachable)

ICMP: Checksum = 1B0F (correct)

ICMP: IP header of originating message (description follows)

ICMP:

IP: —— IP Header ——

IP:

IP: Version = 4, header length = 20 bytes

IP: Type of service = 00

IP: 000. .... = routine

IP: ...0 .... = normal delay

IP: .... 0... = normal throughput

IP: .... .0.. = normal reliability

IP: Total length = 72 bytes

IP: Identification = 32973

IP: Flags = 0X

IP: .0.. .... = may fragment

IP: ..0. .... = last fragment

IP: Fragment offset = 0 bytes

IP: Time to live = 30 seconds/hops

IP: Protocol = 17 (UDP)

IP: Header checksum = 0000, should be 1191

IP: Source address = [132.163.100.1]

IP: Destination address = [132.163.255.255]

IP: No options

ICMP:

ICMP: [First 8 byte(s) of data of originating message]

ICMP:

ICMP: [Normal end of "ICMP header".]

ICMP:

Trace 8.3.4d. TCP/IP Router Confusion ICMP Details

The analyst thus had three strong clues (from ARP, RIP, and ICMP) that NewRouter was causing the problems. He disconnected NewRouter from the internetwork, and went through the reconfiguration process a second time. Several incorrect parameters were found which were re-entered. Upon re-installation, both OldRouter and NewRouter peacefully coexisted with no further difficulties.

As the previous examples have shown, the DOD protocols were designed with multivendor internetworking in mind and provide a great deal of functionality. Given the extensive documentation available, it's no wonder that they've become so popular. In the future, TCP/IP's next development in internetworking and interoperability is expected to be a migration to OSI-compliant protocols at all seven layers of the OSI Reference Model. References [8-41] through [8-44] provide insight into the challenges that network managers are likely to face during the TCP/IP-to-OSI transition.

8.4 References

[8-1] Request for Comments (RFC) documents may be obtained from: SRI International, Room EJ291, 333 Ravenswood Avenue, Menlo Park, CA 94025, 415-859-3695 NIC, @ SRI-NIC.ARPA.

[8-2] Telephone numbers for further information on internet-connected networks are:

NSFNET: (617) 873-3400

CSNET: (617) 873-2777

BITNET: (202) 872-4200

[8-3] Quarterman, John S. *The Matrix: Computer Networks and Conferencing Systems Worldwide*. Digital Press, 1990.

[8-4] DDN Network Information Center. *Defense Data Network Subscriber Interface Guide*. July 1983.

[8-5] DDN Network Information Center. *DDN New User Guide*. February 1991.

[8-6] Miller, Mark. A. *Internetworking: A Guide to Network Communications*. Redwood City, CA: M&T Books 1991.

[8-7] Christian, Robert. "Picking the Right TCP/IP Product." *LAN Technology* (January 1991): 27-35.

[8-8] Spurgeon, Charles. "Guide to Networking Resources Part II: TCP/IP." *LAN Technology* (February 1991): 77-86.

[8-9] Cohen, Dave. "How to Get NetWare and TCP/IP to Coexist." *LAN Technology* (February 1991): 57-67.

[8-10] Malamud, Carl. "TCP/IP: A Dependable Networking Infrastructure." *Network Computing* (April 1991): 84-86.

[8-11] Cohen, Dave. "Alternatives for NetWare and TCP/IP Coexistence." *LAN Technology* (June 1991): 71-80.

[8-12] Stephenson, Peter. "Constructing A Network." *Interoperability* (Fall 1991): 14-18.

[8-13] Glass, Brett. "When it Comes to Protocols, TCP/IP Is Universal." *Infoworld* (August 5, 1991): S63.

[8-14] Romke, John. "Interoperability and the Body Politic: Connecting the TCP/IP World of the Internet." *LAN Times* (August 19, 1 991): 56-57.

[8-15] Jukovsky, Martin. "Managing a Network? TCP/IP Can Help You." *Digital News* (September 2, 1991): 29-36.

[8-16] Scott, Karyl. "Parlez-vous TCP/IP?" *Infoworld* (October 7, 1991): 45-51.

[8-17] Cerf, Vinton G. and Edward Cain. "The DoD Internet Architecture Model." *Computer Networks* (October 1983): 307-318.

[8-18] DDN Network Information Center. *A Standard for the Transmission of IP Datagrams over Ethernet Networks*. RFC 894, April 1984.

[8-19] DDN Network Information Center. *A Standard for the Transmission of IP Datagrams Over IEEE 802 Networks*. RFC 1042, February 1988.

[8-20] DDN Network Information Center. *A Standard for the Transmission of IP Datagrams and ARP Packets over ARCNET Networks*. RFC 1051, March 1988.

[8-21] DDN Protocol Handbook. *A Standard for the Transmission of IP Datagrams Over Public Data Networks*. RFC 877, September 1983.

[8-22] DDN Network Information Center. *Compressing TCP/IP Headers for Low-Speed Serial Links*. RFC 1144, February 1990.

[8-23] DDN Network Information Center. *An Ethernet Address Resolution Protocol*. RFC 826, November 1982.

[8-24] DDN Network Information Center. *A Reverse Address Resolution Protocol*. RFC 903, June 1984.

[8-25] DDN Network Information Center. *Internet Protocol*. RFC 791, September 1981.

[8-26] DDN Network Information Center. *Internet Control Message Protocol*. RFC 792, September 1981.

[8-27] DDN Network Information Center. *User Datagram Protocol*. RFC 768, August 1980.

[8-28] DDN Network Information Center. *Transmission Control Protocol*. RFC 793, September 1981.

[8-29] DDN Network Information Center. *File Transfer Protocol (FTP)*. RFC 959, October 1985.

[8-30] DDN Network Information Center. *Simple Mail Transfer Protocol (SMTP)*. RFC 821, August 1982.

[8-31] DDN Network Information Center. *TELNET Protocol Specification*. RFC 854, May 1983.

[8-32] DDN Network Information Center. *Simple Network Management Protocol*. RFC 1098, April 1989.

[8-33] DDN Network Information Center. *DDN Protocol Implementations and Vendors Guide*, February 1989.

[8-34] DDN Network Information Center. *DDN Protocol Handbook* (4 volume set), December 1985 and February 1989.

[8-35] Comer, Douglas. *Internetworking with TCP/IP Principles, Protocols and Architecture*, second edition. Prentice-Hall, 1991.

[8-36] Comer, Douglas and David L. Stevens. I*nternetworking with TCP/IP Design, Implementation, and Internals*. Prentice-Hall, 1991.

[8-37] DDN Network Information Center. *Assigned Numbers*. RFC 1060, March 1990.

[8-38] Stone, Mike. "Guide to TCP/IP Network Addressing." *LAN Technology* (April 1991): 41-46.

[8-39] Cann, Lawrence. "Glitch Turns into Clue in This TCP/IP Detective Tale." *Data Communications* (June 21, 1989): 53-63.

[8-40] DDN Network Information Center. *Tools for Monitoring and Debugging TCP/IP Internets and Interconnected Devices*. RFC 1147, April 1990.

[8-41] Lynch, Daniel C. "The Transition From TCP/IP to OSI." *Journal of Information Systems Management* (Fall 1990): 48-52.

[8-42] Roynan, James P. "OSI Versus TCP/IP." *LAN Computing* (April 9, 1991): 23-24.

[8-43] Mosher, Robyn E. "A Peaceful Coexistence for TCP/IP and OSI." *Networking Management* (August 1991): 36-40.

[8-44] Harrison, Bradford T. "TCP/IP Versus OSI: The Saga Continues." *LAN Computing* (August 1991): 17-20.

CHAPTER 9

The Costs of Troubleshooting Internetworks

In 1748, Benjamin Franklin observed [9-1]:

"Remember, that time is money."

If this is good advice, then we must develop time-saving troubleshooting techniques to minimize the costs of our internetworks.

Traditionally, the total cost picture for networks and internetworks has included *first costs* and *recurring costs* or charges. First costs are associated with the initial capital investment in the hardware and software. Recurring costs come up over time after the purchase. These include: carrying or interest charges on the capital, lease costs for telecommunications facilities, labor costs, annual maintenance and administration costs (often called *life cycle management costs*), associated permits and licenses, assorted overheads, and so on. However, this method of considering costs does not allow for an easy comparison of the design tradeoffs that always occur in complex internetworks.

A better way to consider the costs of networks and internetworks is to account for the total costs of building and operating the network and the additional cost of network downtime or failure. In this way, all costs can be counted in a format that reflects the tradeoff between time and money.

9.1 The Costs of Network Ownership

A study commissioned by DEC and performed by Dr. Michael E. Treacy and the Index Group developed a model for evaluating network costs [9-2]. The model depicted five cost components and three life cycle phases in a matrix (Figure 9-1). The five cost components were equipment, software, personnel, communications, and facilities. The equipment category tracked the costs of purchasing and maintaining hardware. The software category accounted for any software purchases, one-time license fees, and maintenance contracts. Personnel costs were derived from the time spent in network planning, design, installation, and on-going support activities. The communications line item included the initial installation and monthly tariff charges on communications lines. Finally, the facilities costs added in building and space expenses.

	Acquisition Costs	Operation Costs	Incremental Change Costs
Equipment	• EQUIPMENT PURCHASE	• MAINTENANCE	
Software	• SOFTWARE PURCHASE/ ONE-TIME LICENSE	• ANNUAL LICENSE • SOFTWARE MAINTENANCE	
Personnel	• PLANNING, DESIGN AND SELECTION • EQUIPMENT AND SOFTWARE INSTALLATION	• ROUTINE MONITORING AND OPERATION • NETWORK PROBLEM CORRECTION • USER LIAISON, ADMINISTRATION	• USER CHANGES - MOVES - ADDS - DELETES • SOFTWARE VERSION CHANGES
Communications	• INITIAL HOOKUP CHARGES	• MONTHLY TARIFF CHARGES	
Facilities	• FACILITIES DEVELOPMENT • WIRING COSTS	• SPACE EXPENSE	

Figure 9-1. Cost of Network Ownership Model

(Reprinted with permission, ©1991 CSC Index and Dr. Michael Treacy)

THE COSTS OF TROUBLESHOOTING INTERNETWORKS

These costs accrued over three time periods. *Acquisitions costs* included network planning, design, and installation. *Operations* costs encompassed a five-year period of network maintenance and support. *Incremental change* costs covered the same five-year period, but related to the moves, adds, changes, and other minor reconfigurations that the network required.

Dr. Treacy and the Index Group tested this model with three types of networks: corporate networks (geographically dispersed WANs with over 1,000 users); multiple field office networks (distributed processing environments); and manufacturing site networks (LANs with host access). All networks included either DEC or IBM processing capabilities.

The study came to four significant conclusions. First, the highest costs associated with a network were not the acquisition costs, but rather the cost of operation and incremental change over the five-year period. Thus, efforts to minimize recurring charges could have a significant impact on overall network costs. Second, personnel costs accounted for a significant percentage of the five-year total and nearly equaled the average spent on communications lines. Hiring the best people and giving them the best tools can, therefore, reduce expenses in this area.

Third, the selection of a vendor impacts not only acquisition costs, but also those in the other two time periods. Vendor-related factors that can influence the network costs include the ease/difficulty of administering changes, administrator training time, the availability of a network management system, and the amount of available local or on-site support. This presents a strong argument for selecting a vendor with a good reputation over one with the least-cost bid.

Finally, a network's topology dramatically affects its costs. For the internetworks commonly found in large corporations, a distributed topology costs about half the amount per port as a centralized architecture. This would indicate that the flexibility of the distributed architecture pays economic dividends over the life of the network.

For internetwork analysts, the conclusion to this study is clear: Minimize recurring charges by working smarter, not harder.

9.2 The Cost of Telecommunications Circuits

Given the results of the previous study, we can conclude that recurring internetwork costs exceed the first costs. Perhaps the most significant recurring charge is the monthly cost of the telecommunication circuits such as dial-up circuits, analog or digital leased lines, and Packet Switched Public Data Network (PSPDN) facilities. When monthly costs are fixed, such as with a point-to-point leased line between two locations, the cost analysis is straightforward. For example, if a leased circuit costs $1,000.00 per month for unlimited usage, and the alternative is a dial-up circuit at $0.25 per minute, it's easy to see that the financial crossover point occurs at 4,000 minutes per month (about 67 hours or eight business days). Thus, you could minimize the recurring charges for this circuit by selecting a leased line when the usage exceeded 4,000 minutes per month.

When PSPDN is the transmission facility the analysis becomes more difficult. PSPDN pricing is based upon a flat access charge plus a variable charge for each character transmitted. For example, a 9.6 Kbps link might be priced at around $1,100.00 per month plus $0.02 per kilocharacter (1,000 characters) of data sent or received. Transmitting 30,000 characters (a document about the length of Chapter 1 in this book) would cost $0.60. Thus, you'd need an accurate estimate of the number of characters to be transmitted per month in order to compare the alternatives of dial-up circuits vs. leased lines vs. PSPDN access. References [9-3] and [9-4] give examples of these monthly cost calculations.

9.3 The Cost of Network Downtime

Another significant factor contributing to the recurring costs is network maintenance, which includes supplies, tools, and test equipment. And perhaps even more significant is the cost of network downtime when the network is unavailable to users.

In 1989 Network General Corporation (Menlo Park, CA) commissioned Infonetics Research Institute Inc. (San Jose, CA) to conduct a study of 100 network and internetwork managers [9-5], [9-6]. The company needed at least 40 network devices and 250 employees to participate in the study. The objective was to determine a cost associated with network disabilities. The costs were determined in three areas: lost productivity, lost revenue, and direct expenses. Lost productivity costs included the salaries of the network users and the amount of time they actually used the network. It also took into account other job functions that could be performed without the network's operation as well as the frequency and duration of the network disabilities. Lost revenue was calculated based on the amount of money that the company would lose when the network was down, the seriousness of the disability, and the time of year. The direct expenses of network maintenance included hardware and software maintenance contracts and the salaries of the network troubleshooters.

The results of the study were very revealing. Out of 100 responses, the average network was disabled 23.6 times per year (Figure 9- 2). The minimum number was 0-1 disabilities (12 responses) with a maximum of more than 100 disabilities (seven responses). The average length of disability from 99 responses was 4.9 hours (Figure 9-3). The minimum disability time was 0-0.25 hours (five responses) with a maximum of 25.01 or more hours (five responses). The largest number of respondents (31) recorded disabilities from 0.76 to 2.00 hours in length.

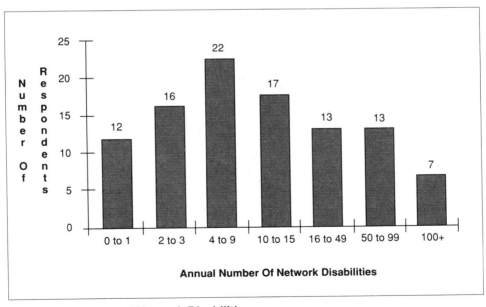

Figure 9-2. Number of Network Disabilities per year
(Reprinted with permission, Infonetics Research Institute, Inc. ©1989)

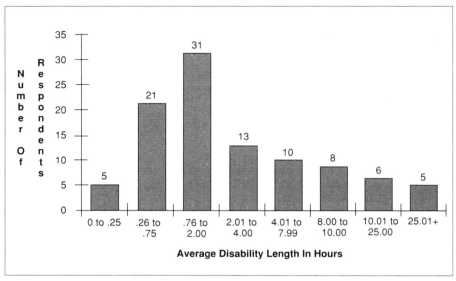

Figure 9-3. Network Disability Length
(Reprinted with permission, Infonetics Research Institute, Inc. ©1989)

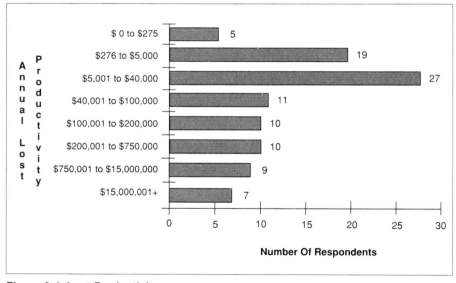

Figure 9-4. Lost Productivity per year
(Reprinted with permission, Infonetics Research Institute, Inc. ©1989)

The study found the costs associated with these disabilities to be as follows. A survey of 98 respondents revealed Lost Productivity averaging $3.48 million per year (Figure 9-4). The minimum lost productivity cost ($0-275) and maximum lost productivity expense ($15,000,001+) seemed extreme, although there were a reasonable number of responses in those categories (five and seven, respectively). Lost Revenue from 99 respondents averaged $606,000 per year (Figure 9-5). The results here were surprising: 14 claimed no lost productivity, while four lost more than $1,000,001. Finally, the Direct Expenses for network support (Figure 9-6) averaged $60,000 annually from a survey of 98 respondents. The median value was considerably less, however, as 78 of the respondents spent $15,000 or less, while 20 spent $15,001 or more. At any rate, this investment was considerably less than the average annual lost productivity ($3.48 million).

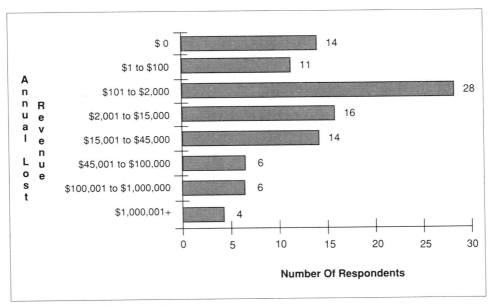

Figure 9-5. Lost Revenue Expenses per year
(Reprinted with permission, Infonetics Research Institute, Inc. ©1989)

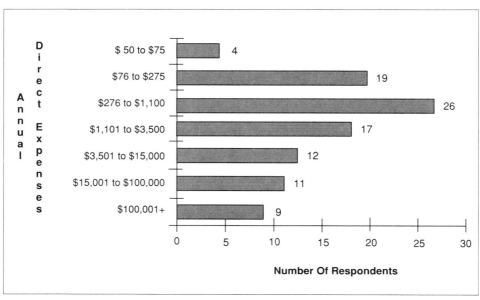

Figure 9-6. Direct Expense Costs per year
(Reprinted with permission, Infonetics Research Institute, Inc. ©1989)

As these figures show, companies are investing very little on prevention despite the potential for enormous losses due to network downtime. Those of us who spend time in the internetwork trenches understand this. But how do we make an effective business case to support the purchase of that new "ultimate analyzer" or the hire of another network engineer? Let's apply these results to a hypothetical network and study the outcome.

For our example, we'll assume that the network is owned by a law firm which uses the network the number of hours indicated below and consists of the following personnel. (The labor costs include benefits, vacation, employment taxes and so on).

	Quantity	Labor Rate/Hour	Network Usage/Day
Attorneys:	100	$200.00	2 hours
Paralegals:	20	100.00	4 hours
Secretaries:	50	20.00	6 hours

THE COSTS OF TROUBLESHOOTING INTERNETWORKS

Let's assume that this network is typical of those in the Infonetics study and fails 23.6 times per year for 4.9 hours at a time. Given this information, we can derive a cost associated with each failure:

	Quantity	Labor Rate/Hour	Downtime	Maximum Productivity Loss
Attorneys	100	$200.00	2 hours	$40,000
Paralegals	20	100.00	4 hours	8,000
Secretaries	50	20.00	4.9 hours	4,900
Total				$52,900

The maximum productivity loss of $52,900 assumes that the office totally shuts down when the network becomes disabled. Since attorneys can find other things to do during downtime, we'll assume that a network failure decreases productivity by 50 percent, meaning the total productivity loss is $26,450 per disability or half the original loss. If we assume 23.6 such disabilities per year, the resulting annual productivity loss would equal $624,220 ($26,450 x 23.6). If you're skeptical, you can make a different assumption regarding productivity decreases, which may yield a lower annual productivity loss.

Now let's assume that the purchase of your "ultimate analyzer" will help you solve these disabilities in half the time it would have taken you before. If you wish to adjust this assumption based upon your internetwork's failure history, revise the calculations accordingly. If you assumed an annual productivity loss of $624,220, you've just saved the company $312,110 (half of the $624,220) in the first year. Keep in mind that this calculation has only considered the productivity loss; a complete analysis would include lost revenues and direct expenses as well. Adding these two costs would increase the true cost of downtime. Subtract the amount that you spent on your "ultimate analyzer" (perhaps $25-50,000), and ask for the rest as a bonus.

In summary, we can draw two significant conclusions from these studies. The initial cost of installing a network is the least of the expenses; recurring costs over a five-year period are far more significant. Second, the cost of downtime can be substantial. However, convincing upper management to supply the right tools and personnel to address these two expenses adequately can be difficult. Fortunately, companies are starting to become more aware of the need for network service and the user satisfaction aspects of keeping the internetwork up and running (see References [9-7] and [9-8]).

One way to minimize both recurring costs and downtime costs is by reducing the downtime [9-9]. Let's see how to do this.

9.4 Saving Internetwork Expenses

So far, we've taken a somewhat pessimistic approach—assuming that everything we do to the internetwork will "cost" something. In today's uncertain economic times, with employee layoffs and tenuous financial projections, it may be difficult to justify the cost of a new analyzer or additional internetwork support personnel. Minimizing internetwork expenses may be the best course of action to take until it's possible to expand support systems, such as test equipment, or install an integrated network management system [9-10]. So let's consider a plan to save internetwork expenses and internetwork downtime.

We'll base this discussion on the factors outlined in Chapter 1 that increase the complexity of internetworks: advances in workstations, protocol interoperability, LAN/WAN connectivity, and network management systems. Let's re-examine these four key areas from the perspective of cost savings.

9.4.1 Saving Workstation Expenses

Three parameters measure the reliability of internetwork components: Mean Time Between Failure (MTBF), Mean Time to Repair (MTTR), and Availability. The MTBF is the average (mean) time between the failure of a component and another failure of that same component. MTBF is measured in hours, where 8,760 hours equals one year. MTTR is the average (mean) time required to identify a failure then repair or replace that component with a good one. A typical MTTR would be eight hours or less (one day). (Do not confuse MTTR with a service vendor's measure of "response time," since the "response" may or may not repair the failed component.) Availability is expressed as a ratio of MTBF and MTTR:

Availability $=$ $$\frac{\text{MTBF}}{(\text{MTBF} + \text{MTTR})}$$

Both MTBF and MTTR must be measured in the same unit, such as hours. For example, the motherboard of a workstation has the following reliability metrics:

MTBF = 105,000 hours
MTTR = 26 hours (overnight shipping of replacement)

Availability $=$ $$\frac{105,000}{(105,000 + 26)} = 99.97\%$$

To improve availability, you can either increase MTBF or decrease MTTR. The only way to increase MTBF may be to purchase a more reliable (and more expensive) workstation. You can, however, decrease MTTR by having a spare motherboard on hand, thus eliminating the overnight shipping time and expense. Let's recalculate availability with this new assumption:

MTBF = 105,000 hours
MTTR = 2 hours (diagnose and replace only)

Availability $=$ $$\frac{105,000}{(105,000 + 2)} = 99.99\%$$

If the workstation is considered a "mission critical" internetwork component, then stocking a replacement can pay for itself. If we assume that stocking the spare part reduced the downtime from 26 hours with overnight shipping to two hours to diagnose the problem and replace the component, we've actually saved 24 hours of downtime. But realistically, let's say that we've saved one business day (eight hours). Multiply your average cost of downtime per hour by eight hours and you'll have the savings realized by having the spare motherboard. For an accurate savings estimate, however, make sure that the spare parts really are "mission critical" and not components that can be easily patched around or temporarily replaced with another device.

9.4.2 Saving Protocol Interoperability Expenses

We've all heard travel stories that ended, "You can't get there from here." Unfortunately, internetworking stories can end on a similar note if the underlying protocols are incompatible. For example, your DECnet network doesn't have the necessary gateway to communicate with the SNA host; or workstations on two token rings cannot communicate because one ring supports the source routing algorithm and the other doesn't. When you identify interoperability problems such as these, the solution may mean additional expense: You may have to purchase a gateway, upgrade a bridge, install a different network operating system, and so forth.

To save these expenses, develop an interoperability matrix similar to the one created by the Clark Burton Corporation [1-15]. Select a transport protocol, such as TCP/IP, as your standard. Then, when selecting other internetwork components, verify that they're compatible with your transport protocol of choice. For example, it would be relatively straightforward to integrate both Banyan VINES and Novell NetWare into a TCP/IP environment since both network operating systems support those protocols. Implementing AppleTalk, however, would require additional components since the TCP/IP protocols are not native to the AppleTalk architecture (review Figure 3-1). As we've studied, extra components impact both first and recurring expenses. You'll minimize these costs if you define an interoperability plan for your internetwork before installation.

9.4.3 Saving LAN/WAN Connectivity Expenses

Update your internetwork documentation drawings and compare them with the documentation from six to 12 months ago. Is your internetwork growing in an orderly (planned) or random (unplanned) fashion? If it's growing randomly, you're probably spending a lot of time and effort fighting fires. For example, if different departments of a university each attached a different sub-network architecture to a backbone, the system would be far more costly and difficult to support than if they had adopted a consistent architecture. So implement a standard network architecture for sub-networks, such as token ring running IBM OS/2 LAN Server or Ethernet running Novell NetWare. Now you'll have fewer operating systems to learn, fewer protocol interpreters to purchase for your analyzer, and so on. The end result will be lower expenses.

9.4.4 Saving with Network Management Systems

Many minicomputer, PABX, and mainframe vendors have developed systems to help manage complex internetworks. (Isn't it interesting that the vendors who designed these complex systems and components are now selling additional systems to manage them?) These management systems offer the advantage of integrating all the information from a number of disparate systems (LAN and WAN) into a single output. For example, if the bandwidth utilization of a voice-only T1 link between two offices is low, consider voice/data integration. Purchasing a LAN interface to the T1 multiplexers might make more sense than installing a separate transmission line for LAN-to-LAN communication. In another case, the management system might record LAN statistics such as collisions or framing errors over a period of time. Such historical trends can offer an early warning of impending network disasters. Whenever the network management system averts a disability, it saves expenses.

A related issue is whether the savings justify the expense of new test equipment. LAN/WAN analyzers can cost upwards of $50,000. But while this may seem costly, consider the alternative of foregoing the tools. Estimate the amount of network downtime the appropriate equipment will save. If your internetwork is typical, the payback period for a complete set of tools will be less than one year. After that, these tools are saving, not costing, money.

Working smarter, not just harder, in the internetwork decade of the 1990s can be a challenge. Let's recap our solution:

1. Appreciate the complexity of the internetwork you are managing. Technology is advancing rapidly, and your skills must advance as well.

2. Obtain the best tools for the job. Select the "ultimate analyzer" to provide the management information your internetwork requires.

3. Understand the protocols of your internetwork. Use the analyzer as a window, peering into the operation of the workstations and hosts. Know the steps involved in establishing internetwork connections. It's very difficult to troubleshoot a system that you don't understand.

4. Consider all the costs associated with your internetwork. Don't buy the low bid today if it will cost you dearly in the future.

Finally, remember that many share your challenges. Frustrating problems can make for a rewarding education. The internetworks of the 1990s are indeed exciting systems to manage.

9.5 References

[9-1] Franklin, Benjamin. "Advice to Young Tradesman," *Writings*, volume ii, 1748.

[9-2] Treacy, Michael E. "The Costs of Network Ownership." Index Group, Inc., Cambridge, MA, 1989.

[9-3] Bossom, John Jr. "Techniques to Control Packet Network Usage and Cost." *Journal of Network Management* (Spring 1989): 30-38.

[9-4] Bolles, Gary A. "Downshifting: Issues & Trends: Choosing the Right Bandwidth for your Wide Area Links." *Network Computing* (September 1991): 56-59.

[9-5] Infonetics Research Institute, Inc. "The Cost of LAN Downtime." San Jose, CA, September 1989.

[9-6] Saal, Harry. "LAN Downtime: Clear and Present Danger." *Data Communications* (March 21, 1990): 67-72.

[9-7] Damian, Jacqueline. "Does Your Company Pass or Fail Service?" *Electronics* (May 1991): 48-56.

[9-8] Kirvan, Paul. "How to Conduct a Full Audit of Your Network." *Communications News* (May 1991): 42-43.

[9-9] Byrd, Mark A. "How to Minimize Downtime." *LAN Technology* (May 1991): 67-76.

[9-10] Gantz, John. "White Paper to Management: A Practical Guide to Cutting Network Costs." *Networking Management* (May 1991): 33-34.

APPENDIX A

Addresses of Standards Organizations

AT&T Publications

AT&T Technologies

Commercial Sales

P.O. Box 19901

Indianapolis, IN 46219

Telephone (317) 352-8557 or (800) 432-6600

Bellcore Standards

Bell Communications Research

Information Management Services

60 New England Ave., DSC 1B-252

Piscataway, NJ 08854-4196

Telephone (201) 699-5800 or (800) 521-2673

CCITT Recommendations and Federal Information Processing Standards (FIPS)

U.S. Department of Commerce

National Technical Information Service

5285 Port Royal Road

Springfield, VA 22161

Telephone (703) 487-4650

CSA Standards

Canadian Standards Association
178 Rexdale Boulevard
Rexdale, ONT M9W 1R9
Canada
Telephone (416) 747-4363

ECMA Standards

European Computer Manufacturers Association
114, Rue de rhone CH-1204
Geneva, Switzerland
Telephone 41 22 35-36-34

ECSA Standards

Exchange Carriers Standards Association
5430 Grosvenor Lane
Bethesda, MD 20814-2122
Telephone (301) 564-4505

EIA Standards

Electronic Industries Association
Standards Sales
2001 Eye Street, NW
Washington, DC 20006
Telephone (202) 457-4966

Federal Standards Sales:

General Service Administration

GSA Specification Unit (WFSIS) Room 6039

7th & D Streets SW

Washington, DC 20407

Telephone (202) 472-2205

FIPS Publication Sales:

National Technical Information Service

5285 Port Royal Road

Springfield, VA 22161

Telephone (703) 487-4650

IEEE Standards

Institute of Electrical and Electronics Engineers

445 Hoes Lane

Piscataway, NJ 08855

Telephone (908) 981-1393 or (800) 678-IEEE

ISO and ANSI Standards

American National Standards Institute

1430 Broadway

New York, NY 10018

Telephone (212) 354-3300

Sales Department (212) 642-4900

ISO Standards

International Organization for Standardization

1, Rue de Varembe Case Postale 56

CH-1211

Geneva 20, Switzerland

Telephone 41 22 34 12 40

Military Standards Sales:
Naval Publications and Forms Center
Commanding Officer
NPFC 43
5801 Tabor Avenue
Philadelphia, PA 19120
Telephone (215) 697-3321

National Communications Systems
Federal Telecommunications Standards
8th Street & South Courthouse Road
Arlington, VA 22204

**National Institute of Standards
and Technology**
Standards Processing Coordinator
Technology Building
Gaithersburg, MD 20899
Telephone (301) 975-2816

Selected Manufacturers of Internetworking Products

Accton Technology Corp.
46750 Fremont Blvd. #104
Freemont, CA 94538
(510) 226-9800
(800) 926-9288
Fax: (510) 226-9833

ADC Kentrox
P.O. Box 10704
Portland, OR 97210
(503) 643-1681
(800) 733-5511
Fax: (503) 641-3341

**Advanced Computer
Communications (ACC)**
720 Santa Barbara Street
Santa Barbara, CA 93101
(805) 963-9431
(800) 444-7854
Fax: (805) 962-8499

Advanced Logic Research
9401 Jeronimo
Irvine, CA 92718
(714) 581-6770
(800) 444-4257
Fax: (714) 581-9240

Advanced Systems Concepts Inc.
33-41 Newark St.
Hoboken, NJ 07030
(201) 798-6400
(800) 229-2724
Fax: (201) 798-9203

Alantec
47800 Westinghouse Drive
Freemont, CA 94539
(510) 770-1050
(800) 727-1050
Fax: (510) 770-1054

Alisa Systems, Inc.
221 E. Walnut, Suite 175
Pasadena, CA 91101
(818) 792-9474
(800) 992-5472
Fax: (818) 792-4068

Allen-Bradley
555 Briarwood Circle
Ann Arbor, MI 48108
(313) 998-2000
(800) 280-4362
Fax: (313) 668-2922

Alloy Computer Products
2082 Michelson Drive #212
Irvine, CA 92715
(714) 955-0633
Fax: (714) 955-0745

Alloy Computer Products, Inc.
1 Brigham Street
Marlboro, MA 01752
(508) 481-5115
(800) 800-2556
Fax: (508) 481-7711

American Power Conversion
132 Fairgrounds Road
West Kingston, RI 02892
(401) 789-5735
(800) 541-8896
Fax: (401) 789-3710

Andrew Corporation
2771 Plaza Del Amo
Torrance, CA 90503
(213) 320-7126
(800) 733-0331
Fax: (213) 618-0386

Andrew Corporation
6034 W. Courtyard Drive
Austin, TX 78730
(512) 338-3000
(800) 331-4144
Fax: (512) 338-3193

Apple Computer, Inc.
20525 Mariani Avenue
Cupertino, CA 95014
(408) 996-1010
(800) 776-2333
Fax: (408) 974-6726

Applitek Corporation
100 Brickstone Square
Andover, MA 01810
(508) 475-4050
(800) 526-2489
Fax: (508) 475-0550

Asante Technologies
404 Tasman Drive
Sunnyvale, CA 94089
(408) 752-8388
(800) 662-9686
Fax: (408) 734-4864

AST Research, Inc.
16215 Alton Parkway
P.O. Box 19658
Irvine, CA 92713-9658
(714) 727-4141
(800) 876-4278
Fax: (714) 727-9355

AT&T Computer Systems
Gatehall Drive
Parsippany, NJ 07054
(201) 397-4800
Fax: (201-397-4918

Atlantix
4800 N. Federal Highway #301B
Boca Raton, FL 33431
(407) 362-9700
Fax: (407) 362-9772

Attachmate Corp.
13231 S.E. 36th St.
Bellevue, WA 98006
(206) 644-4010
(800) 426-6283
Fax: (206) 747-9924

Avatar
65 South St.
Hopkinton, MA 01748
(508) 435-3000
(800) 282-3270
Fax: (508) 435-2470

Aydin Corporation
700 Dresher Rd.
P.O. Box 349
Horsham, PA 10944
(215) 657-7510
Fax: (215) 657-5470

Banyan Systems, Inc.
115 Flanders Road #5
Westboro, MA 01581
(508) 898-1000
(800) 828-2404
Fax: (508) 836-1810

BBN Communications Corp.
70 Fawcett Street
Cambridge, MA 02138
(617) 873-2000
Fax: (617) 491-0921

Belden Wire and Cable/Cooper
Industries
P.O. Box 1980
Richmond, IN 47375
(317) 983-5200
(800) 235-3361
Fax: (317) 983-5656

Best Power Technology
P.O. Box 280
Necedah, WI 54646
(608) 565-7200
(800) 356-5794
Fax: (608) 565-2221

BICC Communications
103 Millbury St.
Auburn, MA 01501
(508) 832-8650
Fax: (508) 832-8689

Black Box Corporation
1000 Park Drive
P.O. Box 12800
Pittsburgh, PA 15241
(412) 746-5500
Fax: (412) 746-0746

Brightwork Development, Inc.
766 Shrewsbury Avenue
Jerral Center W.
Tinton Falls, NJ 07724
(908) 530-0440
(800) 552-9876
Fax: (908) 530-0622

Bytex
120 Turnpike Rd.
Southborough, MA 01772
(508) 480-0840
(800) 227-1145
Fax: (508) 481-5111

Cabletron Systems, Inc.
P.O. Box 5005
Rochester, NH 03867-0505
(603) 332-9400
(800) 526-8378
Fax: (603) 332-4616

Caci Products
3344 N. Torey Pines Ct.
La Jolla, CA 92037
(619) 457-9681
Fax: (619) 457-1184

Calan
1776 Independence Dr.
Dingmans Ferry, PA 18328
(717) 828-2356
(800) 544-3392
Fax: (717) 828-2472

California Microwave
985 Almanor Ave.
Sunnyvale, CA 94086
(408) 732-4000
(800) 772-5465
Fax: (408) 732-4244

Canoga-Perkins
21012 Lassen St.
Chatsworth, CA 91311
(818) 718-6300
Fax: (818) 718-6312

Cayman Systems, Inc.
26 Landsdowne St.
Cambridge, MA 02139
(617) 494-1999
(800) 473-4776
Fax: (617) 494-9270

CBIS, Inc.
5875 Peachtree Industrial Blvd.
Bldg 100/170
Norcross, GA 30092
(404) 446-1332
Fax: (404) 446-9164

Cheyenne Software, Inc.
55 Bryant Avenue
Roslyn, NY 11576
(516) 484-5110
Fax: (516) 484-3446

Chipcom Corporation
118 Turnpike Rd.
Southborough, MA 01772
(508) 460-8900
(800) 228-9930
Fax: (508) 460-8950

cisco Systems Inc.
1525 O'Brien Drive
Menlo Park, CA 94025
(415) 326-1941
(800) 553-6387
Fax: (415) 326-1989

Cleo Communications
3796 Plaza Dr.
Ann Arbor, MI 48108
(313) 662-2002
(800) 233-2536
Fax: (313) 662-1965

CMC/Rockwell International
125 Cremona Dr.
Santa Barbara, CA 93117
(805) 968-4262
(800) 262-8023
Fax: (805) 968-6478

Codenoll Technology
1086 N. Broadway
Yonkers, NY 10701
(914) 965-6300
Fax: (914) 965-9811

Codex/Motorola
20 Cabot Blvd.
Mansfield, MA 02048
(508) 261-4000
Fax: (508) 261-7105

Comdisco Systems, Inc.
919 E. Hillsdale Blvd. #300
Foster City, CA 94404
(415) 574-5800
Fax: (415) 358-3601

Comm/Scope-Network
Cable Division
3642 Hwy. 70 E.
Claremont, NC 28610
(704) 459-5000
(800) 982-1708
Fax: (704) 459-5099

Communication Machinery Corp.
125 Cremona Drive
Santa Barbara, CA 93117
(805) 968-4262
Fax: (805) 968-6478

Communications Research Group
5615 Corporate Boulevard
Baton Rouge, LA 70808
(504) 923-0888
(800) 242-5278
Fax: (504) 926-2155

Compatible Systems Corporation
4730 Walnut St. #102
Boulder, CO 80301
(303) 444-9532
(800) 356-0283
Fax: (303) 444-9595

COMPAQ Computer Corporation
P.O. Box 692000
Houston, TX 77269
(713) 370-0670
(800) 345-1518
Fax: (713) 374-1740

Computer Network Technology
6500 Wedgwood Rd.
Maple Grove, MN 55369
(612) 550-8000
Fax: (612) 550-8800

Concord Communications Inc.
753 Forest St.
Marlborough, MA 01752
(508) 460-4646
Fax: (508) 481-9772

Corvus Systems
160 Great Oaks Blvd.
San Jose, CA 95119-1347
(408) 281-4100
Fax: (408) 578-4102

CrossComm Corporation
140 Locke Drive #C
Marlboro, MA 01752
(508) 481-4060
(800) 388-1200
Fax: (508) 481-4216

Cross Information Company
1881 Ninth St., Suite 302
Boulder, CO 80302
(303) 444-7799
Fax: (303) 444-4687

Cryptall Communications Corp.
2 Thurber Blvd.
Smithfield, RI 02917
(401) 232-7600
Fax: (617) 255-5885

Crystal Point, Inc.
22122 20th Ave. S.E. #148
Bothell, WA 98021
(206) 487-3656
Fax: (206) 487-3773

CXR/Digilog
900 Business Center Dr. #200
Horsham, PA 19044-3453
(215) 956-9570
(800) 344-4564
Fax: (215) 956-0108

Cylix
2637 Towngate Rd. #200
Westlake Village, CA 91361
(805) 379-3155
Fax: (805) 379-4551

Data General Corporation
4400 Computer Drive
Westboro, MA 01580
(508) 366-8911
(800) 328-2436
Fax: (508) 366-1744

Data Interface Systems, Corp.
8701 N. MoPac Expressway #415
Austin, TX 78759
(512) 346-5641
(800) 351-4244
Fax: (512) 346-4035

Datapoint Corporation
8400 Datapoint Drive
San Antonio, TX 78229-8500
(512) 593-7900
(800) 733-1500
Fax: (512) 593-7472

Data Set Cable
748 Danbury Rd.
Ridgefield, CT 06877
(203) 438-9684
(800) 344-9684
Fax: (203) 431-4657

David Systems Inc.
701 East Evelyn Avenue
Sunnyvale, CA 94088-3718
(408) 720-8000
(800) 762-7848
Fax: (408) 720-1337

Dayna Communications Inc.
50 South Main - 5th Fl.
Salt Lake City, UT 84144
(801) 531-0203
Fax: (801) 535-4204

Daystar Digital, Inc.
5556 Atlanta Hwy.
Flowery Branch, GA 30542
(404) 967-2077
(800) 962-2077
Fax: (404) 967-3018

DCA
1000 Alderman Drive
Alpharetta, GA 30202
(404) 442-4000
(800) 348-3221
Fax: (404) 442-4366

DCA 10Net Communications
7887 Washington Village Drive
Suite 200
Dayton, OH 45459
(513) 433-2238
(800) 782-1010
Fax: (513) 434-6305

Demax Software Inc.
999 Baker Way, Ste. 500
San Mateo, CA 94404
(415) 341-9017
(800) 283-3629
Fax: (415) 341-5809

Digital Communications Associates (DCA)
1000 Alderman Dr.
Alpharetta, GA 30201
(404) 442-4000
(800) 348-3221
Fax: (404) 442-4366

Digital Equipment Corporation (DEC)
146 Main St.
Maynard, MA 01754
(508) 467-5111
(800) 343-4040
Fax: (508) 493-8787

Digital Link
252 Humboldt Ct.
Sunnyvale, CA 94089
(408) 745-6200
(800) 441-1142
Fax: (408) 745-6250

Digital Research
70 Garden Ct.
Monterey, CA 93940
(408) 649-3896
(800) 274-4374
Fax: (408) 646-6248

Digital Technology
2300 Edwin C. Moses Blvd.
Dayton, OH 45408
(513) 443-0412
(800) 852-1252
Fax: (513) 226-0511

Digitech Industries
66 Grove St.
Ridgefield, CT 06877
(203) 438-3731
Fax: (203) 438-4184

D-Link Systems
5 Musick
Irvine, CA 92718
(714) 455-1688
Fax: (714) 455-2521

447

DMA
1776 E. Jericho Tpke.
Huntington, NY 11743
(516) 462-0440
Fax: (516) 462-6652

Dowty Communications Inc.
9020 Junction Dr.
Annapolis, MD 20701
(301) 317-7710
(800) 359-7710
Fax: (301) 317-7220

Dove Computer
1200 N. 23rd St.
Wilmington, NC 28405
(919) 763-7918
Fax: (919) 251-9441

Du Pont Electro-Optic Products
P.O. Box 13625
Research Triangle Park, NC 27709
(919) 481-5100
(800) 888-5261
Fax: (919) 481-0753

Eicon Technology Corporation
2196 32nd Ave.
Montreal, QUE Canada H8T 3H7
(514) 631-2592
Fax: (514) 631-3092

Emerald Systems
12230 World Trade Drive
San Diego, CA 92128
(619) 673-2161
(800) 767-7267
Fax: (619) 673-2288

Emerging Technologies Inc.
900 Walt Whitman Rd.
Melville, NY 11747
(516) 271-4525

Emerson Computer Power
5041 Bake Pkwy., Suite L
Irvine, CA 92718
(714) 380-1005
(800) 222-5877
Fax: (714) 380-0456

Everex Systems Inc.
48431 Milmont Dr.
Fremont, CA 94538
(510) 498-1111
(800) 821-0806
Fax: (510) 683-4520

Farallon Computing Inc.
2000 Powell St., #600
Emeryville, CA 94608
(415) 596-9100
Fax: (415) 596-9020

FEL Computing
10 Main Street
P.O. Box 72
Williamsville, VT 05362
(802) 348-7171
(800) 639-4110
Fax: (802) 348-7124

FiberCom Inc.
3353 Orange Ave. N.E.
Roanoke, VA 24012
(703) 342-6700
(800) 423-1183
Fax: (703) 342-5961

Fibermux Corporation
9310 Topanga Canyon Blvd.
Chatsworth, CA 91311
(818) 709-6000
(800) 800-4624
Fax: (818) 709-1556

Fibronics International Inc.
1 Communications Way
Independence Park
Hyannis, MA 02601
(508) 778-0700
(800) 327-9526
Fax: (508) 778-0821

Forest Computers Inc.
1749 Hamilton Road
Okemos, MI 48864
(517) 349-4700
Fax: (517) 349-2947

Frontier Technologies Inc.
10201 N. Port Washington Rd. 13
West Mequon, WI 53092
(414) 241-4555
Fax: (414) 241-7084

FTP Software, Inc.
338 Main St.
Wakefield, MA 01880
(617) 246-0900
Fax: (617) 246-0901

Gandalf Data Inc.
1020 S. Noel
Wheeling, IL 60090
(708) 541-6060
(800) 426-3253
Fax: (708) 541-6803

Gateway Communications, Inc.
2941 Alton Avenue
Irvine, CA 92714
(714) 553-1555
(800) 367-6555
Fax: (714) 553-1616

449

General DataCom, Inc.
1579 Straits Turnpike
Middlebury, CT 06762-1299
(203) 574-1118
Fax: (203) 758-8507

Gigatrend
2234 Rutherford Road
Carlsbad, CA 92008
(619) 931-9122
Fax: (619) 931-9959

Gupta Technologies
1040 Marsh Rd.
Menlo Park, CA 94025
(415) 321-9500
(800) 876-3267
Fax: (415) 321-5471

Halley Systems, Inc.
1590 Oakland Rd.
San Jose, CA 95131
(408) 441-2190
Fax: (408) 441-2199

Hayes Microcomputer Products, Inc.
P.O. Box 105203
Atlanta, GA 30348
(404) 840-9200
Fax: (404) 447-0178

Hewlett-Packard Company
3000 Hanover St.
Palo Alto, CA 94304
(415) 857-1501

Hewlett-Packard
Colorado Telecommunications
Division
5070 Centennial Blvd.
Colorado Springs, CO 80919
(719) 531-4000
Fax: (719) 531-4505

Hughes LAN Systems Inc.
1225 Charleston Road
Mountain View, CA 94043
(415) 966-7300
(800) 321-7251
Fax: (415) 960-3738

IBM
Old Orchard Road
Armouk, NY 10504
(914) 765-1900
(800) 426-2468
Fax: (800) 232-9426

IDEAssociates Inc.
29 Dunham Road
Billerica, MA 01821
(508) 663-6878
Fax: (508) 663-8851

IMC Networks
16931 Milliken Avenue
Irvine, CA 92714
(714) 724-1070
(800) 624-1070
Fax: (714) 720-1020

Information Builders Inc.
1250 Broadway
New York, NY 10001
(212) 736-4433
(800) 969-4636
Fax: (212) 695-3247

Infotron Systems Corp.
9 North Olney Avenue
Cherry Hill Industrial Center
Cherry Hill, NJ 08003
(609) 424-9400
(800) 937-1010
Fax: (609) 751-4370

IN-NET Corporation
15150 Ave. of Science #100
San Diego, CA 92128
(619) 487-3693
(800) 283-3334
Fax: (619) 487-3697

InterComputer Communication Corp.
8230 Montgomery Rd.
Cincinnati, OH 45236
(513) 745-0500
Fax: (513) 745-0327

Intercon Systems Corporation
950 Herndon Pkwy., Ste. 420
Herndon, VA 22070
(703) 709-9890
Fax: (703) 709-9896

InterConnections Incorporated
14711 N.E. 29th Place
Bellevue, WA 98007
(206) 881-5773
(800) 950-5774
Fax: (206) 867-5022

Interlan Inc.
155 Swanson Rd.
Boxborough, MA 01719
(508) 263-9929
(800) 835-5526 or
(800) 526-8255
Fax: (508) 263-8655

Interlink Computer Sciences, Inc.
47370 Freemont Blvd.
Freemont, CA 94538
(510) 657-9800
(800) 422-3711
Fax: (510) 659-6381

International Data Sciences
7 Wellington Rd.
Lincoln, RI 02865
(401) 333-6200
(800) 437-3282
Fax: (401) 333-3584

Internetix, Inc.
8903 Presidential Parkway #210
Upper Marlboro, MD 20772
(301) 420-7900
(800) 562-7292
Fax: (301) 420-4395

Interphase
13800 Senlac
Dallas, TX 75234
(214) 919-9000
Fax: (214) 919-9200

IQ Technologies, Inc.
22032 23rd Dr. S.E.
Bothell, WA 98021
(206) 483-3555
(800) 752-6526
Fax: (206) 485-8949

Irwin Magnetics
2101 Commonwealth Blvd.
Ann Arbor, MI 48105
(313) 930-9000
(800) 421-1879
Fax: (313) 995-8287

J & L Information Systems
9238 Deering Avenue
Chatsworth, CA 91311
(818) 709-1778
Fax: (818) 882-1424

Jensen Tools
7815 S. 46th St.
Phoenix, AZ 85044
(602) 968-6231
(800)366-9662
Fax: (602) 438-1690

Jointer Software Inc.
P.O. Box 5630
Madison, WI 53705-0630
(608) 238-8637
Fax: (608) 238-8986

Kodiak Technology
1338 Ridder Pk. Dr.
San Jose, CA 95131
(408) 436-5850
(800) 777-7704
Fax: (408) 441-1273

Lancer Research
140 Atlantic
Pomona, CA 91768
(714) 396-8100
Fax: (714) 396-8111

Lanex Corp.
7120 Columbia Gateway Dr.
Columbia, MD 21046
(301) 312-3000
(800) 638-5969
Fax: (301) 312-2251

Lanmaster
1401 North 14th St.
P.O. Box 845
Temple, TX 76503
(817) 771-2124
Fax: (817) 771-2379

Lannet Data Communications Inc.
7711 Center Ave. #600
Huntington Beach, CA 92647
(714) 891-1964
(800) 428-4723
Fax: (714) 891-7788

Lantana Technology
4393 Viewridge Ave., Ste. A
San Diego, CA 92123
(619) 565-6400
Fax: (619) 565-0798

Larse Corporation
4600 Patrick Henry Drive
P.O. Box 58138
Santa Clara, CA 95052
(408) 988-6600
Fax: (408) 986-8690

Legacy Storage Systems
200 Butterfield Drive
Unit B
Ashland, MA 01721
(508) 881-6442
Fax: (508) 881-4116

Legent Corporation
711 Powell Ave. SW
Renton, WA 98055-1291
(206) 228-8980
Fax: (206) 235-7560

Luxcom Inc.
3249 Laurelview Ct.
Fremont, CA 94538
(510) 770-3300
Fax: (510) 770-3399

Madge Networks, Inc.
42 Airport Pkwy.
San Jose, CA 95110
(408) 441-1300
(800) 876-2343
Fax: (408) 441-1335

Maynard Electronics Inc.
36 Skyline Drive
Lake Mary, FL 32746
(407) 263-3500
(800) 821-8782
Fax: (407) 263-3668

McData Corporation
310 Interlocken Pkwy.
Broomfield, CO 80021
(303) 460-9200
(800) 752-0388
Fax: (303) 465-4996

Micom Systems, Inc.
4100 Los Angeles Ave.
Simi Valley, CA 93062
(805) 583-8600
(800) 642-6687
Fax: (805) 583-1997

Mirimar Systems, Inc.
201 N. Salsipuedes, Suite 204
Santa Barbara, CA 93103
(805) 966-2432
Fax: (805) 965-1824

Microcom, Inc.
500 River Ridge Drive
Norwood, MA 02062-5028
(617) 551-1000
(800) 822-8224
Fax: (617) 551-1006

Micro Decisionware
2995 Wilderness Pl.
Boulder, CO 80301
(303) 443-2706
(800) 423-8737
Fax: (303) 443-2797

Micro Integration
215 Paca Street
Cumberland, MD 21502
(301) 777-3307
(800) 832-4526
Fax: (301) 777-3462

Microsoft Corporation
One Microsoft Way
Redmond, WA 98052-6399
(206) 882-8080
(800) 227-4679
Fax: (206) 883-8101

Micro Technology
5065 E. Hunter Ave.
Anaheim, CA 92807
(714) 970-0300
(800) 999-9684
Fax: (714) 970-5413

Micro Tempus Corporation
800 South St. #295
Waltham, MA 02154
(617) 899-4046
Fax: (617) 899-2604

Microtest, Inc.
3519 E. Shea Boulevard, Suite 134
Phoenix, AZ 85028
(602) 971-6464
(800) 526-9675
Fax: (602) 971-6963

Miramar Systems
201 N. Salsipuedes St. #204
Santa Barbara, CA 93103
(805) 966-2432
Fax: (617) 965-1824

Mod-Tap
285 Ayer Rd.
P.O. Box 706
Harvard, MA 01451
(508) 772-5630
Fax: (508) 772-2011

Mohawk Wire and Cable
9 Mohawk Dr.
Leominster, MA 01453
(508) 537-9961
(800) 422-9961
Fax: (508) 537-4358

Motorola
3215 Wilke Rd.
Arlington Heights, IL 60004
(708) 632-4723
(800) 233-0877
Fax: (708) 632-7811

Motorola Codex
20 Cabot Blvd.
Mansfield, MA 02048
(508) 261-4000
(800) 544-0062
Fax: (508) 261-7118

Mountain Network Solutions Inc.
240 E. Hacienda Ave.
Campbell, CA 95008
(408) 379-4300
(800) 458-0300
Fax: (408) 379-4302

Multi-Tech Systems
2205 Woodale Dr.
Mounds View, MN 55112
(612) 785-3500
(800) 328-9717
Fax: (612) 785-9874

Mux Lab
165 Graveline Rd.
St. Laurent, Quebec H4T 1R3
CANADA
(514) 735-2741
(800) 361-1965
Fax: (514) 735-8057

National Semiconductor
2900 Semiconductor Dr.
Santa Clara, CA 95052
(408) 721-5020
(800) 538-8510

NCR Corporation
1334 S. Patterson Blvd.
Dayton, OH 45479
(513) 445-5000
(800) 225-5627
Fax: (513) 445-1847

NEC America
10 Rio Robles
San Jose, CA 95134
(408) 433-1250
(800) 222-4632
Fax: (408) 433-1239

NetFrame Systems
1545 Barber Lane
Milpitas, CA 95035
(408) 944-0600
(800) 852-3726
Fax: (408) 434-4190

Netronix
1372 N. McDowell Blvd.
Petaluma, CA 94954
(707) 769-3300
(800) 282-2535
Fax: (707) 763-6291

Network and Communication Technology
24 Wampum Rd.
Park Ridge, NJ 07656
(201) 307-9000
(800) 488-4628
Fax: (201) 307-9404

Network Application Technology Inc.
1686 Dell Ave.
Campbell, CA 95008
(408) 370-4300
(800) 543-8887
Fax: (408) 370-4222

Network Equipment Technologies Inc.
800 Saginaw Dr.
Redwood City, CA 94063
(415) 7366-4400
(800) 234-4638
Fax: (415) 366-5675

Network General
4200 Bohannon Drive
Menlo Park, CA 94025
(415) 688-2700
(800) 395-3151
Fax: (415) 321-0855

Networking Dynamics
3959 Foothill Blvd., Ste. 201
Glendale, CA 91214
(818) 248-0670
(800) 275-6321
Fax: (818) 248-5253

Network Interface Corp.
15019 W. 95th St.
Lenexa, KS 66215
(913) 894-2277
(800) 343-2853
Fax: (913) 894-0226

Network Resources Corp.
736 S. Hillview Drive
Milpitas, CA 95035
(408) 263-8100
Fax: (408) 263-8121

Network Software Associates
39 Argonaut
Laguna Hills, CA 92656
(714) 768-4013
Fax: (714) 768-5049

Network Systems Corporation
7600 Boone Ave. N.
Minneapolis, MN 55428
(612) 424-4888
(800) 248-8777
Fax: (612) 424-1661

Networth, Inc.
8101 Ridgepoint Drive
Irving, TX 75063
(214) 869-1331
(800) 544-5255
Fax: (214) 556-0841

Newbridge Networks
593 Herndon Pkwy.
Herndon, VA 22070-5241
(703) 834-3600
(800) 332-1080
Fax: (703) 471-7080

Newport Systems Solutions, Inc.
4019 Westerly Pl., Suite 103
Newport Beach, CA 92660
(714) 752-1511
(800) 368-6533
Fax: (714) 752-8389

Niwot Networks
2200 Central Avenue Suite b
Boulder, CO 80301
(303) 444-7765
Fax: (303) 444-7767

Norton-Lambert Corp.
P.O. Box 4085
Santa Barbara, CA 93140
(805) 964-6767
Fax: (805) 683-5679

Novell, Inc.
122 East 1700 South
Provo, UT 84606
(801) 429-7000
(800) 453-1267
Fax: (801) 429-5155

Novell, Inc.
2180 Fortune Drive
San Jose, CA 95131
(408) 473-8333
(800) 243-8526
Fax: (408) 435-1706

Nuvotech
2015 Bridgeway - Suite 204
Sausalito, CA 94965
(415) 331-7815
(800) 468-8683
Fax: (415) 331-6445

**Nynex Information Solutions Group
Inc.**
Four W. Red Oak Lane
White Plains, NY 10604
(914) 644-7800

Objective Systems Integrators, Inc.
1002 River Rock Drive #221
Folsom, CA 95630
(916) 987-0310
Fax: (916) 987-0510

Octocom Systems Inc.
255 Ballardvale St.
Wilmington, MA 01887
(508) 658-6050
(800) 822-4234
Fax: (508) 658-0376

Oneac
27944 N. Bradley Rd.
Libertyville, IL 60048
(708) 816-6000
(800) 327-8801
Fax: (708) 816-6797

OpenConnect Systems Inc.
2033 Chennault Dr.
Carrollton, TX 75006
(214) 490-4090
Fax: (214) 490-5052

Open Networks Engineering
777 E. Eisenhower, Ste. 315
Ann Arbor, MI 48108
(313) 996-9900
Fax: (313) 996-9908

Optical Data Systems (ODS)
1101 E. Arapaho Road
Richardson, TX 75081
(214) 234-6400
Fax: (214) 234-4059

Oracle Corp.
500 Oracle Pkwy.
Redwood Shores, CA 94065
(415) 506-7000
Fax: (415) 506-7255

Pacific Micro Data
1682 Langley Ave.
Irvine, CA 92714
(714) 756-8198
Fax: (714) 756-0672

Palindrome Corp.
850 E. Diehl Road
Naperville, IL 60563
(708) 505-3300
Fax: (708) 505-7917

Penril DataComm Networks
1300 Quince Orchard Blvd.
Gaithersburg, MD 20878
(301) 921-8600
(800) 473-6745
Fax: (301) 921-8376

Performance Technology
800 Lincoln Center
7800 IH-10 West, Ste. 800
San Antonio, TX 78230
(512) 349-2000
(800) 327-8526
Fax: (512) 366-0123

Persoft Inc.
465 Science Dr.
Madison, WI 53711
(608) 273-6000
(800) 368-5283
Fax: (608) 273-8227

Phaser Systems, Inc.
651 Gateway Boulevard #400
South San Francisco, CA 94080
(415) 952-6300
(800) 234-5799
Fax: (415) 952-1239

Prime Computer, Inc.
100 Crosby DrivePrime Parkway
Natick, MA 01730
(508) 655-8000
Fax: (617) 275-1800

Promptus Communications Inc.
207 High Point Ave.
Portsmouth, RI 02871
(401) 683-6100
(800) 777-5267
Fax: (401) 683-6105

Proteon, Inc.
2 Technology Drive
Westborough, MA 01581
(508) 898-2800
(800) 545-7464
Fax: (508) 366-8901

ProTools
14976 N.W. Greenbrier Pkwy.
Beaverton, OR 97006
(503) 645-5400
(800) 743-4335
Fax: (503) 645-3577

PureData
180 W. Beaver Creek Rd.
Richmond Hill, Ontario L4B 1B4
CANADA
(416) 731-6444
Fax: (416) 731-7017

Quam-MNC
2817 Anthony Ln. South
Minneapolis, MN 55418
(612) 788-1099
Fax: (612) 788-9365

Rabbit Software Corp.
7 Great Valley Pkwy. E.
East Malvern, PA 19355
(215) 647-0440
(800) 722-2482
Fax: (215) 640-1379

Racal-Interlan, Inc.
155 Swanson Road
Boxborough, MA 01719
(508) 263-9929
(800) 526-8255
Fax: (508) 263-8655

Racal Data Communications
1601 N. Harrison Pkwy.
Sunrise, FL 33323-2899
(305) 846-1601
(800) 722-2555
Fax: (305) 846-5510

Racal-Quanta
160 S. Old Springs Rd.
Anaheim, CA 92808
(714) 282-7700
(800) 328-2668
Fax: (714) 282-7889

Racore Computer Products
170 Knowles Dr. #204
Los Gatos, CA 95030
(408) 374-8290
(800) 635-1274
Fax: (408) 374-6653

RAD Data Communications Inc.
151 West Passaic Street
Rochelle Park, NJ 07662
(201) 587-8822
(800) 969-4723
Fax: (201) 587-8847

RAD Network Devices Inc.
7711 Center Ave., Suite 600
Huntington Beach, CA 92647
(714) 891-1964
(800) 969-4723
Fax: (714) 891-7788

Raycom Systems Inc.
6395 Gunpark Drive #N
Boulder, CO 80301
(800) 288-1620
Fax: (303) 530-3982 (in state)
Fax: (818) 909-4186 (out of state)

Retix
2644 30th Street
Santa Monica, CA 90405
(310) 399-2200
(800) 255-2333
Fax: (310) 458-2685

Samsung Information Systems
3655 N. First St.
San Jose, CA 95134
(408) 434-5400
(800) 624-8999
Fax: (408) 434-5686

Sankyo
2649 Campus Drive
Irvine, CA 92715
(714) 724-1505
Fax: (714) 724-1501

Server Technology
2332-B Walsh Ave.
Santa Clara, CA 95051
(408) 988-0142
(800) 835-1515
Fax: (408) 988-0992

Shiva Corporation
One Cambridge Center
Cambridge, MA 02142
(617) 252-6300
(800) 458-3550
Fax: (617) 252-6852

Siecor
489 Siecor Park
P.O. Box 489
Hickory, NC 28603-0489
(704) 327-5000
(800) 634-9064
Fax: (704) 327-5973

Silicon Graphics Inc
2011 N. Shoreline Blvd.
Mountain View, CA 94043
(415) 960-1980
(800) 326-1020
Fax: (415) 960-1284

Sitka Corporations (TOPS)
950 Marina Village Parkway
Alameda, CA 94501
(510) 769-9669
(800) 445-8677
Fax: (510) 769-8773

SMC
35 Marcos Blvd.
Hauppauge, NY 11788
(516) 273-3100
(800) 992-4762
Fax: (516) 434-9314

Softronics
5085 List Drive
Colorado Springs, CO 80919
(719) 593-9540
(800) 225-8590
Fax: (719) 548-1878

SoftSwitch Inc.
640 Lee Rd. #200
Wayne, PA 19087
(215) 640-9600
Fax: (215) 640-7550

Software Results Corporation
940 Freeway Dr. N.
Columbus, OH 43229
(614) 785-0282
(800) 772-3282

Spectrum Concepts
150 Broadway 20th Fl.
New York, NY 10038
(212) 766-4400
(800) 365-9266
Fax: (212) 571-6077

Spider Systems
12 New England Executive Park
Burlington, MA 01803
(617) 270-3510
(800) 447-7807
Fax: (617) 270-9818

St. Clair Systems Corp.
2680 Marshfield Dr.
Pittsburgh, PA 15241
(412) 835-5000
(800) 326-5267
Fax: (412) 835-5319

Standard Microsystems Corporation
35 Marcus Blvd.
Hauppauge, NY 11788
(516) 273-3100
(800) 992-4762
Fax: (516) 273-7935

Star Tek Inc.
71 Lyman St.
Northborough, MA 01532
(508) 393-9393
(800) 225-8528
Fax: (508) 393-6934

Sun Microsystems, Inc.
2550 Garcia Avenue
Mountain View, CA 94043
(415) 960-1300
(800) 872-4786
Fax: (415) 336-3475

Sybase Inc.
6475 Christie Ave.
Emeryville, CA 94608
(510) 596-3500
Fax: (510) 658-9441

Synernetics Inc.
85 Rangeway Rd.
North Billerica, MA 01862
(508) 670-9009
(800) 992-2446
Fax: (508) 670-9015

SynOptics Communications, Inc.
4401 Great America Pkwy.
Santa Clara, CA 95054
(408) 988-2400
Fax: (408) 988-5525

Systems Center Inc.
1800 Alexander Bell Dr.
Reston, VA 22091
(703) 264-8000
(800) 533-5128
Fax: (703) 260-0063

Systems Strategies Inc.
225 W. 34th St.
New York, NY 10001
(212) 279-8400
Fax: (212) 967-8368

Tallgrass
11100 W. 82nd Street
Lenexa, KS 66214
(913) 492-6002
(800) 736-6002
Fax: (913) 492-2465

Tandberg Data Inc.
2649 Townsgate Road
Suite 600
Westlake Village, CA 91361
(805) 495-8384
Fax: (805) 495-4186

Tangent Computer Inc.
197 Airport Blvd.
Burlingame, CA 94010
(800) 223-6677
Fax: (415) 342-9380

Technically Elite Concepts Inc.
2615 Pacific Coast Highway #322
Hermosa Beach, CA 90254
(310) 379-2505
(800) 659-6975
Fax: (310) 379-5985

Tecmar
6225 Cochran Road
Solon, OH 44139-3377
(216) 349-0600
(800) 624-8560
Fax: (216) 349-0851

Tekelec
26580 W. Agoura Rd.
Calabasas, CA 91302
(818) 880-5656
(800) 835-3532
Fax: (818) 880-6993

Tektronix, Inc.
P.O. Box 1197
Redmond, OR 97756
(503) 923-0333
(800) 833-9200
Fax: (503) 923-4434

Telecommunications Techniques Corporation
(Successors to LP COM)
270 Santa Ana Ct.
Sunnyvale, CA 94086
(408) 749-8008
Fax: (408) 736-1951

Telecommunications Techniques Corp.
20410 Observation Dr.
Germantown, MD 20876
(301) 353-1550
(800) 638-2049
Fax: (301) 353-0731

The AG Group
2540 Camino Diablo #202
Walnut Creek, CA 94596
(510) 937-7900
Fax: (510) 937-2479

The Santa Cruz Operation
400 Encinal Street P.O. Box 1900
Santa Cruz, CA 95061-1900
(408) 425-7222
Fax: (408) 458-4227

Thomas-Conrad Corporation
1908-R Kramer Ln.
Austin, TX 78758
(512) 836-1935
(800) 332-8683
Fax: (512) 836-2840

3Com Corporation
5400 Bayfront Plaza
Santa Clara, CA 95052
(408) 764-5000
(800) 638-3266
Fax: (408) 764-5032

Tiara Computer Systems
1091 Shoreline Blvd.
Mountain View, CA 94043
(415) 965-1700
(800) 638-4272
Fax: (415) 965-2677

Timeplex Inc.
400 Chestnut Ridge Road
Woodcliff Lake, NJ 07675
(201) 391-1111
(800) 755-8526
Fax: (201) 573-6470

Touch Communications
250 E. Hacienda Ave.
Campbell, CA 95008
(408) 374-2500
(800) 878-1674
Fax: (408) 374-1680

Touch Technologies Inc.
3655 Nobel Dr. #650
San Diego, CA 92122
(619) 455-7404
(800) 525-2527
Fax: (619) 455-7413

Trellis Software, Inc.
85 Main Street
Hopkinton, MA 01748
(508) 435-3066
Fax: (508) 435-0556

Tri-Data Systems, Inc.
3270 Scott Blvd.
Santa Clara, CA 95054
(408) 727-3270
(800) 874-3282
Fax: (408) 980-6565

Tripp Manufacturing
500 N. Orleans
Chicago, IL 60610
(312) 329-1777
Fax: (312) 644-6505

Triticom
P.O. Box 444180
Eden Prairie, MN 55344
(612) 937-0772
Fax: (612) 937-1998

Triton Technologies
200 Middlesex Tpke.
Iselin, NJ 08830
(908) 855-9440
(800) 322-9440
Fax: (908) 855-9608

TRW Inc.
1760 Glenn Curtiss St.
Carson, CA 90746
(213) 764-9467
Fax: (213) 764-9491

Ungermann-Bass, Inc.
3900 Freedom Circle Blvd.
Santa Clara, CA 95052
(408) 496-0111
(800) 873-6381
Fax: (408) 970-7386

Unisync, Inc.
1380 W. Ninth Street
Upland, CA 91786
(714) 985-5088
Fax: (714) 982-0929

Unisys
P.O. Box 500
Blue Bell, PA 19424
(215) 986-4011
Fax: (215) 986-6850

UDS Motorola, Inc.
5000 Bradford Drive
Huntsville, AL 35805-1993
(205) 430-8000
(800) 451-2369
Fax: (205) 430-7265

Verilink Corp.
145 Baytech Drive
San Jose, CA 95134
(408) 945-1199
(800) 543-1008
Fax: (408) 946-5124

Vitalink Communications Corp.
6607 Kaiser Drive
Fremont, CA 94555
(510) 794-1100
(800) 443-5740
Fax: (415) 795-1085

Viteq Power Systems
P.O. Box 1440
Rockville, MD 20849-1440
(301) 731-0400
Fax: (301) 731-5995

Walker Richer and Quinn

2815 Eastlake Ave. E.
Seattle, WA 98102
(206) 324-0407
(800) 872-2829
Fax: (206) 322-8151

Wall Data, Inc.

17769 NE 78th Place
Redmond, WA 98052-4992
(206) 883-4777
(800) 487-8622
Fax: (206) 885-9250

Wandel & Goltermann

2200 Gateway Centre Blvd.
Morrisville, NC 27560
(919) 460-3300
(800) 346-6332
Fax: (919) 481-4372

Wang Laboratories

1 Industrial Ave.
Lowell, MA 01851
(508) 459-5000
(800) 225-0654
Fax: (508) 967-7020

WellFleet Communications Corp.

15 Crosby Drive
Bedford, MA 01730
(617) 275-2400
Fax: (617) 275-5001

Western Digital Corporation

8105 Irvine Center Drive
Irvine, CA 92718
(714) 932-5000
Fax: (714) 932-6098

Wilcom Products

Rt. 3 Daniel Webster Hwy.
Laconia, NH 03246
(603) 524-2622
Fax: (603) 528-3804

The Wollongong Group, Inc.

1129 San Antonio Road
Palo Alto, CA 94303
(415) 962-7100
(800) 872-8649
Fax: (415) 969-5547

Xerox Corporation

100 Clinton Ave. S., 5-B
Rochester, NY 14644
(716) 423-5090
Fax: (716) 423-5733

Xircom

26025 Mureau Road
Calabasas, CA 91302
(800) 874-7875
(818) 878-7600
Fax: (818) 878-7630

Xyplex, Inc.
330 Codman Hill Rd.
Boxborough, MA 01719
(508) 264-9900
(800) 338-5316
Fax: (508) 264-9930

Zenith Electronics Corporation
Communication Products Division
1000 Milwaukee Avenue
Glenview, IL 60025
(708) 391-8000
(800) 788-7244
Fax: (708) 391-8919

Zytec Systems Inc.
5323 Spring Valley Rd. #100
Dallas, TX 75240
(214) 991-9966
Fax: (214) 991-9897

LAN and WAN Analyzer Manufacturers

LAN Analyzer manufacturers include:

AG Group
2540 Camino Diablo
Suite 202
Walnut Creek, CA 94596
(510) 937-7900
Fax: (510) 937-2479

Bytex Corporation
120 Turnpike Road
Southborough Office Park
Southborough, MA 01772-1886
(508) 480-0840
Fax: (508) 460-0098

Cabletron Systems Inc.
35 Industrial Way
P.O. Box 5005
Rochester, NH 03867
(603) 332-9400
Fax: (603) 332-4616

CXR/Digilog Inc.
900 Business Center Drive
Suite 200
Horsham, PA 19044-3453
(215) 956-9570
(800) 344-4564
Fax: (215) 956-0108

Digital Technology Inc.
2300 Edwin C. Moses Blvd.
Dayton, OH 45408
(513) 443-0412
Fax: (513) 226-0511

FTP Software Inc.
338 Main St.
Wakefield, MA 01880
(617) 246-0900
Fax: (617) 246-0901

Hewlett-Packard Company
5070 Centennial Blvd.
Colorado Springs, CO 80919
(719) 531-4000
Fax: (719) 531-4505

International Data Sciences, Inc.
7 Wellington Road
Lincoln, RI 02865
(401) 333-6200
(800) 437-3282
Fax: (401) 333-3584

Micro Technology Inc.
5065 E. Hunter Ave.
Anaheim, CA 92807
(714) 970-0300
(800) 999-9684
Fax:(714) 970-5413

Network General Corp.
4200 Bohannon Drive
Menlo Park, CA 94025
(415) 688-2700
(800) 395-3151
Fax: (415) 321-0855

Novell Inc.
2180 Fortune Drive
San Jose, CA 95131
(408) 473-8333
(800) 243-8526
Fax: (408) 435-1706

Protools Inc.
14976 NW Greenbrier Pkwy.
Beaverton, OR 97006-5733
(503) 645-5400
(800) 743-4335
Fax: (503) 645-3577

Spider Systems Inc.
12 New England Executive Pk.
Burlington, MA 01803
(617) 270-3510
(800) 447-7807
Fax: (617) 270-9818

Telecommunications Techniques Corp.
(Successor to LP COM)
270 Santa Ana Court
Sunnyvale, CA 94086
(408) 749-8008
Fax: (408) 736-1951

Wandel &Goltermann Technologies
2200 Gateway Centre Blvd.
Morrisville, NC 27560
(919) 460-3300
(800) 346-6332
Fax: (919) 481-4372

WAN Analyzer Manufacturers include:

Ando Corporation
7617 Standish Place
Rockville, MD 20855
(301) 294-3365
Fax: (301) 294-3359

Telenex Corp.
7401 Boston Blvd.
Springfield, VA 22153
(703) 644-9000
Fax: (703) 644-9011

CXR/Digilog Inc.
900 Business Center Drive
Suite 200
Horsham, PA 19044-3453
(215) 956-9570
(800) 344-4564
Fax: (215) 956-0108

Digital Technology Inc.
2300 Edwin C. Moses Blvd.
Dayton, OH 45408
(513) 443-0412
Fax: (513) 226-0511

Digitech Industries Inc.
66 Grove St.
P.O. Box 547
Ridgefield, CT 06877
(203) 438-3731
Fax: (203) 438-4184

Frederick Engineering Inc.
10200 Old Columbia Road
Columbia, MD 21046
(301) 290-9000
Fax: (301) 381-7180

G N Elmi
661 Bay Circle
Suite 190
Norcross, GA 30071-9878
(404) 446-2665
Fax: (404) 446-2730

GN Navtel Inc.
55 Renfrew Drive
Markham, Ontario
Canada L3R 8H3
(416) 479-8090
Fax: (416) 475-6524
U.S. Office:
661 Bay Circle
Suite 190
Norcross, GA 30071-9878
(404) 446-2665
(800) 262-8835
Fax: (404) 446-2730

Hewlett-Packard Company
5070 Centennial Blvd.
Colorado Springs, CO 80919
(719) 531-4000
Fax: (719) 531-4505

Idacom Electronic Ltd.
Division of Hewlett-Packard
4211 95 Street
Edmonton, Alberta
Canada T6E 5R6
(403) 462-4545
(800) 661-3868
Fax: (403) 462-4869

International Data Sciences, Inc.
7 Wellington Road
Lincoln, RI 02865
(401) 333-6200
(800) 437-3282
Fax: (401) 333-3584

Kamputech Inc.
20 Meridian Road
Suite 4
Eatontown, NJ 07724
(908) 389-6464
Fax: (908) 389-646

Network Communications Corp.
10120 West 76th Street
Eden Prairie, MN 55344-9814
(612) 944-8559
(800) 451-1984
Fax: (612) 944-9805

Network General Corp.
4200 Bohannon Drive
Menlo Park, CA 94025
(415) 688-2700
(800) 395-3151
Fax: (415) 321-0855

Progressive Computing Inc.
814 Commerce Drive
Suite 101
Oak Brook, IL 60521-1919
(708) 574-3399
Fax: (708) 574-3703

Realtime Techniques
15807 Crabbs Branch Way-Unit A
Rockville, MD 20855
(301) 840-3942
Fax: (301) 840-9337

Tekelec
26580 W. Agoura Road
Calabasas, CA 91302
(818) 880-5656
(800) 835-3532
Fax: (818) 880-6993

Telecommunications Techniques Corporation
(Successor to LP COM)
270 Santa Ana Court
Sunnyvale, CA 94086
(408) 749-8008
Fax: (408) 736-1951

Wandel & Goltermann Technologies
2200 Gateway Centre Blvd.
Morrisville, NC 27560
(919) 460-3300
(800) 346-6332
Fax: (919) 481-4372

Acronyms

A	Ampere
AARP	AppleTalk Address Resolution Protocol
ABP	Alternate Bipolar
ACK	Acknowledgement
ACS	Asynchronous Communication Server
ACTLU	Activate Logical Unit
ACTPU	Activate Physical Unit
ADSP	AppleTalk Data Stream Protocol
AEP	AppleTalk Echo Protocol
AFP	AppleTalk Filing Protocol
AFRP	ARCNET Fragmentation Protocol
AGS	Asynchronous Gateway Server
AI	Artificial Intelligence
AMI	Alternate Mark Inversion
AMT	Address Mapping Table
ANSI	American National Standards Institute
API	Applications Program Interface

APPC   Advanced Program-to-Program Communication

ARE   All Routes Explorer

ARI   Address Recognized Indicator Bit

ARP   Address Resolution Program

ARPANET   Advanced Research Projects Agency Network

ASCII   American Standard Code for Information Interchange

ASP   AppleTalk Session Protocol

ATP   AppleTalk Transaction Protocol

B8ZS   Bipolar with 8 ZERO Substitution

BC   Block Check

BIOS   Basic Input/Output System

BIU   Basic Information Unit

BOC   Bell Operating Company

BPDU   Bridge Protocol Data Unit

bps   Bits Per Second

BPV   Bipolar Violation

BRI   Basic Rate Interface

BSC   Binary Synchronous Communication

BTU   Basic Transmission Unit

CCIS   Common Channel Interoffice Signaling

CCITT   International Telegraph and Telephone Consultative
                Committee

CICS	Customer Information Communication System
CLNS	Connectionless-mode Network Services
CMIP	Common Management Information Protocol
CMOL	CMIP on IEEE 802. Logical Link Control
CMOT	Common Management Information Protocol Over TCP/IP
CONS	Connection-mode Network Services
CPE	Customer Premises Equipment
CRC	Cyclic Redundancy Check
CRS	Configuration Report Server
CSMA/CD	Carrier Sense Multiple Access with Collision Detection
CSU	Channel Service Unit
CTERM	Command Terminal Protocol
DAP	Data Access Protocol
DARPA	Defense Advanced Research Projects Agency
DAT	Duplicate Address Test
DCE	Data Circuit-Terminating Equipment
DDCMP	Digital Data Communications Message Protocol
DDN	Defense Data Network
DDP	Datagram Delivery Protocol
DECmcc	DEC Management Control Center
DEMPR	DEC Multiport Repeater
DIX	DEC, Intel and Xerox

DL	Data Link
DLC	Data Link Control
DMA	Direct Memory Access
DOD	Department of Defense
DPA	Demand Protocol Architecture
DRP	DECnet Routing Protocol
DSAP	Destination Service Access Point
DSU	Data Service Unit
DSU/CSU	Data Service Unit/Channel Service Unit
DTE	Data Terminal Equipment
DTR	Data Terminal Ready

EBCDIC	Extended Binary Coded Decimal Interchange Code
ECL	End Communication Layer
ECSA	Exchange Carriers Standards Association
EDI	Electronic Data Interchange
EGA	Enhanced Graphics Array
EIA	Electronic Industries Association
ELAP	EtherTalk Link Access Protocol
EOT	End of Transmission
ESF	Extended Superframe Format

FAL	File Access Listener
FAT	File Access Table
FCC	Federal Communications Commission
FCI	Frame Copied Indicator Bit
FCS	Frame Check Sequence
FDDI	Fiber Data Distributed Interface
FDM	Frequency Division Multiplexing
FID	Format Identifier
FM	Function Management
FMD	Function Management Data
FT1	Fractional T1
FTAM	File Transfer Access and Management
FTP	File Transfer Protocol
G	Giga-
GB	Gigabyte
GHz	Gigahertz
GUI	Graphical User Interface
HDLC	High Level Data Link Control
HLLAPI	High Level Language API
Hz	Hertz

ICMP	Internet Control Message Protocol
ICP	Internet Control Protocol
IDP	Internetwork Datagram Protocol
IEEE	Institute of Electrical and Electronics Engineers
I/G	Individual/Group
I/O	Input/Output
IOC	Inter-Office Channel
IP	Internet Protocol
IPC	Interprocess Communications Protocol
IPX	Internetwork Packet Exchange
IR	Internet Router
ISDN	Integrated Services Digital Network
ISO	International Organization for Standardization
ITU	International Telecommunication Union
IXC	Inter-Exchange Carrier
Kbps	Kilo Bits per Second
KHz	Kilohertz
LAA	Locally-Administered Address
LAN	Local Area Network
LAP	Link Access Procedure
LAPB	Link Access Procedure-Balanced

LAPD	Link Access Procedure D Channel
LAT	Local Area Transport
LATA	Local Access Transport Area
LAVC	Local Area VAX Cluster
LEC	Local Exchange Carrier
LF	Largest Frame
LLAP	LocalTalk Link Access Protocol
LLC	Logical Link Control
LMMP	LAN MAN Management Protocol
LSL	Link Support Layer
MAC	Medium Access Control
MAN	Metropolitan Area Network
Mbps	Mega Bits per Second
MHS	Message Handling Service
MHz	Megahertz
MIPS	Millions Instructions Per Second
MIS	Management Information System
MLID	Multiple Link Interface Driver
MNP	Microcom Networking Protocol
MOP	Maintenance Operations Protocol
MSAU	Multistation Access Unit
MTBF	Mean Time Between Failure

MTTR	Mean Time To Repair
MUX	Multiplex, Multiplexor
NACS	NetWare Asynchronous Communications Server
NAK	Negative Acknowledgement
NASI	Netware Asynchronous Service Interface
NAU	Network Addressable Unit
NAUN	Nearest Active Upstream Neighbor
NBP	Name Binding Protocol
NCP	Network Control Program
NCP	NetWare Core Protocol
NCSI	Network Communications Services Interface
NDIS	Network Driver Interface Standard
NetBEUI	NetBIOS Extended User Interface
NetBIOS	Network Basic Input/Output System
NFS	Network File System
NIC	Network Interface Card
NICE	Network Information and Control Exchange
NIS	Names Information Socket
NLM	NetWare Loadable Module
NOS	Network Operating System
NSP	Network Services Protocol
NT	Network Termination

OC1	Optical Carrier, level 1
ODI	Open Data Link Interface
OSI	Open Systems Interconnection
OSPF	Open Shortest Path First
PABX	Private Automatic Branch Exchange
PAD	Packet Assembler and Disassembler
PAP	Printer Access Protocol
PBX	Private Branch Exchange
PCI	Protocol Control Information
PCM	Pulse Code Modulation
PDN	Public Data Network
PDU	Protocol Data Unit
PEP	Packet Exchange Protocol
POP	Point of Presence
POSIX	Portable Operating System Interface - UNIX
POTS	Plain Old Telephone System
PSP	Presentation Services Process
PSPDN	Packet Switched Public Data Network
PTP	Point-to-Point
PUC	Public Utility Commission

RARP   Reverse Address Resolution Protocol

RC   Routing Control

RD   Route Descriptor

RFC   Request for Comments

RH   Request/Response Header

RII   Route Information Indicator

RIP   Routing Information Protocol

RJE   Remote Job Entry

RPC   Remote Procedure Calls

RPS   Ring Parameter Service

RSX   Realtime resource-Sharing eXecutive

RT   Routing Type

RU   Request/Response Unit

SABME   Set Asynchronous Balanced Mode Extended

SAP   Service Advertising Protocol

SCS   System Communication Services

SDLC   Synchronous Data Link Control

SLIP   Serial Line IP

SMB   Server Message Block

SMDS   Switched Multimegabit Data Service

SMTP   Simple Mail Transfer Protocol

SNA   System Network Architecture

SNADS	Systems Network Architecture Distribution Services
SNAP	Sub-Network Access Protocol
SNMP	Simple Network Management Protocol
SOH	Start of Header
SONET	Synchronous Optical Network
SPP	Sequenced Packet Protocol
SPX	Sequenced Packet Exchange
SR	Source Routing
SRF	Specifically Routed Frame
SRI	Stanford Research Institute
SRT	Source Routing Transparent
SSAP	Source Service Access Point
STE	Spanning Tree Explorer
SUA	Stored Upstream Address
SVC	Switched Virtual Circuit
TB	Terabyte
TCP	Transmission Control Protocol
TCP/IP	Transmission Control Protocol/Internet Protocol
TDM	Time Division Multiplexing
TELNET	Telecommunications Network
TH	Transmission Header
TLAP	TokenTalk Link Access Protocol

TLI	Transport Layer Interface
TP	Transport Protocol
TSR	Terminate-and-Stay Resident
UA	Unnumbered Acknowledgement
UDP	User Datagram Protocol
U/L	Universal/Local
ULP	Upper Layer Protocols
UNMA	Unified Network Management Architecture
UTP	Unshielded Twisted Pair
V	Volt
VAN	Value Added Network
VAP	Value-Added Process
VARP	VINES Address Resolution Protocol
VFRP	VINES Fragmentation Protocol
VGA	Video Graphics Array
VICP	VINES Internet Control Protocol
VINES	Virtual Networking System
VIP	VINES Internet Protocol
VIPC	VINES Interprocess Communications
VLSI	Very Large-Scale Integration
VMS	Virtual Memory System

VRTP	VINES Routing Update Protocol
VSPP	VINES Sequenced Packet Protocol
VT	Virtual Terminal
WAN	Wide Area Network
XID	Exchange Identification
XNS	Xerox Network System
ZIP	Zone Information Protocol
ZIS	Zone Information Socket
ZIT	Zone Information Table

Ethernet Protocol Types

Hexadecimal	Description
0000-05DC	IEEE 802.3 Length Field (0-1500 decimal)
0101-01FF	Experimental (for development) — Conflicts with 802.3 length fields
0200	Xerox PUP — Conflicts with 802.3 length fields
0201	PUP Address Translation — Conflicts with 802.3 length fields
0600	Xerox XNS IDP
0800	DOD IP
0801	X.75 Internet
0802	NBS Internet
0803	ECMA Internet
0804	CHAOSnet
0805	X.25 Level 3
0806	ARP (for IP and for CHAOS)
0807	XNS Compatability
081C	Symbolics Private

0888-088A	Xyplex
0900	Ungermann-Bass network debugger
0A00	Xerox 802.3 PUP
0A01	PUP 802.3 Address Translation
0BAD	Banyan Systems Inc.
1000	Berkeley trailer negotiation
1001-100F	Berkeley Trailer encapsulation
1600	VALID
4242	PCS Basic Block Protocol
5208	BBN Simnet Private
6000	DEC Unassigned
6001	DEC MOP Dump/Load Assistance
6002	DEC MOP Remote Console
6003	DEC DECnet Phase IV
6004	DEC LAT
6005	DEC DECnet Diagnostics
6006	DEC DECnet Customer Use
6007	DEC DECnet SCA
6008	DEC unassigned
6009	DEC unassigned
6010-6014	3Com Corporation

7000	Ungermann-Bass download
7001	Ungermann-Bass NIU
7002	Ungermann-Bass NIU
7007	OS/9 Microware
7020-7029	LRT (England)
7030	Proteon
7034	Cabletron
8003	Cronus VLN
8004	Cronus Direct
8005	HP Probe protocol
8006	Nestar
8008	AT&T
8010	Excelan
8013	SGI diagnostic type (obsolete)
8014	SGI network games (obsolete)
8015	SGI reserved type (obsolete)
8016	SGI "bounce server" (obsolete)
8019	Apollo
802E	Tymshare
802F	Tigan, Inc.
8035	Reverse ARP
8036	Aeonic Systems

8038	DEC LANBridge
8039	DEC Unassigned
803A	DEC Unassigned
803B	DEC Unassigned
803C	DEC Unassigned
803D	DEC Ethernet CSMA/CD Encryption Protocol
803E	DEC Unassigned
803F	DEC LAN Traffic Monitor
8040	DEC Unassigned
8041	DEC Unassigned
8042	DEC Unassigned
8044	Planning Research Corporation
8046	AT&T
8047	AT&T
8049	ExperData (France)
805B	VMTP (Versatile Message Transaction Protocol, RFC-1045, Stanford)
805C	Stanford V Kernel production, Version 6.0
805D	Evans & Sutherland
8060	Little Machines
8062	Counterpoint Computers
8065	University of Massachusetts, Amherst
8066	University of Massachusetts, Amherst

8067	Veeco Integrated Automation
8068	General Dynamics
8069	AT&T
806A	Autophon (Switzerland)
806C	ComDesign
806D	Compugraphic Corporation
806E-8077	Landmark Graphics Corporation
807A	Matra (France)
807B	Dansk Data Elektronic A/S (Denmark)
807C	Merit Internodal
807D	VitaLink Communications
807E	VitaLink Communications
807F	VitaLink Communications
8080	VitaLink Communications bridge
8081	Counterpoint Computers
8082	Counterpoint Computers
8083	Counterpoint Computers
8088	Xyplex
8089	Xyplex
808A	Xyplex
809B	Kinetics Ethertalk - Appletalk over Ethernet
809C	Datability
809D	Datability

809E	Datability
809F	Spider Systems, Ltd. (England)
80A3	Nixdorf Computer (West Germany)
80A4-80B3	Siemens Gammasonics Inc.
80C0	Digital Communication Associates
80C1	Digital Communication Associates
80C2	Digital Communication Associates
80C3	Digital Communication Associates
80C6	Pacer Software
80C7	Applitek Corporation
80C8-80CC	Integraph Corporation
80CD	Harris Corporation
80CE	Harris Corporation
80CF-80D2	Taylor Inst.
80D3	Rosemount Corporation
80D4	Rosemount Corporation
80D5	IBM SNA Services over Ethernet
80DD	Varian Associates
80DE	Integrated Solutions TRFS (Transparent Remote File System)
80DF	Integrated Solutions
80E0-80E3	Allen-Bradley
80E4-80F0	Datability

80F2	Retix
80F3	Kinetics, AppleTalk ARP (AARP)
80F4	Kinetics
80F5	Kinetics
80F7	Apollo Computer
80FF-8103	Wellfleet Communications
8107	Symbolics Private
8108	Symbolics Private
8109	Symbolics Private
8130	Waterloo Microsystems
8131	VG Laboratory Systems
8137	Novell (old) NetWare IPX (ECONFIG E option)
8138	Novell
8139-813D	KTI
9000	Loopback (Configuration Test Protocol)
9001	Bridge Communications XNS Systems Management
9002	Bridge Communications TCP/IP Systems Management
9003	Bridge Communications
FF00	BBN VITAL LANBridge cache wakeup

Used with permission from FTP Software, Inc.

APPENDIX F

Link Service Access Point (SAP) Addresses

IEEE - Administered LSAPs

Address (hexidecimal)	Assignment
00	Null LSAP
02	Individual LLC Sublayer Management Function
03	Group LLC Sublayer Management Function
06	ARPANET Internet Protocol (IP)
0E	PROWAY (IEC955) Network Management & Initialization
42	IEEE 802.1 Bridge Spanning Tree Protocol
4E	EIA RS-511 Manufacturing Message Service
7E	ISO 8208 (X.25 over IEEE 802.2 Type 2 LLC)
8E	PROWAY (IEC 955) Active Station List Maintenance

AA	Sub-Network Access Protocol (SNAP)
FE	ISO Network Layer Protocol
FF	Global LSAP

Manufacturer-Implemented LSAPs

04	IBM SNA Path Control (individual)
05	IBM SNA Path Control (group)
18	Texas Instruments
80	Xerox Network Systems (XNS)
86	Nestar
98	ARPANET Address Resolution Protocol (ARP)
BC	Banyan VINES
E0	Novell NetWare
F0	IBM NetBIOS
F4	IBM LAN Management (individual)
F5	IBM LAN Management (group)
F8	IBM Remote Program Load (RPL)
FA	Ungermann-Bass

Data Link Layer Frame Formats

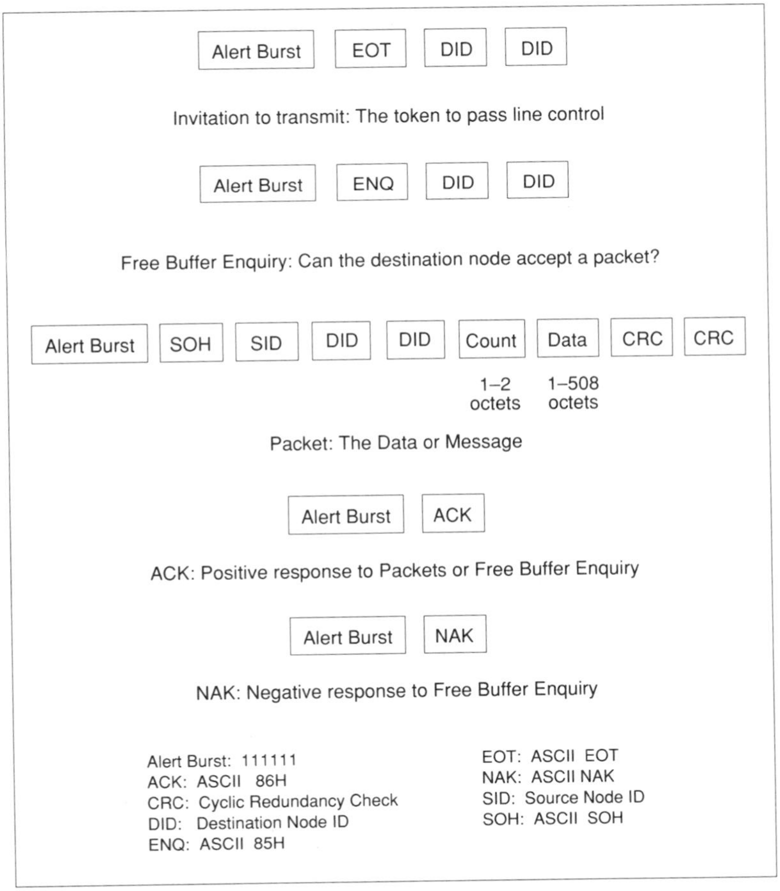

| Alert Burst | EOT | DID | DID |

Invitation to transmit: The token to pass line control

| Alert Burst | ENQ | DID | DID |

Free Buffer Enquiry: Can the destination node accept a packet?

| Alert Burst | SOH | SID | DID | DID | Count | Data | CRC | CRC |

Count: 1–2 octets Data: 1–508 octets

Packet: The Data or Message

| Alert Burst | ACK |

ACK: Positive response to Packets or Free Buffer Enquiry

| Alert Burst | NAK |

NAK: Negative response to Free Buffer Enquiry

Alert Burst: 111111
ACK: ASCII 86H
CRC: Cyclic Redundancy Check
DID: Destination Node ID
ENQ: ASCII 85H

EOT: ASCII EOT
NAK: ASCII NAK
SID: Source Node ID
SOH: ASCII SOH

Figure G-1. ARCNET Frame Formats

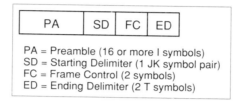

Figure G-2a. FDDI Token Format

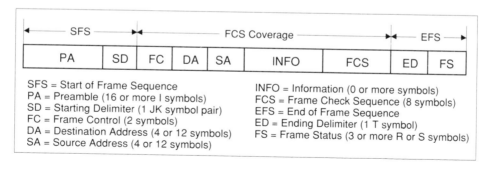

Figure G-2b. FDDI Frame Format

500

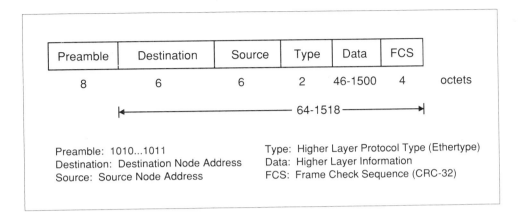

Figure G-3. Ethernet Frame Format

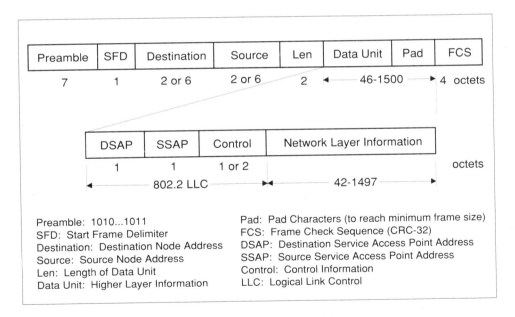

Figure G-4. IEEE 802.3 Frame Format Including 802.2 LLC Header
(Courtesy IEEE)

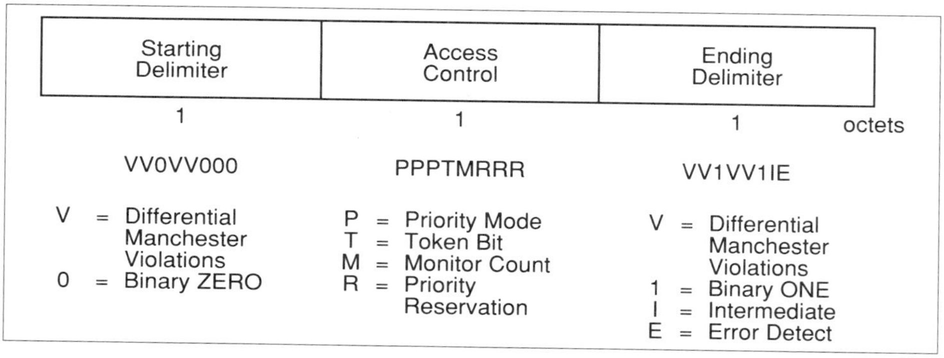

Starting Delimiter	Access Control	Ending Delimiter
1	1	1 octets
VV0VV000	PPPTMRRR	VV1VV1IE

V = Differential Manchester Violations 0 = Binary ZERO	P = Priority Mode T = Token Bit M = Monitor Count R = Priority Reservation	V = Differential Manchester Violations 1 = Binary ONE I = Intermediate E = Error Detect

Figure G-5a. IEEE 802.5 Token Format
(Courtesy IEEE)

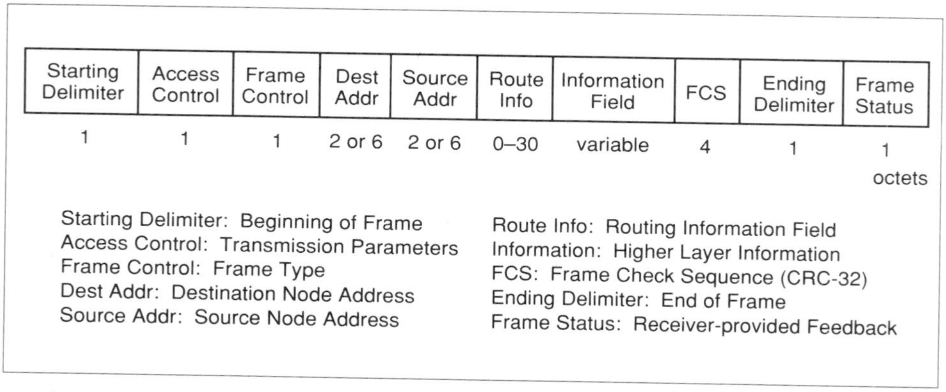

Starting Delimiter	Access Control	Frame Control	Dest Addr	Source Addr	Route Info	Information Field	FCS	Ending Delimiter	Frame Status
1	1	1	2 or 6	2 or 6	0–30	variable	4	1	1 octets

Starting Delimiter: Beginning of Frame
Access Control: Transmission Parameters
Frame Control: Frame Type
Dest Addr: Destination Node Address
Source Addr: Source Node Address

Route Info: Routing Information Field
Information: Higher Layer Information
FCS: Frame Check Sequence (CRC-32)
Ending Delimiter: End of Frame
Frame Status: Receiver-provided Feedback

Figure G-5b. IEEE 802.5 Frame Format
(Courtesy IEEE)

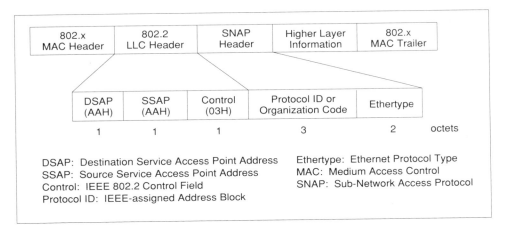

Figure G-6. Sub-Network Access Protocol (SNAP) Header Encapsulated within an IEEE 802.x Frame

(Courtesy IEEE)

APPENDIX H

Physical Layer Connector Pinouts

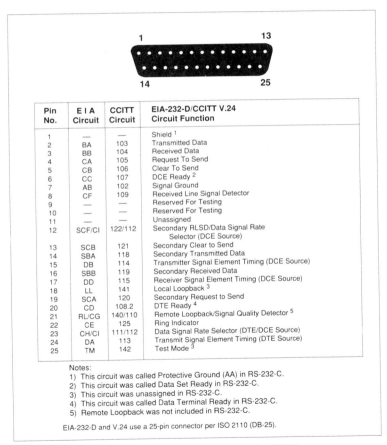

Pin No.	E I A Circuit	CCITT Circuit	EIA-232-D/CCITT V.24 Circuit Function
1	—	—	Shield [1]
2	BA	103	Transmitted Data
3	BB	104	Received Data
4	CA	105	Request To Send
5	CB	106	Clear To Send
6	CC	107	DCE Ready [2]
7	AB	102	Signal Ground
8	CF	109	Received Line Signal Detector
9	—	—	Reserved For Testing
10	—	—	Reserved For Testing
11	—	—	Unassigned
12	SCF/CI	122/112	Secondary RLSD/Data Signal Rate Selector (DCE Source)
13	SCB	121	Secondary Clear to Send
14	SBA	118	Secondary Transmitted Data
15	DB	114	Transmitter Signal Element Timing (DCE Source)
16	SBB	119	Secondary Received Data
17	DD	115	Receiver Signal Element Timing (DCE Source)
18	LL	141	Local Loopback [3]
19	SCA	120	Secondary Request to Send
20	CD	108.2	DTE Ready [4]
21	RL/CG	140/110	Remote Loopback/Signal Quality Detector [5]
22	CE	125	Ring Indicator
23	CH/CI	111/112	Data Signal Rate Selector (DTE/DCE Source)
24	DA	113	Transmit Signal Element Timing (DTE Source)
25	TM	142	Test Mode [3]

Notes:
1) This circuit was called Protective Ground (AA) in RS-232-C.
2) This circuit was called Data Set Ready in RS-232-C.
3) This circuit was unassigned in RS-232-C.
4) This circuit was called Data Terminal Ready in RS-232-C.
5) Remote Loopback was not included in RS-232-C.

EIA-232-D and V.24 use a 25-pin connector per ISO 2110 (DB-25).

Figure H-1. EIA-232-D/CCITT Recommendation Y.24

(© 1987 Hill Associates, Inc.)

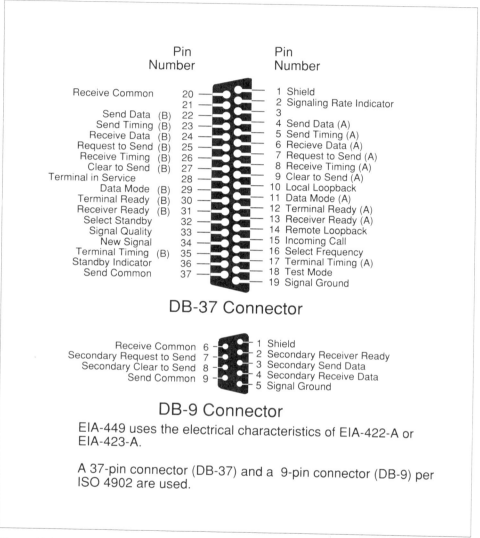

DB-37 Connector

DB-9 Connector

EIA-449 uses the electrical characteristics of EIA-422-A or EIA-423-A.

A 37-pin connector (DB-37) and a 9-pin connector (DB-9) per ISO 4902 are used.

Figure H-2. EIA-449

(© 1987 Hill Associates, Inc.)

Pin No.	E I A Circuit	EIA-530 Circuit Name
1	—	Shield
2	BA (A)	Transmitted Data (A)
3	BB (A)	Received Data (A)
4	CA (A)	Request to Send (A)
5	CB (A)	Clear to Send (A)
6	CC (A)	DCE Ready (A)
7	AB	Signal Ground
8	CF (A)	Received Line Signal Detector (A)
9	DD (B)	Receiver Signal Element Timing, DCE Source (B)
10	CF (B)	Received Line Signal Detector (B)
11	DA (B)	Transmit Signal Element Timing, DTE Source (B)
12	DB (B)	Transmit Signal Element Timing, DCE Source (B)
13	CB (B)	Clear to Send (B)
14	BA (B)	Transmitted Data (B)
15	DB (A)	Transmit Signal Element Timing, DCE Source(A)
16	BB (B)	Received Data (B)
17	DD (A)	Receiver Signal Element Timing, DCE Source (A)
18	LL	Local Loopback
19	CA (B)	Request to Send (B)
20	CD (A)	DTE Ready (B)
21	RL	Remote Loopback
22	CC (B)	DCE Ready (B)
23	CD (B)	DTE Ready (B)
24	DA (A)	Transmit Signal Element Timing, DTE Source (A)
25	TM	Test Mode

EIA-530 uses electrical characteristics of
EIA-422-A or EIA-423-A.

A 25-pin connector per ISO 2110 (DB-25) is used.

Figure H-3. EIA-530
(© 1987 Hill Associates, Inc.)

EIA 530			EIA-449		
Circuit, Name and Mnemonic		Con-tact	Con-tact	Circuit, Name and Mnemonic	
Shield	---	1	1		Shield
Transmitted Data	BA (A)	2	4	SD (A)	Send Data
	BA (B)	14	22	SD (B)	
Received Data	BB (A)	3	6	RD (A)	Receive Data
	BB (B)	16	24	RD (B)	
Request to Send	CA (A)	4	7	RS (A)	Request to Send
	CA (B)	19	25	RS (B)	
Clear to Send	CB (A)	5	9	CS (A)	Clear to Send
	CB (B)	13	27	CS (B)	
DCE Ready	CC (A)	6	11	DM (A)	Data Mode
	CC (B)	22	29	DM (B)	
DTE Ready	CD (A)	20	12	TR (A)	Terminal Ready
	CD (B)	23	30	TR (B)	
Signal Ground	AB	7	19	SG	Signal Ground
Received Line	CF (A)	8	13	RR (A)	Receiver Ready
Signal Detector	CF (B)	10	31	RR (B)	
Transmit Signal	DB (A)	15	5	ST (A)	Send Timing
Element Timing (DCE Source)	DB (B)	12	23	ST (B)	
Receiver Signal	DD (A)	17	8	RT (A)	Receive Timing
Element Timing (DTE Source)	DD (B)	9	26	RT (B)	
Local Loopback	LL	18	10	LL	Local Loopback
Remote Loopback	RL	21	14	RL	Remote Loopback
Transmit Signal	DA (A)	24	17	TT (A)	Terminal Timing
Element Timing (DTE Source)	DA (B)	11	35	TT (B)	
Test Mode	TM	25	18	TM	Test Mode

Figure H-4. Interconnecting EIA-530 with EIA-449

(© 1987 Hill Associates, Inc.)

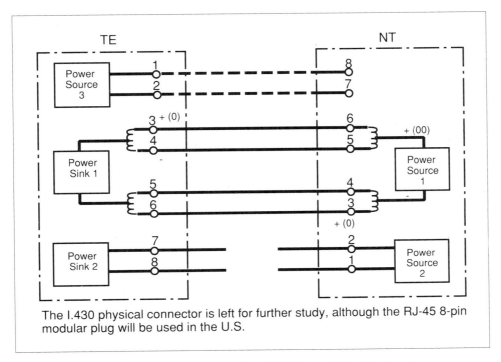

The I.430 physical connector is left for further study, although the RJ-45 8-pin modular plug will be used in the U.S.

Figure H-5. CCITT Recommendation I.430 (ISDN Basic Rate Interface)
(© 1987 Hill Associates, Inc.)

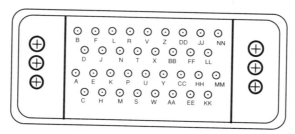

Pin	Circuit Name
A	Chassis ground
B	Signal ground
C	Request to send
D	Clear to send
E	Data set ready
F	Receive line signal detect
P	Transmit data (A)
R	Received data (A)
S	Transmit data (B)
T	Received data (B)
U	Terminal timing (A)
V	Receive timing (A)
W	Terminal timing (B)
X	Receive timing (B)
Y	Transmit timing (A)
AA	Transmit timing (B)

Control signals conform to CCITT Recommendation V.28
A 34-pin connector per ISO 2593 is utilized.

Figure H-6. CCITT Recommendation V.35

(© 1987 Hill Associates, Inc.)

Circuit	Name
G	Signal ground or common return
Ga	DTE common return
T	Transmit
R	Receive
C	Control
I	Indication
S	Signal element timing
B	Byte timing

X.21 uses electrical characteristics from X.26 (V.10)
    or X.27 (V.11)
A 15-pin connector per ISO 4903 (DB-15) is used.

Figure H-7. CCITT Recommendation X.21
(© 1987 Hill Associates, Inc.)

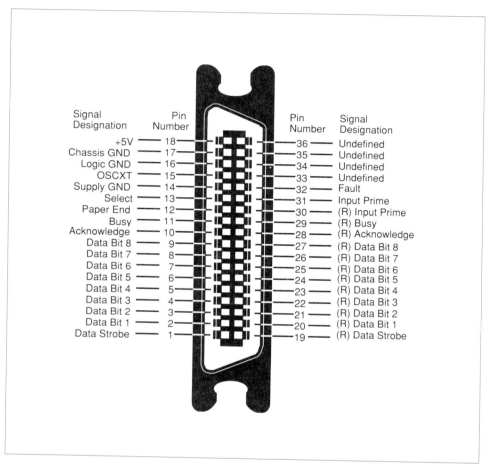

Figure H-8. Centronics® Parallel Interface
(© 1987 Hill Associates, Inc.)

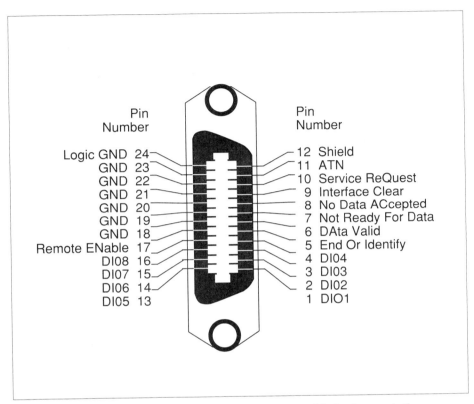

Figure H-9. IEEE-488 Digital Interface for Programmable Instrumentation

(© 1987 Hill Associates, Inc.)

Trademarks

PostScript is a trademark of Adobe Systems.

Apple, the Apple logo, AppleShare, AppleTalk, Apple IIGS,
EtherTalk, LaserWriter,LocalTalk, Macintosh, and TokenTalk
are registered trademarks; and APDA, Finder, ImageWriter and
Quickdraw are trademarks of Apple Computer, Inc.

UNIX is a registered trademark of AT&T and STREAMS, Transport
Layer Interface, and Unix System V Release 4 are trademarks
of AT&T.

Banyan, the Banyan logo, and VINES are registered trademarks
of Banyan Systems Inc; and StreetTalk, VANGuard and NetRPC
are trademarks of Banyan Systems Inc.

COMPAQ is a trademark of COMPAQ Computer Corporation.

CompuServe is a trademark of CompuServe.

Cray is a trademark of Cray Research, Inc.

ARCNET, ARCNET Plus, Attached Resource Computer, and
DATAPOINT are registered trademarks of DATAPOINT Corporation.

DEC, DECnet, LanWORKS, LAT, LAVC, Mailbus, Message Router,
Micro-VAX, MOP, Rdb, ThinWire, Ultrix, VAX, VAX Cluster and
VMS Mail are trademarks, and Ethernet is a registered
trademark of Digital Equipment Corporation.

Proteon is a trademark of Proteon, Inc.

Prime is a trademark of Prime.

Retix is a trademark of Retix.

SMC is a registered trademark of Standard Microsystems Corporation.

Network File System, Open Network Computing, SPARC, Sun, SunOS, and TOPS are trademarks of Sun Microsystems, Inc.

Lattisnet is a trademark of SynOptics Communications.

Tandem is a trademark of Tandem.

3COM is a registered trademark and 3+ is a trademark of 3Com Corporation.

Ungerman Bass is a trademark of Ungerman Bass, Inc.

TransLAN and Vitalink are trademarks of Vitalink.

Clearinghouse, Interpress, Interscript, NS, XNS, and Open Look are trademarks and Ethernet and Xerox are registered trademarks of Xerox Corporation.

Index

A

AARP   67
Activate Logical Unit   235
Activate Physical Unit   235
Active Monitor   78, 79
Active Monitor Present   78, 294, 319
ACTLU   235, 286
ACTPU   235, 249, 291
Address Mapping Table   67
Address port   368
Address Recognized Indicator bit   240
Address Resolution Protocol   364
Advanced Computer Communications   42
Advanced Program-to-Program
    Communication   308
AG Group   37
All Routes Explorer   225
American National Standards
    Institute   437
Analyzer
    combination LAN/WAN   37
    fourth generation   29
    integration with network simulation/
        modeling tool   45
    MAN/WAN   29
    multiport   39
    PC-based   35
    price   48
    requirements   48
    Ultimate   60
Analyzer requirement   30
Apple Computer, Inc.   14, 21

AppleTalk   14, 21, 65
    addressing   70
    analysis techniques   74
    architecture   65
    Data Link layer   65
    Higher layer   69
    Network layer   67
    Phase 1 to Phase 2 transition
        service   91
    Physical layer   65
    Transport layer   68
Application layer   14
AR/Telenex   40, 41, 43
ARCNET   137, 306, 307, 309, 364
ARCNET Fragmentation
    Protocol   310, 314
ASCII   14, 353, 388
AT&T Computer Systems   25, 42, 435

B

B8ZS   27
Bandwidth requirement   9
Banyan Systems Inc.   14, 21, 135
Basic (2B+D) or primary (23B+D)
    rates   41
Basic Information Unit   231, 232
Basic Transmission Unit   231, 234
Bell System   25
Bellcore Standards   435
Bipolar violation   27
Bipolar with eight zero substitution   27
Bit-oriented protocol   28, 230
Byte-count oriented protocol   178
BPV   27

Bridge   15, 236, 277, 319, 341, 372
BTU   231
Bytex   34, 47

C

CAD/CAM   9, 10
Canadian Standards Association   436
Carrier Sense, Multiple Access Bus with
     Collision Detection   192
CCITT   435
Centralized host processor   4
cisco Systems Inc.   42
Clarke Burton Corporation   14
Client/server   7
CMIP   18, 42
CMOL   19
Collision   192
ComDisco Systems, Inc.   45
Command Terminal Protocol   182
Common Management Information
     Protocol   18, 42, 189
CompuServe Information Service   317
Computer memory   3
Configuration Report Server   79, 240
Connection-mode Network Service   189
Connectionless-mode Network Ser-
     vice   189
Connectivity   4, 13
Costs
   acquisitions costs   421
   downtime cost   422
   first costs   419
   incremental change costs   421
   life cycle management costs   419
   network costs   420
   operations costs   421
   recurring costs   419
CSMA/CD   21
CXR/Digilog, Inc.   36, 37, 45

D

DARPA   361
Data Access Protocol   182
Data Link layer   12, 230
   AppleTalk   65
   DECnet Phase IV   178
   DOD   363
   NetWare   309
   SNA/token ring   230
   VINES   137, 140
Data transmission speed   3
Datagram   365
Datagram Delivery Protocol   67
DCONFIG   316
DDCMP   178, 188
DDP   67
DEC   21, 42
   Multiport Repeater   196
   VT-100   5
DEC, Intel, and Xerox   180
Decade of Internetworking   26
DECnet   15, 177
   address   184
   architecture and protocol   178
   Data Link layer   178
   DEC VT-100   184
   End Communication layer   192
   host   11
   multicast address   188
   Phase IV   177
   Phase IV End Communication
      layer   182
   Phase IV Higher layer   182
   Phase IV internetwork addressing   187
   Phase IV internetwork
      troubleshooting   192
   Phase IV packet format   184
   Phase IV physical link   178
   Phase IV   190

DECnet (continued)
Phase IV protocol analysis
technique   190
Phase IV Routing layer   180
Phase IV Session Control layer   182
Phase V   188
Phase V compatibility   188
Routing Protocol   180, 181, 192
session establishment   205
Defense Data Network   362
DEMPR   196
DEMSA   214
Department of Defense
DOD Internet Addressing   367
Host-to-Host   362
Internet   362
IP Datagram   369
Network Access or Local Net-
work   362
Process/Application   362
Department of Defense Advanced Re-
search Projects Agency   361
Digital Data Communications Message
Protocol   178
Digital Equipment Corp. (DEC)   21
Digital Technology, Inc.   44
Digitech Industries, Inc.   42
Discovery process   236, 254
Distributed computing   7
Distributed host processing   4
Distributed processing   25
DIX   180, 363, 371
DOD
Host-to-Host Layer Protocols   365
Internet   362
Internet Architecture   362
Internet Layer Protocols   364
IP Datagram Format   367
Local Network Layer
Protocols   363

Process/Application Layer
Protocols   366
DP header   367
DS-1   9
DS-3   9
Duplicate Address   148
Duplicate Address Test
79, 235, 240, 254, 277
Dynamic Microprocessor Associates   44

E
EBCDIC   14, 353, 388
Echo Protocol   311, 315
ECONFIG   316
Economic consideration   20
EIA-232 interface   5
Electronic Industries Association   436
Electronic mail   323, 365
Emerging MAN/WAN protocol   40
End Communication layer   192
End node   181
Error Monitor   348
Error protocol   311, 315
Ethernet/IEEE 802.3
6, 137, 187, 192, 202, 306, 307,
309, 321, 364, 378, 383
Ethernet/IEEE 802.3 frame   138
EtherTalk   140
EtherTalk Link Access Protocol   65
European Computer Manufacturers
Association   436
Evaluating
WAN analyzer   56
Exchange Carriers Standards Associa-
tion   436
Expense
internetwork   428
availability   428
connectivity   430
interoperability   430

Expense (continued)
  mean time between failure 428
  mean time to repair 428
  saving workstation 428
Expert system 31

F
FAL 203
FDDI 9, 16, 40, 188
Federal Communications Commission 8
File Access Listener Process 203
FileTransfer Access and Manage-
  ment 189
File Transfer and Management 362
File Transfer Protocol 366
Fractional 42
Frame 34, 277
Frame Copied Error 348, 350
Frame Copied Indicator 284
Frame Relay 16, 30, 42
Franklin, Benjamin 419
Frederick Engineering Inc.
  36, 37, 39, 49
FTP Software Inc. 36, 43
Function Management Data 232, 294

G
Gartner Group 20
Gateway 6, 15, 284
General Service Administration 437
GN Elmi a/s 41
GN Navtel Inc. 36, 40, 42
Graphical information 9
Graphical User Interface (GUI) 11, 37

H
Hardware performance 11
HDLC 188
Header 27
Hewlett-Packard Co. 34, 36, 49

High-Level Data Link Control 137, 230
Host-centric internetwork 6

I
IBM 14, 21
IBM 3278 5
IBM 8209 bridge 107
IBM host 388
Idacom Electronic Ltd. 41, 42
IEEE 802.1d 223
IEEE 802.2 LLC 230
IEEE 802.3 21, 115, 188, 383
IEEE 802.5
  21, 115, 223, 341, 348, 364
IEEE 802.6 9, 41
IEEE 802.x 137, 312, 364
Index Group 420
Infonetics Research Institute 20, 422
Input/output 5
Institute of Electrical and Electronics
  Engineers 437
Integrated Services Digital Network 9
Intel 11
Inter-Exchange Carrier 8
International Data Sciences, Inc. 37
International Organization for Standardiza-
  tion 437
Internet Control Message Protocol 364
Internet Datagram Protocol 310
Internet Protocol 361, 364, 367
Internet Router 68
Internetix, Inc. 45
Internetwork 361
  analysis 26
  connectivity 12
  Datagram Protocol 307
  expenses 428
  host-centric 6
  Packet Exchange
    Protocol 306

Internetwork (continued)
  troubleshooting methodology   60, 61
Internetworking   25
  Decade of   26
Interoperability   14
Interoperate   361
IP datagram   367, 369
IP header   367
IPX.COM   316
IPX/SPX   14
ISDN   9, 16, 34, 41, 189, 230
  basic rate   41
  primary rate   41
  ISDN Terminal Equipment   41
ISO 7498-4   17
ISO Internetwork Protocol   189
IXC   15

K
Kamputech Inc.   40, 43

L
LAN   11, 202
LAN analysis trends   32
LAN Analyzer
  evaluating   50
  interface   53
  protocol   53
LAN/WAN
  connection   15
Largest frame   228, 341
LAT   196
LAVC   213
Leased line   4
LEC   15
LF   228
Link Access Procedure for the
    D-Channel   230
Link Access Procedure-Balanced   137
Link Support layer   310

Local Access Transport Area   8
Local Area Network   3
Local Area Transport   183, 196
Local Area VAX Cluster   213
Local Exchange   42
Local Exchange Carrier   8
Local network connectivity   12
Locally-Administered Ad-
    dress   235, 312, 317
LocalTalk   140
LocalTalk Link Access Protocol   65
LocalTalk wiring   129
Logical connection   13
Logical Link Control   67,
    83, 166, 225, 242, 356
Logical Unit   230
LU-LU session   294

M
MAC-layer   148
Maintenance Operations Protocol   183,
    212
MAN   11
Medium Access Control   78, 240, 348
Metropolitan Area Network   3
Micro Technology Inc.   43
Microcom Inc.   44
Microprocessor   35
Microsoft Corporation   14, 137
Motorola Computer Systems, Inc.   11
Multi-Station Access Unit   79, 350
Multiport   39

N
National Institute of Standards and
    Technology   438
National Technical Information
    Service   437
Nearest Active Upstream Neighbor   79
NetBIOS   139, 225, 274, 277, 311

NetView   43, 168, 170, 236, 357
NetWare   7, 21
NetWare
   286 architecture   306
   386 architecture   308
   addressing   333
   architectures and protocol   305
   Core Protocol   306, 311
   Data Link layer   309
   Higher layer   311
   internal routing   319
   internetwork addressing   312
   IPX.COM   307, 316
   Loadable Module   308, 317
   management utility   316
   Network layer   310
   NETx.COM   306, 316
   packet format   314
   Physical layer   309
   preferred server   327
   protocol analysis   315
   Requester   312
   server connection   331
   Shell   306, 307, 312
   Source Routing   341
   Transport layer   311
   workstation driver   316
Network   4
   Addressable Unit   231
   Driver Interface Standard   137
   Services Protocol   182, 186, 189
Network Addressable Unit   230
Network communication   42
Network costs   420
Network General Corpora-
   tion   36, 37, 43, 45, 47, 49, 422
Network layer   12
Network management   17
Network Management Protocol   42
Network Management Systems   431

Network Operating System   7, 10
NETx.COM   316
NIC   319, 348, 353
Northern Telecom Inc.   42
Novell Inc.   14, 15, 21, 43

O
OC-1   9
Open Data-Link Interface   308
Open Systems Interconnection   11
Open Systems Interconnection Reference
   Model   12
Optical Carrier, level 1   9
OS/2 LAN Server   7
OSI
   layer   29
OSI Reference Model   229, 362, 413
OSI Transport Protocol   189

P
PABX   14, 42, 431
Packet   34
   AppleTalk packet format   73
   DECnet Phase IV packet format   184
   IP packet format   369
   NetWare packet format   314
   SNA packet format   232
   VINES packet format   142
Packet Switched Public Data Network   4,
   8, 138, 178, 230, 422
PCI   27
Physical   12
Physical Unit   230, 266, 356
Ping   365, 378, 383, 385, 387
Poison route   96
Port   142
PRI   42
Private Automatic Branch Exchange   14
Proteon, Inc.   15, 310

Protocol
  Address Resolution   67, 138, 364
  AppleTalk Data Stream   69
  AppleTalk Echo   68
  AppleTalk Session   70
  AppleTalk Transaction   68, 69
  bit-oriented   28, 230
  byte-count oriented   178
  Command Terminal   182
  Common Management Informa-
    tion   189
  Data Access   182
  DECnet routing   180, 181
  Digital Data Communications Message
    178
  File Transfer 366
  Internet   361, 364, 367
  Internet Control Message   138, 364
  Internet Datagram   307, 310
  Internetwork Packet Exchange   306
  Maintenance Operations   183, 212
  Name Binding   68, 69
  NetWare core   306, 311
  Network Services   182, 186, 189
  OSI Transport   189
  Printer Access   70
  Reverse Address Resolution   364
  Routing Information   306, 311
  Routing Table Maintenance   68
  Sequenced Packet   311
  Sequenced Packet Exchange   306
  Session Control   186, 189
  Simple Mail Transfer   366
  Sub-Network Access   67, 83, 363
  Transmission Control   139, 160, 365
  Upper Layer   366
  User Datagram   139, 365
  VINES Address Resolution   137
  VINES Fragmentation   137, 142
  VINES Internet   137

  VINES Internet Control   137, 138
  VINES Interprocess Communica-
    tions   139
  VINES Routing Update   137, 138
  VINES Sequenced Packet   139
Protocol control information   27, 232
ProTools, Inc.   36
Public Utility Commission   8

Q
Quintessential Solutions, Inc.   47

R
Realtime Techniques Corp.   40, 41
Remote data gathering   43
Remote Job Entry   5
Remote Procedure Call   308
Request For Comment   361
Request Header   291
Request Initialization Frame   277
Request/Response header   231, 232
Request/Response Unit   231, 232
Reverse Address Resolution Proto-
    col   364
RII   224
Ring Parameter Server   79, 274
Ring purge   79
Route   319
Route Descriptor   228
Route Information Indicator   224
Router   15, 321, 372, 395, 396
Routing Control message   181
Routing Domain   180
Routing Information   341
Routing Information Field   242
Routing Information Protocol   306, 311
Routing node   181

S

SCS   213
SDLC   234
segments   366
Sequenced Packet Exchange Protocol   306, 311
Server Message Block   139
Service Advertising Protocol   306, 311
Session Control Protocol   186, 189
Set Asynchronous Balanced Mode Extended   249
Signaling System 7-SS7   34
Simple Mail Transfer Protocol   366
Simple Network Management Protocol   19, 42, 366
Slow host response time   5
SMDS   9, 16, 41
SMTP   160
SMTP command   161
SNA   21, 223
   architecture   228
   connection establishment   241
   Data Flow Control layer   231
   gateway   120, 353
   gateway response time   294
   host   236
   mainframe   353
   packet format   232
   Path Control layer   230
   physical   230
   presentation service   232
   session   266
   Transaction Services layer   232
   Transmission Control layer   231
SNMP   19, 42
SNMP agents/managers   43
SNMP Manager   45
Socket   68, 71, 142, 313, 365
SONET   9, 30, 42
Source   364

Source routing   21, 341
Source Routing Protocol   224
Spanning tree   21
Spanning Tree Explorer   225
Specmanship   30, 49
Spider Systems Inc.   45, 47
SS7/SS#7   41
Standby Monitor Present   78, 240, 319
Startup range   71
Stored Upstream Address   148, 240
StrataCom Corp.   42
Sub-Network Access Protocol   67, 83, 363
Switched Multimegabit Data Service   9, 16, 41
Synchronous Data Link Control   230, 353
Synchronous Optical Network   9, 42
System Communication Service   213
System Network Architecture   4, 223
System Service Control Point   230

T

T1   16, 20, 41
T1 circuit   14
T1 multiplexer   15
T3   16, 20, 41
TCP header   367, 368
TCP three-way handshake   388
TCP/IP   14, 21, 42, 139, 160, 188, 192, 284, 361
TCP/IP connection establishment   376
   protocol analysis techniques   371
   protocols   366
TE   41
Tekelec Inc.   40, 43
Terminal   388
Terminal Communication Protocol   182, 183
Terminal emulation   5, 236, 273, **293**

TEST frame   225, 235, 356
Testing requirements
   LAN   30
   WAN   30
3Com Corporation   14, 137
Token ring   107, 223, 306, 309, 321
Token ring architecture and protocol   224
Token ring/IEEE 802.5   6
TokenTalk   115, 140
TokenTalk Link Access Protocol   65
Transmission
   Control Protocol   160
   Control Protocol/Internet Protocol   361
   header   291
Transmission Control Protocol   139, 365
Transmission header   231, 234
Transport Level Interface   308
Transport layer   12
Troubleshooting methodology   60, 61
Telecommunications Techniques Corpora-
   tion   36, 37, 40, 41, 42

U
UDP   368
UDP header   368
Ultimate analyzer   47, 427
Ungermann-Bass, Inc.   15
UNIX   135, 305, 308, 371
Upper Layer Protocols   366
User Datagram Protocol   139, 365

V
Value Added Process   307, 317
   Data Link Layer   137
VINES   7, 21, 135
   AddressResolution Protocol   137
   addressing   140
   architecture and protocol   135
   Data Link Layer   137, 140
   file   151

Fragmentation Protocol   142
Higher layer   139
internet address   142
Internet Control Protocol   137, 138
Internet Protocol   137
internetwork troubleshooting   146
Interprocess Communications
   Protocol   139
login sequence   146, 148
Network Layer   137, 140
packet format   142
Physical layer   137
protocol analysis technique   143
Routing Update Protocol   137, 138
Sequenced Packet Protocol   139
server   152
SMTP gateway   160
SNA gateway   166
Transport layer   139
version 5.0   139
Virtual route   230
VTAM   298

W
WAN   11, 202
   interface   57
   protocol   57
WAN analysis trends   33

WAN protocol   34
Wandel & Goltermann Technologies,
   Inc.   34, 36, 37, 40,
   42, 43, 44
WellFleet Communications Corpora-
   tion   15
Wide Area Network   3
Wideband requirement   8
Workstation   9
Workstation driver   316

Workstation expenses   428

X
X.25   138, 189, 192, 202, 230
X.25 protocols   364, 371
Xerox Network System   305
XID   235, 242
XID frame   225, 235

Z
ZIP   120
Zone   71
Zone Information Protocol   69, **120**
Zone Information Socket   120
Zone Information Table   120

A Library of Technical References
from M&T Books

LAN Troubleshooting Handbook
by Mark A. Miller, P.E.

This book is specifically for users and administrators who need to identify problems and maintain a LAN that is already installed. Topics include LAN standards, the OSI model, network documentation, LAN test equipment, cable system testing, and more. Addressed are specific issues associated with troubleshooting the four most popular LAN architectures: ARCNET, Token Ring, Ethernet, and StarLAN. Each is closely examined to pinpoint the problems unique to its design and the hardware. Handy checklists to assist in solving each architecture's unique network difficulties are also included. 309 pp.

Book & Disk (MS-DOS)   **Item #056-7**   **$39.95**

Book only   **Item #054-0**   **$29.95**

Building Local Area Networks with Novell's NetWare, 2nd Edition
by Patrick H. Corrigan and Aisling Guy

From the basic components to complete network installation, here is the practical guide that PC system integrators will need to build and implement PC LANs in this rapidly growing market. The specifics of building and maintaining PC LANs, including hardware configurations, software development, cabling, selection criteria, installation, and on-going management are described in a clear "how-to" manner with numerous illustrations and sample LAN management forms. *Building Local Area Networks* covers Novell's NetWare, Version 2.2, and 3.11 for the 386. Additional topics covered include the OS/2 LAN Manager, Tops, Banyan VINES, internetworking, host computer gateways, and multisystem networks that link PCs, Apples, and mainframes. 635 pp. approx.

Book & Disk (MS-DOS)   **Item #239-X**   **$39.95**

Book only   **Item #237-3**   **$29.95**

Available at bookstores everywhere or call
1-800-533-4372 (in CA 1-800-356-2002)

A Library of Technical References
from M&T Books

Blueprint of a LAN
by Craig Chaiken

For programmers, valuable programming techniques are detailed. Network administrators will learn how to build and install LAN communication cables, configure and troubleshoot network hardware and more. Addressed are a very inexpensive zero-slot, star topology network, remote printer and file sharing, remote command execution, electronic mail, parallel processing support, high-level language support, and more. Also covered is the complete Intel 8086 assembly language source code that will help you build an inexpensive-to-install local area network. An optional disk containing all source code is available. 337 pp.

Book & Disk (MS-DOS)	Item #066-4	$39.95
Book only	Item #052-4	$29.95

LAN Protocol Handbook
by Mark A. Miller, P.E.

Requisite reading for all network administrators and software developers needing in-depth knowledge of the internal protocols of the most popular network software. It illustrates the techniques of protocol analysis—the step-by-step process of unraveling LAN software failures. Detailed is how Ethernet, IEEE 802.3, IEEE 802.5, and ARCNET networks transmit frames of information between workstations. Individual chapters thoroughly discuss Novell's NetWare, 3Com's 3+ and 3+Open, IBM Token-Ring related protocols, and more! 324 pp.

Book only	Item 099-0	$34.95

LAN Protocol Handbook Demonstration Disks

The set of seven demonstration disks is for those who wish to pursue the techniques of protocol analysis or consider the purchase of an analysis tool.

The analyzers will give you a clear view of your network so that you can better control and manage your LAN, as well as pinpoint trouble spots. The *LAN Protocol Handbook* demo disks are packed with detailed demonstration programs for LANalyzer®, LAN Watch®, The Sniffer®, for Token-Ring and Ethernet, SpiderAnalyzer® 320-R for Token-Ring, and LANVista®. By surveying the demo programs, you will receive enough information to choose an analyzer that best suits your specific needs.

Requirements: IBM PC/XT/AT compatible with at least 640K after booting. Requires DOS version 2.0 or later. Either a color or monochrome display may be used.

Seven disks	$39.95

Available at bookstores everywhere or call
1-800-533-4372 (In CA 1-800-356-2002)

A Library of Technical References
from M&T Books

Internetworking
A Guide to Network Communications
LAN to LAN; LAN to WAN
by Mark A. Miller, P.E.

This book addresses all aspects of LAN and WAN (wide-area network) integrations, detailing the hardware, software, and communication products available. In-depth discussions describe the functions, design, and performance of repeaters, bridges, routers, and gateways. Communication facilities such as leased lines, T-1 circuits and access to packed switched public data networks (PSPDNs) are compared, helping LAN managers decide which is most viable for their internetwork. Also examined are the X.25, TCP/IP, and XNS protocols, as well as the internetworking capabilities and interoperability constraints of the most popular networks, including NetWare, LAN Server, 3+Open™, VINES®, and AppleTalk. 425 pp.

Book only   Item #143-1 $34.95

LAN Primer
An Introduction to Local Area Networks
by Greg Nunemacher

A complete introduction to local area networks (LANs), this book is a must for anyone who needs to know basic LAN principles. It includes a complete overview of LANs, clearly defining what a LAN is, the functions of a LAN, and how LANs fit into the field of telecommunications. The author discusses the specifics of building a LAN, including the required hardware and software, an overview of the types of products available, deciding what products to purchase, and assembling the pieces into a working LAN system. *LAN Primer* also includes case studies that illustrate how LAN principles work. Particular focus is given to Ethernet and Token-Ring. 221 pp.

Book only   Item #127-X $24.95

Available at bookstores everywhere or call
1-800-533-4372 (In CA 1-800-356-2002)

A Library of Technical References
from M&T Books

NetWare for Macintosh User's Guide
by Kelley J. P. Lindberg

NetWare for Macintosh User's Guide is the definitive reference
to using Novell's NetWare on Macintosh computers. Whether
you are a novice or an advanced user, this comprehensive text
provides the information readers need to get the most from their
NetWare networks. It includes an overview of network operations and detailed explanations of all NetWare for Macintosh
menu and command line utilities. Detailed tutorials cover such
tasks as logging in, working with directories and files, and
printing over a network. Advanced users will benefit from the
information on managing workstation environments and
troubleshooting.
280 pp.

Book only   **Item #126-1**   **$29.95**

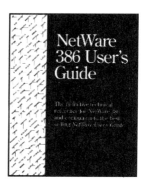

NetWare 386 User's Guide
by Christine Milligan

NetWare 386 User's Guide is a complete guide to using and
understanding Novell's NetWare 386. It is an excellent reference
for 386. Detailed tutorials cover tasks such as logging in,
working with directories and files, and printing over a network.
Complete explanations of the basic concepts underlying
NetWare 386, along with a summary of the differences between
NetWare 286 and 386, are included. Advanced users will benefit
from the information on managing workstation environments
and the troubleshooting index that fully examines NetWare 386
error messages. 450 pp.

Book only   **Item #101-6**   **$29.95**

Available at bookstores everywhere or call
1-800-533-4372 (in CA 1-800-356-2002)

A Library of Technical References
from M&T Books

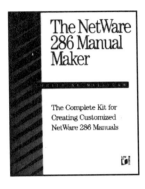

The NetWare Manual Makers
Complete Kits for Creating Customized NetWare Manuals

Developed to meet the tremendous demand for customized manuals, The NetWare Manual Makers enable the NetWare supervisor and administrator to create network training manuals specific to their individual sites. Administrators simply fill in the blanks on the template provided on disk and print the file to create customized manuals and command cards. Included is general "how-to" information on using a network, as well as fill-in-the-blank sections that help administrators explain and document procedures unique to a particular site. The disk files are provided in WordPerfect and ASCII formats. The WordPerfect file creates a manual that looks exactly like the one in the book. The ASCII file can be imported into any desktop publishing or word processing software.

The NetWare 286 Manual Maker
The Complete Kit for Creating Customized
NetWare 286 Manuals
by Christine Milligan

Book/Disk   Item #119-9 $49.95   314 pp.

The NetWare 386 Manual Maker
The Complete Kit for Creating Customized
NetWare 386 Manuals
by Christine Milligan

Book/Disk   Item #120-2 $49.95   314 pp.

The NetWare for Macintosh Manual Maker
The Complete Kit for Creating Customized
NetWare for Macintosh Manuals
by Kelley J. P. Lindberg

Book/Disk   Item #130-X $49.95   314 pp.

A Library of Technical References from M&T Books

NetWare Programmer's Guide
by John T. McCann

Covered are all aspects of programming in the NetWare environment — from basic planning to complex application debugging. This book offers practical tips and tricks for creating and porting applications to NetWare. NetWare programmers developing simple applications for a single LAN or intricate programs for multi-site internetworked systems will find this book an invaluable reference to have on hand. All source code is available on disk in MS-PC/DOS format. 425 pp.

Book/Disk (MS-DOS)	**Item #154-7**	**$44.95**
Book only	**Item #152-0**	**$34.95**

Troubleshooting LAN Manager 2
by Michael Day

The ideal reference for network supervisors responsible for the maintenance of a LAN Manager 2 network. *Troubleshooting LAN Manager 2* builds a functional model of LAN Manager from the ground up, beginning with OS/2 and ending with fault tolerance and printer setup. Key components such as data structures, protocols, services, and applications are placed in a troubleshooting context, examining possible problems and providing hands-on solutions. More than basic hints and tips, this book lays a solid foundation upon which you can build a truly outstanding troubleshooting methodology. 337 pp.

Book only	**Item #161-X**	**$34.95**

Troubleshooting NetWare for the 286
by Cheryl Snapp

The ideal reference for network supervisors responsible for the installation and maintenance of a NetWare 286 network. Contains a thorough overview of the NetWare 286 operating system plus step-by-step instructions for troubleshooting common and not-so-common problems. Detailed chapters emphasize the information most helpful in maintaining a healthy NetWare 286 LAN, including installation, file server and workstation diagnostics, printing utilities, and network management services. Covers NetWare 286 version 2.2. 350 pp.

Book only	**Item #169-5**	**$34.95**

**Available at bookstores everywhere or call
1-800-533-4372 (in CA 1-800-356-2002)**

A Library of Technical References
from M&T Books

Running WordPerfect on NetWare
by Greg McMurdie and Joni Taylor

Written by NetWare and WordPerfect experts, this book contains practical information for both system administrators and network WordPerfect users. Administrators will learn how to install, maintain, and troubleshoot WordPerfect on the network. Users will find answers to everyday questions such as how to print over the network, how to handle error messages, and how to use WordPerfect's tutorial on NetWare. 246 pp.

Book only   Item #145-8 $29.95

The Tao of Objects:
A Beginner's Guide to Object-Oriented Programming
by Gary Entsminger

The Tao of Objects is a clearly written, user-friendly guide to object-oriented programming (OOP). Easy-to-understand discussions detail OOP techniques teaching programmers who are new to OOP where and how to use them. Useful programming examples in C++ and Turbo Pascal illustrate the concepts discussed in real-life applications. 249 pp.

Book only   Item #155-5 $26.95

Object-Oriented Programming for Presentation Manager
by William G. Wong

Written for programmers and developers interested in OS/2 Presentation Manager (PM), as well as DOS programmers who are just beginning to explore Object-Oriented Programming and PM. Topics include a thorough overview of Presentation Manager and Object-Oriented Programming, Object-Oriented Programming languages and techniques, developing Presentation Manager applications using C and OOP techniques, and more. 423 pp.

Book/Disk (MS-DOS)   Item #079-6 $39.95

Book only   Item #074-5 $29.95

A Library of Technical References
from M&T Books

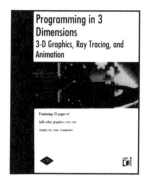

Programming in 3 Dimensions
3-D Graphics, Ray Tracing, and Animation
by Sandra Bloomberg

Programming in 3 Dimensions is a comprehensive, hands-on guide to computer graphics. It contains a detailed look at 3-D graphics plus discussions of popular ray tracing methods and computer animation. Readers will find techniques for creating 3-D graphics and breath-taking ray-traced images as, well as explanations of how animation works and ways computers help produce it more effectively. Packed with examples and C source code, this book is a must for all computer graphics enthusiasts! All source code is available on disk in MS/PC-DOS format. Includes 16 pages of full-color graphics.
500 pp. approx.

Book/Disk (MS-DOS)	Item #218-7	$39.95
Book only	Item #220-9	$29.95

Fractal Programming and Ray Tracing with C++
by Roger T. Stevens

Finally, a book for C and C++ programmers who want to create complex and intriguing graphic designs. By the author of three best-selling graphics books, this new title thoroughly explains ray tracing, discussing how rays are traced, how objects are used to create ray-traced images, and how to create ray tracing programs. A complete ray tracing program, along with all of the source code, is included. Contains 16 pages of full-color graphics. 444 pp.

Book/Disk (MS-DOS)	Item 118-0	$39.95
Book only	Item 134-2	$29.95

Available at bookstores everywhere or call
1-800-533-4372 (in CA 1-800-356-2002)

A Library of Technical References
from M&T Books

Delivering cc:Mail
Installing, Maintaining, and Troubleshooting a cc:Mail System
by Eric Arnum

Delivering cc:Mail teaches administrators how to install, troubleshoot, and maintain cc:Mail, one of the most popular E-mail applications for the PC. In-depth discussions and practical examples show administrators how to establish and maintain the program and database files; how to create and modify the bulletin boards, mail directory, and public mailing lists; and how to diagnose and repair potential problems. Information on using the management tools included with the package plus tips and techniques for creating efficient batch files are also included. All source code is available on disk in MS/PC-DOS format. 450 pp.

Book & Disk	**Item #187-3**	**$39.95**
Book only	**Item #185-7**	**$29.95**

The Complete Memory Manager
Every PC User's Guide to Faster, More Efficient Computing
by Phillip Robinson

Readers will learn why memory is important, how and when to install more, and how to wring the most out of their memory. Clear, concise instructions teach users how to manage their computer's memory to multiply its speed and ability to run programs simultaneously. Tips and techniques also show users how to conserve memory when working with popular software programs. 437 pp.

Book	**Item #102-4**	**$24.95**

Available at bookstores everywhere or call
1-800-533-4372 (In CA 1-800-356-2002)

ORDER FORM

To Order:

Return this form with your payment to M&T books, 501 Galveston Drive, Redwood City, CA 94063 or **call toll-free 1-800-533-4372 (in California, call 1-800-356-2002).**

ITEM #	DESCRIPTION	DISK	PRICE

Subtotal	
CA residents add sales tax ____%	
Add $3.75 per item for shipping and handling	
TOTAL	

NOTE: **FREE SHIPPING** ON ORDERS OF THREE OR MORE BOOKS.

Charge my:
- ❏ **Visa**
- ❏ **MasterCard**
- ❏ **AmExpress**

- ❏ **Check enclosed, payable to M&T Books.**

CARD NO. _____

SIGNATURE _____ EXP. DATE _____

NAME _____

ADDRESS _____

CITY _____

STATE _____ ZIP _____

M&T GUARANTEE: If your are not satisfied with your order for any reason, return it to us within **25** days of receipt for a full refund. Note: Refunds on disks apply only when returned with book within guarantee period. Disks damaged in transit or defective will be promptly replaced, but cannot be exchanged for a disk from a different title.

8057

1-800-533-4372 (in CA 1-800-356-2002)